CU00794048

Praise for

A WORLD OF DARKNESS

"To see the world through someone else's eyes is to be uniquely privileged. David Price has written a beautiful account of Cotton Mather's worldview and cosmology and in the process has transformed how we view Mather himself, and the Salem witch trials. By locating this pivotal episode in American history in its fullest intellectual, religious and social context—evidenced in the writings of its most powerful participant—Dr. Price explains how the forces of belief and of community conspired in tragedy."

—Tim Hitchcock

Professor of Digital History, University of Sussex, United Kingdom

"Wide-ranging reading, careful reasoning, and deep immersion in the life and writings of Cotton Mather have allowed David Price to achieve the nearly impossible—which is to offer a fresh word about the much-studied Salem witch trials of late-seventeenth-century Massachusetts. Price's 'historical-theological' method provides a perspective for showing how both general Puritan theology and Mather's own personal cosmology played out at Salem, but also lets him exploit insightfully many other scholarly viewpoints. In its goal of adding another level of interpretive meaning to a much-studied event, *A World of Darkness* is a significant success."

—Mark Noll

Research Professor of History, Regent College and Professor Emeritus of History, Notre Dame University; Author of *A History of Christianity in the United States and Canada*

"This fascinating and scholarly book provides a new perspective on Salem. David Price reconstructs with forensic care the distinctive worldview of Cotton Mather, in whose end-times vision good and evil were in constant battle, and in so doing, helps us understand how and why the Salem trials happened as they did, and the limited but far-reaching role of Mather himself."

—Laura Gowing

Professor of Early Modern History at King's College London

"David Price's book *A World of Darkness* gives us an historical perspective and current worldview of the intricacies of witchcraft and Salem rituals. You will walk away enlightened and informed with a new perspective after reading this book."

—Dr. Dedra Sibley, JD

Provost, Eastern Florida State College, Cocoa Campus, Florida A&M University

A World of Darkness:

Cotton Mather and the 1692 Salem Witchcraft Trials

by David W. Price

© Copyright 2020 David W. Price

ISBN 978-1-64663-020-2

All rights reserved. No part of this publication may be reproduced, stored in a retrieval system, or transmitted in any form or by any means—electronic, mechanical, photocopy, recording, or any other—except for brief quotations in printed reviews, without the prior written permission of the author.

Published by

köehlerbooks™

3705 Shore Drive
Virginia Beach, VA 23455
800–435–4811
www.koehlerbooks.com

A World of Darkness

COTTON MATHER AND THE 1692 SALEM WITCHCRAFT TRIALS

DAVID W. PRICE

VIRGINIA BEACH
CAPE CHARLES

For my wife, LuAnn, who has spent a lifetime encouraging me to pursue my dreams and walking with me every step of the way.

TABLE OF CONTENTS

A RANGE OF INTERPRETIVE VIEWPOINTS 1

Current Issues in Salem and New England Scholarship......... 7

Seventeenth-Century European Witchcraft Scholarship as a Background to Salem Studies 10

The Salem Trials and Cotton Mather: A Range of Interpretations.................................. 15

The Historical-Theological Model 27

A CONSISTENT COSMOLOGICAL OUTLINE............. 32

The Background of Cotton Mather's Theology 35

A Consistent Cosmological Outline Regarding Witchcraft..... 39

Witchcraft: The Damned Art 53

The Expected Covenant-Nation Response to Witchcraft 58

Conclusion 65

A CONGRUENCE OF BELIEF:
NEW ENGLAND WITCHCRAFT 66

The Widespread Belief in Witchcraft........................ 67

Elite and Popular Cross-Social Conceptions of Witchcraft..... 74

Conclusion 99

PREVIOUS INTERPRETATIONS:
A PARADIGM OF BLAME.............................. 101

Robert Calef's More Wonders of the Invisible World......... 104

Cotton Mather's Pre-Salem Articulation about Witchcraft.... 108

Preexistent and Transcendent Factors in New England....... 112

Conclusion 131

A PREDICTABLE RESPONSE TO SALEM WITCHCRAFT. 132

A Consistent Pattern of Cosmological Interpretation 134

A Correspondence of Belief and
Response to Salem Witchcraft 142

Conclusion 168

THE SALEM TRIALS: COTTON MATHER'S DILEMMA .. 169

Cotton Mather's Proposals for the Salem Adjudications 170

The Stoughton Court and the Course of the Salem Trials 177

Mather's Ambiguous Advice to the
Salem Court about Spectral Evidence 180

A Paradoxical Account: The Wonders of the Invisible World.. 189

Conclusion 203

CONCLUSION 206

ACKNOWLEDGMENTS 221

Endnotes 225

BIBLIOGRAPHY....................................... 275

1

A Range of Interpretive Viewpoints

I have indeed set myself to countermine the whole PLOT of the Devil, against New England, in every Branch of it, as far as one of my darkness, can comprehend such a World of Darkness.

Cotton Mather, *The Wonders of the Invisible World* (1693)

ON 20 APRIL 1692, the family of twelve-year-old Ann Putnam Jr. of Salem Village, Massachusetts, gathered around the bedside of the young girl, one of the original Salem Village girls to suffer witchcraft possession. Since February, Ann had been the subject of attacks from the invisible world by various specters resembling local personages. On that night, the latest torments came from a specter of an unexpected source. Ann cried out, "Oh, dreadful, dreadful. Here is a minister come: what, are ministers witches too?"[1]

Ann Putnam Jr. was "racked and choked" as the specter tempted her to write her name in the Devil's book as a Salem-witch conscript. When Ann demanded to know the specter's name, it revealed itself as George Burroughs, the former minister at Salem Village.[2] Although Ann Putnam Jr. refused to sign the Devil's book, her experience with George Burroughs's specter did not end here. Throughout the months of her possession, Putnam complained that the image of the former minister tormented her several times a day in its attempts to make her a Salem witch.[3]

Burroughs had served the Salem Village church from 1680 until 1683, at which time a growing conflict between the minister and churchmen over salary and political issues forced his angry departure from Salem. Burroughs moved to Maine, accepting another pastorate at Wells.[4]

The move, however, did not prove to be far enough away from Salem Village. As a result of Ann Putnam Jr.'s insistent testimony, on May 4, 1692, nine years after his bitter departure from Salem, George Burroughs was arrested by the authorities in Maine and deported to Salem to face charges of witchcraft.

At his trial on August 5, 1692, George Burroughs's situation worsened when he was accused of witchcraft by his neighbors in Wells, Maine, and then identified by several Andover witch suspects as the leader of a growing witch cult centered in Salem and Andover. According to these testimonies, Burroughs and his followers were developing a satanic church, whose alleged aim was to take over the political and religious structure of New England. The combined evidence led to Burroughs's conviction for witchcraft and subsequent death on the scaffold.

On August 19, 1692, the former Salem pastor and now convicted Salem wizard George Burroughs was transported by cart through the streets of Salem along with four other condemned witches to Gallows Hill. In keeping with the usual pattern of Puritan New England hangings, after being led up the ladder, Burroughs was given an opportunity to speak before being executed. Instead of confessing guilt and warning the assembled crowds of the consequences of sin, Burroughs protested his innocence, and ended his address with a flawless recitation of the Lord's Prayer. Samuel Sewell recorded that Burroughs's perfect repetition of the Lord's Prayer "did much move unthinking persons" who had gathered for the execution, since it was commonly believed that witches could not say the Lord's Prayer without error.[5] Others in the crowd countered that the "Black Man" himself stood beside Burroughs and dictated the words to him.

According to Salem contemporary and Cotton Mather critic Robert Calef, at that moment Mather, a minister at Boston's Old North Church, made his presence known. Mounted and standing in the stirrups of his horse, he stilled the confused crowd. He reminded those assembled that the Devil had often been "transformed into an angel of light," and that Burroughs was not an ordained minister.[6] After Mather's intervention, the hangman carried out his duties, executing the former pastor at Salem Village and four other convicted Salem witches.[7]

Although Robert Calef's account of Mather's actions at the Burroughs execution was printed in Calef's attack on Mather, *More Wonders of the Invisible World*, and is therefore suspect, it nonetheless encapsulates the historical portrait that has come to typify the popular view of Cotton Mather and his role as stern cheerleader and prime mover in the Salem witchcraft trials. Scholars and historians, who have largely ignored the theological elements of seventeenth-century New England witchcraft beliefs, have, following Robert Calef, made Cotton Mather the enigmatic representative of the Salem witch hunt.

The cosmology and theological beliefs which allowed Mather to act out his role in this tragedy form the subject of this book. Historians and scholars have written about Cotton Mather and the Salem trials from a number of perspectives, including those derived from most of the social sciences. However, Mather's own seventeenth-century New England historical-theological context has attracted much less scholarly interest. And yet, in relation to Salem studies, and Cotton Mather's role in them, the theological dimension provides an important and perhaps vital lens through which to study the events at Salem in 1692 to 1693.

This book examines Cotton Mather's personal cosmology and his relationship to the Salem trials. By exploring these events from the perspective of a single individual, a number of benefits will accrue. First, this approach allows for the development of a more fully articulated interpretive model of the relationship between the forces and personalities present during the early 1690s, and allows us to explore a single individual's intellectual and behavioral contribution to a series of events for which that individual, Cotton Mather, has traditionally been held responsible. More than this, the focus on Cotton Mather and the Salem episode provides an opportunity to add a further level of interpretive understanding of Salem witchcraft by reexamining what contemporaries would certainly have identified as the underpinnings of the entire episode: the theological worldview of seventeenth-century New England.

As this introductory chapter suggests, exploring Cotton Mather's cosmology and relating it to the Salem trials provides a new, or perhaps very old, complexity to what is already a very rich historiography. It presents a long-missing explanation of the intellectual framework through which Mather observed and interpreted the events of his era and his own life, in terms of cause and effect. The Calvinistic theology of the Puritans has been well documented within seventeenth-century New England studies. However, with respect to Salem studies, scholars have offered only a very limited explanation of Mather's personal cosmology. Instead, Mather's cosmology has been primarily subsumed within a largely undifferentiated seventeenth-century Puritan theology. Yet, as this study demonstrates, Cotton Mather had a well-developed and articulated personal worldview that was largely in place prior to the Salem events, and which, while it shared many facets with a broader Puritan belief structure, was nonetheless distinct.

Mather's cosmology included specific and personal beliefs about the existence, identity, and powers of the Devil and demons. Examining these beliefs from Mather's individual perspective moves away from the at times banal observations of scholars about Mather's general Puritan theology and lays greater emphasis upon Mather's well-formulated and consistent cosmology prior to, during, and after the Salem trials.

While Mather's perspective was unique and individual, he was also a member of a well-defined social cadre: an intellectual and clerical elite who effectively governed large aspects of late seventeenth-century New England life. Exploring Mather's worldview provides a new insight into the world of the Massachusetts clerical elite. Mather's beliefs about magic and witchcraft serve as an excellent model of early modern clerical views, since his ideas were accepted by most of his ministerial contemporaries. Modern critics have often alleged that Cotton Mather's theology represents an individual, if not aberrant, worldview which was at odds with his clerical and educated contemporaries. Yet, when Mather's conceptions of the supernatural and specifically witchcraft are compared to that of the generality of seventeenth-century clerics, they demonstrate more concurrence than disparity.

Seventeenth-century sources reveal that the clergy of Boston, and more largely New England, preached and published views on the power and dangers of witchcraft similar to those expressed by Cotton Mather. Citing the pre-Salem progression and influence of sermons and published works by other New England clerics, this study shows their persistent attempts to address the growing clerical alarm at the practice of magic and witchcraft among seventeenth-century New England's populace. In addition, these sources bolster the view of a broad consensus of witchcraft beliefs by the New England clerics before, during, and after the Salem trials.

This book brings to the study of Salem a more balanced view of Mather's cosmology within the context of contemporary beliefs. Additionally, it offers an explanation of how the Boston clergy could have largely agreed upon the necessity for the witch prosecutions, despite their undeniable and specific disagreements about the legal process which led to so many deaths.

This study also examines Cotton Mather's reaction to witchcraft cases, and especially those involving possession. An analysis of this area reveals a strong pattern to Mather's pastoral application of the theology of witchcraft to its treatment, an area largely ignored by modern scholars. As a result of Mather's prominent position in the clerical hierarchy, his involvement in suspected witchcraft cases was greater than that of many of his contemporaries. Historically, Mather's involvement in witchcraft cases has been used by critics to give credibility to the caricature of Cotton Mather as a zealot and "witch-hunter" on par with several seventeenth-century counterparts across the Atlantic. Given this common portrayal of Mather, this work engages in a serious examination of Mather's life-long pattern of spiritual warfare, noting specifically his ministry to witchcraft victims.

Mather's application of the biblical principles of fasting and prayer in his attempts to deliver witchcraft victims is contextualized within the larger discussion of the continuity between his beliefs and his overall behavior during the Salem witchcraft trials. The benefit of the examination of this aspect of his beliefs and behavior is that it brings a greater degree of fairness to the historical portrait of Cotton Mather's theology and his application of that theology to the Salem trials. As such, this study presents a more fully contextualized historical treatment of Cotton Mather's reaction toward witchcraft episodes, by examining the consistency of his response to cases preceding and following the Salem trials.

Finally, this study clarifies the issue of the degree to which Cotton Mather's role in the Salem trials influenced the proceedings and their outcome. The characterization of Mather by prior historians and scholars as the initiator or primary proponent of the Salem episode is subjected to a thorough analysis. To do so, an examination is undertaken to show the detail of Mather's stated beliefs about the three primary causes of the Salem situation as expressed in *Wonders of the Invisible World*: divine judgment upon New England's spiritual degeneration, a demonic retaliation for the Puritan settlement of New England, and an end-times precursor of Christ's Second Advent. By comparing these postulates to Mather's response to witchcraft episodes prior to Salem, it can be demonstrated that Mather's response to Salem witchcraft was to a large degree predictable and consistent with his previously expressed views.

In light of this demonstrable integrity, a more equitable assessment of the relationship between Mather's preconceived and demonstrated cosmology and his role in the Salem trials is revealed. This work does not suggest that Mather can or should be absolved from all responsibility for his behavior during the course of the trials. Instead, it argues that, to date, historical perceptions of Cotton Mather have been unduly influenced by a tradition of criticism initiated by Mather's bitter contemporary rival Robert Calef and carried on by modern critics.

To this end, the final chapter of this book compares the advice Cotton Mather gave to the Boston and Salem authorities with the independent actions of the Stoughton Court, providing a more balanced appraisal of the relative importance and roles of Mather and the court. This discussion moves away from the standard condemnation of Mather as a singularly malevolent influence. Although Mather did in fact make mistakes in his handling of his advice to Governor Phips, and in publishing *The Wonders of the Invisible World*, this study gives a fresh understanding of those mistakes and presents a clearer view of Mather's influence upon the proceedings.

Current Issues in Salem and New England Scholarship

MODERN HISTORICAL WRITING ON the history of New England is voluminous and complex. Still, the continuing importance to scholars of what happened at Salem Massachusetts in 1692 and 1693 is beyond doubt. Salem witchcraft remains at the heart of our understanding of the place and the period. As David Levin suggests, "The Salem trials have . . . held a disproportionately large place in American historical consciousness for nearly three centuries."[8] Although the Salem episode was relatively short in comparison to many major historical events in American history, the trials have become a symbol for a number of issues in both the modern popular and scholarly imagination.

Perhaps the easiest place to start in any attempt to characterize this extensive literature is with the broader scholarship on the history of seventeenth-century New England as a whole. Historians and scholars have invested a large degree of research effort into the various political, military, religious, social, and cultural contexts of Puritan New England, as a synopsis of just a few items reveals.

Among modern scholars, one of the most active debates concerns the Puritans' domination of seventeenth-century New England. The nature of the Puritans' elevated initial view of their journey to the New World is being challenged by a number of authors, including Andrew Delbanco, as being constructed from texts that are both limited and of questionable reliability.[9] Based upon such a reassessment, Mark A. Peterson's book *The Price of Redemption* adopts a revisionist interpretation, insisting that Puritan theological compromises such as the Halfway Covenant were not signs of religious declension, but rather progressive attempts by Congregationalist churches to adapt to changing religious, social, and cultural realities.[10]

Another debate within current early modern New England studies deals with the historical perception of the cultural insulation of Puritan New England. While much of New England's historiography has focused upon Puritanism's seventeenth-century internal cultural productions, Phillip H. Round's book *By Nature and by Custom Cursed* insists that Puritanism was not impervious to external and competing discourses. Round asserts that Puritanism was forced to engage a number of opposing transatlantic discourses concerned with a highly diverse set of issues, including ethnicity, gender, genre, and class.[11] A recent book which to some degree echoes this viewpoint is Emerson W. Baker's *A Storm of Witchcraft*. Baker argues that the social homogeneity of Puritan New England was threatened by historical shifts that eventually led to a more independent American consciousness.[12]

In the area of women's studies, New England scholarship has focused on a wide range of issues and has adopted viewpoints which range from the more overtly feminist analytical models of the 1960s and 1970s to more moderate descriptions of women's contributions to New England history. Representing one approach is Elaine Forman Crane's book *Ebb Tide in New England*, an examination of women and womanhood in the colonial seaport towns of Boston, Salem, Newport, and Portsmouth.[13] Crane's central focus is how New England's transformation from a frontier-based economy to an urbanized, specialized, regulated, and essentially male market economy led to the loss of women's prestige and authority, and that this is reflected in their growing social and economic marginalization.[14]

An alternative approach to the gendered history of Puritan New England can be found in studies based on the analysis of discursive norms and controls, which are seen in this literature to represent both individual and community boundaries. A good example of this sort of study is Jane Kamensky's *Governing the Tongue*.[15] In this volume Kamensky looks at specific periods in which "dangerous speech," particularly by women, threatened the Puritan model of godly order, prompting clerical and judicial attempts at control. Adopting an approach similar to that of Bethany Reid, Kamensky places particular emphasis upon the conflict between patriarchal leaders and specific outspoken women such as Anne Hutchinson.[16] Kamensky maps the reaction of New England authorities toward independent women during the Antinomian debate, the Salem witch trials, and the eventual decline of Puritan anxieties about speech by the early eighteenth century.

While women's studies has provided a new and growing historiography, ethnography has also been used to rewrite the history of New England in recent decades.[17] Dedicated to the examination of specific cultures, or subcultures, ethnography encompasses but is not limited to an examination of such themes as religion, social constructs, economics, and spatial organization.[18]

Kathleen J. Bragdon's work *Native People of Southern New England* is a good example of ethnography as applied to colonial New England.[19] Bragdon's book looks at the Native American populations in southern New England, particularly the Ninnimissinuok. Using current ethnology as well as sociology and economic models, Bragdon portrays the various aspects of Ninnimissinuok culture, and the European–Native American relationship from the sixteenth century to the mid-seventeenth.

The historiography of seventeenth-century New England presents a rapidly changing and evolving landscape in which a range of new approaches is evident. Many of the old shibboleths of seventeenth-century history are currently up for discussion, and no single over-arching model has remained either unchallenged or universally accepted. In this context, this study aims to add a further element of complexity to an already complex picture.

Seventeenth-Century European Witchcraft Scholarship as a Background to Salem Studies

AS EVEN THIS SMALL selection of current seventeenth-century literature on New England suggests, Salem studies belong to a much larger body of New England scholarship. Additionally, in recent years there has also been a greater degree of sensitivity to how New England and European witchcraft relate to one another. In essence, historians are increasingly responsive to the claim that Salem witchcraft cannot be understood in the near vacuum of seventeenth-century New England itself. First, New England clerics and authorities were far from intellectually isolated from England and Europe in this period. Some of the prominent figures in the Salem events, such as Cotton and Increase Mather, were active participants in transatlantic discussions on politics, natural philosophy, and witchcraft. Second, the Puritans readily transported their primary English witchcraft beliefs across the Atlantic Ocean, including them in the staple of religious and cultural realities that pervaded their understanding of this not-so-new world.

Because of the interconnectedness of European and American witchcraft beliefs, the impact of European scholarship is also important to the interpretation of the events at Salem. As a theme in European history, the witch trials of the seventeenth century continue to attract the attention of historians. The British scholar James Sharpe has described the witch hunts as "one of those pieces of history . . . to be taken out and reinterpreted, like so many of the best bits of history, at regular intervals."[20]

In the latter half of the twentieth century, a wide variety of approaches to seventeenth-century witchcraft events in Europe were assayed. Partial explanations involving historical or intellectual shifts such as the Reformation,[21] the Counter-Reformation,[22] the rise of the modern state,[23] political consolidation by elite ruling classes,[24] and misogynist-based persecutions[25] have all provided valuable insights and perspectives. However, explanations based entirely upon single historical shifts or events have largely failed to convince, due to the complications inherent in the variety of geographical, political, and religious contexts in which European witchcraft persecutions took place. Mono-causal approaches have, as Brian Levack notes, "proved to be singularly unconvincing, if not demonstrably false."[26]

Consequently, emerging scholarship is increasingly cognizant of the need to view the causes of individual and large-scale seventeenth-century witchcraft episodes as multi-faceted. This approach, which shows greatest promise, is one which crosses a number of research disciplines, including most of the social sciences. The journey to this more interdisciplinary and inclusive approach has, however, been a long one.

Rationalist scholarship, which viewed witch hunts as the product of theological dogmatism, dominated European witchcraft studies up until the 1960s, and is typified by the work of scholars such as

Rossell Robbins, who saw the European witch hunts as barbaric and unintelligible.[27] Perhaps the first small shift away from this type of scholarship can be found in the work of Hugh Trevor-Roper, in his 1969 book, *The European Witch-craze.*[28] Trevor-Roper's study of the larger sixteenth and seventeenth-century European witch hunts, covering a wide range of cultures and geographical locations, took the view that these witch persecutions needed to be placed in a more clearly articulated contemporary early modern European historical context. Still, typical of rationalist studies, Trevor-Roper gave little attention to social-anthropological questions and attributed the eventual demise of witchcraft beliefs to the rise of later philosophical and scientific movements.

As Trevor-Roper's views were being advanced and debated, alternative methods for the analysis of witch hunts were initiated by other European scholars. Several works emerged which suggested that witchcraft needed to be seen "from below," and which incorporated a self-conscious social-science perspective. Peter Burke describes the methodology of these scholars, noting,

> *They tended—like anthropologists—to put rationalism in brackets . . . to write about witches and their accusers without using words like "craze," "credulity," or "hysteria," and to even suggest that accusations of witchcraft served a social function.*[29]

Alan Macfarlane's *Witchcraft in Tudor and Stuart England* and Keith Thomas's *Religion and the Decline of Magic* modeled this largely social-anthropological approach, combining modern anthropological research with that of the early modern English witchcraft studies.[30] Thomas drew comparisons between the early twentieth-century African Azande and seventeenth-century European witchcraft, while Macfarlane looked at the relevance of witchcraft to sixteenth and seventeenth-century English socioeconomic relationships. Macfarlane and Thomas represented witchcraft accusations and purges as endemic to societies in which relationships between villagers and particularly needy neighbors, primarily socially and economically marginalized women, led to the expression of strong social tensions. For these scholars it was a small step from bickering on your back doorstep to the initiation of an accusation of witchcraft.

Historians have continued to use the Macfarlane-Thomas model with variations of emphasis. Their influence, for instance, is seen in William Monter's examination of endemic and epidemic small-scale witchcraft episodes in France and Switzerland, as well as in Erik Middlefort's study of the larger panics of southwest Germany.[31] Similarly, Christina Larner's research on seventeenth-century Scottish witchcraft attributed witch examinations, in part, to attempts by adjudicators to legitimize the monarchy during James VI's reign.[32] Larner's moderate feminist perspective encouraged a number of later studies on women and witch hunts, including Lyndal Roper's recent emphasis upon the theme of motherhood and witchcraft.[33]

During the last decade, one of the most noteworthy developments in European scholarship has been the adoption of the "acculturation model" developed in the late 1960s by sociologists and economists studying delays between cultural and market innovations and their wide-scale acceptance. European witchcraft scholars have used acculturation to study attempts by the elite of the seventeenth century, including clerics and the representatives of the state, to convert peripheral populaces to orthodox and changing intellectual positions. To do so, they diabolized popular magical beliefs, attempting to transform the outer periphery initially by persuasion and subsequently by accusations, trials, and purges.[34]

Among those applying the acculturation concept, Robert Muchembled and Peter Burke have researched the early modern French and Flemish witch trials. In addition, while Carlo Ginzburg has used this model to explain the diabolization of the sabbath myth of the North Italian and Friulian Benandanti, Gustav Henningsen has examined the same process with reference to the fairy and dream cults of Sicily.[35] European witchcraft studies are engaged in expanding multi-causal interpretive approaches to early modern witchcraft, as three examples demonstrate.

Robin Briggs's book *Witches and Neighbors*, based upon hundreds of cases from the Franco-German borderlands, is a consideration of the social dynamics of the creation of the witch figure and witch hunts.[36] Using psychoanalytical concepts such as projection, Briggs relates how in times of economic distress, the imagined and real fears of any village could transform social conflict into witchcraft allegations and prosecutions. James Sharpe's book *Instruments of Darkness* explores English witchcraft beliefs and episodes from 1550 to 1750, focusing upon the complexity of witchcraft allegations and trials and their origins in contemporary structural tensions. In particular, he traces the origins of these trials to a combination of direct interpersonal conflict and the existence of endemic social attitudes within the state and society.[37] Sharpe asserts that witchcraft allegations were often developed slowly, and made toward economically distressed members of society, including women and the elderly.[38]

Finally, Stuart Clark's book *Thinking with Demons* has added significantly to the argument that witchcraft belief in early modern Europe was not marginal or peripheral to elite conceptualizations. In examining the intellectual context of early modern European witch prosecutions, Clark traces the centrality of constructs of and debates about witchcraft to the larger areas of language, science, history, religion, and politics, and relates these in turn to attitudes toward and beliefs about magic, festivals, superstition, women, etc. The analysis found in the work of Clark and other more recent scholars has effectively placed the witch hunts at the center of developments in a broader intellectual and social history, and has suggested that both the rise and decline of witchcraft prosecutions is an epiphenomenon of the fundamental transitions (intellectual, spiritual and economic) which characterized the period.

The Salem Trials and Cotton Mather: A Range of Interpretations

TURNING BACK TO THE historiography of Salem and Cotton Mather, there is a growing recognition of the importance of using a variety of interpretive tools in order to crack this particular historical nut. Recent work has applied the techniques of psychology, sociology, anthropology, and economics. The background to this more recent work is perhaps best explored through a brief review of the extensive older scholarship on Salem, which is itself characterized by a variety of approaches. The origin of the first of these historiographical traditions can be found in attempts by contemporaries to understand events which they themselves contributed to. The basis for much later scholarship can be readily identified in the work of Puritan clerics such as Cotton Mather and John Hale, and in that of their critics, such as Robert Calef.[39]

Perhaps the most vibrant tradition to emerge from this contemporary scholarship encompassed a scholarly attempt to assign blame for the trials and executions. Following late seventeenth-century critics of the trials, several people, individuals and groups, including Samuel Parris, the Salem judges, the Boston clergy, and in particular Cotton Mather, were identified as bearing substantial responsibility for the tragedy. From the early eighteenth to the mid-twentieth century, a number of authors took this approach, including Massachusetts governor Thomas Hutchinson, Salem mayor Charles Upham, and modern American textbook authors such as George Bancroft and Vernon Parrington.[40]

Within their larger arguments, a common theme was the culpability of Cotton Mather for the Salem trials. Upham alleged that, at the least, Mather "took a leading part in fomenting it . . . in order that he might increase his own influence."[41] Bancroft described Cotton Mather as a primary example of "how far selfishness, under the form of vanity and ambition, can blind the faculties, stupefy the judgment, and dupe consciousness itself."[42] Similarly, Vernon Parrington insisted that Cotton Mather "not only ran with the mob, but he came near to outdistancing the most credulous. His speech and writings dripped of devil-talk."[43]

The role of human culpability in the Salem trials continued to be assessed and debated well into the early twentieth century. Historians such as James Truslow Adams insisted that Salem was a typical example of Puritan intolerance, while others such as Samuel Eliot Morse and George Lyman Kittredge portrayed Cotton Mather and the Puritans more moderately.[44]

Kittredge's work on seventeenth-century New England witchcraft, one of the last attempts to explicitly assign blame, was largely based upon the "rationalist approach" to Salem and New England witchcraft studies. His view was typical of European rationalist studies, which predominantly viewed witch hunts in terms of the transmission of beliefs from medieval logic to the Enlightenment. Kittredge suggested the Salem witchcraft trials were "a brief and transitory episode in the biography of a terrible, but perfectly natural superstition."[45] In his *Witchcraft in Old and New England*, Kittredge suggested historians read the events of Salem, "by common consent . . . the darkest page of New England history, in an unemotional and rational fashion."[46]

Kittredge's efforts were followed by those of Perry Miller, whose two-volume *The New England Mind: From Colony to Province* was published in 1953.[47] Perry Miller's viewpoint is typical of a larger body of scholars who present seventeenth-century New England as a homogenous Puritan society defined by their intellectual commitment and covenant mindset.[48] Miller's book dealt primarily with the intellectual constructs of Puritan rhetoric and covenant, examining the Salem events within the overall paradigm of a largely undifferentiated New England Puritanism.[49]

Miller further asserted that in writing *The Wonders of the Invisible World*, Cotton Mather joined the clergy in their abuse of the covenant, concealing the violation of the jeremiad principle of confession and forgiveness perpetrated by the Salem court.[50] Using Cotton Mather as a model, Miller's conclusion was that the Puritans could be rightly blamed by history for what went wrong at Salem, not by the terms of a more "enlightened" age, but specifically in their own terms—in those of the covenant.[51]

In essence, Miller insisted that the Puritans' belief in God's covenant with New England was used as an excuse to hunt down and execute those members of society that did not live up to the demands of that covenant.[52] He blamed the Salem judges for erroneously applying the doctrines of the jeremiad—the sermonic formula specifically used by New England Puritan clerics to threaten the wrath of God for covenant neglect and offer forgiveness for reform.[53] He depicted their methods as ensuring that "meretricious confession went free and sincere denial automatically became guilt."[54]

In the years following Miller's *New England Mind*, the Salem scholarship increasingly came under the influence of the social sciences. As with the European work of Trevor-Roper, Thomas and MacFarlane, a number of historians began using models of seventeenth-century New England witchcraft that relied upon psychology, sociology, physiology, anthropology, and economics. A precursor to this transition to the social sciences appeared in 1943, when medical doctor Ernest Caulfield presented a study to the *American Journal of Diseases of Children*. In an early use of psychoanalysis, Caulfield challenged earlier views of the Salem girls, calling them uncharitable and unfounded.[55] He theorized that Salem had experienced a psychological hysteria understood by contemporaries as physical manifestations of possession.

Caulfield attributed this situation to the Goodwin and Parris children's psychological inability to cope with the strict Calvinistic theology of death and eternal damnation. In short, they were reacting to deep distress over these issues. In this analysis, "demons" indicated repressed instinctive impulses that manifested themselves to the Parris girls and the New England population through the language of witchcraft and demonic possession.[56] Starkey portrayed the Parris girls' possession behavior during the Salem proceedings as an attempt to take "terrible revenge upon a society" that both neglected them and subjected them to the rigors of a Calvinistic childhood.[57] Starkey also viewed the Salem witch hunt as providing the New England community with its own psychological catharsis, through which it was able to deal with "a kind of collective guilt on the part of all Massachusetts in falling away from the high consecration of its founders."[58]

More recently, two other forays into this explanation have been undertaken by Marilynne Roach and Stacy Schiff. Roach's book *Six Women of Salem* underscores what she describes as the severity of life for both Puritan women and preadolescent girls. Her book largely describes the lives of six women accused of witchcraft: Bridget Bishop, Mary English, Rebecca Nurse, Ann Putnam, Mary Warren and Tituba. Schiff suggests that a possible explanation for the early accusations of witchcraft was an interplay between the young girls involved and their adult, female counterparts. She suggests these were, in part, a reaction to their roles and lives as females in Puritan society.[59]

Stacy Schiff has presented her view of the role of both preadolescent and adult women in her book *The Witches: Suspicion, Betrayal, and Hysteria in 1692 Salem*. Schiff asserts the Salem trials were the result of the young girls at the center of the witch accusations reacting to the restrictive expectations of Puritan society. Schiff suggests that what began as an "acting out" of these emotions quickly spiraled out of control as they became the focal point of a dramatic set of events.[60]

Psychological theories would be advanced yet again in 1969, in Chadwick Hansen's book *Witchcraft at Salem*.[61] Hansen attempted to establish the psychological "reasonableness" of seventeenth-century fears of witches based upon the model of a less enlightened era struggling with apparently diabolical events and persons. In doing so, Hansen insisted that the behavior of the girls at Salem and that of their subsequent accusers was pathological rather than fraudulent. In his view, "They were hysterics . . . mentally ill [and] they were ill long before any clergyman got to them."[62] In a controversial vein, Hansen further catalogued evidence that image magic, including that which was intentionally malevolent, had in fact been practiced at Salem and other New England villages. Accompanying this assertion was Hansen's view that in societies that accepted witchcraft, the psychological suggestion of malevolence was physically effective, although the resulting symptoms were "psychosomatic rather than organic."[63]

Hysteria and superstition, the Freudian psychological concepts of mental unbalance and delusion, have not been the only explanation offered for the mental imbalance evident during the Salem episode, since such conditions can also be produced by chemical or organic means. Some scholars have suggested that the latter may have been used to create the illusory memory of flying on sticks or of having participated in the witch's sabbath.[64] Another theory, proposed by Linnda Caporael in an article entitled "Ergotism: The Satan loosed in Salem?" suggested that the same outcome was the result of the inadvertent consumption of ergot. On the basis of the depositions from the 1692 Salem trials, Caporael observed that the general features of the Salem crisis corresponded to the characteristics of convulsive ergotism outbreaks.[65] Caporael theorized that the physiological and psychological distortions of the afflicted and the accusers of witches were the effects of ergotism.[66] She also suggested that some of the Salem trial convictions could be attributed to the fact that the judges at Salem Town may have had their thought processes altered by ergotism as well.

Linnda Caporael's theory that the origins of the Salem trials lay in ergot-poisoned rye was largely refuted by two psychologists, Nicholas

Spanos and Jack Gotlieb.[67] Noting that ergot epidemics are "exclusive to locales where the inhabitants suffered vitamin A deficiencies," they argued that its presence in seventeenth-century Salem Village and Salem Town was very unlikely since both had ample supplies of dairy products.[68] As to the courtroom behavior of the Parris girls and the symptoms of possession, Spanos and Gotlieb took the view that the various manifestations of affliction by the Salem girls seemed connected to certain "social cues," suggesting the disease (as they call it) was of an internal, psychological nature.[69] As to the symptoms of the witnesses, Spanos and Gotlieb adopted Boyer and Nissenbaum's explanation, pointing to the power of social disunity to drive communities into crisis. They also suggested that the rapid conclusion of the Salem trials provided evidence of psychological and social conflict, rather than a chemical one.[70] The debate over ergot poisoning reemerged in 1982 in an article by Mary Matossian, titled "Ergotism and the Salem Witchcraft Affair." Matossian argued that Spanos and Gotlieb's arguments could not rule out the possibility of ergot poisoning, and that it should still be considered with other factors.[71]

Although psychological analysis has continued to preoccupy a segment of the scholarly community, by the 1970s many scholars were entertaining increasingly interdisciplinary approaches to interpretation. From the early 1970s onwards, historians began to place greater emphasis upon the theory of social conflict as an explanation of witch-hunting, emphasizing its origin at the local level, rather than in elite culture. The views of this phalanx of scholars is perhaps best represented by the work of a team of sociologists, Paul Boyer and Steven Nissenbaum, but also includes the work of historians such as John Demos, and Carol Karlsen.

Sociologists Paul Boyer and Stephen Nissenbaum, in their book *Salem Possessed: The Social Origins of Witchcraft*, concluded the Salem episode originated in preexisting social and class conflict between the two main families in the Salem Village church: the Putnams and Porters.[72] In particular, they associated a conflict over the role and suitability of minister Samuel Parris with the relationship between the wealthier mercantile elements of the port town of Salem and the largely marginalized elements of the agrarian village of Salem.[73]

Using a map from Charles Upham's *Salem Witchcraft*, the two scholars suggested that the geographical locations of the landholdings of the families of Salem Village relative to Salem Town suggested that a broad division based on church membership, wealth, and geography separated the Putnam-backed, anti-Parris faction from the Porter-backed, pro-Parris elements.[74] As they depict this issue, the supporters of the trials generally belonged to the pro-Parris faction, while the opponents of the trials were overwhelmingly anti-Parris in persuasion.[75] Boyer and Nissenbaum argue that the explosive nature of the Salem trials was primarily the result of a unique combination of historical factors, which included the internal Putnam-Porter dispute over Salem Village minister Samuel Parris as an all-important component.[76]

While Boyer and Nissenbaum focused on the Salem Village–Salem Town conflict, John Demos employed psychohistory to study New England witchcraft in his 1982 book entitled *Entertaining Satan*.[77] Demos reflects on the theme of witch hunts as a form of persecution, whether interpreted as covert attempts at state-building, societal purges, the imposition of religion, or gender bigotry.[78] Put within the religious context of seventeenth-century New England, Demos viewed the clergy and government as the conservative and cooperative elements within the Puritan communities confronting persons who evidenced individualistic traits. He points to the persecution of married but childless women between forty and sixty years of age, women with long-standing histories of strife with neighbors, and women practicing informal medicine as evidence for this conflict.[79]

Social conflict as an explanation of witch purges has also found a place in feminist scholarship examining European and Salem witchcraft. Beginning with the American suffragist leader Matilda

Joslyn Gage, a number of feminist interpretations have been written which depict the persecution of women for witchcraft as an outgrowth of a broader gendered conflict. The role of women as cunning folk, local healers, peasant revolutionaries, and precursors of later independent feminists have been used to explain their function as scapegoats in this context.[80]

A noted feminist study of Salem is Carol Karlsen's *The Devil in the Shape of a Woman,* which is based upon case studies and statistics from New England witch trials from the years 1620 to 1725.[81] In Karlsen's opinion, the 1692 Salem trials represent a watershed in a seventeenth-century gender conflict, which was endemic to colonial Puritanism, and indicative of the fear men felt toward women whose individualistic and non-conforming life patterns challenged the social order.[82] Karlsen particularly points to antagonism felt toward local healers and midwives who turned their traditional skills to profit, and older widows who by their disruption of the pattern of primogeniture were felt to deprive men of their rightful property.[83]

In Karlsen's view, these women came into direct conflict with the accepted social order, and inadvertently brought into being the wide-scale accusations and persecutions of New England women by a society unable to deal with the tensions created. Consequently, driven by these tensions, Puritan society and the religious and legal establishment went into action during the Salem trials, attempting to both restore social order and to eradicate the cause of the disruption—the women who refused to fit into their traditional role.

During the last couple of decades, Salem scholarship has benefited from studies which have, at their core, insights derived from the "acculturation" model of European scholarship as represented in the work of Peter Burke and others.[84] This research illustrates how the elite, learned classes of seventeenth-century clerics either accommodated popular beliefs or forced their own views of witchcraft upon a populace which held different views of magic and maleficium. Salem scholars have begun to ask new questions of this society. Exemplifying this trend is the work of Richard Weisman, David D. Hall, and Richard Godbeer.

Richard Weisman's book *Witchcraft, Magic, and Religion* represents a significant strand in this tradition. He argues that conflicting pre-Salem and Salem trial clerical and popular beliefs about witchcraft ensured that the Salem trials would end in failure.[85] Weisman draws attention to the dissonance between the clergy and the populace in two critical areas of pre-Salem and Salem witchcraft proceedings. First, he argues that the normal pattern of witch accusations and examinations found prior to the 1690s allowed Salem villagers to resolve long-standing disputes with women representing unacceptable communal attributes. He goes on to suggest that this pattern was distorted in the Salem court proceedings, as the court prosecuted people often unknown to their accusers, and who did not fit the commonly held stereotypes of the witch.[86]

Weisman's second point relates to matters of evidence. He suggests that because most pre-Salem accusations were characterized by the lack of provable criminality, the clergy and magistracy was able to accommodate popular conceptions about witchcraft. The creation of witch tests and the banishment of individuals found innocent suggests to Weisman that the New England establishment had chosen an ill-defined middle way between elite and popular beliefs, in their response to the problem.[87] In the context of the Salem trials, Weisman believes this accommodation broke down, as the court became the focus for the essentially elite, legal persecution of witchcraft. By using confessions and spectral evidence to identify and prosecute people, forms of evidence based on an essentially elite view of spiritual causality, the court lost its ability to claim legitimacy in the eyes of the populace as a whole. The result was the execution of persons who formerly would have been acquitted for a lack of evidence.

Weisman's conclusion is that the decline in witchcraft prosecutions in New England after 1692, rather than being "a sudden reversal in public policy," was "an understandable resolution to a long standing predicament."[88] As the popular conceptions of pre-Salem witchcraft and the clergy's faith in the adjudication process were shaken by the perception that the actions of the Court of Oyer and Terminer were either illegitimate or unwarranted, the Salem trials represented a turning point in popular and elite constructions of witchcraft crimes and, perhaps more importantly, the nature of the relationship between these two worldviews.[89]

When David D. Hall attempted to recreate a seventeenth-century Puritan worldview in his book *Worlds of Wonder, Days of Judgment*, he presented New England's mindset as a "fluidity of power and culture" in which religion had much in common with folk beliefs.[90] Hall portrayed the clerics and the populace as sharing religious thought, whether distinctively Calvinistic or otherwise, allowing a "hegemonic system" which included both magic and counter-magic to exist.[91] As in Weisman's work, Hall's analysis of the Salem trials suggested that it represented the breakdown of this system of shared beliefs.

By examining both almanacs and the wonder stories, and the clergy's response to them, Hall suggests that the clergy actively attempted to engage with popular views, and to influence the reception of this printed popular culture. Hall then suggests that the 1692 Salem witchcraft episode represented a crisis which stemmed from the failure of the clergy to perform this mediating role. The key ritual of confession, followed by restoration to God and community, found in the clergy's interpretation of almanacs and wonder literature collided with the witchcraft adjudications.

As Hall describes it, the result was the transformation of confessions from "a means of reconciling with the covenanted community" to a method whereby magistrates could justify the execution of those who refused to confess, as a way of cleansing the land of malevolent witches, appeasing God, and reestablishing the righteousness of the community of believers.[92] In the final analysis,

David Hall viewed the Salem trials as the point at which the prior successful mediation of popular beliefs by clerics collapsed. The trials and deaths of 1692 were the disastrous result.

A third model based on acculturation can be found in Richard Godbeer's work. In his book *The Devil's Dominion*, Godbeer argues that far from holding shared beliefs about the power of witchcraft and magic, New England's seventeenth-century elite and general populace were substantially in conflict.[93] Godbeer's assessment is that, despite clerical opposition, New England Puritans and non-Puritans alike resorted to magic, counter-magic, and maleficience on a regular basis, to "enable . . . them to harness the world and adapt it to their own ends: to heal the sick, to protect against harm, and also to inflict harm."[94] Godbeer argues that by the later seventeenth century, clerical insistences that these practices were attempts to overturn God's providence and to access occult realms created an ideological power struggle within New England. For Godbeer, the first signs of witchcraft possession at Samuel Parris's home renewed the ministers' and judges' determination to "rid Christianity of magical accretions and to suppress folk magic," a magic which the clergy insisted be understood under the umbrella of diabolism.[95] Godbeer argues that unlike earlier New England witch trials, it was the evidence of diabolism, under attack by the clergy and searched for by the Salem judges, that made the Salem trials so deadly. He asserts that the Salem trials were "crippled by what was in effect a clash between magical and theological principles."[96]

Besides center-to-periphery acculturation and that associated with distinctions of class and power, some recent scholars have added an analysis of more narrowly defined seventeenth- century Puritan aspects of faith and belief. Relative to the Salem episode, two authors advancing a limited shift toward theological studies are Elizabeth Reis and Peter Lockwood Rumsey.

In her book *Damned Women*, Elizabeth Reis focuses on the relationship between religion and gender within the constructs of

Puritan New England's "underside of theology; sin, predestination, and witchcraft."[97] Questioning earlier studies which appealed to an ill-defined misogyny, Reis points out the correlation between the theological dynamics of Puritanism and the association of witchcraft with women.[98] She assesses the ways the 1692 Salem witchcraft trials reveal the place of women in the larger context of the theology of women and sin within Puritanism.

Reviewing Puritan literature, Reis links the unequal ratio of female witches and accusers to the Puritan emphasis upon the innate depravity of women, a depravity derived from the close association of women "with their inner nature, the unregenerate [and feminine] soul."[99] Reis articulates seventeenth-century Puritan ideas about the Devil in relation to the idea that women would be uniquely susceptible to his blandishments.[100] Reis suggests that during the Salem trials, when women confessed to witchcraft or accused other women, they were following a culturally transmitted and highly gendered script, which affirmed the proper Puritan view of Christian womanhood and supported a process of identifying those who stood outside its definition.[101]

In addition, Reis points out that women's views of their own individual, inward depravity reduced their resistance to the idea that other women could or would covenant with the Devil. She argues that by accusing other women of witchcraft, testifying against them, or by speaking in their defense, women "helped produce or reproduce particular gender categories and arrangement, and helped construct or reconstruct female subjectivity in Puritan New England."[102]

In Peter Lockwood Ramsey's book *Acts of God and of the People, 1620-1730,* he examined the transformation of the Puritan doctrine of special providences from one which emphasized passive, theologically unimproved acts of God, to a doctrine that could be used by the clergy in the 1680s to insist upon God's active role in events within New England.[103] According to Rumsey, in the 1680s the Puritan clergy increasingly complained of the spiritual decline of their generation, and, more than this, the doctrine of special providences became hopelessly enmeshed in the clergy's understanding of their contemporaries' position.[104] Charting Puritan reactions to comets and natural disasters, found in almanacs, sermons, complex theological discourses, and eschatological predictions, Rumsey shows the clergy's extension of special providences within seventeenth-century New England to cover all types of negative and non-serial events, including witchcraft.

To Rumsey, the issue of spectral evidence, the most disastrous issue for the Salem court, was an extension of the use of special providences. This was the result of the inherent antithetical role of the secular court in weighing tangible, accusative evidence versus the elusive and invisible theological evidence used to try cases of witchcraft.[105] Rumsey suggests that the adverse effects of special providences on the Salem trials forced the clergy to retreat to their prior cautious approach to special providences, having been exposed to the dangers created by their own unchecked rhetoric.

As this abstract of twentieth-century literature demonstrates, historians have used a number of interpretive models in an attempt to understand both why the 1692 Salem witch hunt occurred, and why witch prosecutions diminished in the aftermath of the Salem trials. Most theoretical models available to modern scholars have been applied to these issues. What historians, with a few notable exceptions discussed above, have largely failed to undertake is serious consideration of the detailed theological framework within which late seventeenth-century clerics and laypeople worked. This book, in part, attempts to rectify this notable lacuna.

The Historical-Theological Model

WITH THE RECENT WORK of writers who are more willing to take religion and its theologies seriously, Salem scholarship has to some extent come full circle. Despite this progress, Puritan theology in the Bible Commonwealth during the seventeenth-century Salem trials remains what Michele Lise Tarter has called "the much neglected and yet central lens."[106] More than this, one of the original questions posed by the Salem trials, why Cotton Mather conducted himself as he did—why he appears to have promoted them—remains largely unanswered. To date, Salem scholarship has offered a less than satisfactory explanation of the theology of the late seventeenth century, and of Mather's behavior and motivation. There are certainly unquestioned assumptions about both these issues in the whole corpus of Salem scholarship, which have remained either naively unexamined or, where analyzed, approached in a way which ahistorically ignores the beliefs and assumptions of the original participants.

Indeed, and perhaps surprisingly, it can be argued that what Salem scholarship has yet to do is examine Cotton Mather's cosmology as it relates to the 1692 Salem trials, placing it in an appropriate contemporary context. This study is an attempt to do just this. It returns to the theological dimensions of Salem witchcraft, contending that Cotton Mather's view of New England witchcraft was the natural and logical result of his cosmology. Taken within its historical period, this concentration deserves consideration as a way of understanding Salem witchcraft and Cotton Mather's responsibility in relation to it.

A word is in order here about the intention of this book. First, while it acknowledges the principle of acculturation and the role it played at Salem, it is not a study in acculturation. Nor is it a defense of Cotton Mather. Returning to a mono-causal approach for the purpose of defending either Cotton Mather or colonial Puritanism is neither practical, possible, nor appropriate, since, as the breadth of recent scholarship so ably demonstrates, the Salem situation can only be viewed as a combination of cultural, social, psychological, political, and religious constructs.

Nevertheless, there are interpretive benefits to be derived from focusing precisely upon the historical-theological approach to the study of Cotton Mather and the Salem witchcraft trials. In the process, the study engages the following areas:

Chapter one examines the historiography of the Salem trials, beginning with the latter nineteenth century. It looks at the various interpretive viewpoints that have been applied to the Salem trials and used as explanations of Cotton Mather's role within them. Beyond this, a number of both European and American interpretations of seventeenth-century witch hunts are identified, and the relative scarcity of work which takes a historical-theological approach to the study of Salem and Cotton Mather is noted.

Chapter two investigates the cosmology of Cotton Mather as it relates to witchcraft, drawn from four of his major works on the subject: *The Wonders of the Invisible World, The Magnalia Christi Americana, The Diary of Cotton Mather* and *The Armour of Christianity*. After tracing the early development of Cotton Mather's cosmology within the context of his Puritan upbringing, the balance of the chapter defines the specific components that formed Cotton Mather's personal theology. This chapter demonstrates that prior to the 1692 Salem trials Mather had developed a consistent theological outline related to witchcraft as a whole.

After this examination of Cotton Mather's personal cosmology, chapter three considers seventeenth-century New England witchcraft beliefs as found in pre-Salem, Salem episode, and post-Salem journals, publications, and court records of New England. The relative unity of witchcraft beliefs across social groups is presented, taken from these extant historical records. This chapter shows the compatibility of Cotton Mather's views of witchcraft to those of his contemporaries, demonstrating the shared witchcraft beliefs of the elite and common seventeenth-century New England populace.

Chapter four analyzes Robert Calef's censure of Cotton Mather as detailed in *More Wonders*, and reviews the background of the Calef-Mather dispute. Subsequently it considers the historical insistence initiated by Calef and repeated by Salem historians, that the Salem trials and executions resulted from Cotton Mather's pre-Salem and Salem preaching and publications.

Next, the historical climate of New England relative to witchcraft is investigated, through an examination of the major preexistent and transcendent factors within New England that had a formative impact on the Salem events. This evidence leads to a rebuttal of the historical allegation that Mather caused the Salem ignominy and suggests that the Salem witch trials can be more accurately described as another cycle of witchcraft accusations and adjudications within a preexistent and dominant culture.

Chapter five assesses the continuity between Cotton Mather's cosmology and his response not only to the Salem adjudications, but also to the broader scope of New England witchcraft episodes. First, the chapter looks at Mather's pattern of using his cosmology in interpreting contemporary personal, national and international events in terms of spiritual warfare and end-times portents. This pattern is expressed in several documents written by Mather before, during, and after the Salem trials. Next, the chapter examines Mather's application of his cosmology to several witchcraft episodes besides the Salem trials. Included in this is Mather's use of fasting and prayer to combat witchcraft invasions, as opposed to any adjudicatory procedures. The rest of the chapter presents Mather's primary postulates about the meaning of the Salem events, and the consistency of his corresponding conduct during the trials.

The sixth and final chapter begins with a contextual sketch of the challenges the New England government and magistrates faced in the Salem witchcraft trials. Following this, a fuller examination of Mather's advice to the Court of Oyer and Terminer is given, outlining Mather's plan for the examination and prosecution of the Salem witches. This chapter shows Cotton Mather allowed his relationship to the judges to prevent him from challenging their abuse of spectral evidence, and that he presented ambidextrous advice to the Salem court about its use. Last, this chapter shows that *The Wonders of the Invisible World* inadvertently became a self-contradictory and paradoxical account of the Salem trials as Mather attempted to distance himself from the principal personages involved in the Salem adjudications.

In its conclusion, this study presents the view that without identifying Cotton Mather as the initiator of the Salem trials, his role as an advisor to the Salem court and his publication of *Wonders of the Invisible World* created a legacy for him in later scholarship which has allowed historians to censure him, without ever entirely understanding him.

2

A CONSISTENT COSMOLOGICAL OUTLINE

Go tell Mankind, that there are Devils and Witches; and that tho those night-birds least appear where the Day-light of the Gospel comes, yet New-Engl. has had Exemples of their Existence and Operation; and that not only the Wigwams of Indians, where the pagan Powaws often raise their masters, in the shapes of Bears and Snakes and fires, but the Houses of Christians, where our God has had His constant Worship, have undergone the Annoyance of Evil spirits.

Cotton Mather, *Memorable Providences* (1689)

BY THE TIME THE curtain fell on the Salem witchcraft trials in the late fall of 1692, twenty New Englanders had been executed and another three hundred were in custody awaiting trial or execution.[107] Rather than subsiding, additional witchcraft accusations surfaced regularly. On 29 October 1692, Governor Phips ordered a halt to all of the proceedings, and later replaced the special court of Oyer and Terminer with the regular Superior Court. Sitting in January 1693, the Superior Court abruptly ended the previous judicial activities and exonerated all of the accused.[108] There would be no further executions.

It was at this moment that Cotton Mather released his latest book, entitled *The Wonders of the Invisible World*.[109] Written at the request of the Court of Oyer and Terminer, with Governor Phips's permission, it was a hurried compilation of sermons, accounts of Indian atrocities, and a chronicle of five select cases from the recent witch trials and executions. More importantly, it would be Mather's theological defense of the reality of witchcraft and an attempt to show that witchcraft had been genuinely present in the colonies and, in particular, at Salem.

Wonders was not immediately distributed in the colonies because Governor Phips felt it might have an inflammatory influence upon a population already deeply divided over the trial procedures and executions. Because of Phips's delay in releasing *Wonders* in New England, the same 1693 publication sold more copies in England than in North America. When *Wonders* was finally released to the New England public, it was received with a mixture of both compliments and criticism in spite of the fact that it was endorsed by several prominent Puritans, including Chief Justice Stoughton.[110]

In the hands of his critics, however, Mather's defense of the Salem court was equated with the tragic outcome of the trials themselves. In the writings of Robert Calef, in particular, Mather's name was effectively linked to the trials. In 1700, Calef wrote a scathing attack on Cotton Mather in his own account of the proceedings, entitled *More Wonders of the Invisible World*.[111] As previously noted, Calef's criticism has informed the work of many more recent historians, including Perry Miller. In Miller's analysis, he specifically singled out Cotton Mather and his defense of the Salem trials and executions, alleging Mather knew they were a shameful disgrace. In doing so, he portrayed Mather's publication of *The Wonders of the Invisible World* as an attempt to cover the Salem atrocity perpetrated by the ministers and the court of Oyer and Terminer. Miller describes Mather's motives this way:

> *He was commissioned to absolve them [the court]; to his undying infamy, he accepted the assignment. . . . The Wonders of the Invisible World, has ever since scarred his reputation. . . . He tried to make those killings legitimate when he knew they were murders by dressing them in the paraphernalia of the federal doctrine.*[112]

Miller's viewpoint is important as it typifies the belief of modern critics that Mather defended the results of a judicial proceeding in which he had no faith, by means of a hurriedly created and ill-conceived book. The allegation becomes incriminating when it is taken to its logical conclusion: that in the fallout of the Salem trials, Mather wrote *Wonders* as a theological defense of witchcraft beliefs, in a craven attempt to save the reputations of Boston's ministers and judges, and his own.

At the time of its publication in 1693, *Wonders* was Cotton Mather's most detailed and widely read work on witchcraft. Nonetheless, it was hardly his only study of the issue. Four other major works by Mather either exclusively or partially deal with witchcraft. These include *Memorable Providences* (1689), *Magnalia Christi Americana* (1702), *The Armour of Christianity* (1704), and his then unpublished diaries (1681-1724). Written before and after the events at Salem, these works encompass Mather's main cosmological beliefs, and reinforce the positions on witchcraft found in *Wonders.*

In all of Cotton Mather's works there is the obvious pervasive influence of the dogmatic theology of Puritanism. This cosmology served as the mental grid through which Mather perceived and interpreted events in his personal life and historical era both in terms of causation and effect. One cannot begin to fathom Salem witchcraft or Mather until the theology behind these subjects is taken seriously. The Puritan worldview had everything to do with how Cotton Mather and his generation perceived and dealt with witchcraft. As Richard Weisman puts it, "If Puritan theology can be adequately interpreted without reference to witchcraft, it remains the case that witchcraft in Massachusetts cannot be understood outside the context of Puritan theology."[113] As a result, no assessment can be made of the credulity of Mather's *The Wonders of the Invisible World,* or his role in the Salem trials, without first reviewing Mather's seventeenth-century cosmology relative to witchcraft.

This chapter will do just that—examine Mather's personal

cosmology related to witchcraft. What follows will demonstrate that Cotton Mather possessed a specific worldview in relation to witchcraft that was in agreement with the basic premises the court used in the Salem adjudications. Far from being a post-Salem creation, Mather's cosmology had been largely formed between the period of his graduation from Harvard college in 1678 and his publication of *Memorable Providences* in 1689.

This chapter will look at Cotton Mather's theology in relation to witchcraft from the perspective of his pre-Salem, Salem, and post-Salem works, rather than focusing exclusively upon Mather's publication of *Wonders*. After briefly surveying Mather's theologically formative years, this chapter addresses three dominant parts of his cosmology related to witchcraft. First, the chapter identifies Cotton Mather's theological explanation of the existence of Satan and demons. This section shows not only Mather's personal understanding of these entities, but also the compatibility of Mather's views with those of his seventeenth-century clerical contemporaries. Next, the chapter explores Mather's analysis of the practice of witchcraft, including his explanation of how witchcraft was initiated, developed, and operated in his era. Finally, while Mather's specific recommendations to the Salem court will be discussed in the final chapter of the book, this chapter makes a number of preliminary observations of Mather's overall beliefs concerning how the covenant people of New England were expected by God to respond to witchcraft.

The Background of Cotton Mather's Theology

THE PURITANS OF SEVENTEENTH-CENTURy New England subscribed to a basic cosmology predicated upon what they believed to be God's revelation to humanity: the Bible. For the Puritans the Bible was the singular authority for their corporate faith, as presented through the framework of their Calvinistic theological predisposition.

This was particularly and adamantly true of Cotton Mather. He was a third-generation Puritan minister, and the maternal grandson of one of the great architects of the Puritan faith, John Cotton. Mather was the epitome of Puritan society's product in terms of his belief in the concepts of the Puritan community and covenant faith.

As the son of Boston minister Increase Mather, Cotton spent his formative years in the setting of a ministry. Having learned to read at about the age of seven, Mather's early interest in the Bible resulted in his routine reading of some fifteen chapters from the scriptures each day. When at age eleven and a half Mather became the youngest student in Harvard College's history to be admitted, he already had a working knowledge of Latin and Greek, and showed signs of academic promise.[114] At Harvard, Mather simultaneously devoted much of his time to studying theology and natural philosophy (science), including contemporary astronomy and Copernican theories, and medicine. This trilogy of disciplines had a profound impact upon Mather's later life as a minister and scholar, as is evidenced in a number of his works and endeavors.

During some point in the last two years of Cotton Mather's college education, he felt he had received the assurance of salvation, and began to apply himself to the work of the ministry. He became an amanuensis for his father, Increase, transcribing important documents. Mather graduated from Harvard College in 1678, at the age of fifteen. Two years later he was appointed a probationary pastor, assisting his father at the historic Old North Church in Boston. With as many as two thousand people in the congregation, it was one of the largest and most influential churches of Mather's day. By the time Cotton received his MA degree in 1681, he was being courted by churches seeking a pastor, but he chose to remain at the Old North Church. In May 1685 the Boston ecclesiastical authorities ordained Cotton Mather as a co-pastor with his father, Increase.

By age twenty-two, Cotton Mather's position at the Old North Church had contributed greatly to his visibility as both a minister and scholar. Among his early published and unpublished works, Mather's notebooks of sermons and his diaries are most notable. His diaries in particular, beginning in 1681 and ending in February 1725, are, as Silverman notes, "the lengthiest surviving of any American Puritan."[115] The sheer volume of Mather's published and unpublished writings is impressive. During the forty-seven years of his active ministry he produced over four hundred works for both publication and private use and circulation.[116]

Between the years of 1678 and his 1689 publication of *Memorable Providences Relating to Witchrafts and Possessions*, Mather gradually developed his own worldview, including that part which dealt with witchcraft. Of particular importance is the fact that Mather's cosmology was quite compatible to that of his contemporaries, although it was at points more fully articulated in that he was in a powerful position from which to apply that cosmology to the specifics of seventeenth-century life. Mather's fuller expression of his views can be primarily attributed to his clerical prominence, which allowed him to publish his sermons and historical narratives.

It would be inaccurate to say that Mather made witchcraft a central focus of his studies before the Salem trials. Mather's ongoing publications were reflective of his varied interests in the Bible, natural philosophy, medicine, and pietistic works. With this in mind, it is nevertheless helpful to briefly describe his writings specifically on witchcraft: *Memorable Providences* (1689), *Magnalia Christi Americana* (1702), *The Armour of Christianity* (1704), and *The Diary of Cotton Mather* (1681-1724).

Beyond periodic sermons and diary entries, Cotton Mather's 1689 publication of *Memorable Providences* was arguably his clearest pre-Salem account of his theology relative to witchcraft to that date. It summarizes the events surrounding the 1688 possession of the young daughters of Boston native John Goodwin, a member of Mather's congregation, and reveals as much about Cotton Mather's personal ministry approach to deliverance as it does his theology of witchcraft.

Within its pages, *Memorable Providences* details the biblical and contemporary views of seventeenth-century New England witchcraft beliefs as seen in the Goodwin children's possession and Cotton Mather's application of Puritan theology to affect their spiritual liberation. This experience had a particularly profound impact upon Mather's personal belief in the power of witchcraft:

> *I am resolved after this, never to use but just one grain of patience with any man that shall go to impose upon me a Denial of Devils, or of Witches. I shall count that man Ignorant who shall suspect, but I shall count him down-right Impudent if he Assert the Non-Existence of things which we have had such palpable Convictions of.*[117]

Mather's theology of witchcraft found in *The Wonders of the Invisible World* was not theologically innovative compared to his contemporaries. Cotton Mather may have been more specific in his articulation of Puritan clerical beliefs about the power of Satan and witches, but he did not present any substantially new ideas.

In the years after the Salem trials, despite some introspection about his involvement in these events, Mather's belief in the nature of witchcraft or the power of Satan did not diminish. This is evident in Mather's publication of *Magnalia Christi Americana,* his church history of New England. Finished in 1698, but not published until 1702, the pages of *Magnalia* bear the marks of Mather's consistent and continuing application of theology to all forms of witchcraft, including predictive astrology. *Magnalia* also repeated much of the information found in *The Wonders of the Invisible World,* reinforcing Mather's insistences on the validity of the Salem trials.

The Armour of Christianity, published in 1704, would be one of Mather's most detailed publications relating his views of Satan and the powers of the demonic to attack both believers and non-believers. Mather's depiction of Satan in this work was far from that of a mere symbol of evil; instead Satan was depicted as a personal and powerful adversary, bent on the corruption and destruction of humanity. *The Armour* was originally preached by Mather at the Thursday Lectures in Boston from June to October of 1703 and entitled "The Wiles of the Devil." Mather subsequently published this series of sermons expressing his intent to "undermine the Kingdome and Interest of the Devil," by exposing Satan's devices and arming his readers with biblical guidelines for overcoming diabolic and malignant influences.[118]

Last in this list of Mather's major works reflecting his cosmology as it related to witchcraft are his diary entries for 1681 to 1724, published later as *The Diary of Cotton Mather*. These provide insight into Mather's ongoing interpretation of seventeenth-century events. Since Mather never intended to publish his journals, these entries record Mather's personal and often introspective insights without the mitigating influences seen in publications meant for his contemporary audience.

Taken together, these works provide a valuable resource from which it is possible to establish that Mather produced a rather detailed and consistent cosmological outline concerning Satan, demons, witchcraft, and the covenant people's expected response toward them.

A Consistent Cosmological Outline Regarding Witchcraft

TO COTTON MATHER'S MIND, the Bible taught that the world was made up of two critical spheres. One could be identified as the visible world and the other as the invisible world. The visible world was by all accounts a difficult realm. It was not only the domain in which everyday events occurred, but also where the great battle of the ages was waged, and won or lost. Then there was the invisible world. It was more glorious and menacing by far. It was the environment of both benevolent and malevolent forces in which the former functioned as marvelous protectors and the latter as terrible adversaries. On the whole, the invisible world was a mysterious realm into which few persons, including Mather, had ever been privileged by God to see.

It was the manner in which these two realms interacted that arrested the imagination and attention of Cotton Mather. It was the subject of not only his scholarship but his pietism as well. Almost all of his life he studied and postulated about this interaction, but it was New England witchcraft and the events connected to the Salem witch episode that provided him a real-life laboratory in which these two worlds could be seen to have collided. As it turned out, it was an experiment of unique and tragic proportions.

When it came to the diabolical entities of the invisible realm, the first and most easily identifiable individual in Cotton Mather's writings was Satan. Mather believed in the real and personal entity known as Satan, not merely as a symbol of evil, but as evil embodied. The subject of the Devil was never to be treated lightly, for Satan was an invisible and formidable enemy.

In fact, to Mather, questioning the existence of Satan was tantamount to denying the existence of God and the validity of the Bible itself. Mather says it this way in *Magnalia Christi Americana*: "Come hither, ye prophane Saducees, that will not believe the being of a devil, for fear lest you must thence infer the being of a God."[119] After all, the same Bible that said God was a real person said Satan was also. Only a defiant Sadducee (Mather's favorite term of condemnation for his antagonists) would fail to recognize Satan's existence. Satan was the foremost entity connected to witchcraft and the Bible the foremost authority that supported this fact. He states this categorically when he writes,

> *That there is a Devil, is a thing doubted by none but such as are under the influence of the Devil. For any to deny the being of a devil must be from ignorance of profaneness, worse than diabolical. About this Devil, there are many*

things, whereof we may reasonably and profitably be inquisitive: such things, I mean, as are in our Bibles reveal'd unto us.[120]

There was no debate therefore in Mather's mind as to the reality of Satan. It was a foregone conclusion. This should come as no surprise: It was an opinion shared by the vast majority of biblical scholars, both Mather's contemporaries and his predecessors. The majority of seventeenth-century Christians, including Puritan clerics, would have agreed with Mather's portrayal of Satan as a personal entity capable of extreme diabolism. Puritan minister Edward Taylor described Satan as having "laid his Train to blow up all the world by sin."[121] Though rarely used as the central or singular theme of Puritan sermons, Satan was ever present in the writings of New England clerics, as Elizabeth Reis indicates, "not as a metaphorical character, but as an actual embodiment of worldly and spiritual attractions: he was cunning, manipulative, and above all, persistent."[122]

As to the nature of Satan, Mather repeats the common Puritan interpretation. He sees him as a fallen angel who is involved in the affairs of this world as an adversary to man and God, and at times a tool of God. In *The Armour of Christianity*, Mather writes, "Those Apostate Angels, are all United under one Infernal Monarch, in the Designs of Mischief."[123]

As Mather and his Puritan clerical contemporaries such as Samuel Willard and Jonathan Mitchell understood it, Satan's fall stemmed from his post-creation status within the divine hierarchy. They explained that Satan's ill-fated discontent was provoked when God signified that Satan and his subservient angels' role in the universe would include ministering to the needs of the newly created human race.[124] Citing humanity's apparent inferiority to themselves, Satan and the angels rebelled against God. Consequently, as Mitchell described it, the "witting and wilfull Sin and pride" of Satan caused his irretrievable fall from grace.[125] As Mather would further expound,

> *He was once in that Order of Heavenly Creatures, which God in the Beginning made Ministering Spirits, for his own peculiar Service and Honour, in the Management of the Universe; but we may now write that Epitaph upon him, How art thou fallen from Heaven! Thou hast said in thine Heart, I will Exalt my Throne above the Stars of God; but thou art brought down to Hell.*[126]

The Devil, however, was not to be viewed as a uniquely powerful entity, apart from the demonic hosts. Instead, he was to be regarded as one being in the same category of divinely created but fallen beings. Further, even the term "Devil" was adaptable, since, as Godbeer notes, "it could signify not only a specific being, but also evil in a collective . . . to designate the fallen angels by a singular name was not inappropriate, since it underlined their oneness and union in sundry respects."[127] For Mather, then, Satan's actual prominence is due to the fact that he occupies an elevated position in the hierarchy of evil angels. This is reflected in Mather's descriptions of the Devil:

> *When we speak of, the Devil, 'tis, A name of Multitude; it means not One Individual Devil, so Potent and Scient, as perhaps a Manichee would imagine; but it means a Kind, which a Multitude belongs unto. . . . A Devil is a Fallen Angel, an Angel fallen from the Fear and Love of God, and from all Celestial Glories; but Fallen to all manner of Wretchedness and Cursedness.*[128]

This description by Mather is similar to those penned by a number of his seventeenth-century counterparts. The English minister Henry Smith would remind his readers that "when Christ asked [the demon] his name, he called himself Legion, which imports a multitude, as if he should brag of his number."[129] Jonathan Mitchell declared Satan the leader of "a numberless number of those

Invisible Immortall created spirits."[130] Similarly, Samuel Willard indicated that while Satan connoted all of the devils, he was also "the ringleader of the rest called the prince of Devills."[131]

Although, like his contemporaries, Mather's intent was to put the emphasis upon the fact that Satan is not an omnipotent, omnipresent personality, the effect is nonetheless just the opposite. Mather's understanding tends to give Satan a ubiquitous presence, for in folding him into the general scheme of ever-present evil angels, Satan does indeed become practically pervasive. In the process, Mather depicts Satan as the root cause of what evil activities transpire in the world. This line of thought acquires an increasingly important element in Mather's reaction to the evil perceived to be at work at Salem. In Mather's view, the Devil is responsible for what is happening, because the evil spirits are in his command. Mather describes it this way when he writes,

> *Tis probable, That the Devil, who was the Ringleader of that mutinous and rebellious Crew, which first shook off the Authority of God, is now the General of these Hellish Armies; Our Lord, that Conquered him, has told us the name of him; 'tis Beelzebub; 'tis he that is the Devil, and the rest are his angels, or his Souldiers.*[132]

Mather believed Satan's role in witchcraft to be a deliberate and orderly process: that the Devil was always at the core of witchcraft troubles. This was true whether one was referring to the Salem affair or any other historical case of witchcraft. He took great pains in *Wonders* to record events found in other parts of the world, including several reported accounts from cases in Sweden in the year 1669.[133]

To Mather, Satan's overarching design was always the same—to seduce humanity away from God and to enslave it to himself. This remained true whether Satan's attack was focused upon the elect or damned, the individual or the community, since all humans were his prey in the cosmic battle against God. In the case of the unregenerate, Mather insisted that Satan acted to "employ as many and subtle wiles to divert every man living from ever being a Christian."[134] Far more frightening to Mather, however, was the Devil's ability through witchcraft covenants to persuade the godly to renounce Christ, and become his slaves. In such cases, Mather warned, "All the vice, all the baseness, all the darkness that could render a man a devil incarnate, would presently seize upon the soul of that man."[135] Mather indicates the age-old, persistent approach of the Devil toward humanity, remarking that "the Devil whose Malice and Envy prompts him to do what he can in his assaulting of us: he that assail'd our First Parents, in a Serpent, will still Act Like a Serpent."[136] This battle, which had gone on throughout human history, would find its culmination in eschatology; as William Perkins suggested, "These are the last times, and Satan seeth, that he hath but a short time to continue, therefore he bestirreth himself."[137]

In all cases, the Devil's first tool was that of recreating in humans the same damning sin of pride that had been present at the Devil's rebellion, thus alienating men and women from saving grace.[138] In *Wonders*, Mather detailed this attack, writing,

> *The Temptations of the Devil, aim at puffing and bloating us up, with Pride: as much perhaps as any iniquity. . . . Pride is the Devil's own sin: and he affects especially to be, The King over the Children of Pride. . . . He [the Devil] is a Fallen spirit Himself, and it pleases him to see the Falls of Men.*[139]

By the end of the Salem trials, Mather believed that Satan's method was to consistently work from one population center to another until he accomplished a grandiose design of ruining not just individuals, but the churches and government of God's commonwealth. Mather found ample evidence to support this belief in Andover witches' testimonies verifying Satan's intention to "set up his own worship, abolish all the churches in the land, to fall next upon Salem and so go throughout the country . . . to set up the kingdom of the Devil."[140]

Just how did the Devil intend to implement this? Was there a pattern which Mather could detect and identify in all that was happening? The answer to these questions is found in a system of evil that Mather lays out for the reader in his book *Wonders*, and amplifies in other writings.

Satan's first objective in his longer campaign was to gain access to the various communities and populations. Mather's view was that Satan could not act without the permission of God in such matters. As a result, Satan's first role was to act as an accuser before the throne of God, with his primary activity centered on pointing out where such individuals and societies had sinned and when they deserved punishment. This was the starting point. Mather says of this,

> *The Devil first goes up as an accuser against us. He is therefore styled The Accuser; and it is on this account, that his proper Name does belong unto him. There is a Court somewhere kept; a Court of Spirits, where the Devil enters all sorts of Complaints against us; he charges us with manifold sins against the Lord our God . . . whereupon he urges, Lord, let'em now have the death which is wages, paid unto'em!*[141]

Mather would repeat this version of events in his 1704 publication of *The Armour of Christianity*, when he wrote,

> *The Devil sees, that by sin against God, men bring upon themselves the Wrath of God; and he hopes to be the Executioner of that wrath. . . . It is the Office of the Devil, to be the Executioner.*[142]

In this process, the fate of the accused is determined by the truthfulness of the charges. The hope, of course, is an acquittal. Mather's courtroom portrayal continues this way:

> *There he loads us with heavy Imputations of Hypocrysie [sic], Iniquity, Disobedience. . . . If our Advocate in the Heavens do not now take off his Libel; the Devil, then, with a Concession of God, comes down, as a destroyer upon us. Having first been an Attorney, to bespeak that the Judgements of Heaven may be ordered for us, he then also pleads, that he may be the Executioner of those Judgements.*[143]

If the charges are just and no acquittal materializes, then God grants Satan permission to afflict the population for their crimes against God. The effect of this consent is to give Satan a powerful additional role, that of implement of God's punishment. Putting it in explicitly judicial terms, Mather says, "The God of Heaven sometimes after a sort, signs a Warrant, for this destroying Angel, to do what has been desired to be done for the destroying of men."[144]

Mather saw Satan's actions in the visible and invisible realms, in both tangible and intangible forms. He portrays Satan's visible punishments as infectious plagues, human wars, and natural storms and disasters. However, by far the worst are the intangible signs. These are "spiritual woes," the working of Satan's wrath and God's judgement as evidenced among covenant nations by heresies, persecutions, the turning of pious men to acts of wickedness, and yet the most damning of all: witchcraft in the population.

Witchcraft, then, is one of Satan's greatest instruments against God's chosen people. It becomes a two-pronged dilemma. First, Satan gains permission to distress the populace through the temptations of witchcraft participation, and then he tyrannizes the population through witchcraft possessions and attacks, all as a prelude to their submission to him.

What, then, is Satan's goal in the use of witchcraft assaults against the nations? As Mather sees it, without God's intervention the outcome of Satan's diabolical effort is the enslavement of the nation to himself, destroying the populace as well as God's historical and salvific plan in the process. As Mather puts it,

> *You may both in Sacred and Profane History, read many a direful Account of the woes, which they that are possessed by the Devil do undergo: And from these conclude, What must the children of Men hope from such a Devil. . . . Furthermore, the servile, abject, needy circumstances wherein the Devil keeps the Slaves, that are under his more sensible Vassalage, do suggest unto us, how woful the Devil would render all our Lives.*[145]

The only thing that prevents Satan from accomplishing his final objective is the mercy of God. As a true Puritan, Mather believed that God may punish the sin of his people through allowing Satan room to afflict them, but that his initial and concluding purpose is always redemptive. It should be clearly stated that Mather's great concern was that his country's afflictions be recognized as God's judgement so that a repentant nation would stop the cause of judgement: sin.

In viewing Satan's role, Mather effectively portrayed him as the adversary of humanity. Satan appears in the court of heaven accusing the covenant people of crimes against God. If his charges are truthful, he gains authorization to execute the judgement of God. Witchcraft is the preeminent tool of Satan because by it he can both execute his wrath against the populace and bring it under his own control.

In Satan's plot to enslave humanity he was not alone in his diabolical endeavors. For Cotton Mather, if in this invisible cosmos Satan was a formidable opponent, there were quantitatively even more menacing evil entities about: the devils themselves. Satan was a devil, to be sure, but he was only one devil: powerful, but limited in the scope and range of his ability to do evil. On the other hand, his underlings, the demons, were so many they could not be numbered, nor was it any use to guess what their combined strength might be.

Mather held that the general dwelling place of this demonic host was the atmosphere that surrounded the earth. He envisions this when he writes,

> *The Sovereign God hath, with infinite Wisdom and Justice confined the Fallen Spirits unto this atmosphere; But with their confinement, they have so much liberty . . . they may range and rove about, and molest the poor children of men. Our air is filled with them, as with flies in midsummer. We draw our breath in the place of Dragons.*[146]

The world, the very place that humans walked, was filled with demons. Within *Wonders* Mather insists, "We are continually surrounded with swarms of those devils, who make this present world become so evil."[147] This translated into a perilous picture of evil entities all seeking an opportunity to enter the general rank and file of human beings to carry out their horrid designs. Mather's Boston colleague Peter Thatcher would claim that the number of demons among humans was sufficient to "beleaguer the whole Earth," as there was "not a place under Heaven where Satan had not his Troops; not a person without some of these cursed Spirits haunting and watching him."[148]

Added to the dangers posed by these invisible co-conspirators of Satan was the fact that Christians were not even safe from the work of demons in their own New England meeting houses. Preaching to his congregation at the Old North Church, Mather admonished them to consider,

> *In our Church-Assemblies, O how many Devils, do you imagine, crowd in among us! There is a Devil that rocques [sic] one to Sleep, there is a Devil that makes another to*

be thinking of, he scarce knows what himself; and there is a Devil, that makes another to be pleasing himself with wanton and wicked speculations.[149]

Within the visible world, Mather believed that the demons had specific spiritual and geographic areas that they were authorized to control. He reasoned, "Tis to be supposed, that some devils are peculiarly Commission'd, and perhaps Qualify'd, for some Countries, while others are for other."[150] Mather derives this view from the gospel of Mark, chapter five, where the demons ask Christ not to cast them out of the country of the Gadarenes. Mather conjectures from this that the power of those demons was limited to the area in which they had already enslaved a portion of the population. According to Mather, "Each devil, as he sees his advantage, cries out, Let me be in this Countrey, rather than another."[151]

In terms of structure, Mather believed that the demons were well organized. Their work is one of cooperation and mutual support in the cause of Satan. They are seen as "united under One Monarch and upon One design."[152] Mather often uses terms denoting organization to describe them, such as an *invisible army*, a *horde*, or *confederate spirits*. In each instance he wants his addressees to understand that these powers are not arbitrary, not random, but a well-ordered unit capable of careful strategy and coordinated attack upon humanity.

One of the chief advantages possessed by such entities is their vast knowledge gained through centuries of existence in the world. Mather deems the devils to be extremely intelligent adversaries, though like Satan they are not omniscient. He writes that the "education of all Devils is not alike,"[153] and as such, they are not all equal in knowledge. This does not make them any less dangerous, for in Mather's opinion they are still more knowledgeable than humans. He states it this way: "Doubtless, the knowledge of a Daemon is vastly beyond any of ours. . . . And the vast knowledge and understanding of the Devil is improved by a long experience."[154]

What then is their field of operation? Mather sees this in terms of ordinary vexations and extraordinary works. They are commissioned by Satan to bring about the judgement of God upon mankind in the form of visible and invisible afflictions.

Within the category of the ordinary vexations caused by demons, the role of these co-conspirators of Satan was to destroy the kingdom of God through their seduction and perversion of humanity. To do so, the fallen angels focused their attacks on recreating their own sin of rebellion within their human counterparts, using the soul as the battlefield between the kingdom of God and the kingdom of Satan.[155]

Mather and his contemporaries believed this attack upon the soul could take various forms, one of which was the attempt to distract humans from spiritual matters to the enjoyment of the sinful pleasures of the flesh.[156] Mather noted in the beginning of *The Armour of Christianity* that "the enemies that War against our Souls are the Flesh, the World, and the Devil: the Trinity of Hell!"[157] For Mather and his contemporaries, sinful flesh served the purposes of the demons well. They were able to use it, as Jonathan Mitchell noted, as "the principle agent in all disobedience."[158] As Mather put it in *Wonders*, "How did the Devil assault the First Adam? It was with Temptations drawn from Pleasure, and Profit, and Honour . . . Whereby the Devil would be Ensnaring us."[159]

Additionally, the devils attempted to vex New England through dissension within the Puritan churches. Such divisions were characteristically attributed to the work of malevolent demons working to undermine pastoral authority and harmony within the godly community. As the Puritan minister William Hubbard wrote, "Divisions, especially in the Church of God, [were] in a great measure to be ascribed to the policy of Satan."[160] Finally, the cohorts of Satan worked in the lives of the believers to bring them into false beliefs or to get them to denounce God altogether. As far as Cotton Mather was concerned, the most effective demonic vexation, short of witchcraft, was that of bringing people into heresy. In *Wonders*, Mather identifies these attempts, warning, "O Never does the Devil make such dangerous passes at us . . . when the Devil would poyson with false Doctrines."[161] Mather observed that heresy had not only been the fall of many humans, but also the tool of the Devil in the hands of the promoters of heresy. Mather puts it in this manner, writing,

> *That Serpent the Devil has acted his cursed Seed in unwearied endeavors . . . By the impulse of the Devil, 'tis that first the old Heathens, and then the mad Arians . . . and the Papists that came after them, have out done them all for Slaughters.*[162]

In the context of seventeenth-century Massachusetts, as Richard Weisman notes, the demons were not limited to any one form of heresy, but "encouraged all forms of religious error, from Antinomianism at one extreme to Arminianism and Catholicism at the other."[163]

As much as Cotton Mather underscored the ordinary vexations of the demons, the *extraordinary* vexations were a greater concern for him. These were the supernatural works of devils connected to the world of witchcraft. It was one of their areas of specialization, and perhaps the single greatest tool they possessed. In reading Mather's publications, the work of the demons in this matter can be readily divided into three activities.

Their first endeavor involved enticing persons to enter the practice of witchcraft through promises of supernatural assistance. As Mather described it, the demons were permitted by God to "Range with their Poisonous Insinuations among Ignorant, Envious, Discontented People, till they have cunningly decoyed them into some sudden act, whereby the Toyls of Hell [were] inextricably cast over them."[164] This would be the case in Mather's post-Salem account of the witchcraft torments of the young Boston woman Mercy Short. Mather wrote that the demons had "used a thousand

Flatteries and Allurements to induce her into a compliance" in their (unsuccessful) attempts to convince Mercy Short to become a Salem-witch conscript.[165]

The second activity was that of persuading the subject to inscribe their name in the Devil's covenant book, thus sealing an alliance with the Devil. In *Wonders* Mather noted that the Devil had convinced a "fearful knot" of persons to "lift themselves in his horrid service, by entering their names in a Book by him tendered to them."[166] As Mather saw it, the demons' success in persuading individuals to seal a covenant with the Devil extended to the individual's children as well. Mather described the inverted nature of the demons' works when he wrote,

> *It would break the heart of stone to have seen what I have lately seen: Even poor Children of several ages, even from seven to twenty, more or less, Confessing their Familiarity with Devils . . . that made a little Pourtratiture [sic] of Hell itself.*[167]

In certain cases, the demons took on the visage of particular witches in order to persuade persons, either by promises or by threats, to sign their names in the Devil's book. Mather records that the specter of Bridget Bishop, a Salem tavern-keeper, had taken one victim "from her [spinning] Wheel, and carrying her to the River-side, threatened there to Drown her, if she did not Sign to the Book mentioned."[168]

Last of all, Mather sees the demons bringing the witches themselves into the Devil's snare through their individual practice of witchcraft. Mather's point was that in those cases in which people allowed themselves to covenant with the Devil, the demons assigned to them would eventually prove to be their adversary. One danger was that once the demon was employed, the witch could not sever ties with it. In these cases, Mather explained that the "devil is evermore invited to the service of the Person that shall practise these Witchcrafts

. . . and so assume their Livery, that they cannot shake him off in any way."[169] Another dire effect of making a covenant with demons was that they would maliciously retaliate against witches who attempted to repent by the confession of their crimes. Mather recorded in *Wonders* that those witches who had testified against George Burroughs, the former minister of Salem, "ever since their Confessions, had been themselves terribly Tortured by the Devils" and "therein undergone the Pains of many Deaths for their Confessions."[170]

One could not covenant with the Devil and demons with impunity. Having used the witches to afflict and destroy others, the final goal of the demons was the damnation of the witches' souls. In the end, humanity lost, and the demons were the victors in Satan's plot. As this section demonstrates, in the years prior to the first signs of witchcraft at Salem, Cotton Mather had developed the overarching outline of his theology relative to the existence and activities of Satan and demons. The chapter now examines Mather's conceptions of witchcraft within the context of seventeenth-century New England.

Witchcraft: The Damned Art

JUST AS MATHER'S UNDERSTANDING of the invisible world of Satan and demons had been largely developed by the publication of *Memorable Providences* in 1689, it is equally true that Mather had also created a consistent theological perspective in relation to the practice of witchcraft itself. Again, the importance of Mather's statement of his theology of witchcraft is not so much found in any novel theoretical aspect as in the fact that his theology was in agreement with the preponderance of witchcraft beliefs in his own era. This section therefore surveys the main tenets of Mather's personal beliefs about witchcraft as identified in *Wonders*. Later, in chapter four, the specific application of Mather's theology of witchcraft to the Salem trials will be examined.

Cotton Mather, like almost all of his contemporaries, readily accepted the reality of witchcraft. He had only to go to his Bible and a plethora of established authorities on the subject to find evidence to validate the assertion that witches and witchcraft were not fictional, but rather a dark and evil reality. This view was expounded by Mather and nearly all of seventeenth-century New England. As Weisman notes,

> *That witchcraft and witches existed as real occurrences was as thoroughly uncontroversial an assertion to the colonial of New England as it was to his contemporaries in western Europe. The proof consisted merely of pointing to the relevant biblical texts.*[171]

For Mather therefore it was unnecessary to go to any great lengths to defend such a belief. His preface to *Wonders of the Invisible World* simply declares, "For the Dogmatical part of my Discourse, I want no Defense."[172]

In an attempt to define witchcraft, Mather essentially paraphrased the definition penned by the Cambridge theologian Joseph Glanville. Mather described it as "the doing of Strange (and for the most part ill) Things by the helpe of Evil Spirits, Covenanting with (and usually representing of) the woful Children of Men."[173] His and Glanville's definition is insightful, for it describes not only the activity of witchcraft, but also its operational basis.

As will be seen in greater detail in the next chapter of the book, witchcraft also had an inversionary aspect, since like salvation it was seen as a systematic progression of evil. In this respect, as Mather put it, witchcraft was a "Renouncing of God and Advancing of a filthy Devil into the Throne of the Most High . . . preferring of the Communion of a loathesome lying Devil before all the Salvation of the Lord Redeemer."[174] Therefore, witchcraft possessed a recognizable pattern and an identifiable result.

Drawing upon prior and contemporary sources on witchcraft, Mather proposed what he believed to be a plausible explanation for how witchcraft was initiated, developed, and operated. To begin with, witchcraft was understood to have a preparatory phase. The person who became a fully empowered witch was first preconditioned to such a state. In the minds of the New England clergy, this pre-entanglement consisted of the nurturing and practice of sin. The sins most usually cited as precursors to witchcraft were pride, greed, lust, anger, hatred, unbelief, revenge, or discontent. All these sins of impiety created avenues that Satan used to prepare one for his service. Mather expresses this when he writes,

> *When persons through discontent at their poverty, or at their misery, shall be always murmuring, and repining at the Providence of God, the Devils, do then invite them to an Agreement with, and a Reliance on them for help. Downright Witchcraft is the upshot of it.*[175]

There were more direct preparatory routes to witchcraft which Mather identified as dabbling in the practice of "white magic" or "little witchcrafts." These included such activities as fortune-telling, using spells or conjurations to heal sicknesses, and water-witching. These could be easily identified with seventeenth-century folk religion, which had been largely imported from Europe.[176]

Mather often warned his congregation and all of New England that such dabbling would lead to witchcraft activities. In *Wonders,* he asks "Whether a World of Magic Tricks often used in the World, may not insensibly ablige Devils to wait upon the Superstitious Users of them."[177] In his mind, the use of any type of magic called forth demonic powers as the active agents in the practice of such magical arts. This was equivalent to becoming partners with demons.

Up to this point, such entrances to witchcraft might be called "innocent" entrapments. However, they led the individual down the much more serious path to the practice of "black magic," which itself implied conscious acts of occultism. These were most commonly called Sorceries. In *Wonders,* Mather would only describe them as the use of demons to perform functions to gratify the curiosities or to prevent inconveniences to individuals and beasts. He feared to give any further descriptions as he explained, "I should by naming, Teach them."[178] These actions were considered the swiftest and most dangerous path by which one became caught in witchcraft.

The most crucial progression occurred when the witch sealed a covenant with Satan, who then promised to assign a demon to actively provide them assistance. The covenant was composed of several parts. Mather describes it on the basis of the confession of several witches convicted at the Salem proceedings:

> *We have seen a horrible thing done in our land! O 'tis a most humbling thing, to think, that ever there should be such an abomination among us, as for a crue of humane race to renounce their Maker, and to unite with the Devil, for the troubling of mankind, and for People to be, (as if by some confess'd) Baptized by a Fiend . . . afterwards communicating in a Hellish Bread and Wine, by that Fiend admitted to them.*[179]

Here, the crux of the matter is presented. The imitations of the Lord's Supper and the Book of Life were the tangible and horrible counterparts to the covenant of salvation so ardently believed in by the Puritans. In the mind of Mather and the rest of the New England clergy, this was the ultimate expression of sin. Nothing could be more treacherous, for the witch shunned God's grace and mocked the salvific covenant, but far worse, matriculated to the leagues of the damned. Peter Hoffer refers to this when he writes, "They were to sign the Devil's book. . . . It made the contract secure against the new witch's backsliding. The Devil gained possession—in law 'seisin'—of the signer's soul."[180] In essence, it was the purposeful renunciation of God and willing conscription into Satan's war against God and the objects of God's love, his chosen people. In the framework of Puritan theology, it was the equivalent of committing treason.

The most powerful stage of witchcraft emerged after one entered a covenant with the Devil. One or more demons assigned to the initiate would be called upon to become the "engines of malice" for them. They took the form of poltergeists, or "specters," and attacked both humans and animals, with invisible and often visible weapons. Their attacks on humans were evidenced by the witch's prey being tormented. In Mather's words, "The specters would proceed then to wound them with Scalding, Burning, Pinching, Pricking, Twisting, Choaking, and a thousand preternatural Vexations."[181] In certain extreme cases the victim either died suddenly or was driven to commit suicide. Cotton and Increase Mather had each documented such occurrences in their respective books, *Memorable Providences*, and *Remarkable Providences*. Both ardently reported, with noticeable public credibility, the number of previous cases of demon attacks in New England and elsewhere.

Demon representatives of the witch, using the witch's visage, would make the desired attacks. This was undoubtedly a great advantage, but it also became a chief danger because in a court of law the victim could easily identify his/her tormentor because the demon had appeared in their form. As will be seen in the later chapters, the whole issue of "spectral evidence" became increasingly problematic as many began to believe that "specters" could take the form of innocent persons. As demonstrated later, this issue would be the most significant problem that the Court of Oyer and Terminer faced. It would also become the issue which, more than any other, ended the Salem trials and brought Cotton Mather into disrepute.

As this section has shown, Cotton Mather truly believed in the power of witchcraft. Those who became fully empowered witches were preconditioned by their own sin of either "innocent" dabbling with "white magic" or the purposeful use of the dark arts. When persons involved in such activities accepted the promises of supernatural assistance from demonic entities and signed their names in the Devil's covenant book, they were assigned demons to aid their practice. The crucial aspect of this covenant was its sheer mockery of the covenant of grace and the act of enlisting in Satan's army against God and his chosen people. This was the most diabolical and horrific act that Cotton Mather and his generation could imagine. In the context of seventeenth-century Massachusetts, Puritanism and malevolent witchcraft could not be reconciled. What was left to be decided was how a covenant people should respond. For Cotton Mather, this was also a part of his cosmology, one that was largely in place prior to the 1692 Salem trials. The final section of this chapter discusses Cotton Mather's view of what seventeenth-century New England's response to witchcraft should be.

The Expected Covenant-Nation Response to Witchcraft

THE GREATEST QUESTION THAT faced Cotton Mather's generation was not the authenticity of witchcraft, since this was well documented and largely uncontested. On their migration to the Massachusetts Bay Colony the Puritans brought their cosmological model, and it was still intact eighty years later. As Karlsen points out, the "continuities rather than the differences stand out. . . . Indeed belief in the existence and danger of witches was so widespread, at all levels of society, that disbelief was itself suspect."[182] As a consequence, for the Puritans the question they struggled with above all others was what should be done when witchcraft was discovered in their midst. The last major component of Mather's cosmology relating to witchcraft dealt with this very inquiry and details his own method for the eradication of this danger. In all of his writings, he presents this outline dogmatically.

To counter any crisis linked to witchcraft, Mather advised

creating a system of shared responsibility on several levels. He proposed dealing with the problem spiritually and judicially. There were certain steps he insisted were necessary to ensure the success of such an undertaking.

The first consideration was what a covenant nation should do spiritually. In *Wonders*, Mather suggested the first step was to address the nation's failure to serve God properly. Mather says to his readers, "Let the Devils coming down in great wrath upon us, cause us to come down in great grief before the Lord."[183] Clearly, the attitude to be adopted was humility. By doing so, perhaps the Lord would be moved to pull back the chain which held the great "mastiff" called Satan. This was fundamental.

Because he believed that national sin brought about God's judgement, the initial response to witchcraft was centered around the concept of national repentance and reformation. In *Wonders,* he takes this position:

> *O let us set ourselves to make our peace with our God, whom we have displeased by our iniquities: and let us not imagine that we can encounter the Wrath of the Devil, which there is the Wrath of God Almighty to set that Mastiff upon us. REFORMATION! REFORMATION! has been the repeated Cry of all the Judgements that have hitherto been upon us.*[184]

Mather could see no end to the witchcraft dilemma unless the nation called upon God and turned from the very sins that had given Satan a platform from which to launch his fiendish plot. In other words, it was sin that brought the horrible circumstances about, and only the elimination of sin through repentance could change the situation.

Next, he maintained that the nation be cautious to eliminate the circumstances in which Satan could "lodge" among them. He cites

Ephesians 4:27, which states, "Neither give place to the Devil." Here he is suggesting that in the acts of accusing and judging one another of witchcraft, the whole "thorny business" could get out of control. This would result in the Devil accomplishing far more with the help of the people than he could have expected by his own unaided powers.

With this caution, Mather thought the nation should then take a third step in seeking to rid itself of any occult practices that were present. Keeping in mind the belief that witchcraft was often preceded by occult dabbling, Mather warns the nation to put away anything of the sort because

> *by these Courses 'tis, that People play upon The Hole of the Asp, till that cruelly venomous Asp has pull'd many of them into the deep Hole of Witchcraft it self. It has been acknowledged by some who have sunk the deepest into this horrible Pit, that they began at these little Witchcrafts: on which 'tis pity but the Laws of the English Nation, whereby the incorrigible repetition of those Tricks, is made Felony, were severally Executed.*[185]

The danger was that the same activities that caused the original witch invasion would bring others. The best method of escaping further trouble was prevention.

The last spiritual step that Mather points to is what he describes as "laying hold on the Covenant of God." In essence, this is the return to piety. Mather urged New England to return to its spiritual roots. If the judgement of God was upon the nation, it was because it had failed to give God glory by living out the covenant of grace he gave her. Throughout *Wonders*, Mather's tone is emphatic as he implores New England to return to God in this manner:

> *With Great Zeal, we should lay hold on the Covenant of our God, that he may secure Us and Ours, from the Great*

Wrath, with which the Devil Rages. Let us come to the covenant of Grace, and then we shall not be hook'd into a Covenant with the Devil, not be altogether unfurnished with Armour against the Wretches that are in that Covenant.[186]

In Mather's mind, a return to piety would have more power to heal New England of its wounds and put to rest the problem of witchcraft than any other method. It was his country's failure to live out the covenant that allowed for the horrible events that had transpired. God's purpose in allowing the witch invasion was to bring his people back to the place of spiritual vitality. New England needed to return to the life of the covenant nation, and then, and only then, would the colony be secured from evil.

The second major aspect of Cotton Mather's proposed response to witchcraft centered on the adjudication process. Mather was firm in his belief that witchcraft needed to be dealt with jointly by the Church and the government. The judicial process, however flawed it may or may not have been, was a tangible outworking of the theology of the Puritan community. The Puritans saw themselves, as Silverman attests, "as a small independent church-state, a purified American Israel separated from a corrupt Old World."[187]

No better term could be employed here than that of a church-state. Much like John Calvin's Geneva, New England was designed by its architects to be a state in which the Law of God was to be the law of the land. As such, when the Law of God was broken, it was not only the right but also the obligation of the state to be responsible for carrying out the adjudication process, under the moral guidance of the Church. Hoffer notes this important connection when he writes,

The close ties between ministerial roles and magisterial roles in New England made the judges' recourse to the ministers a natural step. . . . They were adepts in a time

when moral judgement and natural truths were not severed from each other.[188]

When it came to the unpleasant subject of witchcraft, Cotton Mather and the New England ministers called for no less than this. The Bible, the Law of God (upon which the laws of New England were based) had to be consulted in the determination of what was a crime, and what the prescribed punishment must be. This was the position of not only Mather but also all of seventeenth-century New England.

It certainly required them no great amount of study to arrive at the conclusion that witchcraft was expressly condemned by the Bible. In Exodus 22:18 God explicitly commanded, "You shall not suffer a witch to live." In Leviticus 20:6 God warned, "And the soul that turneth after such as have familiar spirits, and after wizards, to go awhoring after them, I will even set my face against that soul, and will cut him off from among his people." Countless other passages condemned all acts of occultism and witchcraft. In particular, the Old Testament judgement for such unrepentant and malevolent activities was quite consistent; it always ended in capital punishment for the offenders.

With regard to New England's legal statutes, one of its earliest constitutional documents, *The Body of Liberties*, specifically outlawed witchcraft activities. Drawn up in 1641 by John Cotton, Cotton Mather's grandfather, this document was patterned after the scriptures and specifically the Pentateuch. *The Body of Liberties* stated the biblical penalty for witchcraft categorically: "If any Man or Woman be a Witch they shall be put to Death."[189]

New England's prohibitions against and prosecutions of witchcraft were not the exception of the day; they were the norm. Similar laws were in use throughout the countries of Europe from the medieval era to more than fifty years after the Salem situation. By the end of the seventeenth century there had been extensive witchcraft allegations in the French and German parts of Europe in which, as Robin Briggs indicates, "the most reasonable modern estimates suggest perhaps 100,000 trials between 1450 and 1750, with something between 40,000 and 50,000 executions."[190]

Given this propensity toward the prosecution of witches in both Europe and the American colonies, perhaps it would be natural to expect that Cotton Mather's initial reaction when faced with a witch molestation would be that of calling for the immediate execution of all suspected witches. This was definitely not the case. Mather's writings and actions concerning the prosecution and punishment of suspected witches reveal a dichotomous approach which would cause him great grief in the aftermath of the Salem tragedy.

As chapter five will show in detail, Mather discriminated between two situations in the adjudication process. The first was that of the prosecution of malicious witches. He recognized the biblical injunction so often quoted by the Court of Oyer and Terminer: "You shall not suffer a witch to live" (Exodus 22:18). In the cases where the witchcraft was deemed to be deliberate and malicious, Mather saw no reason to waive the execution of the guilty fiend.

In one of the historical cases he records in *Magnalia Christi Americana,* that of Ann Cole, Mather reports that in 1662 she had been terribly afflicted by a local witch. After a thorough examination, the witch at last confessed and was sentenced by the judges to die. Mather records that "the woman was executed . . . whereupon Ann Cole was happily delivered."[191]

In the Salem cases, when Mather felt assured of the evidence and verdict of the court, he would intimate that the convictions and executions were biblically and socially deserved. This is manifest in the case of Tituba, the slave woman who was an early participant in the Salem affair. Although her conviction did not end the Parris family's ordeal, to Mather it was perfectly in order because it exposed what he deemed to be a plot of Satan against New England.[192]

Perhaps one of the best examples of this viewpoint may be taken from a letter that Cotton Mather wrote to his uncle, John Cotton, in which he commended the proceedings of the court in hanging five of six convicted witches on August 5, 1692. Among those executed were two persons accused by the Andover witches of being the leaders of their coven: George Burroughs of Maine and Martha Carrier of Andover. His letter specifically signified his approval of the executions, identifying Burroughs as the "Ringleader" and Martha Carrier as a "Rambling Hag." It was evident to Mather that the leaders of the entire devilish plot had been righteously executed, since, as Silverman notes, "for him, the persons being executed included the veritable King and Queen of American Hell."[193]

The second part of Mather's attitude was his reluctance to execute those who he felt had no malicious or devilish intentions in their practice of witchcraft. For these, Mather held out the grace of God and his personal sympathy. In Goody Glover's situation and similar cases, Mather went so far as to visit them personally in prison and to pray for them. Mather cautioned the court not to move too quickly in sentencing the convicted witches when their involvement in the Salem atrocities did not appear purposeful. He felt compassion for the common "neighbors" that were caught in the Devil's web, as evidenced by the following passage from *Wonders*:

> *With great regard, with great pity we should lay to heart the condition of those, who are cast into affliction, by the great wrath of the Devil. There is a number of our good neighbors, and some of them very particularly noted for goodness and virtue, of whom we may say, Lord, they are vexed with Devils.*[194]

In Mather's mind there was a judicial responsibility to execute the dangerous witches and yet an equal need to protect both the "innocent" and the inadvertently guilty. He reasoned that this dichotomy needed to be kept in tension. It was this very dichotomy that caused Mather to vacillate on his opinion of the trials and the executions of the convicted witches. It would also lead to Mather's eventual historical characterization as the person primarily responsible for the Salem tragedy.

Conclusion

AS THIS CHAPTER HAS shown, it can be demonstrated that Cotton Mather held a consistent theological view concerning the existence and activities of Satan and demons, the practice of the damned art of witchcraft, and the response toward witchcraft that God expected of the covenant nation. Mather did not, as his critics contend, develop an entire cosmology about witchcraft in the aftermath of the Salem tragedy. Instead, it was this preconceived cosmology that would form the basis for his response toward the Salem witchcraft trials. Accordingly, in Mather's mind and heart New England had a spiritual and judicial responsibility to actively deal with the witchcraft assault.

With Mather's cosmology relating to witchcraft in focus, the focus now turns to an examination of seventeenth-century beliefs about magic and witchcraft, within the historical context of Puritan New England.

3

A CONGRUENCE OF BELIEF: NEW ENGLAND WITCHCRAFT

Witchcraft is a most monstrous and horrid evil. Indeed there is a vast heap of bloody roaring impieties contained in the bowels of it. Witchcraft is a renouncing of God, and an advancing of a filthy Devil into the throne of the most high. Tis the most nefandous High Treason against His Majesty on High.

Cotton Mather, *Memorable Providences*

THE INTELLECTUAL LANDSCAPE OF seventeenth-century New England was filled with elements of the supernatural. Within this world, frightening supernatural entities such as demons and apparitions existed and were used to account for a number of strange but true events. Demons at New Hampshire, Newbury in Massachusetts, and Hartford, Connecticut, assaulted the homes of three families during the 1680s.[195] A strange scythe-shaped light appeared in the New England sky during 1681, seen by large numbers of people. Near Lynn, Massachusetts, a ghost ship was observed floating atop the waters of the bay.[196] In one incident, a woman murdered by her husband appeared to a young woman to report the homicide.[197] At Marblehead, Massachusetts, residents heard the eerie screams of a girl killed by pirates each year on the anniversary of her death. Another such apparition appeared at regular intervals during the 1680s in Cavendish, Vermont.[198]

Beyond the Puritan faith and sporadic wonders, however, the most generally accepted elements of the supernatural within early modern New England were embodied in the belief in witchcraft. As the previous chapter has shown, Cotton Mather's well-developed personal theology reflected a belief in the existence and work of Satan and demons, as well as the dangers of witchcraft. Nonetheless, a critical question that needs to be addressed concerning Mather's relationship to the 1692 events at Salem is whether his personal cosmology conforms to or is incompatible with that of his own contemporaries.

This chapter examines early modern New England elite and popular notions concerning magic and witchcraft by looking at pre-Salem, Salem episode, and post-Salem journals, publications, and court records. The chapter begins by exploring the widespread belief in witchcraft in early modern New England, with an emphasis upon historical sources and interpretive difficulties. This section cites elite and popular conceptions of witchcraft practice among groups threatening Puritan Massachusetts's security or homogeneity, including the Native Americans and radical dissenters. The balance of the chapter is given to an examination of the cohesiveness of elite and popular conceptions of four significant categories of witchcraft within seventeenth-century New England: magic, malefic witchcraft, counter-magic, and covenant witchcraft.

The chapter illustrates the broader "congruence" in elite and popular conceptions of the supernatural within seventeenth-century New England. The ultimate benefit of doing so is to establish the compatibility of Cotton Mather's personal cosmology with that of his contemporaries, both elite and plebeian. This examination lays the groundwork for a critical assessment of the historical condemnation of Cotton Mather for initiating the 1692 Salem witchcraft trials.

The Widespread Belief in Witchcraft

FOR THE PEOPLE OF seventeenth-century New England, witchcraft was not a theoretical matter, but a historical and contemporary reality based upon a plethora of common human experiences. The belief in the person of Satan, the power of demons, and the dangers of witchcraft extended in some measure to every branch of New England society. One Dutch visitor to New England in 1679 was particularly conscious of this pervasive belief. In his journal he wrote he had "never been in a place where more was said about witchcraft and witches."[199]

This does not imply that seventeenth-century New England lacked anything by way of intellectual sophistication. It would be too simplistic to attribute the belief in magic and malevolent witchcraft to superstition and ignorance. James Sharpe, referring to English witchcraft during the same era, notes the dangers of such an approach when he writes,

> *The belief in witches was shared by many people who were in the context of their own times as intelligent as we are. . . . The issue is not to show that people who believed in witchcraft were unintelligent; it is rather to explain how a wide variety of people, ranging from the very intelligent to the fairly stupid, were able to hold that belief.*[200]

Certainly, what Sharpe suggests is equally important to understanding witchcraft beliefs in seventeenth-century New England. New Englanders held a wide range of witchcraft beliefs similar in depth to their sixteenth and seventeenth-century English counterparts. Their witchcraft postulations were also largely derived from their English heritage and experiences. This becomes clear when one compares central English and New England witchcraft beliefs of the same era.

Seventeenth-century New England witchcraft beliefs do nonetheless present scholars with certain interpretive difficulties. Among these, one of the greatest challenges is that of determining the congruity of witchcraft definitions and beliefs between the elite, learned class and the larger population of early modern New England.

This is largely due to the fact that the specific nature of popular beliefs in witchcraft are difficult to ascertain, especially during periods in which little official documentation is produced. However, there are sources for studying beliefs in either the European or North American context that arise primarily from the various witchcraft narratives. These documents tend to give the greatest information about learned and popular views.

Relative to New England clerical and popular witchcraft beliefs, one helpful source is the accounts and trial transcripts of pre-Salem and Salem prosecutions. Of course, caution is necessary in examining this testimony, since these documents themselves present profound problems of interpretation. Witchcraft trial transcripts reveal neither complete agreement nor widespread dissension between the learned and popular culture of New England about the various aspects of witchcraft beliefs. This divergence of clerical and popular beliefs exhibits itself, at times, in ambiguity and confusion during witch examinations. For example, whether the adjudicators define witchcraft in response to the evidence provided during interrogation, or whether the outcome of interrogation reflected the shared beliefs of both the interlocutor and accused, is frequently unclear. As Keith Thomas put it, "Legal proceedings for witchcraft, in other words, represent the tip of an iceberg of unascertainable dimensions."[201]

Beyond trial transcripts, another major source of witchcraft beliefs is the writings of the clergy. The New England Puritan clergy, who were "interdisciplinary" in their education, believed quite literally in the powers of the Devil and the dangers of witchcraft. Their testimonies reveal that the divergence of beliefs at least between the Puritan clergy and the populace had little to do with the existence or efficacy of magic, whether beneficent or malevolent. Richard Godbeer brings this issue into focus when he states,

> *Puritan sermons, treatises, diaries, and correspondence also testify to the persistence of magical practices: in*

> *these writings the godly reported and condemned popular recourse to magic. None of those describing magical experiments, whether in court testimony or elsewhere, ever suggested that such activities were in any way unusual.*[202]

For the Puritan leadership, the real issue was not the efficacy of such activities, but rather the biblical and moral legitimacy of them. This insistence is repeated throughout the writings of the clergy as well as in the transcripts of the pre-Salem and Salem episode examinations. The Puritan clergy and government based the illegitimacy of magic and witchcraft upon three underlying assumptions examined in this chapter. In the first place, the clergy maintained a determined stance against the practice of all forms of witchcraft. In their view, whether beneficent or malevolent, witchcraft was an effort to manipulate or overturn the will of God through human and, worse yet, diabolical means.[203] Second, the use of magic (especially in the case of physical healing) was a departure from faith and dependence upon God, which was to be primarily exhibited through prayer and perseverance. Consequently, the use of magic was clearly outside of those means of relief solely ordained by God. Third, the clergy taught that magic, including but not limited to incantations, fortune-telling, and divination, created a dangerous propensity toward greater levels of witchcraft and possible damnation.

A second interpretive question that arises in the examination of seventeenth-century witchcraft beliefs concerns the level of witchcraft practice within New England prior to and concurrent with the Salem trials. John Hale, the minister at Beverly, seems to indicate that at least the first generation of Puritans did not in fact believe they faced any real threat of witch invasions. He noted, "Our fathers in the beginning of times of this Land, did not see so far into these mysteries of iniquity, as hath been since discovered."[204] By the latter part of the seventeenth century, this situation had obviously changed, since the historical evidence confirms that multiple levels of witchcraft belief and witchcraft practice existed throughout the New England populace, although to what degree cannot be ascertained.[205]

Beyond this, competing elements of magic and religion had become a part of an ongoing point of contention in the relationship between the clerics and general populace of New England. As this chapter will show, by this time New England's clerics were becoming more vocal about the illegitimacy of all forms of magical practices. The preaching and publications of this era are punctuated with clerical attempts to both warn their flocks of the inherent dangers of magical practices and to convince them to adhere to the Puritan supplicative means afforded by the Church.

The New England clerics were not alone in their attempts, since their colleagues on the other side of the Atlantic were pursuing similar ends. Stuart Clark has demonstrated that during the sixteenth and seventeenth century Protestant clerics throughout Europe were also attempting to dissuade their congregates from all magical practices. Identifying this conflict, Clark indicates that, to the extent that services like healing, divination, and counter-witchcraft had become professionalized in the hands of "cunning" practitioners, the churches were probably correct to think that they were being challenged by a rival institution.[206]

If indeed the seventeenth-century Massachusetts clergy considered magic and witchcraft practitioners to be their rivals, such persons were not exclusively found in a small portion of aberrant New England Puritan adherents. Clerical and government documents within later seventeenth-century New England demonstrate that groups challenging Puritan ideology and unity were also presumed to have implicit or explicit links to witchcraft practices. As chapter five shows, Cotton Mather and his clerical contemporaries would interpret these conflicts as divine judgments upon Puritan spiritual decline and as millennial anticipators.

For example, the Puritans not only insisted that the "Native-American culture was of diabolical origin," but also that the Native Americans had long been in collusion with Satan through witchcraft practices.[207] Indian hostilities such as Metacomet's War of 1675 to 1676 strengthened late seventeenth-century views that the Indians continued to be, as Alfred Cave suggested, "villains in a sacred drama" wherein God and the Devil struggled for control of the American wilderness.[208] Both clerics and settlers believed that Indian diabolism and English witchcraft were intertwined at several points. Accordingly, one former Indian captive claimed that specters of "Indian Sagamores" she had known during captivity appeared to her, urging her to sign the Devil's book.[209]

To Increase Mather, such claims of Indian-Satanic collusion seemed verified by post-conversion admissions of Indian shamans that they had previously "by the hands of Evil Angels murdered their neighbors."[210] Puritan clerics also attributed witchcraft activities to seventeenth-century dissenters, including the Antinomians, Anabaptists, and Quakers. When the Massachusetts General Court formally tried Antinomian leader Anne Hutchinson and her accomplices Jane Hawkins and Mary Dyer for heresy, they informally identified them as witches. According to Governor Winthrop, Jane Hawkins's activities involving midwifery and informal medicine "grew into great suspicion [that she was] a witch."[211] Hutchinson and Dyer were also suspected of witchcraft, in part because of miscarriages that allegedly produced "monstrous births" indicative of diabolical conception.[212]

In the case of the Anabaptists' radical millenarianism and denial of pedobaptism and church membership, the Puritan clerical response was to decry them as heretics and to insist that the magistrates enforce whatever punishments were afforded by New England laws.[213] As this chapter will later demonstrate, Puritan clerics and witch suspects alike portrayed the witches' rebaptism, by means of "dipping" initiates' heads in water, in similar terms to the

Anabaptists' pattern of rebaptizing adult converts who had thereby rejected Congregationalist traditions.

The Puritans attributed diabolism to the Quakers quite specifically. This was evident as early as the 1677 trial of Margaret Brewster, when one witness insisted that during Brewster's recent disruption of a Boston church service, "she had appeared in the shape of a devil."[214] In short, it was reasoned that because the Quakers were heretics, closely aligned with the Devil, it followed that they were also involved in witchcraft. As Carla Pestana notes,

> *If the heretics were witches, their success at converting English men and women to their blasphemous views was much easier to explain. Thus, Quakers as a group were described as witches. . . . Quaker leaders were accused of witchcraft, and individual Quakeresses were believed by New England authorities to be witches.*[215]

Beyond spectral sightings, within the seventeenth century, the New England Quakers' physical quaking during either prophecy or revelatory receptions would also be equated with Native Americans' demonic possession. In *Illustrious Providences*, Increase Mather clearly made this association, when he recorded a form of demonic possession among Quakers at wilderness meetings. He reported that after singing and dancing as a sign of conversion Quaker converts "were murdered, driven insane, inspired to dance naked, believed they were the risen Christ, or were urged to participate in ritual blood sacrifices."[216] The identification of the Quakers with Indian possession also took the form of accusations that the Quakers joined Native Americans in Devil worship. As such, Salem merchant Edmund Batter testified that Quakeress Elizabeth Kitchen had been "apawawing," meaning attending nocturnal devil worship with Indians.[217]

Turning back to the New England populace, it is not surprising that, within this broader context of late seventeenth-century New

England, clerics were battling another perceived challenge to Puritan homogeneity. This one, however, did not come from external forces threatening destruction, or heretics disturbing the tranquility of the Commonwealth. Instead, it came from insidious powers operating in portions of the Puritan population, to the degree that, as Richard Godbeer describes it, "magic, countermagic, and maleficience . . . proved to be less susceptible than either dissent or sectarianism to control by the guardians of spiritual purity."[218]

Despite disagreements about its biblical validity, the clergy and general populace still agreed about the power of witchcraft. This agreement can be traced in New England's seventeenth-century experience. Carol Karlsen notes this consensus, indicating that "what is most striking about the Salem outbreak was the congruence of belief it featured between Puritan leaders and townspeople."[219]

It is this "congruence of belief" that is the focus of the remainder of this chapter. The pre-Salem trial records and the literature stemming from the Salem situation present strong evidence for the widespread belief in witchcraft within the New England populace. The next section therefore concentrates on depicting the relative unity of witchcraft beliefs across social groups evident in the extant historical records of New England. Specifically, four types of elite and popular common conceptions of witchcraft are presented: magic, malefic witchcraft, counter-magic, and covenant witchcraft.

Elite and Popular Cross-Social Conceptions of Witchcraft

THE FIRST LEVEL OF seventeenth-century New England shared beliefs in witchcraft centered in magic or "white witchcraft." In England and Scotland, persons practicing this variety of magic were known as "blessers" or "cunning folk." In New England, the latter description was often used. The work of cunning folk was believed to involve the use of supernatural powers to perform acts benevolent to humans, often involving some payment for services rendered.[220]

The use of such arts was well known to both the clergy and populace, and both groups attested to its existence and power. Clerical documents and court records from both the pre-Salem and Salem witch trials indicate the use of magic by many who were later accused of malevolent acts. The techniques used by each varied, but all of them tended to employ charms, spells, and incantations, often based upon Christian prayers or scriptures.

One of the more common reasons that New Englanders consulted cunning folk had to do with physical healing. At least some of the populace went beyond the Puritan teaching of God's sovereignty in such matters, to attempts at securing healing outside of the covenant. Those who did so evidently did not have to go far to find one of cunning folk. Cotton Mather acknowledged as much in his *Paper on Witchcraft* when he wrote of a woman "who upon uttering some Words over very painful Hurts and sores, did . . . presently cure them."[221] In a similar reflection within *Wonders of the Invisible World,* Mather insisted, "They say, that in some Towns it has been an usual thing for People to cure Hurts with Spells."[222]

In Easthampton, Connecticut, a small farming town on the eastern tip of Long Island, neighbors sought one of its residents, Elizabeth Garlick, on many occasions when in search of healing.[223] In Massachusetts, Margaret Jones was also widely known for her healing powers and medicinal advice, which reportedly had "extraordinary violent effects" on those who followed them.[224] Jones's healing powers may have been too successful, since they also became a source of evidence against her during her later trial for maleficium.

In both Old and New England, a second use for magic entailed efforts to find lost or stolen objects. William Byg of England, who was arrested in 1647 for heresy and sorcery in the court of the Archbishop of York, confessed under examination that he employed a twelve-year-old apprentice who successfully used a crystal in locating stolen goods for others as well as ascertaining the identity of the thieves.[225] In New England, Governor John Winthrop noted a Massachusetts resident who alleged that he spoke to the dead "in order to discover either future events or locate stolen goods."[226] Cotton Mather also reported in his *Paper on Witchcraft* that he knew of a person who, "missing anything, would use to sitt down and mutter a certain Charm and then immediately by an Invisible Hand be directly led unto the place where the Thing was to be found."[227]

Predictive astrology was another cunning skill that a portion of the New England populace employed. Standard forms of the seventeenth-century English almanac contained astrological prognostications and zodiacal symbols based upon astrological lore, in which the influence of celestial bodies was linked to natural events. When these were used for the study of heavenly movements and their effect on weather conditions, agriculture, or medical treatment, the Puritan clerical attitudes ranged from ambivalence to tacit approval. However, the use of judicial or prognosticative astrology—the use of astrology by fortune-tellers, etc.—to predict or coordinate human activities was severely condemned by clerics as a violation of God's providential dealings.

Puritan clerical attitudes toward such uses of astrology are clearly enunciated by Cotton Mather: "It is a disgrace to the English Nation, that the Pamphlets of such idle, futile, trifling Stargazers are so much considered; and the Countenance hereby given to a Study . . . perilous to the Souls of Men."[228] Clerics construed the use of horoscopes to predict the course of a person's life, to determine favorable times for specific activities, or to ask specific questions based upon the position of stars as a variant of witchcraft.[229]

The Salem trial transcripts indicate Dorcas Hoar had acquired an astrology book from John Samson containing "streaks and pictures in it." Among other things, she used astrology to decide which dates were most propitious for stealing from her employer, John Hale.[230] At her trial in Salem, Mary Toothaker owned that the Andover witches had consulted astrology books as well, and "especially one book that treated of the twelve signs, from which book they could tell a great deal."[231] Their avowed purpose, however, rather than stealing, involved predicting the best time for their assault upon the New England religious and governmental establishment.

As the use of astrology might suggest, cunning folk might also practice fortune-telling. Some twenty years before the Salem trials, Dorcas Hoar confessed to her pastor, John Hale, that she had "borrowed a book of Palmistry, and there were rules to know what should come to pass."[232] Dorcas Hoar was obviously not the only New Englander to practice this art, since throughout the Salem trials evidence of fortune-telling was used against those facing maleficium indictments.

Andover resident Samuel Wardwell accurately predicted the gender, birth order, and number of children Ephraim Foster's wife would bear.[233] When Wardwell was later charged with maleficium by the Salem court, he confessed to Essex County authorities that he was "sensible he was in the snare of the devil" and that he had been "foolishly led along with telling of fortunes, which sometimes came to pass."[234] This confession gave credence to the clergy's insistence that practicing the lesser forms of witchcraft would ensnare individuals into yet greater degrees of the damned art. According to Wardwell, the Devil had promised to extend his life to some sixty years if he would sign a compact. The Devil's word, however, proved undependable since at the age of forty-six Samuel Wardwell was executed alongside Alice Parker on 22 September 1692.[235]

Before the Salem outbreak, the New England clergy also expressed concern about an increased use of divination among young persons. Their fears seem well founded in light of the Salem records. For example, during the examination of Sarah Cole of Lyne, she confessed that she had, along with other young girls, "toyed with a Venus glass and egg . . . [to see] what trade their sweet hearts should be of."[236] It was a similar attempt at satisfying youthful curiosity that precipitated the possession episode of Samuel Parris's daughters leading to the entire Salem tragedy.

During the Salem trials, several New Englanders were either charged with or confessed to using divination. The Salem sheriff arrested Abigail Faulkner Sr. for witchcraft after neighbors reported that she knew how to "conjure with a sieve."[237] Rebecca Johnson also owned that she used divination, but she did so for more personal reasons—to determine "if her brother Moses Haggat was alive or dead." Johnson testified that after using the words "By Saint Peter and Saint Paul, if Haggat be dead let this sieve turn round," it did so. Johnson subsequently learned through more conventional means that at the time of her experiment her brother was indeed dead.[238]

Foreknowledge, a companion to fortune-telling and divination, was also part of New England magic. This held particular importance because in contrast to divine revelations, foreknowledge endowed the witch with a unique body of information not available to others and useful for beneficent—or as the case often turned out, for malevolent—reasons. Peter Pitford obviously believed in the witch's foreknowledge as he had once complained to a neighbor about Ann Dolliver's insight, saying, "That old witch knows every thing that is done in my house."[239]

Martha Dutch expressed similar misgivings in her deposition against suspected witch Alice Parker. She testified that one day as the two were watching the crew of a ship coming ashore Dutch commented that it had been by God's grace that her own sailor husband had returned safely from many extended periods of duty at sea. At this point, the conversation changed dramatically. As Dutch recalled it, "I did say unto the said Parker that I did hope he would come home this voyage well also and the said Parker made answer unto me and said 'No Never more in this world.'"[240] Sadly for Martha Dutch, Parker's prediction came true, for seaman Dutch died on that voyage. As for Alice Parker, her prediction was partially responsible for her execution at Salem on 22 September 1692.[241]

By the seventeenth century, the ability to use magic to do harm was also a part of the imagining of both the elite and popular culture. Put simply, those magic practitioners who brought about good might employ the same supernatural arts for sinister purposes, with or without remuneration. Despite some degree of interpretive difficulty, the Salem trial transcripts reveal that many of the confessors believed their diabolical methods to have real effect.[242] The records involving pre-Salem and Salem witchcraft adjudications are resplendent with accounts of malefic acts of witchcraft, enumerating common elements of maleficium as purported by accusers, adjudicators, and the accused themselves.

One of the forms of maleficium perhaps most often cited by accusers and adjudicators was the alleged power of the witch to bring about dire effects through verbal curses. Taken in the Puritan context, the witch's cursing represented the use of diabolical powers to reverse or harm the natural world order. Such powers presented a threat to the wellbeing of individuals and communities. Jane Kamensky describes this threat:

> *The witch's words struck at the very foundation of local life: the dominion of man over their wives and farmers over their crops and livestock, the ability of parents to protect and nurture their children. . . . The impact of her words in the community setting was more literal and immediate. Babies and animals dropped dead. Inanimate objects moved at will. Luck ran out.*[243]

In the American colonies and in England, within early modern society verbal curses were part of a broader set of dangerous activities. Both slander and verbal curses were associated with persons who stood outside the boundaries of acceptable social behavior, whether on the interpersonal or community level. Verbally abusive persons, therefore, were part of the process of defining and maintaining social boundaries, as well as differentiating between "deviant" and "normal" persons with reference to morals and, at times, witchcraft suspicion.[244]

As Laura Gowing has demonstrated, this pattern can be seen in English verbal slander cases involving sexual accusations, in which "sexual insult and its prosecution became woven into the fabric of neighborhood dispute."[245] In New England, similar protracted village disputes involving slander and verbal curses often culminated in witchcraft accusations. As Jane Kamensky puts it, "Hectoring, threatening, scolding, muttering mocking, cursing, railing, slandering . . . reads like a handbook of verbal etiquette for witches."[246]

In both England and New England, relative to witchcraft, a suspect's speech weighed heavily against them both at the point of neighborly conflict and in the context of judicial examination. In 1608 the English theologian and witchcraft scholar William Perkins indicated in his treatise *A Discourse on the Damned Art of Witchcraft* that the witch acquired the powers of verbal maleficium in a covenant with Satan. He observed that the Devil had "his words and certain outward signs to ratify the same to his instruments." He further directed judges to note any accusations of maleficium that followed either the direct curse uttered by witches or was a result of quarreling or threatening relatives or neighbors.[247]

The power of the tongue was a much-attested danger within the Salem trials as well. Curses were often directed at either property or animals. In the case of Benjamin and Sarah Abbot (husband and wife), their misfortunes began after they were granted an enviable parcel of land by Andover Township, when their neighbor Martha Carrier accosted Benjamin about it and "gave out threatening words." Shortly afterward, Benjamin Abbot developed an acute inflammation in his side and feet, and Sarah Abbot testified,

> *Strange and unusual things has happened to his [Benjamin's] cattle, for some have died suddenly and strangely . . . and some of the cattle would come out of the woods with their tongues hanging out of their mouths in a strange and affrighted manner, and many such things,*

which we can give no account of the reason of, unless it should be the effects, of Martha Carrier's threatenings.[248]

The ability of malevolent practitioners to cause either loss of life or property was not limited to verbal means. Indeed, "cunning people" turning to malefic practices might utilize more insidious and less obvious methods. One of these was the "overlooking" or "casting of the eye" upon animals, belongings, and persons. New England literature is replete with examples of this. When a sow belonging to John Bly suddenly became violent, he was certain that it had been "overlooked" by a witch. At the suggestion of a neighbor, Bly fed the animal a mixture of "red okra and milk" as a remedy against a witch attack and later found the sow normal again.[249] During the Salem proceedings many of the witnesses attested to the dangers of the "evil eye." In the case of suspected witch Mary Taylor, when she was directed to look upon her accusers, Simon Willard records that one of them was "struck down by it."[250] The power to "overlook" was possessed by both male and female witches. The Salem court clerk recorded that during Job Tookey's appearance before the judges "the said Tuky lookeing upon the afflicted struck them down with his eyes and recoverd them by taking on them Severally by the hand or wrist."[251]

At other times, the witch might perform maleficium through image magic—charms, images, or spells used to cause harm or death to others. As a scholar, Cotton Mather wrote of the ability of witches to cause harm using puppets made to resemble the witch's victim. In his *Paper on Witchcraft* he told his readers of an unnamed man who was "tortured with a cruel, pricking, Incurable pain in the Crown of the head." In the end, the authorities caught the man's sister with "a Poppet in Wax, resembling him, with a pin stuck in the head of it; which being taken out, he Recovered Immediately."[252] As a minister, and in a more personal encounter, Cotton Mather watched image magic being performed at the Salem jail while visiting Goody

Glover, an Irish witch. Mather wrote in *Memorable Providences* that "she took a stone, a long and slender stone, and with her Finger and Spittle fell to tormenting it . . . though whom or what she meant, I had the mercy never to understand."[253] Mather was obviously uneasy about being the only person present with Glover during this activity.

Short of killing their victims, perhaps the most striking manifestation of the witch's power occurred in possession cases. Richard Godbeer suggests that "diabolical possession was one of the most dramatic and disturbing manifestations of the supernatural world to which early modern Europeans and seventeenth-century New Englanders were exposed."[254] In short, diabolic possession was defined as the inhabitation and control of a human body by one or more demonic powers, manifested through the victim's speech, physical movements, and behavior.

In cases involving diabolical witchcraft possession, there were, however, significant difficulties. The first was the issue of the diagnosis of witchcraft possession by the seventeenth-century clergy and medical establishment. Both, of course, gave credence to witchcraft. For example, Sir Thomas Browne in his treatise *Religio Medici* wrote, "I have ever believed and do now know that there are witches. They that doubt of these are . . . of a sort, not of infidels, but atheists."[255] Such a belief on the part of medical practitioners was not always on a professional basis. In Old England, an Elizabethan doctor at Wells complained the Devil was appearing to him more often than he liked. Trained by Jesuits, he dispensed with the Devil by throwing rosary beads at him.[256]

This seventeenth-century agreement concerning possession cases by the clergy and physicians was normal. Cooperation between the disciplines in theological and medical education was a long-established tradition harking back to the English Puritan era. This cooperation, however, could also create a propensity toward dangerous speculation or medical diagnoses of witchcraft when unexplainable physical and mental manifestations occurred.

Of course, not all possession cases in seventeenth-century New England could be automatically attributed to demonic possession. What historians have labeled "spirit-possession" took a number of specific forms, indicating either the manifestation of God or Satan, depending upon the context. This was an era in which, as Clarke Garrett has pointed out, "the Millennium seemed to be at hand, [and] spirit possession manifested itself in many forms."[257]

As previously noted, when Pennsylvania Quakers and other radical dissenters experienced spirit possession, they believed that the Holy Spirit had taken control in order to grant them access to "Inner Light" revelations. The Puritans of course shunned enthusiastic possession while finding diabolic possession more credible in the battle between the Puritan community and the Devil's end-time forces. The latter approach, as Stuart Clark observes, reveals that

> *in an age accustomed to polarize the moral categories on which history ultimately rested, possession and its treatment were the most vivid possible demonstration of the relative strengths of good and evil in the world.*[258]

As to diabolical possession, despite diagnostic difficulties, three discernible explanations had become established for how persons came to this condition. The first possibility was that the possessed might have given themselves over to the Devil of their own free will. A second was that the Devil might have taken over victims without their permission or desire.[259] Lastly, and perhaps the most prevalent explanation, was that possession had occurred as a result of the malevolent mediation of a witch.[260] The third explanation, possession by witchcraft, would have a definite hold on the New England populace within the middle to latter part of the seventeenth century. In fact, during the thirty years before the Salem episode, and well after it, a number of possession cases were attributed to witch attacks within New England. Godbeer makes this clear when he writes, “For New England alone, we know of seventy-eight cases that occurred during the first century of settlement.”[261]

The information available on these disturbing events stems from clergy journals and sermons, official court records (where prosecutions occurred), and from firsthand accounts of observers. Possession cases often became public events, drawing significant numbers of people either out of curiosity or for fasting and prayer for deliverance. Karlsen gives a telling account of the common elements attributed to possession cases when she writes,

> *They typically included strange fits, with violent, contorted body movements; prolonged trances and paralyzed limb; difficulty in eating, breathing, seeing, hearing, and speaking; sensations of being beaten, pricked with pins, strangled, or stabbed; grotesque screams and pitiful weeping, punctuated by a strange but equally unsettling calm between convulsions, when little if anything was remembered and nothing seemed amiss.*[262]

A classic case of witchcraft possession occurred in 1662 at Hartford, Connecticut. Ann Cole experienced possession as a direct result of the malevolent witchcraft practiced by several witches, including Judith Varleth. According to Increase Mather, during Cole’s possession by demons, she manifested supernatural knowledge, as well as astonishing her attendants with her ability to “so exactly imitate the Dutch-tone in the pronunciation of English.”[263] The latter ability seemed particularly important to the judges since Judith Varleth was Dutch by ancestry.

Another case of possession occurred in 1671. Samuel Willard’s servant, Elizabeth Knapp, underwent thirty-four days in the hold of unseen powers. Her invisible captors caused her to alternate between the inability to speak and verbal torrents, while at other times she was either paralyzed or “leaped and skipped” about the house. The clergy and her family eventually recovered Knapp through fasting and prayer.[264] No counter-magic or Catholic ritual had been employed, for reasons one Elizabethan preacher had stated decades before: Possession was not to be dealt with by "conjuration and incantation as Popish priests profess and practice, but by entreating the Lord humbly in fasting and prayer."[265]

Acts of maleficium, however powerful, were not always final in their effect. New England witchcraft beliefs attested to by both clergy and populace also extended to the possibility of their reversal as well. Although denounced by the Puritan clergy, counter-witchcraft, also called counter-magic, was deemed capable of powerful effects. New England minister Deodat Lawson, in his *Christ's Fidelity the Only Shield against Satan's Malignity,* wrote that these "unwarrantable projects" included "burning the afflicted persons hair; paring of nails, stopping up and boyling the urine; [and] Their scratching the accused, or otherwise fetching Blood of them."[266]

Lawson's condemnation of these "unwarrantable projects" underscored contemporary and deep-rooted clerical fears about witchcraft progressions through counter-magic. They were not alone in such fears, as the English cleric George Gifford had said much the same when he warned his congregation about counter-magic:

> *A man is tormented sore in his body; he feareth that it is some witch that hath done it. He is advised by his neighbors to send unto some cunning man. Word is sent back, that indeed he hath bad neighbors. Let him do such an such a thing and he shall have ease. Well, he doth it and hath ease. What, shall we think that the Devil is driven out? A woeful driving out. He doth cease from tormenting the body [of the man] for a time, that he may enter deeper into the soul. He winneth by this driving out.*[267]

Despite the Puritan clerics' warnings that the use of counter-witchcraft to reverse maleficium would eventually lead to the Devil's ensnarement, some New Englanders willing to take such risks used this power anyway. Perhaps they did so because counter-witchcraft provided the person suffering from the effects of witchcraft recourse beyond the religious forms that were wielded exclusively by professional clergymen like Lawson and Gifford. Beyond its transgressive and empowering nature, counter-magic had a range of characteristics which made it particularly attractive for seventeenth-century New Englanders.

The first purpose of counter-magic was to reverse or remove a witch's spell. Trial records seem to indicate that, in part, counter-magic was attractive to common people because it depended primarily upon the correct use of reverse image ritual or spoken words, as opposed to skill or education. As such, its efficacy rested on the fact that the initial use of witchcraft by anyone created the environment in which malevolent and reversal witchcraft operated. As Godbeer explains it, "When someone used image magic to injure a person or damage an object, a two-way channel of communication was believed to open between practitioner and victim."[268] Therefore, the witch's victim might attempt to reverse the maleficium personally or secure this service from one of the cunning folk.

Second, beyond reversing or removing the witch's spell, counter-witchcraft could be used to identify the individual or agency responsible for the victim's suffering or reversals. In these circumstances, items taken from the victims themselves were often burned or boiled to identify the witch. Beverly minister John Hale noted the use of boiling and burning experiments, writing, "I observed that people laid great weight upon this; when things supposed to be bewitched were burnt, and the suspected persons came to the fire in the time of it."[269]

Hale's insistence is verified by an incident recorded in 1685. A local doctor diagnosed a young Quaker child in Salem to be "under an evil hand." When the boy had been ill for some time, the neighbors suggested cutting off a lock of the boy's hair and boiling it in water.

Though Quakers, like Puritans, forbade the use of counter-magic, because of his failing health, they proceeded. According to the boy's father, Samuel Shattock, while the hair was boiling the child began to "shreek out as if he had bin tormented."[270] During this episode, Mary Parker, a neighbor long rumored to be a witch, came asking if Shattock desired to purchase some chickens. Shattock's visiting neighbors felt this strange, since they believed Parker had none available for sale. Clearly, they believed that boiling the afflicted boy's lock of hair had drawn the guilty witch to Shattock's home.

In specific cases, counter-witchcraft took on its third and most serious purpose: the punishment of the witch responsible for the damage to personal property or bodily affliction. When used in this manner, the purpose of counter-witchcraft moved beyond the healing of the person or restoration of the items corrupted by the witch: the intent was to exact revenge. A case in point is that of Henry Grey, a Connecticut farmer who suspected witchcraft was the cause of his ailing heifer's sad condition. Grey attempted to verify bewitchment by cutting off a piece of the heifer's ear and burning it. After this failed, he beat the animal, intending to transfer harm to the responsible person. To Grey, the effect was seemingly immediate and convincing since his heifer recovered, but his neighbor Mercy Disborough, whom he suspected had bewitched his heifer, was discovered collapsed in agony as if from a beating.[271]

This adaptation of counter-witchcraft might also involve the use of "urine tests." The prevalence of these experiments within New England led to its formal prohibition by the courts. To this end the Bay Colony authorities noted that the "urinary experiment . . . was an unwarrantable way to find out Witches."[272] Cotton Mather wrote of these experiments in *Memorable Providences*, identifying the practice of putting nails and pins, items commonly reported to be manifested by possession victims, into a urine bottle.[273] Showing his familiarity with such methods he explained that the "urine must be bottled with . . . instruments in it as carry a show of torture with them."[274]

Mather clearly was not the only New Englander familiar with the urinary experiment. At the onset of the Salem episode, Tituba, the Parris family servant, had employed another version of the "urine experiment" while attempting to identify the person responsible for the affliction of the Parris girls. At her later trial, Tituba confessed her "mistress in her own country" had taught her the "means to be used for the discovery of a Witch." Tituba employed this method when she mixed some of the urine of the possessed girls with meal, baked it, and fed it to the family dog. There is no record of how the dog fared in the matter, but the Parris girls were able to identify their tormentors. Tituba, on the other hand, nearly went to her death as a convicted witch, in part due to the experiment.[275]

During the 1662 Hartford witch outbreak, one of the magistrates asked suspected witch Rebecca Greensmith, "Have you made an express covenant with the Devil?"[276] Thirty years later, at one of the 1692 Salem trials, Judge Hathorne recorded a similar confession taken from suspected witch Deliverance Hobbs's examination, noting, "She continued in the free acknowledging herself to be a Covenant Witch."[277] These examinations, separated by three decades, are significant as they describe a third level of shared witchcraft beliefs within seventeenth-century New England—that of covenant witchcraft.

The idea of the witch compact, as previously noted, was not an invention of the seventeenth-century populace. Keith Thomas notes the antiquity of such ideas when he writes,

> *In itself, the idea of a compact with the Devil was as old as Christianity. Pagans had been regarded as devil-worshippers, and the Legend of Theophilus, the monk who transferred his allegiance to Satan, was familiar to the late Anglo-Saxons. It was a commonplace of medieval theology to assert that any magical activity, however beneficent in intention, necessarily involved a tacit compact with the Devil and should therefore be punished. The church courts*

often treated crystal-gazing and similar activities as a kind of heresy. But there was a great deal of difference between this idea of a tacit compact implicit in an individual's magical dabblings and the myth of explicit covenants with Satan made by bands of self-conscious devil-worshippers.[278]

Despite this ideological difference, the Devil's compact became part of the fabric of witchcraft beliefs throughout the seventeenth-century world. Kittredge indicates that by 1590 Continental witch trials were detailing the covenant witchcraft in what he describes as "an elaborate form."[279] By 1612, confessions from English witch trials began to give at least an outline of an "oral compact" with the Devil. By the 1640s, the examinations of English demonologist Matthew Hopkins would include detailed depositions admitting to a written covenant with the Devil, although, as Thomas remarks, "even then it was far from being an indispensable feature."[280]

In seventeenth-century New England, the compact seems to have made significant advances in the popular imagining. In keeping with their views of maleficium, the New England learned and popular culture held similar views about those who had matriculated to Satan's kingdom through witchcraft. Rebecca Greensmith's testimony is notable, for in it she described several elements of New England witch beliefs that had become common by the later seventeenth century.[281] Greensmith admitted that

she had had familiarity with the Devil . . . she promised to go with him when he called . . . and that the Devil told her that at Christmas, they would have a merry Meeting, and then the covenant between them should be subscribed. Moreover, she said that the Devil had frequently the carnal knowledge of her Body. And that the witches had meetings at a place not far from her house.[282]

Taken within the context of seventeenth-century New England, and in much of Europe, the "express covenant" that Greensmith confessed to must be seen as part of a systematic progression. Just as the Puritans of New England had sought to define salvation in terms of inward and outward signs of election, witchcraft would be cast in a similar, though diabolical, light. Robert Rowland explains this when he writes, "The world of witches often constitutes a systematized structure of negation, an inversion of the world in which people who hold these beliefs live."[283]

The depositions from the pre-Salem and Salem trials offer a good look at the beliefs of seventeenth-century New England concerning maleficium. These elements are important, for if they are observed in parallel with Cotton Mather's beliefs as detailed in the previous chapter, they give an outline of what the judges, the witch victims, and the accused themselves believed about the concept of an organized aspect of witchcraft within New England relevant to the Salem and Andover cases. Again, these records demonstrate how witchcraft beliefs existed and were propounded in a cross-social setting within seventeenth-century New England.

As previously mentioned, the covenant with the Devil had its necessary preconditions apart from the precursor sins of greed, lust, anger, hatred, unbelief, revenge, or discontent usually cited by the clergy. Richard Gildrie observes, "Preceding the pact was the temptation, which, by definition, involved gaining an improper goal or acquiring something by improper means."[284] The Puritans believed the Devil might offer a number of initiatives to the elect, just as he had to Christ in the wilderness.[285]

One of the Devil's initiatives might entail economic assistance or material possessions. This was the case on both sides of the Atlantic. John Rogers of England would confess later in life that as a young man, too financially distressed to get into Cambridge University, he experienced the powers of the Devil's temptations. In his own words, "The devil did often tempt me to study necromancy and nigromancy and to make use of magic, and to make a league with him, and that then I should never want."[286]

As it turned out, John Rogers did not study necromancy or make a contract with Satan. In New England, however, the Devil's temptations proved to be too much for Tituba, Reverend Parris's Barbados servant. Perhaps, like Rogers, it was her sense of marginalization that set in motion the set of circumstances which forever linked her personally to the outbreak of the Salem witch hunt. At her examination, she told Judge Hathorne, "A man come to me and say serve me. . . . He had a yellow bird that kept with him and he told me he had more pretty things that he would give me if I would serve him."[287]

Tituba would not be the only Salem witch suspect to make this confession. Others told of similar promises made by the Devil in exchange for their cooperation. William Barker of Andover was promised that the Devil "would pay all his debts and he should live comfortably." Steven Johnson was offered a pair of "French fall Shouses [shoes]," which Johnson confessed he had never received in spite of having been baptized at Shaw Shim River. Mary Bridges Jr. was promised "money and fine Cloathes" and Andrew Carrier "new cloathes and a horse."[288]

The Devil's bargain might also be for protection from prosecution or execution. In a notable Salem case, Thomas Putnam's daughter, while in the throes of possession, had seen the specter of a man who claimed that Giles Corey had pressed him to death with his feet. After Ann's visitation, Thomas Putnam notified Judge Samuel Sewell that local court records did indeed confirm that a man who had lodged with Corey had died suddenly. When Dr. Endicot examined the man's body, he recorded that he had been "bruised to death, having clodders of blood about his Heart." The inquest jury issued a determination of murder, without naming a suspect.

What was not in the inquest record was the apparition's insistence that not only had Giles Corey committed the murder, but that the Devil had been involved. The Devil's timing was excellent, for, as Putnam reports it, "the Devil there appeared to him [Corey] and covenanted with him, and promised him He should not be hanged."[289] In truth, Corey did not suffer hanging for murdering his houseguest. Instead, during the Salem witch trials he was arrested for maleficium. In a rather ironic twist of fate, on 16 September 1692 Corey died during the Salem sheriff's attempt to make him enter a plea to the charges. Corey died by pressing.

Finally, one of Satan's temptations seems to have applied specifically to women: the offer of sexual pleasure. Richard Baxter had attributed the success of this tactic by the Devil to "lustful, ranks of girls and young widows that plot for some armourous, procacious design, or have imaginations conquered by lust. . . . [There] Satan oft sets in."[290] This is not to say that sexual intercourse with the Devil was a common feature of Salem witchcraft, nor of the English versions. Sharpe notes, "Sexual intercourse between the Devil and the witch was rarely a salient feature in accounts of English witchcraft, but it was clearly not a totally alien concept."[291] Sharpe relates that when Mother Samuel, the eighty-year-old central figure in the Huntingdonshire Warboys witchcraft case, sought to avoid execution by claiming to be pregnant, a jury of women reported her not to be, "unless, (as some saide) it was with the divell."[292]

In New England, such confessions were also to be found. In a pre-Salem witch trial, Mary Johnson confessed to covenanting with the Devil after he offered "the best service he could do for her." Evidently this service included sexual favors, since Johnson confessed that "she had been guilty of Uncleanness with . . . Devils."[293] Similarly, during the Salem trials, local authorities suspected Sarah Bishop of witchcraft, but her husband suspected her of adultery with the Devil. He complained to the magistrates that "the Devill Did Come bodyly unto her [Sarah Bishop] and that she was familiar with the devil and that she sate up all the night Long with the Devill."[294] Bishop's husband obviously assumed that in these "all night visits" his wife had transferred her affections to the Devil.

If the Devil was successful in his temptation of the elect, the initial consummation of the witch's compact would entail signing the Devil's (covenant) book. At the Salem trials, this would be a standard allegation as a few examples demonstrate: Sarah Bridges confessed when Satan came to her in the form of a man, urging her signature, "I did Sign the book and the Mark was Red [and] he told me I must . . . Renounce God and Christ."[295] Hannah Post also admitted to signing the Devil's book, but not with ink. Instead, the trial transcripts state, "she also Showed her finger tep where it had been Cut and said she made the Red mark In the Divels book w'th the blood of that [finger]."[296]

Mercy Lewis complained to her examiners that the specter of former Salem minister George Burroughs had appeared to her, threatening that if she did not sign the Devil's book, "he had severall books in his studdy [by which] . . . he could raise the Divell." When she refused, Lewis was forced to endure "a temptation of Christ" experience. As she testified,

> *On 9th May Mr. Burroughs carried me up to an exceeding high mountain and shewed me all the kingdoms of the earth and tould me that he would give them all to me if I would writ in his book and if I would not he would throw me down and brake my neck; but I tould him they ware non of his to give and I would not wirt if he throde me down on 100 pitchforks.*[297]

Mercy Lewis had obviously understood the Devil's book was an inversion of both church membership and the Book of Life, and that to inscribe her name would damn her soul eternally. Cotton Mather would reflect on such dire consequences in *Wonders*, writing, "The unpardonable sin, is most usually committed by professors of the Christian Religion, falling into Witchcraft."[298]

By Mercy Lewis's refusal, she had narrowly escaped the Devil's snare and the second element of covenant witchcraft: the witch's mark or teat. After the witch signed the covenant, the Devil marked the new initiate with a sign which took the form of a spot in the flesh insensitive to pain, or an excrescence of flesh from which demonic imps might suckle. The Devil's mark had become a common allegation in English witch cases by 1579. Some insisted it was "a common token to know all witches by."[299] Sharpe observes the chronology of this belief:

> *In the early pamphlet accounts the place where the witch was sucked varied: face, nose, chin, and forefinger, but also thigh, shoulder and wrist. By the end of James I's reign, however, the mark was most often thought to be located on the genitalia or near the rectum of the witch.*[300]

Within seventeenth-century New England, the Devil's mark had become an essential part of the witch's compact with the Devil. Karlsen notes of this, "Puritan doctrine had it that the mark was placed on the witch's body by the Devil at the signing of the covenant, to seal their bargain, and allow him to recognize her as one of his followers."[301] One outcome of this belief led to a specific practice in the courts in Scotland, England, and New England: the impaneling of committees to conduct body searches for the witch's mark.

These searches followed a pattern already at work in formal and informal seventeenth-century inquiries primarily related to women. In England, adjudications involving suspicion of bastardy or infanticide often included formal tests to determine pregnancy or recent pregnancy. Under these circumstances, juries of matrons were assigned to do such tests as squeezing the breasts of female suspects for signs of milk.[302] Laura Gowing notes that in one such case in Yorkshire an unmarried woman suspected of an illegitimate birth was "searched by midwives who found fresh milk in her breasts." The woman subsequently confessed to having delivered "a man child dead and stillborn."[303] While impaneled juries were used to search for signs of pregnancy in women, the parallel practice used during the 1692 Salem trials searched for witch signs. In this instance, however, the searches were not sex specific since men also underwent accusations of and searches for witch marks or teats.

Susannah Sheldon alleged that "Good man Core [Giles Corey] had two tircels [turtles] which he put to his brest and gave them suck."[304] Sheldon's testimony influenced the Salem judges to the degree that Corey and his wife, Martha, were both searched for witch marks.[305] Besides searching Giles Corey, sometime between July and August of 1692 a seven-man court panel also searched former Salem minister George Burroughs and George Jacobs Jr. While no witch marks were observed on George Burroughs, the panel reported finding on Jacobs's body "three Teets w'ch according to the best of our Judgements wee think is not naturall for we runn a pinn through two of them and he was not sensible of it."[306]

After becoming an initiate witch by signing the Devil's covenant book and receiving the witch's mark, one was obliged to attend the witch's sabbath. Although it was not an indispensable part of New England witch lore, by the latter part of the seventeenth century both elite and popular witchcraft beliefs included witches meeting for an inverted form of church service and sacrament. Although there are no extant pre-Salem documents verifying inverted sabbaths, in the Salem trials there are accounts of at least two specific witch sabbaths. Deliverance Hobbs and Mary Lacey insisted that at least one major witch sabbath had taken place at Salem Village attended by some seventy people.[307] According to Sarah Bridges, a second witch's sabbath took place at Chandler's garrison house in Andover, at which she recalled "there were about 200 witches there."[308]

Whether located in Salem or Andover, the witch's flight to these meetings on poles or sticks would be another point of general agreement among those examined during the Salem trials. Conversely, across the Atlantic, pole riding by witches would rarely appear in the transcripts of the English witch trials. Thomas observes, "The notion that witches could fly . . . and the broomstick, made famous by subsequent children's fiction, occurs only once in an English witch-trial."[309]

Witches riding poles would not be so rare in New England. Tituba, the first Salem witch, gave evidence of such transport in her response to Judge Hathorne's question of "How did you go?" Tituba responded, "We ride upon stickes and are there presently."[310] Mary Osgood and others would verify Tituba's testimony. Osgood claimed to have journeyed along with three other persons toward a witch meeting "carried upon a pole . . . through the air in company."[311] Still another Salem witch, Mary Bridges Jr., told the court of her personal ride with the Devil to a Salem Village meeting. She claimed they rode "upon a pole and the black man carried the pole over the tops of the trees."[312]

True to its inverted formula, the Devil's sabbath would also include two important sacraments: baptism and the eucharist. For the Puritan clergy, these imitations of baptism, the Lord's Supper, and the Book of Life were the tangible and devilish counterparts to the covenant of salvation. For the Devil, the perversion of these two elements of the Puritan community would be the powerful counterpart of his hellish synergy with the witches, since, as Gura points out, "to the New England Puritans, the Abrahamic covenant was the corner stone of the ecclesiastical edifice that housed God's visible saints."[313]

Throughout the Salem trials, accounts were given of rebaptism by the Devil. These baptisms were not, however, in accordance with the Puritan formulas. As previously mentioned, this devilish rebaptism resembled the various versions used by the Anabaptists and other radical sects.[314] Most often, the confessors indicated that the Devil baptized them by "ducking their heads" in a pond, a river, or even a bucket of water. Salem witch suspects Mary Barker and Sarah Hawkes confessed that upon becoming witches they were both baptized by the Devil at Five Mile Pond.[315] Hawkes lamented that she was forced to renounce "her former Baptism" at which time "the Divel dipt her face in the Watt'r."[316]

In 1694, Massachusetts minister Joshua Scottow identified the second of these counterfeit sacraments, the Devil's eucharist, describing it as "a Damned Crew of Devils" feasting on "Red Bread and Wine, in derision of our Lord's Body and Blood."[317] Scottow's disgust for this inversion of the eucharist was well founded in the 1692 Salem witch examinations. Abigail Williams testified against Sarah Cloyce that not only had some forty Salem witches met in the woods near Samuel Parris's house, but that "Goody Cloyse and Goody Good were their Deacons."[318] In terms reflecting Roman Catholic transubstantiation, another witness to this witch's meeting stated that the Devil's priest "administered the sacrament unto them . . . with Red Bread, and Red Wine like Blood."[319] With respect to this testimony Gildrie comments, "Among the orthodox, and particularly in the preaching of Samuel Parris, the Salem village pastor, Catholic ritual was a form of witchcraft in any case."[320]

As outlined in the previous chapter, in the minds of the seventeenth-century New England populace, the most powerful and dangerous stage of witchcraft emerged after the witch's acceptance of the Devil's compact. At this point, the Devil assigned to the initiate one or more demons called "familiars" who would become the witch's invisible operatives. As such, demons representative of the witch, using the witch's visage, would take the form of poltergeists or specters, as they attacked both humans and animals with visible or, most often, invisible weapons. The attacks on humans were evidenced by numerous manifestations. In the words of Cotton Mather, "The Spectres would proceed then to wound them with Scalding, Burning, Pinching, Pricking, Twisting, Choaking, and a thousand preternatural Vexations."[321]

Beyond whatever injury the witch and his/her familiar might cause individuals, by far the greatest threat the Puritans feared was the Devil's invasion and overthrow of both religion and government.

Richard Gildrie observes, "The pact with Satan, which began a witch's career, was a decision not only to reject proper society but also to wage war upon it."[322] In this light, the standard form for witchcraft indictment used in New England is clear about the religious and governmental aspects of the charges. In the case of Edward Farrington, the bill of indictment by the Province of Massachusetts Bay reads, in part, as follows:

> *The Jurors for o'r Sov'r Lord and Land the King and Queen Present That Edward Farington of Andivor in the County of Essex . . . is become a detestable witch against the peace of o'r Soveraign Lord . . . and the Laws in this Case made and provided.*[323]

If one takes the testimony of the Salem and Andover witches seriously, the Massachusetts courts should have been concerned about the threat of the witch invasions. As chapter five demonstrates, near the onset of the Salem trials testimony was given insisting that an organized witch sect in New England was actively planning to "bewitch all in the Village . . . gradually and not all att once."[324] According to one witness, the witches' unified task was to "afflict persons and over come the Kingdome of Christ, and set up the Divels Kingdome . . . throughout the whole country."[325]

Apparently, in this invasion the human witches were not left to their own devices, since, as suspected wizard William Barker indicated, the Devil had assigned spectral spiritual warriors to the witches. Barker claimed, "At Salem Village, there being a little off the Meeting-House, [were] about an hundred five Blades, some with Rapiers by their side, which was called and might be more for ought I know."[326] Such testimonies effectively stated that Satan was tempting New Englanders to sign a compact with him and empowering initiates to destroy the religious, political, and societal structuring of New England.

To the Puritan populace, both learned and plebian, this was undoubtedly a frightening and unthinkable horror. Thomas Putnam, in his letter to Judges Hathorne and Corwin, summed it up well when he wrote, "We [are] beholding continually . . . not only every day but every hour," things which are "high and dreadful: of a wheel within a wheel, at which our ears do tingle."[327] Nor would such fears of diabolical witches plotting to overthrow society end with the Salem witchcraft trials, as is apparent from Richard Boulton's 1715 *An Account of the First Rise of Magicians and Witches*. Among tantalizing reports, Boulton promised to detail "the contracts they make with the Devil and what Methods they take to accomplish their infernal Designs."[328]

Conclusion

IN COTTON MATHER'S SEVENTEENTH-CENTURY world, both the elite, learned class and the ordinary New England inhabitant shared a common set of witchcraft beliefs despite differences in specific interpretations and definitions. Within this framework, the New England population accepted witchcraft as an everyday reality of life. The clerical and popular shared beliefs in witchcraft are identifiable in four major categories of witchcraft: magic, maleficium, counter-magic, and covenant witchcraft. These are abundantly evidenced through the pre-Salem, Salem episode, and post-Salem journals, publications, and court records of New England.

Cotton Mather's theology of Satan, demons, and witchcraft, as demonstrated in chapter two, was not incompatible or exaggerated within his contemporary context. As the remaining chapters of this study will suggest, perhaps what made the Salem witchcraft trials a particularly Puritan witch hunt is not to be found only in Puritan dogma, but also in the context of what the Puritan clerics perceived to be a falling away from the Puritan errand, as well as the growing threats to unity presented by Indians, dissenters, and

Puritans practicing witchcraft. In essence, elite and popular beliefs about witchcraft served to set the stage for what followed in the Salem witch outbreak. Taken in this light, as Phillip Gura observes,

> *what remained inviolate at least through the seventeenth century . . . was the colonists' sense of their specialness as guardians of the Christian faith against the attacks of any and all enemies, be they Indians, Papists, witches, or, eventually opponents of "enthusiastic" religion, colonial agents, and deists.*[329]

Having outlined the predominant witchcraft beliefs of seventeenth-century New England, held by both elite and popular classes, the dissertation now moves on to an examination of Robert Calef's charges that Cotton Mather should be blamed for the initiation of the Salem witchcraft trials.

4

PREVIOUS INTERPRETATIONS: A PARADIGM OF BLAME

I am far from insensible that at this extraordinary time of the devils coming down in great wrath upon us, there are too many Tongues and hearts set on fire of hell; that the various opinions about the witchcrafts which of later time have troubled us, are maintained by some with so much cloudy fury, as if they could never be sufficiently stated, unless written in the liquor wherewith witches use to write their covenants; and that he who becomes an author at such a time, had need be fenced with iron, and the staff of a spear.
Cotton Mather, *The Wonders of the Invisible World* (1693)

IN THE WAKE OF the Salem dilemma, the single most energetic and dogmatic effort to place the blame for the Salem trials and executions at the feet of Cotton Mather was Robert Calef's. This is reflected in his book *More Wonders of the Invisible World,* published in London in 1700. Calef's characterization of Cotton Mather in *More Wonders* led to the creation of a historical portrait of Mather as a seventeenth-century Puritan witch-hunter and instigator of the Salem trials.

Calef's stinging criticism of both the trials and more specifically Cotton Mather has also become central to subsequent scholarly treatment of the subject.[330] Charles Upham, for instance, adopted

Calef's views with little amendment, and this pattern has been echoed well into the twentieth century.[331] Upham in particular based much of his two-volume historical assessment, entitled *Salem Witchcraft,* upon the evidence supplied by Robert Calef in his *More Wonders of the Invisible World.* Like Calef, Upham castigated Cotton Mather, alleging that he not only instigated the Salem witch hunt but also continued his witch-hunting activities even after the Salem trials had ended. As Upham put it,

> *There is some ground for suspicion that he was instrumental in originating the fanaticism at Salem. . . . At any rate . . . it can be too clearly shown that he was secretly and cunningly endeavoring to renew [the proceedings] during the next year in his own parish in Boston.*[332]

Upham's assertions about Salem and Cotton Mather became what Marc Mappen has labeled "the standard interpretation, repeated for generations in textbooks on American History."[333] A succession of nineteenth and twentieth-century authors have repeated this view, and have collectively created the popular American public image of both the Puritans and specifically Cotton Mather. The nineteenth-century descendant of Salem judge John Hathorne, Nathaniel Hawthorne, depicted Cotton Mather as "the one bloodthirsty man, in whom were concentrated those vices of spirit and errors of opinions that sufficed to madden the whole surrounding multitude."[334] Over a century later this view would still have resonance for the European rationalist scholar H. Trevor Roper. In his volume *The European Witch-craze,* he includes Mather in a list of infamous witch-hunters:

> *Perkins in England, Rivetus and Voetious in Holland, Baillei and Rutherford in Scotland, Desmarets and Jurieu in France, Francis Turrettini in Switzerland, Cotton*

> *Mather in America—what a gallery of intolerant bigots, narrow-minded martinets, timid conservative defenders of repellent dogmas, instant assailants of every new or liberal idea, inquisitors and witch-burners!*[335]

Late twentieth-century scholarship, with only a few exceptions, repeats this well-worn litany of Cotton Mather's purposeful malignancy. George Malcolm Yool, for instance, asserts that Cotton Mather, as "a zealous witch hunter, wanted nothing less than to see them [witch suspects] brought to justice."[336]

In light of the continuing acceptance of Calef's perspective on Mather and the Salem trials, and subsequent historians' use of his version of the historical record, we need to examine Robert Calef's censure of Cotton Mather in detail. This chapter commences by reviewing Robert Calef's background and the Calef-Mather dispute, detailing Calef's adamant insistence that the trials and executions were the direct result of Cotton Mather's preaching and his publication of the Margaret Rule possession case. In doing so, Mather's pre-Salem articulation of witchcraft is outlined relative to his published and unpublished sermons and his publications, showing the degree to which he kept the subject before his Boston congregation and the larger New England populace.

Next, the historical climate of New England in relation to witchcraft is examined, demonstrating the existence of three major preexistent and transcendent factors within New England that had an overriding impact on the Salem events. These factors include the prevalence of prior witchcraft publications, seventeenth-century contemporaneous preaching on witchcraft, and a legacy of prior witch trials and executions. Finally, this chapter maintains that the indictment of Cotton Mather's preaching and publications as the single most important influence on the initiation and course of the Salem trials is unsustainable.

Robert Calef's More Wonders of the Invisible World

LITTLE IS KNOWN ABOUT Robert Calef's history prior to his emigration from England to Boston. He was known as a "Merchant of Boston and a Dealer in woolen goods."[337] And although Cotton Mather's description of Calef as a "weaver" emphasized his relatively low social status, after the Salem trials he did hold at least two political offices in Boston. He was elected as "Hayward and Fence-viewer" in 1694 and served as an "Overseer of the Poor" in 1702. In 1706 he was also subsequently chosen as an "Assessor," but declined to serve.[338]

Calef was living in Boston at the time of the witchcraft proceedings at Salem Village and Boston. It seems that even during the trials Calef was looking for some way to express his consternation at what was happening at Salem. Not finding a suitable venue, in 1693 Calef took the initiative to denounce the matter personally and pointedly, in print.

Two specific events precipitated Calef's initiative. First, the publication and distribution in New England of Mather's *The Wonders of the Invisible World,* perceived by some as an attempt to legitimize the recent adjudications. Second, a further case of "diabolical possession" had emerged in Calef's hometown of Boston. While *Wonders* had a profoundly negative effect on Calef, he feared that the case of Margaret Rule would initiate another deadly witchcraft episode.

The Margaret Rule case is particularly important for our understanding of Calef's perspective. During the five weeks from September 10 until the end of October, Margaret Rule, a young Boston woman, suffered what her family and the clergy assumed to be a form of demonic torment. On September 13, 1693, Calef visited Rule's home on an occasion when both Increase and Cotton Mather were present. In the company of some thirty or forty others, Calef watched as the Mathers examined the seventeen-year-old, made inquiries into her condition, and attempted to effect her deliverance.

Afterwards, Calef wrote to Cotton Mather asking for an explanation of his views about witchcraft, as laid out in *Wonders*, and for specific scriptural passages supporting these beliefs.[339] Meanwhile, Calef quietly circulated a copy of his own observations to some of his and Cotton Mather's friends who had been present that evening at the Rule house. His stated objective was to allow these spectators to verify the accuracy of his account. Several modern authors have reproduced that letter, but here a summary will suffice.[340]

Calef began by asserting that Cotton Mather had asked leading questions to get Margaret Rule to tell him the names of the witches tormenting her. He also alleged that Increase Mather had prayed for half an hour and sought God to reveal the names of the specters tormenting the young woman. More incriminating than all of this was Calef's accusation that Cotton Mather had lewdly fondled the afflicted young woman. Using ambiguous but graphic language, Calef wrote that Mather "brushed her on the face with his glove, and rubbed her stomach (her breast not covered with the bedclothes) and bid others do so too, and said it eased her."[341]

When Cotton Mather was shown a copy of the observation he was horrified. After complaining to Calef that the account had "contributed to make people believe a smutty thing," Mather promptly castigated Calef from his pulpit at the Old North Church.[342] Cotton and Increase Mather underscored this censure by having Calef arrested for scandalous libel, but because they failed to appear and testify at the court session, the suit was dismissed.

The conflict, though, was far from finished. Calef had gathered documents related to the Salem events for a book but was unable to find a publisher in New England. One can only assume that this was partly a result of Cotton Mather's local influence. Calef sent the manuscript to London for printing, choosing the title *More Wonders of the Invisible World*, as an obvious play on the title of Mather's recent work, *The Wonders of the Invisible World*. Realizing the potential impact of Calef's publication, Cotton Mather indicates in his diary that he prayed against its success, asking God to rescue his "opportunities of serving [the] Lord Jesus Christ, from the attempts of the man [Calef] to damnify them."[343] When the book arrived in Boston during November of 1700, as president of Harvard College, Increase Mather had a copy of it publicly burned in the college yard.[344]

The release of *More Wonders* in New England proved to be more significant than Increase's actions. While Upham reported that it "burst like a bomb shell upon all who had been concerned in promoting the witchcraft prosecutions," Richard Lovelace asserts that *More Wonders* was an "inarticulate, poorly organized, but telling attack."[345] Indeed, *More Wonders of the Invisible World* was not a literary masterpiece. Calef's imitation of Cotton's book approximated it too well in that it suffered from equal if not worse organization, rambling from cover to cover.

Despite these defects, *More Wonders* should not be underestimated. Its impact far outdistanced its lack of coherency and structure. Calef's basic premise was that the trials been a deadly charade "disguised under the mask of zeal for God," in which the ministers and the magistrates of New England had branded innocent persons as witches, "insulting over the [true] sufferers at execution."[346] Where directed specifically at the Court of Oyer and Terminer, Calef's attack was a blow at the theological foundation of the trials, a castigation of the adjudication process, and a censure of the ethical integrity of the members of the court and clergy. Calef's criticism of Cotton Mather, as this next section shows, was much more specific and incriminating.

Calef's first allegation detailed in *More Wonders* was that Cotton Mather had created the environment which led to the Salem accusations and trials through his preaching about the Devil, demons, and witchcraft and by publishing his works on the subject in the period before and during the Salem episode, which he dates from the 1689 Goodwin possession until the end of the Salem tragedy in 1693. This charge is most clearly reflected in two passages in *More Wonders*. The first is from an open letter to the Boston area ministers dated March 18, 1694, and reproduced in *More Wonders.* In it Calef wrote,

> *I medle not now to say, but cannot but suppose his strenuous and Zealous asserting his opinions, has been one cause of the dismal Convulsions we have here lately fallen into. . . . His books Memorable Providences relating to Witchcraft, and also his Wonders of the Invisible World, did contain in them things not warrantable, and very dangerous.*[347]

The second statement is found in the postscript to *More Wonders,* where Calef insists,

> *Mr. Cotton Mather was the most active and forward of any Minister in the Country in those matters, taking home one of the Children, and managing such intreagues [sic] with that Child, and after printing such an Account of the whole, in his Memorable Providences, as conduced much to the kindling of those flames, that in Sir Williams time threatened the devouring this Country.*[348]

Again, as previously noted, Calef's allegations can be traced to those of modern scholars. Peter Hoffer's 1996 book, *The Devil's Disciples,* echoes this opinion that Cotton Mather's involvement in the Salem trials outdistanced that of his peers and created a dangerous platform for trying and executing witches. Hoffer suggests that through Mather's insistence upon relating supernatural providence to witchcraft outbreaks in his publication of such books as *Memorable Providences*

> *no divine had more to do with the forthcoming trials than Cotton Mather. His story is inextricably interwoven with the cases, for he was more than an elite spokesman for a book-*

> *bound priesthood. Mather was a believer in the invisible world. . . . With a mixture of arrogant carelessness and true belief Mather aspired to bridge the gap between the popular and the elite across a span of miraculous prodigies.*[349]

These accusations against Mather raise two questions. First, do the extant historical records confirm that Cotton Mather made witchcraft a prominent issue of his ministry during the period of 1689 to 1693? And second, does a clear historical connection exist between Mather's pre-Salem publications and preaching, and the initiation of the Salem trials?

Cotton Mather's Pre-Salem Articulation about Witchcraft

THE FIRST QUESTION CAN be addressed through a chronological sampling of Mather's publications and sermons. To begin with, in 1689 Cotton Mather published *Memorable Providences,* a collection of supernatural experiences. The book itself, as will be seen later, was little different from the myriad of similar publications which described wonderful miracles, strange preternatural occurrences, unique judgments of God upon sinners (such as deformed monstrous births), divine vindications and rescues, and of course, demon possessions and witchcraft manifestations. Mather added another feature to this genre by the addition of a postscript to the book in which he detailed a recent situation in a Boston family. His conclusion hinted that witchcraft had been involved and further suggested that God might be preparing to expose more witches.

Mather's pulpit ministry at the Old North Church in Boston is also relevant. For some time prior to 1692 he had been preaching to Boston and all New England about their spiritual condition. In the years before the witch invasion he had preached several messages in which he called New England to repentance, without which he warned dire punishments were in store. What Mather was doing, as was common for his day, was to preach the "jeremiad" style of sermon, a rhetorical formula that had been used in both Protestant and Catholic churches throughout Europe from the medieval era onwards. As Sacvan Bercovitch describes it, the jeremiad "decried the sins of the people—a community, a nation, a civilization, mankind in general—and warned of God's wrath to come."[350] The clerics of New England, however, modified this type of sermon, creating a distinctively Puritan formula. As Emory Elliot observes,

> *Taking their texts from Jeremiah and Isaiah, these orations followed—and reinscribed—a rhetorical formula that included recalling the courage and piety of the founders, lamenting recent and present ills, and crying out for a return to the original conduct and zeal.*[351]

In their adaptation, the clerics included an insistence that the people of New England were special to God, and that therefore they would at times face God's corrective wrath because of their very place in God's end-times salvific plan. By Cotton Mather's era, such jeremiads were often preached after political elections. They commonly consisted of describing the sins of the people, predicting God's eminent judgments upon their continuance, and delivering a plea for repentance and revival among the elect.

Cotton Mather preached and published no less than five jeremiads between the 1689 publication of *Memorable Providences* and the first signs of the troubles of 1692. In each of them he warned of God's imminent judgment upon New England, reminding the people of the power of the Devil and demons, and pointing to witchcraft as a possible means of this judgment.

The first of such jeremiads came on March 20, 1690. As Mather was preparing his Thursday lecture, he changed his sermon topic to reflect the recent news of a renewed French and Indian attack on the outlying settlements of New England. In his revised sermon, entitled

"The Present State of New England," Mather reminded his audience that during the preceding year there had been "devastations upon the more pagan skirts of New England." He then declared that the recent attacks of the French and Indians were an outcropping of spiritual warfare, saying that the "devils are stark mad, that the House of the Lord our God, is come into these remote corners of the world."[352]

Mather's words about Indian invasions called to mind recent Indian hostilities such as Metacomet's War of 1675 to 1676, in which as many as one-tenth of all colonial males were killed and over twelve thousand homes were burned. The death of Metacomet in 1676 put an end to that particular round of hostilities, but the population centers in the lightly defended northern frontier in Maine, New Hampshire, and western Massachusetts continued to suffer sporadic attacks by Indians accompanied by their French allies.[353] Since, as the previous chapter noted, the Puritans believed that Native Americans were part of a diabolical alliance with Satan to destroy New England, Mather's sermon reminded Bostonians of this ever-present threat.

Mather would use this same framework, which pitted the Devil against New England again, while speaking to the Artillery Company of Massachusetts at their annual meeting on June 1, 1691. In a message entitled "Things to be Looked For," Mather reflected on the economic and emotional strains brought about by the failure of the recent Canadian expedition, the intensity of the recent Indian raids, and the colonists' foreboding about the new charter. As Increase Mather was in London attempting to gain the new agreement, Cotton was preaching a message of judgment and hope to the Artillery Company. Within the second point of his sermon, alluding specifically to the military conflicts, Mather noted, "As now, tis the Divel that is the Make-hate of the World . . . the same Divel that makes Demoniacks to tear and cut themselves, do's also cause men to Wound one another."[354]

Third, casting spiritual warfare in the human terms of religious unorthodoxy, Mather wrote a tract against the Quakers in September of 1691 entitled "Little Flocks guarded against Grievous Wolves." Using portions of several tracts written by the Quaker George Keith, Mather presented five specific arguments against the tenets of the Society of Friends.[355] Among his arguments, he compared the "strange quaking" of the Quakers to the "diabolical possession" of witchcraft.[356]

Another sermon would come from Mather on December 24, 1691, entitled "Fair Weather" (not published until 1692). In the wake of the recent revolt, Mather found himself preaching to a discontented group of Bostonians. He suggested to his audience that witchcraft was already at work within the Boston and broader New England population. In rhetorical fashion he stated, "How many doleful wretches, have been decoy'd into witchcraft itself, by the opportunities which their discontent has given the Devil, to visit 'em and seduce 'em."[357]

The last in this progression, and one of the best examples of a published Cotton Mather jeremiad, is entitled "A Midnight Cry." Mather first preached this sermon in April of 1692, only a month before the Salem trials began in earnest. In hopes of a national revival, not unlike the Protestant Reformation, he delivered this alarming message describing the state of New England as that of a nation asleep in sin, unprepared for the coming of Christ. Mather instructed his audience, among other things, to "Look upward and see a God Angry . . . Look inward, and see our Cursed hearts [and] . . . Fly to the Lord Jesus Christ, as the Refuge that has been set before us." In stark terms, Mather portrayed a devilish invasion as one possible judgment of God upon New England should the nation refuse to repent.[358]

Considering this, and the many other unpublished works by Cotton Mather during this period, it is apparent that preceding the Salem outbreak and afterwards, Mather kept the concept of a malevolent spiritual world in front of his own congregation and of his broader New England audience.[359] The question that remains is not whether witchcraft was one of the subjects of Mather's 1689 to 1693 ministry but whether the publication of *Memorable Providences* and Mather's preaching significantly contributed to the creation of Salem events or whether his actions were an indirect and general influence on a preexisting propensity toward episodes of the sort which descended upon Salem in 1692. To fully understand the significance or indeed lack of significance of these publications, we need to place them in their context. The rest of this chapter describes three historical and theological factors that arise out of New England's early history which provide such a context: the prevalence of prior witchcraft publications, contemporaneous preaching about the invisible world, and New England's legacy of prior witchcraft trials and executions.

Preexistent and Transcendent Factors in New England

COTTON MATHER'S *MEMORABLE PROVIDENCES* and *Wonders* added to an already established genre of witchcraft publications in New England. Such books had been in existence since the nation's New World inception.[360] When the Puritans made their journey to the New World they took with them much of their Old World. The new adventure was bound to be colored by the old beliefs. As a result, Puritans included in their spiritual and intellectual luggage two types of publications that related to the supernatural, including witchcraft: the Bible and the wonder stories.[361]

To the Puritans, the first and foremost publication that attested to the existence of witchcraft was the Bible itself. Though this may seem obvious, the fact is that much of what has been written on New England witchcraft undervalues this integral factor. Like the Protestant Reformers themselves, the long tradition of Puritan biblical scholars held to the belief that the Bible was the grid through which every subject was to be studied.[362] Basing their overall religious and social ordering upon the Bible and Calvinistic doctrine, Puritans took their basic beliefs about witchcraft directly from the Bible.

The Bible's importance is given further impact as a result of two additional factors: high literacy rates and the prevalence of Bible ownership among the New England populace. Literacy rates were high because the founders of the colony had insisted upon a rigorous attempt to teach the skills of reading and writing. David Hall notes that beginning with the hornbook, "apart from the Bible (and especially the Book of Psalms), the crucial texts were the primer and the catechism."[363] Hall indicates that in 1660, even though only 60 percent of men and 40 percent of women were able to write, a large majority of people of all classes were able to read.[364]

Like their seventeenth-century counterparts across the Atlantic, New England clerics pointed to the biblical references about witchcraft. As Stuart Clark observes, whether Protestant or Catholic, "the thing that defined witchcraft for clerics . . . is its universal placement in the Decalogue as a sin against the first Commandment."[365] Cotton Mather's generation had little trouble defending their belief in witchcraft since both the Old and New Testament give indications of the various acts of witchcraft, albeit without dividing them into beneficent or malevolent categories.

The Bible defines witchcraft by depicting the witches' activities rather than focusing specifically on the identity of witches. Leviticus 19:26 banned both divination and sorcery, including the use of spells and enchantments. Leviticus 19:31 warned, "Regard not them that have familiar spirits, neither seek after wizards." Deuteronomy 18:10 spoke of the practices of divination, sorcery, the interpretation of omens, and the practice of witchcraft. In I Samuel 15:23, the prophet Samuel compared rebellion to the "sin of witchcraft." Acts 19:19, referring to the city of Ephesus, mentions that many witchcraft scrolls had been burned by those who had converted to Christianity. Finally, Galatians 5:19-20 lists witchcraft among "the works of the flesh."

The Bible also indicated that practitioners of witchcraft could be male or female, and identified certain individuals as witches, sorcerers, or sorceresses. Exodus 22:18 commanded Israel to "not allow a sorceress to live." I Samuel 28:7 says that Israel's king Saul inquired about the future from a female witch at Endor. II Kings 9:22 describes Queen Jezebel as a witch, noting that "Jezebel and her witchcrafts are many." Conversely, in Numbers 24:1 Balaam is identified as the sorcerer who attempted to "curse" Israel in exchange for money from King Baalak. Similarly, Manasseh, the king of Israel, is condemned for his use of witchcraft, including child sacrifices, necromancy, and consulting with wizards. In the New Testament, in Acts 8:9 the figure Simon was known to have "practiced sorcery in the city of Samaria." Again, in Acts 13:6 Paul the Apostle is met with the opposition of a sorcerer named Bar-Jesus or Simon at Paphos.

Last of all, witchcraft and especially maleficium was a capital crime under the Old Testament law. Leviticus 20:6 cautioned that "such as turn after such as have familiar spirits, and wizards . . . I will even cut him off." Leviticus 20:27 gave instructions that any persons consulting "familiar spirits" or known to be male witches should be exterminated. In II Kings 23:24, King Josiah is mentioned to have exterminated a number of persons known as "mediums" and "spiritists." For both the clergy and the populace, the Bible was the unquestionable and ubiquitous authority upon which all witchcraft beliefs were based.

The Bible did not, however, provide the only seventeenth-century discourse on witchcraft. The founders of New England brought to the New World a cosmology that was also heavily influenced by medieval Continental and English ideas about the supernatural. This was manifest in an extensive literature that recorded and popularized a conception of an invisible world of angels, demons, and witches. Hyder Rollins notes the nearly universal acceptance of these publications by both elite and common persons in seventeenth-century England when he suggests that they presented

> *the same subjects as those to which learned men like Glanvill were devoting themselves—the same subjects as*

> *[the] Royal Society . . . listened to and published; accounts of human and animal monstrosities, of wheat rained from the sky, of ghosts and witchcraft, of enchantment, earthquakes, and judgments of God.*[366]

In seventeenth-century New England, such books were readily available as the book trade in Boston was one of the most active in the British colonies. Although the local authorities and clerics exercised strict control over printing, these books were regularly imported by booksellers. Such books, including those written by Samuel Clarke and Thomas Beard, which are examined in this section, easily found their way into the hands of both the general populace and the elite, learned class. For example, as a Harvard student during the 1670s, Edward Taylor copied the story "An account of ante-mortem visions of Mr. John Holland" from Clarke's book.[367] Increase Mather often quoted from both Samuel Clarke and Thomas Beard's collections of wonder stories. Similarly, John Foster, the founder of the Boston press, incorporated almost all of Beard's work in his own 1679 adaptation of a London broadside, entitled *Divine examples of God's Severe Judgements against Sabbath Breakers*.[368]

The "wonder pamphlets" helped shape and reinforce the beliefs in the supernatural present within New England both before and after the Salem trials engulfed the colony. Richard Godbeer cites the presence of these publications and their link to Old and New England when he writes that "for all their determination to break with the 'superstitions' of the past, the Puritan colonists maintained the lore of wonders that pervaded seventeenth-century English culture."[369]

These imported "wonder stories" established and repeated three specific themes within seventeenth-century supernaturalism. The first theme was reflected in those stories which manifested God's ability to suspend the normal course of nature or events in order to save the "elect" or even to identify the wicked. Peter Lake, describing English murder pamphlets, notes the emphasis upon "an even more powerful force" correcting these wrongs "for over against the forces of sin and the devil was ranged the awesome power of divine providence."[370] The working of this providence is reflected in John Trundle's work *A Miracle of Miracles* in which he recorded the case of a Holnhurst criminal whose demise was representative of "a sodaine and strange death upon perjured persons . . . including the execution of God himself from his holy fire in heaven."[371]

The second class of wonder stories were those which showed the Devil's ability to disrupt the natural order. One such story well known in both Old and New England was that of St. Cainnicus, who remained dry in spite of traveling through a downpour. During the Salem trials Sarah Atkinson may have applied this legend in sinister terms when she testified that the accused witch Susannah Martin did not get wet on her journey to Atkinson's home during a rainstorm. As Atkinson put it, "I should have been wet up to my knees if I should have come so far."[372]

A third category of the wonder stories promoted the seventeenth-century elite and popular concept of the rapid winding down of history in which signs or portents did not indicate the promises of the future, but the certainty of the "end of the age" coming upon the world. This theme was one of the predominant messages of the seventeenth-century New England clergy, including Cotton Mather.[373]

Among the most active writers and printers of volumes of wonder stories were Londoners Nathaniel Crouch (who went by the pseudonym Robert Burton), John Hart, and John Trundle. Trundle's reputation was primarily based on his extensive plagiarism of earlier works. David Hall indicates that the scope of these volumes included a wide variety of subjects:

> *Their product line included histories and merriments that told of cuckolds or astrology or repeated Chaucer's vulgar stories. Humor, sex, romance—we may add to these another vein of proven popular appeal, the violence*

that pervaded narrative of witchcraft, war, death and supernatural wonders.[374]

Although the New England ministers warned their congregations against those books which dealt with the more "vulgar" side of life, they could at times accommodate the use of wonder stories in their attempts to promote more acceptable moral values. Just as Puritan clerics had patiently worked to reform the standard form of the English almanac, they also chose to reinforce the biblical concepts of morality by the selection of and adaptation of the wonder stories. They used, among many examples, tales such as the one describing the fate of "Margery Perry, whose soul was carried away by the Devil in person after she perjured herself. Equally terrible was the story of the punishment inflicted by the Devil on Gabriel Harding for having murdered his wife."[375]

Beyond attempts at accommodation, the New England clerics encouraged the populace to read publications dealing with the issues of evangelical faith and the fate of the unconverted. Often written by clerics, such books were abundantly available to the New England populace. The latter theme, the fate of the unconverted, was reflected in such works as *The Progress of Sin*, by Benjamin Keach. Among other things it equated sin with a "commission from the Devil," who practiced his abilities to lead the godly into perils and the ungodly into damnation.[376] Others include John Bunyon's *Sighs from Hell: Or, The Groans of a Damned Soul*,[377] Stephen Batman's 1581 work, *The Doome warning all men to Judgment*,[378] and Thomas Beard's book *The Theatre of God's Judgements*, which first appeared in 1597.[379]

Another version of the wonder stories included models of spiritual warfare, which were widely circulated among the clergy and laity alike. Two popular examples include John Downame's *The Christians Warfare Against the Devill, the World, and Flesh*,[380] written in 1604, and William Gurnall's *The Christian in Compleat Armour*,[381] originally published in 1655. Similarly, Michael Wigglesworth's 1661 ballad-styled folio entitled *The Day of Doom*[382] also had great success in New England, selling some eighteen hundred copies in the first year.[383] A minister and Harvard graduate, Wigglesworth capitalized on the population's interest in the supernatural and perhaps more importantly their fears of the power of the Devil and witches.

In 1597, Samuel Clarke produced one of the truly great masterpieces of this genre, *A Mirrour or Looking Glasse both for Saints, and Sinners, Held forth in about two thousand Examples.* The Puritans came to know it simply as *Clarke's Examples.*[384] They referred to it for examples of preternatural events, and its influence can be seen during the Salem witchcraft trials themselves, including testimonies of Satan's appearances as black bears or dogs.[385]

The last in this line of publications important for the present purpose is that of Nathaniel Crouch's *The Kingdom of Darkness* (1688). Its full title is perhaps more helpful: *The History of Daemons, Spectres, Witches, Apparitions, Possessions, Disturbances and other supernatural Delusions, and malicious Impostures of the Devil.* With respect to the Salem trials, *The Kingdom of Darkness* is relevant in two specific ways. First is its historical proximity to the Salem trials. Written just four years before the Salem trials, this book was essentially a retelling of a number of well-known wonder stories gathered from and at times plagiarized from several other authors, including Alexander Roberts and Increase Mather.[386] Second, Crouch gave the New England populace a compendium of demonological stories involving witchcraft possessions, magic, demonic resurrections, and Satan's appearances in the forms of common village animals.

Many of these seventeenth-century publications propounded wonder stories that served as an additional authority beyond the Bible for what New Englanders commonly believed about supernatural events. Cotton Mather's two works in this genre, *Memorable Providences* (1689) and *Wonders of the Invisible World* (1692), were little more than minor additions to an extensive and popular body of literature.[387]

At times, historians have treated Cotton Mather's sermonizing about the hostile invisible world and witchcraft as if it were a singular, ill-fated practice. As previously detailed, Mather had preached extensively on the subject during the eighteen months between the Goodwin case and the Salem problems of 1692. However, before the Salem episode, during the period of 1689 to 1692 the rest of the New England clergy had also been regularly preaching against all forms of sin, including magic and witchcraft.

One of their main concerns was the apparent spiritual decline of the New England populace. An early example of this outlining of spiritual deficiencies can be seen in Michael Wigglesworth's 1662 sermon in which he charged that the hearts of New Englanders had become filled with "luke-warm Indifferency" and "key-cold Dead-heartedness."[388] This indictment would grow during the years directly preceding the Salem trials, as the clergy insisted with growing intensity that New England had failed to live up to her covenant responsibilities.[389] As the Salem era drew closer, the clergy added to their lists of indications of spiritual decline the use of magic, counter-magic, and malevolent witchcraft, seeking, as Godbeer maintains, "to purge their communities of magic."[390]

Examples abound. One may begin with Jonathan Mitchell, the pastor at Cambridge. As early as 1656 he found it necessary to preach to his congregation against the use of divination and astrology, declaring popular astrology was centered in "things secret . . . forbidded, and concealed from discovery by lawful means" by God. He went further to demand that anyone using such arts was falling into "the Devills policie and invention" designed to draw them away from "God and his providence and word into an irreligion."[391]

Increase Mather's ministry included similar efforts. Before his son, Cotton, preached his first jeremiad against witchcraft in 1690, Increase had already felt the need to preach a lengthy series on the subject in 1683. In a 1684 sermon later published as *Illustrious Providences*, Increase told the Old North congregation that some

New Englanders were in fact using counter-magic techniques. He warned them that "for men to submit to any of the Devils Sacraments is implicitly to make a covenant with him."[392]

Increase followed this sermon with another extended series on witchcraft in 1685. Even after the Salem trials, Increase Mather's preaching would include much of the text of his 1696 publication of *Angelographia*, in which he would give notice of God's severe condemnation for those who went to "fortune tellers, to reveal such things, as cannot be known, but by the help of Evil Angels."[393]

In a 1691 pre-Salem sermon, Samuel Willard, a contemporary of Cotton Mather, decried the use of magic formulas intended either for "the keeping of Devils out of places, or for the Curing of . . . Maladies." Willard went on to insist that such measures were nothing short of "plain conjuration, and an horrible abusing of the Name of God . . . establishing the Devils Kingdom." Subsequent to this, in a sermon preached during the first month of the Salem inquiries, he told his congregation that he believed that Elizabeth Knapp had been possessed by demons, admonishing them to "examine by this Providence what sins [had] given Satan so much footing in this poor place."[394]

Charles Morton, a Charlestown pastor, also propagated a view of the hostile and invisible world of demons and witches. Preaching in 1688, Morton claimed that in some natural disasters God "improves Evil angels as his Instruments and Executioners."[395] It was Morton who, along with James Allen, Joshua Moodey, and Samuel Willard, signed the preface to Mather's *Memorable Providences* attesting to be witnesses of the supernatural things Mather recorded connected to the Goodwin case.

Deodat Lawson also had a significant place in these matters. Preaching against the use of all forms of magic in a message published as *Christ's Fidelity*, he remonstrated his congregation that the use of magic experiments with the "Sive and Seyssors, the Bible and Key; the White of an Egge in a Glass . . . are from the Devil, not from God."[396]

Similarly, on March 24, 1692, as he preached from Zechariah 3:2, Lawson declared that in carrying out his diabolical plans Satan would especially choose persons who, like recently accused witches Rebecca Nurse or Martha Cory, appeared to be the very elect. He insisted, "It is certain that he never works more like the Prince of Darkness than when he looks most like an angel of light."[397]

Finally, it would be a serious error to disregard the one New England pastor whose church and household had more to do with the initiation of the Salem trials than any other: Samuel Parris. Throughout his tenure as the Salem Village pastor, Parris's sermons reflected the social and political rivalries in his church. Yet, more importantly, as Cooper and Minkema observe,

> *His preoccupation with hidden evil in the church, his frequent references to the struggles between the forces of Christ and Satan . . . and his insistence upon the imminence of an invasion of "devils," all helped to create a propitious climate for witchcraft accusations.*[398]

Samuel Parris would be vociferous throughout the Salem ordeal, beginning with the first Sunday that he chastised Salem Village church member Mary Sibley for "going to the Devil for help against the Devil" by having Tituba use the urine-cake experiment to discover the source of Parris's own children's possession. Both during and after the Salem trials, Parris would use his pulpit as a public forum to both explain the witch invasions, and at times defend the adjudication process.[399] Peter Hoffer, in his book *The Devil's Disciples,* makes an insightful comment on this issue when he writes,

> *Although others may have had unsavory motives for accusing their neighbors of witchcraft, Parris truly believed the Devil had made converts within his own congregation,*

> *had insinuated himself into Parris's own family, and had done it to reduce the minister's life to a living hell.*[400]

The pre-Salem and Salem event sermons of Cotton Mather's contemporaries demonstrate that he was not the only one to preach on the invisible world and witchcraft during the period in question. Mather's position as the pastor of the Old North Church in Boston simply afforded him a greater weekly audience than any other pulpit in New England and allowed for a greater proportion of his sermons to be published than most clerics. Even so, Mather's preaching cannot be deemed as singular, either in its emphasis on witchcraft or in relation to its role in the Salem tragedy. One has to agree with David Levin's assessment when he writes,

> *[Mather's] sermons, preached before the first witchcraft accusations of 1692, could hardly have affected anybody in Salem Village until the irrevocable crying-out had resounded through the village and the town for many weeks.*[401]

Salem was not New England's first or final witchcraft incident. The propensity toward accusations and prosecution for witchcraft represents the third major preexisting condition within New England society that predates the 1690s.

From the inception of the American colony, the Puritans transferred the basic premises of English law to the New World. Choosing the Mosaic Code as their core ethics, as Robert Oaks indicates, the New England clerics and judges "incorporated verbatim into statutes the proscriptions of Leviticus."[402] By combining English practice with Mosaic law, the Puritan clergy in the New World greatly affected their system of jurisprudence. Justifying their adoption of the Old Testament standards, they insisted that if reason through legal precedent revealed a code of proper and improper behavior, the Bible most certainly set forth injunctions against sin compatible with that older legal system. That the New England settlers accepted this argument can be observed in the cooperation between the courts and the clergy in matters of the prosecution and punishment of offenders. Francis Hill, in her book *A Delusion of Satan*, describes it in these terms:

> *The Massachusetts Bay Colony was governed by a secular body called the General Court, but its laws were based on the edicts of the Old Testament. . . . In practice it was a dictatorship by an elite of Puritan politicians and clergymen.*[403]

In reality, the enforcement of moral order within the Massachusetts Bay Colony was no more severe than it had been in Reformation Geneva or Scotland. A review of the laws of England itself during the same seventeenth-century period suggests that in general, the moral standards demanded by the English legal system were not far removed from those imposed on New England. The modern historical belief in the peculiarity of Puritan justice is perhaps exaggerated not so much by the seventeenth-century judicial code itself as by the exactness of its implementation. This exactness was not limited to cases of witchcraft, since the Puritans took an identical approach to other capital crimes defined in the Bible.[404] To this end, both the initial laws of Plymouth Colony and the 1641 *Body of Laws and Liberties* of the Massachusetts Bay Colony included multiple types of offenses punishable by death.[405]

While the punishment for such crimes as murder and treason might seem self-evident in early modern New England, other specific crimes potentially punishable by death included rape and homosexuality. In colonial New England the death penalty was prescribed for rapes involving "carnal copulation" with any "woman child under ten years old" (with or without her consent), or an engaged or married woman. The latter two instances were applied to rape cases since under the Old Testament law intercourse with an engaged or married woman was defined as "adultery" and punishable by death.[406]

Similarly, in a particular application of the Old Testament code, homosexuality was defined as a capital offense within seventeenth-century New England and throughout colonial America. This continued to be the case until the 1790s, at which time from state to state sodomy was largely made non-capital. The New England and colonial American penal codes for homosexuality were not unusual for the seventeenth century. Sodomy was a capital crime throughout most of Europe until the Napoleonic code of the 1790s and specifically within Britain until 1861. The Bay Colony adopted for their laws against homosexuality the word-for-word translation of Leviticus 20:13 which said, "If a man lyeth with mankinde as he lyeth with a woman, both of them have committed abhomination, they both shall surely be put to death."[407] Colonial clerics and judges demonstrated their commitment to enforcing the Old Testament prohibition against this crime when, as Louis Crompton relates, twice in early modern America they executed persons convicted of homosexual activities.[408]

As applied to witchcraft, the laws recognizing and punishing the "damned art" existed because the colonists had a practical purpose in prohibiting what they believed had dangerous social and spiritual implications. By the seventeenth century numerous New England statutes were in place condemning both benevolent and malevolent witchcraft.

The Massachusetts Bay Colony laws of 1641 and 1648 stated categorically, "If any man or woman be a witch (that hath or consulteth with a familiar spirit), they shall be put to death. Exodus 22:18 Leviticus 20:27 Deuteronomy 18:10-11." The 1671 and 1685 laws of Plymouth Colony specifically expressed, "If any Christian (so called) be a witch, that is, hath, or consulteth with a familiar spirit;

he or they shall be put to death." The Rhode Island and Providence Plantation's judiciary used similar language. The 1647 statute declared, "Witchcraft is forbidden by the present Assembly to be used in this colony; and the penalty imposed by the authority that we are subjected to is felony of death."

The New Haven Colony law of 1656 warned, "If any person be a witch, he or she shall be put to death according to Exodus 22:18 Leviticus 20:27 Deuteronomy 18:10-11." Connecticut records show a 1672 ordinance demanding that "if any man or woman be a witch, that is, hath or consulteth with a familiar spirit, they shall be put to death, Exodus 22:18 Leviticus 20:27 Deuteronomy 18:10-11." Finally, the 1679\80 Cutt Code of New Hampshire pronounced, "If any Christian, so-called, be a witch, that is, hath or consulteth with a familiar spirit, he or they shall be put to death."[409]

A perusal of New England's clerical and court records reveal that from the 1620s to 1646, there were few witchcraft allegations within New England that reached official hearings and were brought to trial. Even though the Antinomian controversy was deemed to have diabolical overtones, the Hutchinson crisis was adjudicated as a case of heresy instead of a witchcraft trial.

This seemingly quiet period would come to a halt when in 1647 Alice Young and Elizabeth Kendall were both executed for witchcraft.[410] The pace of formal complaints and trials steadily increased with the June 1648 trial of Margaret Jones, in the city of Charlestown. Governor Winthrop presided at Jones's trial in which she was accused of having a "malignant touch" that caused others to become sick or deaf. Jones became the first accused witch in Massachusetts to be executed, initiating the now familiar pattern of New England witch trials.[411]

Beginning with the same year, 1648, and until 1665, Hartford, Connecticut, became the location of the first serious outbreak of witch trials and executions, with only a few acquittals. In 1648, Mary Johnson of Hartford was tried as a witch and executed upon her confession of having had "familiarity with the Devill."[412] Hartford was also the site of the trial of Mary and Hugh Parsons, a husband and wife. Mary Parson faced witchcraft allegations in 1651 and 1674. Hugh Parsons was tried in 1652. Neither husband nor wife was convicted. In 1663 a woman named Greensmith was tried and hanged for diabolical practices. And in 1665, Elizabeth Segur was condemned at Hartford but released by the court before her sentence could be carried out.

In 1670 at Northampton, Mary Webster of Hadley was examined, sent to Boston for further interrogation and finally acquitted by that court. This, however, was not the end of the situation. When she returned home, she was accosted by a group of young men who dragged her from her home and hung her upside down until she nearly died of suffocation. Essex County, in Massachusetts, had a similar history from 1652 until the onset of the Salem trials. During this period witchcraft accusations resulted in no less than three trials and the execution of a woman named Hibbins.[413]

It should also be noted that New England was not the only American setting for witch trials and executions during the seventeenth century. New York, Pennsylvania and Virginia saw similar cases regularly within this same period. As Silverman points out, the "Colonial courts tried more than eighty such cases from 1647 to 1691 resulting in twenty executions and many more fines, banishments, and whippings."[414]

Beyond the pattern of periodic witch outbreaks and prosecutions, the New England witch trials also demonstrate a consistency with that of their English and Continental counterparts in one other important aspect: the high percentage of alleged witches who were female. In Europe, James Sharpe indicates that "as a whole, something like 80 percent of those accused of witchcraft at the courts were women, while in England, a figure nearer 90 percent was not uncommon in samples of cases tried at the assizes."[415] Similarly, in early modern New England witch trials, and specifically the Salem outbreak, the majority of accused witches were women. Of these, sixty-one were married, twenty widowed, and twenty-nine were single.

The linking of women and witchcraft has roots in earlier witchcraft scholarship. In the sixteenth and seventeenth centuries alone, a number of sources alleged this propensity of women toward witchcraft. A few examples are relevant here: Nicolas Remy, the Lorraine judge and witch prosecutor in the 1590s, did not find it "unreasonable that this scum of humanity [witches] should be drawn chiefly from the feminine sex."[416] Nor would Henri Boguet, the witch-hunter and prosecutor in the Burgundian Franche-Compte. He agreed with this analysis, writing, "The Devil knows that women love carnal pleasures, and he means to bind them to his allegiance by such agreeable provocations."[417]

In his 1608 treatise *The Damned Art,* English witchcraft expert William Perkins observed that "the woman, being the weaker sex, is sooner entangled by the devil's illusions with this damnable art than the man."[418] In 1616, Alexander Roberts had made a similar connection in his *A Treatise of Witchcraft,* writing, "Women more easily receive the impression of the Divell."[419]

Recognizing this evidence, scholars have offered varying explanations for this historical association of women with witchcraft. As noted in the introduction, one approach taken by some feminist writers argues that the explanation can be found in the misogynistic mindset of the male-dominated early modern society. Christina Larner's monumental work on Scottish witchcraft beliefs and prosecutions, *Enemies of God,* concluded that witchcraft could be shown to be sex-related though not sex specific, whether examined in the Continental, English, or New England setting. She suggests that the Scottish witch hunts were primarily a result of the emergence of a new type of post-Reformation Christianity and Catholic Counter-Reformation thought within seventeenth-century Scotland.[420] She focused on what has been described as the "validating ideologies such as moral purity, moral control and, by extension, law and order consciousness . . . pre-existent misogynistic notions interacted with new religious, political and social processes."[421]

In a similar vein, Carol Karlsen portrays the witchcraft persecutions in New England as being predominantly a byproduct of misogynistic viewpoints in Puritan society. Karlsen argues that women were identified with witchcraft when their behavior challenged the male-dominated societal ordering. The Puritans were, for Karlsen, marked by their purposeful teaching and ordering of women, and their attempt to train women to submission. Karlsen suggests that witch hunts and persecutions were often the result of what she calls "the fear of female sexual power" mediated through the practice of magic, midwife practice, and other female-centered activities.[422]

Elizabeth Reis suggests in her book *Damned Women* that the unequal ratio of female to male witches and accusers was a direct outcome of the application of Puritan theology.[423] Citing seventeenth-century Puritan sermons, as well as midwifery and medical tracts in circulation in New England, Reis indicates a shared assumption by men and women that although "women and men would be equal before God and the Devil, . . . women were more likely than men to submit to Satan and become witches."[424] Reis suggests that although the Salem witch-trial process was clearly in the control of the male adjudication panel, both accused and accusing women reaffirmed the role of women in society through their response to cultural expectations both while on the witness stand and in acting as examiners. In short, Reis argues that they were following a culturally transmitted script on gender roles, which affirmed the proper Puritan view of womanhood, while at the same time agreeing with a process that identified those who did not fit the proper model of a Christian woman.[425]

Finally, in bringing a balance to the discussion of linking women and witchcraft, it is important to note that despite the higher numbers of seventeenth-century women witch suspects, witchcraft and maleficence was not an exclusively "female" crime. Robin Briggs makes this point when he writes,

> *Although every serious historical account recognizes that large numbers of men were accused and executed on similar charges, this fact has never really penetrated to become part of the general knowledge on the subject.*[426]

The historical evidence points to the fact that men were not believed to be any less capable of engaging in white magic, maleficium, or compact witchcraft. In some individual witch hunts, particularly in Continental Europe, the number of men prosecuted was equal to or greater than that of women, especially in cases where witches were prosecuted primarily as heretics or for treason.[427] As Brian Levack suggests,

> *In some of the woodcuts and engravings produced during the sixteenth and seventeenth centuries, especially those illustrating the pact with the Devil, male and female witches are shown in equal numbers.*[428]

Seventeenth-century legal structures did not necessarily mandate or point to a specifically female identity for the witch. Within Old and New England, men were just as "eligible" to be examined since there was nothing in the definitions or legal prohibitions that excluded males from witchcraft allegations. In reference to English witchcraft, Sharpe places this in perspective:

> *In our discussion of women and witchcraft we should not lose sight of one basic point: men were accused of witchcraft. . . . The current interpretation would suggest that most men accused of witchcraft were related to a female witch, either through blood or though marriage. . . . Occasionally however, it is possible to find a male witch who seemed to enjoy an individual career.*[429]

In seventeenth-century New England, men figure generally as witchcraft participants in the Salem court transcripts, but also specifically, as in the case of George Burroughs. The former Baptist minister and accused Salem-Andover witch-cult leader seems to have enjoyed the "individual career" Sharpe describes.

Nonetheless, as this material suggests, the consistency of gender bias in witchcraft prosecutions throughout European and North American perceptions strongly reinforces the evidence for a trans-Atlantic community of belief and function, in relation to witchcraft, drawn from intellectual and legal sources.

In light of the preexisting pattern of witch trials within New England, a pertinent question regarding this would be whether anything relative to witchcraft prosecutions had changed near the end or after the Salem events. In other words, had the colonists changed their minds about the necessity for laws or prosecutions against witchcraft? They had not. One indication of this continuing pattern is the passage of A Bill Against Conjurations, Witchcraft, and Dealing with Evil and Wicked Spirits ratified by the Boston legislature in December 1692, just before the termination of the Salem trials. The thrust of the reenacted prohibition against all forms of witchcraft is evident in the General Court's adoption of this statute warning the New England populace that

> *if any persons shall use, practice or Exercise any Invocation or Conjuration of any evil and wicked Spirit, Or shall consult, covenant with, Entertain, Employ, feed or reward any evil and wicked Spirit for any intent or purpose . . . or shall use, practice or Exercise any Witchcraft Inchantment charm or Sorcery, whereby any persons shall be killed, destroyed, wasted, consumed, pined or lamed in his or her body or any part thereof, That then every such Offender or Offenders, their Aiders, Abetters, and Counsellors . . . shall suffer pains of death as a Felon or Felons.*[430]

Nor would the Salem events end New England's witch trials, since arrests and trials for witchcraft would continue well into eighteenth century, demonstrating the continuing fear of witches and their malevolent powers.

Conclusion

THE SALEM WITCH TRIALS were simply one more turn in an ever-present cycle of witchcraft accusations, trials, and executions. Cotton Mather's presence in Boston could not have been the key factor that led to the trials, since, as Kenneth Silverman insists, "the enormous likelihood is that the girls at Salem would have become possessed, and their alleged tormentors would have been tried and hanged, had Cotton Mather never existed."[431]

There are significant reasons for believing this. First, as the previous chapter demonstrated, seventeenth-century New Englanders maintained a largely congruent set of witchcraft beliefs that predated the Salem episode. Second, as this chapter has shown, against the backdrop of seventeenth-century New England witchcraft beliefs, a better argument can be made that the Salem events were predisposed by the prevalence of prior witchcraft publications in New England, contemporaneous preaching about witchcraft, and a legacy of prior witchcraft trials and executions.

Accordingly, it is now appropriate to proceed to an explanation of Cotton Mather's theology as it applies to the specific circumstances of the events at Salem.

5

A Predictable Response to Salem Witchcraft

A Malefactor, accused of Witchcraft . . . Executed in this place more than Forty Years ago, did then give Notice of, an Horrible plot against the Country by WITCHCRAFT then laid, which if it were not seasonably discovered, would probably Blow up, and pull down all the Churches in the Country. And we have now with Horror seen the Discovery of such a Witchcraft!

Cotton Mather, *The Wonders of the Invisible World* (1693)

WHEN THE PREEXISTING FACTORS integral within New England's religious and social structure prior to the Salem trials are examined, it becomes clear that Cotton Mather could not have had a decided effect upon the initiation of the trials. No precise link between Cotton Mather and the initiation of the trials can be demonstrated. Instead, Mather had a conspicuous but limited part in the trials, the scope of which derived more from New England's judicial cooperation between the judges and clergy and Mather's personal ministerial prominence in Boston.

It is equally true, however, that an equitable historical analysis cannot be allowed to end with this conclusion or anything like a total denial of the allegations critical of Cotton Mather. Rather, it leads us to an assessment of his conduct as it related directly to the entire Salem affair. In the light of Mather's preconceived, cohesive cosmology, the issue that must be addressed is the extent to which those beliefs were acted out prior to and during the Salem trials. This chapter will begin the process of doing just this.

There are a number of complications in assessing the evidence for what that behavior in fact was. Perhaps the most difficult of these lies in the nature of Mather's own most comprehensive statement of events. Scholars have criticized not only Cotton Mather's behavior during the trials, but also the integrity of Mather's main statement on the subject of Salem witchcraft, *The Wonders of the Invisible World*. That publication has been identified by various scholars as Mather's justification for the entire Salem situation. Peter Hoffer, for instance, complains, "Would that we could trust that tract, but its author was a partisan. . . . Mather lionized the judges and approved everything they did, casting some doubt upon the validation process."[432] *Wonders* alone is therefore not sufficient as a source from which to form an analysis of the integrity and consistency of Mather's conduct in Salem's witchcraft episode. Such an analysis would be compromised by the singularly complicated account contained in *Wonders*, an account by a prominent Boston pastor with some serious personal doubts about what had transpired.

Fortunately, although *Wonders* is Mather's most comprehensive work detailing both his cosmology and the historical outline of the trials, it is not the only Mather document contemporary to the Salem trials. *Wonders* was the culmination of Mather's thinking about witchcraft up to the year 1693 rather than a coherent pronouncement of a well-articulated cosmology. There are supporting documents Mather wrote before, during, and after the Salem episode, including his personal letters, and his unpublished diary, as well as tracts such as *Remarkable Providences* and *Magnalia Christi Americana*. Using these resources in a corroboratory and comparative manner creates a much broader portrait of Mather's cosmology and the nature of his overall response to witchcraft events within New England and specifically the New England of the early 1690s.

The purpose of this chapter is to explore the continuity between

Cotton Mather's cosmology and conduct pertaining to the Salem witch episode. Using several of Mather works, the first half of the chapter will demonstrate Mather's pattern of interpreting his era's international, local, and personal events within his preconceived worldview as spiritual warfare and end-times indicators. The balance of the chapter outlines the three main points of Mather's propositions about the meaning of the Salem witchcraft episode as detailed in *The Wonders of the Invisible World.* Using *Wonders* as a benchmark, Mather's other major works, *Diary*, *Remarkable Providences*, and *Magnalia Christi Americana*, are examined to show how Mather's cosmology was employed in several episodes of witchcraft within New England, including that of Salem. This includes Mather's pattern of spiritual intervention in witchcraft cases through fasting and prayer, as opposed to any involvement in adjudicatory matters as expressed in the final chapter of this book. The result is a portrait of the interrelationship between Mather's stated beliefs and his response to witchcraft episodes.

A Consistent Pattern of Cosmological Interpretation

IN KEEPING WITH THE model of his Puritan forefathers, Cotton Mather observed the events and circumstances of his generation through a specifically Puritan, biblical and eschatological understanding. His theological disposition, which affected his interpretation, is critical because it largely determined Cotton Mather's response not only to Salem witchcraft, but also to all incidents of New England witchcraft. As the historical evidence bears out, Mather's reaction to "preternatural" events stemming from malevolent witchcraft was both predictable and consistent.

Apart from his attitudes toward witchcraft, Cotton Mather's writings reveal that he employed a distinct pattern of interpreting seventeenth-century events on multiple levels in relation to contemporary events both in New England and on the international stage. He also analyzed the world in light of much more personal circumstances. Consequently, his habits of interpretation affected not only what he understood, but also how he responded.

Throughout his life, Cotton Mather's propensity was to place the world's more pronounced incidents into the scheme of his cosmology. Mather viewed seventeenth-century international religious and political situations, national revolts, and military conflicts in this way. This was equally true when the situation dealt with witchcraft. He consistently saw world events as the battleground in which God and Satan vied for the control of the human race, interpreting those events in the light of the Biblical prophecies.

One area from which Mather drew cosmological implications was that of natural disasters. An example of this is Mather's commentary on the earthquake that struck the island city of Port Royal, Jamaica, on June 7, 1692. When word of the earthquake reached Boston, Mather changed his August 4, 1692, lecture-day message to reflect the news of this catastrophe. Calling Port Royal "the Tyrus of the whole English America, but a very Sodom for wickedness," Mather declared that God had judged the wicked city since

> *just before the earthquake the People were violently and scandalously set upon going to Fortune-Tellers upon all Occasions; much notice was taken of this Impiety generally prevailing among the People; But none of those wretched Fortune-Tellers could foresee or forestall the direful Catastrophe.*[433]

Mather then drew a parallel between Port Royal and Boston, referring to "Fortune-Tellers in this Town [Boston] consulted by some of the sinful inhabitants."[434] He went on to warn the assembly that the Port Royal catastrophe was an end-times portent of the judgment to come for the "high treason" of fortune-telling and other forms of witchcraft in New England.

International political and religious persecutions such as the revocation of the Edict of Nantes in 1685 and the resulting immigration of the French Protestants to America could also be understood this way. This political reversal ended any hopes of pluralism in France, precipitating the closure of the final one-third of French Protestant churches. Although it was illegal, many French Protestants immigrated to New England through the West Indies, but not without extreme physical and financial hardships.

Cotton Mather also identified these events as an end-times indicator, insisting that Satan was clearly the active force behind the revocation of the Edict of Nantes and the persecution of French Protestants. In *Wonders of the Invisible World*, Mather writes,

> *The late French Persecution is perhaps the horriblest that ever was in the World: And as the Devil of Mascon seems before to have meant it in his out-cries upon the Miseries preparing for the poor Hugenots! Thus it has been all acted by a singular Fury of the old Dragon inspiring of his Emissaries.*[435]

Using much of the same biblically illustrative and prophetic language, Cotton Mather also sought to explain New England's own political, religious and catastrophic events. In *Magnalia Christi Americana*, Mather's extensive historical rendering of New England's New World experiment, Mather describes a number of ecclesiastical, political and military challenges faced by New England. One notable example is Mather's approach to the Quakers' incursion into seventeenth-century New England. As radical millenarians, with similarities to the English Fifth Monarchy Men, the Quakers saw their task as preparing the world for the Second Coming of Christ. Like many other seventeenth-century Christians, the Puritans also played this millenarian strain, but the Quakers' representation of these ideas stood in stark opposition to the Puritans.' Whereas the

Puritans' preparation was seen in external, visible manifestations, the Quakers' emphasis was upon the internal, invisible realization of this truth. Subsequently, as Phillip Gura writes, the Quakers

> *confirmed their worst fears about the final tendency of radical spiritism [which] undermined the Puritans' elaborately constructed Bible Commonwealth and threatened New England with the religious anarchy that in England eventually led to the reinstatement of Anglicanism as the nation's official faith.*[436]

Throughout New England, the official reaction to the Quakers came in two forms: persecution and accusations of diabolism. Carol Karlsen records the response of the New England leadership to the arrival of the first two female Quaker preachers in Boston in 1656. Ann Austin and Mary Fisher were arrested as witches before they ever reached shore. Acting Governor Richard Bellingham ordered both Austin and Fisher stripped naked on board the ship and their bodies examined for signs of Devil worship. Their possessions were searched for books containing "corrupt, heretical, and blasphemous Doctrines."[437]

Despite the authorities' rough treatment and deportation of Austin and Fisher, during the decades that followed the Quakers eventually made inroads into New England. In 1682 when William Penn arrived in the New World, he carried a charter from Charles II to establish a new colony and the monarch's decree for the colonies to repeal many of their punitive laws against the sect. Consequently, by the late seventeenth century, the Quakers, with their stronghold in Pennsylvania, had ruptured the religious monopoly held by the New England Puritan institutionalized church.

Like other clerics, Cotton Mather believed that God intended New England to be Puritan throughout. Mather therefore viewed the introduction of religious sects into New England as a work of the

Devil to destroy "Christian" and more importantly "Puritan America." Mather's view that the growth of Quakerism posed a genuine spiritual threat to Protestantism is clear in his explicit opposition to them.

In the introduction to his sermon "Little Flocks guarded against Grievous Wolves," published in 1691, Mather charged that the physical manifestations and powers of the Quakers were nothing less than the work of Satan. Mather claimed that the conversion of one young woman to the Society of Friends in the 1680s was simultaneous with her possession by demons. Quoting his father, Mather wrote in *Magnalia Christi Americana*, "Diabolical Possession was the Thing which did dispose and encline Men unto Quakerism."[438] In a further coupling of Quakerism and demonic possession, he stigmatized the notable manifestations of the Quakers this way:

> *The quaking which distinguished these poor creatures was a symptom of diabolical possession . . . there could be nothing less than a diabolical possession in many other things that attended and advanced Quakerism.*[439]

The Quakers and other radical separatists were not the only religious threats to New England's "errand in the wilderness." There were also struggles internal to New England Puritanism itself, such as the establishment of successive Puritan churches within New England and specifically Boston. Some resulted from divisions within the congregational churches themselves. First had come the debate over the Halfway Covenant Synod of 1662. By the 1690s, certain segments of Puritans were again straying from the original premises of New England's Congregationalist pattern of baptism and church membership predicated upon evidence of salvific grace. The result was a move toward allowing participation in the sacraments to a wider portion of the population.

This controversy would gain importance in the years after the Salem events. Out of this debate the Brattle Street Church formed in 1699, providing a rival of Cotton Mather's Old North Church. The Brattle Street Church founders included some former Mather supporters, such as Solomon Stoddard and the wealthy Thomas Brattle, from whom the church derived its name.

The church had two distinctive features: its architectural and ecclesiastical structure. The Brattle Street Church construction imitated the churches of England, with a full tower and a spire at one end rather than the central turret common to New England Congregationalist buildings. The church also adopted more ecumenical standards, claiming its governing structure to be in the spirit of the United Brethren of England—the recently aligned English Presbyterian and Congregational churches. This included the admission of members to communion and baptism without requiring a conversion statement and allowing the church membership to elect its ministers. Cotton Mather's reaction to this was direct and wrathful. He rejected the new church, likening its formation to an assault by Satan against Puritan New England:

> *I see Satan beginning a terrible shake unto the Churches of New England; and the Innovators, that have sett up a new Church in Boston (a new one indeed!). . . . The Men are ignorant, arrogant, obstinate, and full of Malice and Slander, and they fill the Land with Lyes.*[440]

Near the end of his life, Mather would continue to place New England's events within this framework, as an example from 1721 demonstrates. That year, New England would suffer one of its worst smallpox epidemics. Cotton Mather fought ardently for the inoculation of the population against the disease and succeeded despite volatile opposition. Mather drew parallels between the battle to institute inoculations, the suffering of the infected, and spiritual warfare. Placing these within a cosmological framework, Mather wrote in his *Diary*,

> *The Destroyer being enraged at the Proposal of anything, that may rescue the Lives of our poor People from him, has taken a strange Possession of the People on this Occasion. They rave, they rail, they blaspheme.*[441]

Cotton Mather also perceived the situations and phenomenon of his own life, whether positive or negative, within the boundaries of his cosmology. His worldview held considerable sway over his analysis of incidents related to the invisible and supernatural realm. Included in Mather's journals are claims of Divine guidance through visions, dreams, scriptural illumination, and angelic visitations.[442]

Cotton Mather's personal contact with the hostile invisible world was equally consequential. Whether preaching from his Boston pulpit or writing in his journal, Mather often described personal incidents and obstacles through the lens of this conflict with Satan. No greater primary records of this conflict exist than Cotton Mather's then unpublished diary, and *Magnalia Christi Americana*, which detail many of his attempts at comprehending both the will of God and the mystery of God's actions in his personal life.

Beyond any doubt, Mather believed himself to be personally and decidedly locked in a battle with the Devil. Within his *Diary*, Mather details this battle in terms of spiritual oppression used by Satan to dissuade Mather from his ministerial duties:

> *Satan has made violent and surprising Assaults upon me . . . it is an incredible Force, with which the Satanic Energy hath at certain Times, bore in upon my Soul . . . and the presence of it hath made the Confusion of my Mind unutterable, and unsupportable.*[443]

Spiritual oppression was not the Devil's only weapon. Mather frequently mentions in his diary his anticipation of the Devil's assault against his person, family, or possessions. An example that illustrates this is a personal tragedy that Mather experienced in March 1693 during the Salem witchcraft episode. In his *Diary*, Mather relates that his then pregnant wife, Abigail, "a few weeks before her Deliverance, was affrighted with an horrible Spectre, in our Porch, which Fright caused her Bowels to turn within her."[444]

When Abigail gave birth to a male infant, it died within a few days. Afterwards, Mather either conducted or assisted in an autopsy, which linked the infant's death to a deformity in its lower intestinal tract. Given the context of Mather and New England's contemporary struggle with the witches, the medical evidence seemed to verify Mather's "great Reason to suspect a Witchcraft, in this praeternatural Accident."[445]

Six months later, after the Salem trials, Mather was scheduled to preach at Salem Village. While there, he intended to gather some further documents on the recent witch trials for preservation in his forthcoming "Church History" of New England, *Biblia Americana*. During the journey, Mather lost three sermon manuscripts, about which he wrote in his diary: "These Notes, were before the Sabbath, stolen from mee, with such Circumstances, that I am somewhat satisfied, The Spectres, or Agents in the invisible World, were the Robbers."[446] Mather equated the manuscript theft with a satanic attempt to prevent him from preaching at the seat of the recent witch trials.

When Mather returned to Boston, he was asked to pray for Margaret Rule, a young neighbor woman suffering from an apparent witch possession. Before her deliverance, Rule claimed Mather's sermon notes had been stolen by the very specters tormenting her and predicted the notes would be returned. A few days later, when the manuscripts were found scattered about the streets of Lynn Village and returned to Mather, he marveled at the "exactness of their Praeservation," writing triumphantly in his journal that "God helped me . . . so that the Divel got nothing!"[447]

At times, Mather could be excessive in this insistence of a personal battle with the Devil. In a particularly self-absorbed moment, writing in his *Diary* Mather implied that the Salem witch assault might have been Satan's retaliation against Mather's own evangelizing efforts in New England:

> *This Assault of the Evil Angels upon the Countrey, was intended by Hell, as a particular Defiance, unto my poor Endeavors, to bring the Souls of men unto heaven . . . it enflamed my Endeavors this Winter to do yett more, in a direct opposition unto the Divel.*[448]

Whether or not Mather really believed that the Salem invasion was a direct attack of Satan upon Mather's endeavors, he was certain the ongoing criticism of Robert Calef over the theological and adjudicatory issues connected to the Salem trials was. Without specifically naming Calef, Mather depicts a recent letter from Calef in his journal in explicitly diabolical terms:

> *This day I was buffeted with a libellous Letter from a Merchant in this Town, fill'd with Scurrilities that I suppose were hardly ever aequalled in the World. The Divel stared in every Line of it. A Legion together could scarce have out done it.*[449]

As these examples demonstrate, Cotton Mather maintained a consistent pattern of interpreting the events of his era cosmologically and eschatologically. Whether it was the minor loss of some sermon notes or the cataclysmic destruction of an entire city by an earthquake, nothing transpired in Mather's world that did not possess some spiritual, if not supernatural, significance.

A Correspondence of Belief and Response to Salem Witchcraft

COTTON MATHER'S GENERAL PATTERN of interpreting

contemporary international, New England, and personal events through the grid of his cosmology would find a significant application during the Salem witchcraft chapter. Mather interpreted the Salem trials as an extension of God's judgment, as well as the outcropping of the war between New England and the Devil.

In reviewing three of Mather's main works, *The Wonders of the Invisible World*, his *Diary*, and *Magnalia Christi Americana*, the salient points of his conviction concerning Salem witchcraft can be seen. Within *Wonders*, the synthesis of Mather's eschatological expectations and pre-Salem assessment of New England's moral state, Mather argues that genuine witchcraft had been present at Salem. Viewed together these propositions suggest he believed Salem Village's witchcraft invasion was the focal point of three converging situations: God's judgment upon New England's spiritual decline, a demonic retaliation due to the Puritan settlement of America, and an end-time plot of Satan to destroy the establishment of New England.

For each of Mather's postulates as to the meaning of the Salem episode, he displayed a pattern of behavior consistent with his own interpretation of the predicament the New England clergy and government faced. This section suggests that he not only believed in the reality of the threats, but that this belief informed his conduct at every level.

As far as Cotton Mather was concerned, seventeenth-century Puritans had largely failed to live out the vision of their forefathers typified by John Winthrop's theme of "A City Set on a Hill." In *Wonders*, Mather extols the piety and holiness of the first-generation New World–Puritans who, desiring "Reformation . . . embraced a voluntary Exile in a squalid, horrid, American Desert, rather than to live in Contentions with their Brethren."[450] To Mather, the expression of this first-generation piety could be seen in Giles Firmin's speech to Parliament, in which he boasted that in his first seven years of life in New England he "never saw one man drunk, or heard one oath sworn, or beheld one beggar in the streets."[451]

Cotton Mather saw the New England of 1692 as a society suffering a significant spiritual relapse. Mather's jeremiads at the Old North Church in Boston insisted that New England had "miserably degenerated from the first Love" of their predecessors.[452] To Mather, the former "true Utopia" of New England had become "a nest of swearing, Sabbath-breaking, whoring, drunkenness."[453]

Wonders was in part a denunciation of the sins of the people of the day.[454] Within its pages, Cotton Mather pointed to the recent adverse conditions New England had experienced, for which the colony had "all the reason to ascribe it unto the Rebuke of Heaven" for their "manifold Apostates." He warned his generation that "we make no right use of our Disasters: if we do not, Remember whence we are fallen, and repent, and do the first Works."[455]

These disasters, repeatedly cited by Mather, were an ever-increasing series of "judgments" which had befallen New England in the form of severe calamities. Religious threats had abounded in the form of the Antinomian error,[456] the rise of the Quakers, the incursion of the Baptist-Arminian influence, and the worrisome presence of the Crown's Episcopal churches. Hostilities or threats of war had also either occurred or loomed close, such as the Indian attacks, the distant but still frightening European wars (i.e., the Glorious Revolution with the warfare in Scotland and Ireland), and the ever-present threat of a French invasion in the New World. Added to this, there had been inexplicable crop failures, disease-related plagues, droughts, fires, and storms. Finally, there had been the revocation of the Bay Charter, the conflict with Governor Andros, and the threat of English military rule in New England under Kirke.

To Mather, if God's judgment on New England's backsliding had not been evident enough, there came another prodigious calamity; the onset of Salem witchcraft. For Mather, it was God's climactic sentence upon a people in spiritual decline. In Peter Hoffer's words,

Mather correctly reckoned the crucial ministerial issues

> *for his generation were moral and social, part of the goal of recovering the founders' community spirit and the purity of worship. Against this, he judged, the threat of witchcraft was primarily directed, for witchcraft did not raise doctrinal problems so much as social ones.*[457]

In a multitude of references within *The Wonders of the Invisible World*, Mather intimates that Salem witchcraft was the equivalent of God's judgement on Salem. In writing the first half of *Wonders*, Mather presents several postulates by which he details this view.

First, Mather points out that God severely judged New England by witchcraft because their place of prominence demanded greater allegiance to him than they had offered. Here is his contention:

> *The Kingdoms of Sweden, Denmark, Scotland, yea and England itself, as well as the Province of New-England, have had their Storms of Witchcrafts breaking upon them. . . . And it is not uneasie to be imagined, that God has not brought out all the Witchcrafts in many other Lands with such a speedy, dreadful, destroying Jealousie, as burns . . . here in the Land of the Uprightness: Transgressors may more quickly here than elsewhere become a Prey to the Vengeance of Him.*[458]

In Mather's mind, it would come as no surprise if "witch storms" might break upon nations he considered lesser in godliness and teleological importance. Even Old England might experience these trials as part of the judgment of God for its unfaithfulness and spiritual decline. However, New England, the site of God's great Puritan colony, naturally attracted God's sentence more quickly and more severely enacted precisely because of God's jealousy over New England's "High Treason": her idolatry connected to Satan.

Mather also describes the invasion and execution of the witches as the chastisement of God for New England's corporate sins. The villages had been rife with those errors the clergy had long been preaching against: backbiting, talebearing, scandal mongering, card playing, drunkenness, lawsuits, complaints, clamors, and the lack of church attendance. In addition, as previously demonstrated, some portions of the New England populace had transgressed through lesser magical practices. Mather reprimands New England's populace for using the various forms of lesser witchcraft such as fetishes, fortune-telling, superstitious health remedies, "water witching," and, of course, uttering imprecations over their enemies. These lesser sins had led to the dangerous sin of witchcraft. Hence, God permitted the devils to hook the "ignorant, envious, discontented people" of New England as a form of punishment.[459]

A third proposition suggested by Mather was that God had used Satan's own wrath as a means of judgment. As Mather put it, "There is a Devilish wrath against Mankind, with which the Devil is for God's sake inspired."[460] Satan received God's express permission to afflict the nation, but as Mather put it, God's purpose in the Salem situation was not destruction, but rather the awakening of the nation:

> *It is not without the wrath of God himself, that the Devil is permitted thus to come down upon us in his wrath . . . Blessed Lord! Are all the other Instruments of thy Vengeance, too good for the chastisement of such transgressors as we are? Must the very Devils be sent out of their own place, to be our troublers.*[461]

If in Mather's thinking Salem witchcraft was God's judgment upon New England's spiritual degeneration, what then was the solution? Mather spells it out in twin spiritual terms: repentance and reformation. Mather saw a new Reformation, created by true repentance, as the only means for turning back Satan's wrath and averting God's certain judgment. This belief is confirmed by one important aspect of Mather's pre and post-Salem activity: a call for repentance.

Mather had in fact been calling New England to repentance long before the 1690s, making use of every opportunity to do so. For example, in 1685, he delivered the customary "execution sermon" at the hanging of convicted murderer James Morgan. Preaching to an enormous crowd representative of a wide cross section of New England's population, Mather pointed to Morgan as a "frightening example of the results of brothels, swearing, and other prevalent vices."[462] Soon afterwards, Mather included a full account of Morgan's execution and this sermon in "The Call of the Gospel," Mather's first published call for a national reformation.

Again, as previously noted, on March 20, 1690, Mather preached a jeremiad entitled "The Present State of New England." Reflecting on the French and Indian attack on New England's outlying settlements, Mather called for a renewed commitment to England's monarchs before going on to an overlapping subject: the colony's moral state. After saying that this new calamity was a result of the "anger of The righteous God" against New England, Mather appended to the sermon a proclamation calling for a "Speedy REFORMATION."[463] He also called upon the magistrates to enforce the laws against "Blasphemy, Cursing, Prophane Swearing, Lying, Unlawful Gaming, Sabbath breaking, Idleness, Drunkenness, Uncleanness."[464]

A final extract illustrating Mather's call for repentance and reformation was published in 1692, just weeks before the culmination of the Salem trials. At that moment, suspicion, trepidation, and paranoid confusion seemed to reign throughout New England. Entitled "A Midnight Cry," it was one of Mather's most powerful sermons. Preaching from the pulpit of the Old North Church in Boston, Mather called for a return to God similar to Europe's Protestant Reformation. Mather punctuated his sermon with emotionalism, and sporadic threats of impending judgment. Referring to the Salem witchcraft events, Cotton Mather called the populace to "Look upward, and see a God Angry; Look Downward, and see an Hell Gaping; Look Inward, and see our Cursed Hearts; Look Backward, and see our Wicked Lives."[465]

Mather's call for reformation continued well past the Salem trials. In a lecture that was later included in *Magnalia,* called "The Boston Ebenezer," Mather warned,

> *Tis notorious that the Sins of this Town have been many Sins, and mighty Sins; the Cry thereof hath gone up to heaven. If the Almighty God should from heaven Rain down upon the Town an horrible Tempest of Thunderbolts, as he did upon the Cities which he overthrew in his Anger, and repented not, it would be no more than our unrepented Sins deserve.*[466]

With this in view, it is evident Cotton Mather believed that the Salem witchcraft events were at least partially the result of New England's spiritual decline. Salem witchcraft equaled God's judgment on Salem. What was necessary to restore the spiritual vitality of New England and avert God's wrath was a wholehearted return to the covenant.

When the main body of the Puritans landed at Massachusetts Bay in June of 1630, they saw themselves at the beginning of a new era of Christianity. Although their spiritual vision focused upon establishing a truly theocratic society, they nonetheless understood that colonizing the territory would include numerous physical, agricultural, financial and political challenges.

At least one other major concern existed: the presence of a large population of native Indians. The early Puritans lived in a state of alarm with respect to Indian attacks. Although the frequency of the Indian raids upon the main settlements eventually lessened, the fear of them was still very palpable nearly six decades later in the now large city of Boston.

The Puritans came to the New World believing that it had long been Satan's particular preserve. Joseph Mede had expressed this view as early as 1634, when he said that Satan had chosen and established the Indians as his people even before Christ's incarnation. As Mather put it, for centuries Satan, "like a Dragon," had ruled America completely unopposed, keeping "a Guard upon the spacious and mighty Orchards of America."[467]

According to the Puritans, Satan's primary influence over his "chosen ones" involved empowering them through ceremonial magic and demonic covenants. William Bradford recorded in his history of the Plymouth Colony that soon after the Indians of Cape Cod first sighted the Puritans, they "got all the Powachs of the country, for three days together in a horrid and devilish manner, to curse and execrate them with their conjurations."[468] Similarly, Roger Williams stated categorically that the Bay Colony "Indians' priests were no other than our 'English witches,' the Devill drives their worships."[469] This witchcraft, in which the "pagan Powaws often raise their masters, in the shapes of Bears and Snakes and fires," included spectral agents used to torture human targets.[470]

Predictably, the original Puritan settlers concluded that the Indians were the subjects of Satan's evil dominion and a real threat to the Puritans' American colonization. In inheriting and retaining this view, it was only natural then for Cotton Mather to believe that the Puritan colonists would continue to face the Devil's opposition.[471] Returning to the position that Satan was the master of the devils, the same in nature and malice as Satan himself, Mather derived particular meaning from the Salem calamity.

In both *Wonders* and *Magnalia*, Mather details the calamities that the settlement had endured, intimating that some were demonically induced. He further noted that as if this had not been enough, the Indians had not only "watered the soil" of New England with the "blood of many hundreds of our inhabitants,"[472] but often forced their captives to observe as "their friends [were] made a sacrifice of devils before their eyes."[473] His intent was to show that the Indians had historically been demonically energized and commissioned to attack the Puritans. Contemporary to Mather's era, this was evident in the Indians' frequent assistance in the attacks by the French, whom the Puritans regarded as the Catholic minions of the papal Antichrist.

Certainly, the Indians induced a considerable degree of terror for the populace of New England.[474] James Kences notes that witchcraft episodes in New England villages often occurred simultaneously with the population's fear of either war or Indian atrocities. Kences gives a telling account of this propensity when he records that

> *in July [1692], soldiers guarding the approaches to the town of Gloucester fired their muskets at what they believed to be . . . a hoard of Indians with "Black bushy hair." But their bullets passed right through the wavering images of the attackers. In panic, the soldiers called for reinforcements, crying that the town was besieged by spectral Indians.*[475]

In relation to the Salem dilemma, the 1692 reinterpretation of this theme suggested that just as the demons had enticed previous generations of Indians into a compact with Satan, the same devils were now carrying out an identical strategy. This time, however, they were ensnaring subjects from within the Puritan community, as Cotton Mather reported:

> *The People that were Infected and Infested with such Daemons, in a few Days time arrived unto such a Refining Alteration upon their Eyes, that they could see their Tormentors; they saw a Devil of Little Stature, and of a Tawny Colour, attended still with Spectres that appeared in more Humane Circumstances.*[476]

Mather's insistence on Indian and demonic cooperation was not limited to his personal observations, since various Salem witchcraft suspects and victims would claim that a Native American–Salem witchcraft connection existed. Witch suspect Sarah Osborne claimed that she was "more like to be bewitched than that she was a witch," having been assaulted by "a thing like an indian all black."[477] Mercy Short, a possession subject, would tell Cotton Mather that she had been tormented by specters of "Indian Sagamores" she had known during her Indian captivity, who urged her to sign the Devil's book.[478] Another Salem victim testified that Captain John Alden, a prominent New England figure involved in negotiating a truce with warring Indian tribes, was also involved with Salem witchcraft. Alden was in attendance at one of the Salem proceedings when one of the young women cried out that he sold "Powder and Shot to the Indians and French, and lies with the Indian Squaes, and has Indian Papooses."[479] This indictment is a poignant illustration of the perceived relationship between the Indians and New England witchcraft in which, as Alfred Cave puts it, "suspicion of collusion with Indians, in this case, led to charges of collusion with the Devil."[480]

As these citations show, Cotton Mather saw Salem witchcraft as a demonic retaliatory attack upon the Puritan settlement of America. With this belief firmly fixed in his mind, Cotton Mather went on to express the solution to this second cause for the Salem outbreak. He referred to what had been his personal and official response in every case of New England witchcraft he had encountered—a period of spiritual warfare against Satan through fasting and prayer. If repentance and reformation were the twin elements able to remove God's judgment upon the colony, prayer and fasting were the twin weapons able to defeat the demons molesting the populace through witchcraft.

If Mather clearly displayed a single course of action before, during, and after Salem's ordeal, it was his dedication to spiritual warfare as the primary means of countering demonic invasions. This was Mather's solitary approach to dealing with Satan's incursions into his personal life and the only means he employed in delivering those suffering "diabolical possessions" caused by demons in covenant with witches. The next section reviews Mather's methodology of fasting and prayer in connection to spiritual warfare.

In reading Mather's *Diary* for the summer of 1692, it is evident that it was a difficult time for Cotton Mather for more than one reason. His health had been "lamentably broken" for some period, through what he described as "excessive Toyle" connected to his personal and public life. He found it difficult to prepare properly for his preaching, and even more difficult to recover after exercising his pulpit ministry. There was also another exceptional reason—the Salem Village troubles. Mather describes the events in these terms:

> *The Rest of the summer, was a very doleful Time, unto the whole Countrey. The Divels, after a most praeternatural Manner, by the dreadful Judgement of Heaven took a bodily Possession, of many people, in Salem, and the adjacent places; and the Houses of the poor People, began to bee filled with horrid Cries of Persons tormented by evil Spirits. There seem'd an execrable Witchcraft, in the Foundation of this wonderful Affliction.*[481]

Because of illness, Cotton Mather did not actively attend the witch trials or the executions during that summer and the next fall. His friends advised him to forego any excessive traveling to attend the trials at Salem Village, fearing that any extra burden on his fragile health, as Mather records, "would at this time threaten perhaps my life itself."[482]

Although Mather could not be present in Salem for the trials, he could nonetheless exercise what he believed would ultimately prove to be the most powerful weapons against the witch attack: fasting and prayer. In his diary he writes about this often, emphasizing that the Salem Village experience had become a primary focus of personal intercession. This spiritual methodology is also evident in several examples during the periods before, during, and after the Salem trials.

During a pre-Salem episode, in February of 1685, Mather faced circumstances involving witchcraft possession. Mather notes his determination that,

> *whereas those Divels may bee cast out by Fasting and Prayer, [I will] sett apart still a Day of secret Prayer, with Fasting . . . to supplicate for such Effusions of the Spirit from on high as may redress, remove, and vanish such Distempers from the Place.*[483]

Seven years later, Mather would make similar notations about spiritual warfare during Salem's dark hour. His journal entry for April 1692 records, "But my Prayers did especially insist upon the horrible Enchantments, and Possessions, broke forth upon Salem Village: things of a most prodigious Aspect."[484] Later that year, Mather details in his journal his ongoing intercession about Salem:

> *However, for a great part of the Summer, I did every Week, (mostly) spend a Day by myself, in the Exercises of a sacred FAST, before the Lord . . . not only for my own Praeservation from the Malice and Power of the evil Angels, but also, for . . . this miserable countrey.*[485]

Although Salem scholars have generally offered little concerning Mather's method of fasting and prayer, this was Cotton Mather's primary answer to the Salem witch outbreak. It would continue to be the course that Mather pursued with absolute faith. Viewed within Mather's cosmology, witchcraft stemmed from a malevolent spiritual source, and thus necessitated a spiritual solution. As such, Mather believed that incursions of the evil invisible world would be defeated by the intercession of God's servants.

Cotton Mather did not confine this approach to his personal life. When he was confident that an alleged witch victim was truly "diabolically possessed," his initial response was to call for a season of prayer and fasting. This activity would break the hold of demons acting for their confederates, the witches. To Mather's Calvinistic mindset, deliverances were acts of God's sovereign grace. As Kenneth Silverman remarks,

> *Like all other Puritans, he [Mather] regarded holy water, crosses, and the entire Catholic rite of exorcism as gross superstition. . . . Abjuring exorcism and magic, he followed Mark 9:29: "This kind can come forth by nothing, but by prayer and fasting."*[486]

It is a historical fact that Mather originally suggested to the Salem judges that the witchcraft victims be scattered throughout Boston, personally offering to take charge of six of them to prove "whether without more bitter methods, Prayer and Fasting would not putt an end unto these heavy Trials."[487] For reasons which remain unclear, the Court of Oyer and Terminer did not accept Mather's offer. Even so, at least three examples of Mather's use of this method to liberate witch victims, occurring in varying points in time, can be cited. Each bears a considerable degree of consistency on the part of Cotton Mather.

The first recorded case of Mather's public ministry to the bewitched began at midsummer 1688, about three and a half years before the Salem incident. Martha Goodwin, the eldest daughter of Bostonian John Goodwin, "became variously indisposed in her health, and visited with strange Fits"[488] after an altercation over stolen linens with the elderly mother of their family's laundress, Goody Glover.

After Martha told her story, Glover was arrested and examined by the magistrates. When "puppets and babies" stuffed with rags and goat hair were found in her home, Glover was convicted by the court and sentenced to die by hanging. As Cotton Mather accompanied her to the gallows, Goody Glover revealed the names of her accomplices, including one close relative, and warned him that her execution alone would not end the Goodwin affliction. Cotton Mather never revealed those names.[489]

Soon afterwards, Martha's sister, Mercy, and two of her brothers also began manifesting elements of possession. Dr. Thomas Oakes, a locally renowned physician, concluded that "nothing but an hellish Witchcraft could be the original of these maladies."[490] Cotton Mather then offered to take Martha Goodwin into his own home to "observe the extraordinary circumstances" and to serve as a "critical eyewitness." Mather studied Martha's condition, tried various tests used to detect witchcraft and wrote copious notes. Goodwin displayed some remarkable manifestations, including choking on a ball about the size of an egg and riding an invisible horse (without touching the floor). Demons attempted to pull her into the fireplace using invisible chains. Mather confided, "Once I did with my own hand knock it [the chains] off as it began to be fastened about her."[491]

Mather initiated several intense periods of fasting and prayer, imploring God for her deliverance. Finally, on November 27, Mather invited three other ministers and some neighbors to keep another set of days in fasting and prayer for the young woman. Through this procedure, Martha Goodwin and her siblings were all permanently released from the power of witchcraft.

When these events were over, in 1689 Mather released his book *Memorable Providences*, which related his recent and successful attempt to deliver the Goodwin children. The book commenced by stating that "prayer is the powerful and effectual remedy against the malicious practices of devils and those that covenant with them."[492] At the end of the introductory passage, Mather concluded, "All that I have now to publish is, that Prayer and Faith was the things which drove the devils from the children."[493]

Mather used this spiritual remedy in a later encounter with another young woman, Mercy Short, a seventeen-year-old Boston servant girl. In the early summer of 1692, Mercy was on an errand to the prison in Boston when she encountered Sarah Good, an imprisoned witch.[494] When Sarah Good asked Mercy for some pipe tobacco, Mather records that Mercy "affronted the hag by throwing an handful of shavings at her, saying 'that's tobacco enough for you.'"[495] In return, Sarah Good cursed Mercy Short, causing her to have strange fits suggesting bewitchment. Consequently, her family contacted Cotton Mather, who aided by others fasted and prayed for some twelve days before attaining Mercy's freedom. Unfortunately, sometime around November 22, two months after the last round of executions at Salem, Mercy Short's possession recurred, complicated by worse manifestations than before.

Although the experience of Mercy Short was in many respects analogous to the Martha Goodwin case, it included other remarkable features. Mercy saw a specter of the Devil himself, who appeared in the "figure of a short and a black man."[496] At each appearance, Satan cast Mercy Short into a "horrible Darkness" in which she would see "hellish harpyes" and hear demonic voices urging her to sign the "Book of Death" to become a "Devoted Vassal of the Divel."[497] At times, Mercy Short also learned information about the Devil's own campaign against Cotton Mather and Boston. For example, it was revealed that the demons were planning to burn the city of Boston. Mather reports that the night after this "the Town had like to have been burn't; but God wonderfully prevented it."[498]

Considering the horrible possession of Mercy Short, one might ask what Cotton Mather's course of action would be. The answer comes from Mather's own pen, as he writes, "The methods that were taken for the Deliverance of Mr. Goodwin's afflicted Family, four years ago, were the very same that wee now follow'd for Mercy Short . . . Prayer with Fasting."[499] It took four months of prayer and periods of fasting to effect Mercy Short's cure, but, as Mather records, "she was finally and forever delivered from the hand of evil angels."[500] In time Mercy gave evidence of grace and became a full member of Cotton Mather's Old North Church. It was a glorious ending to a terrible chapter.[501]

The last case presented here is that of Margaret Rule, of Boston. Her experiences at the hand of evil angels began on September 10, 1693, after the Salem affair ended. On that day, Rule "fell into odd fits" during the public assembly and had to be carried home by her friends. After an examination, a physician declared her to be "diabolically possessed." She too suffered horribly from the physical and emotional effects of witchcraft attested to by Martha Goodwin and Mercy Short. She experienced some unique phenomena as well. Mather reports that "once her tormentors pull'd her up to the cieling [sic] of the chamber, and held her there before a very numerous company of spectators, who found it as much as they could all do to pull her down again."[502] Rule not only saw evil specters, but at one point she also saw a "White Spirit" which specified that Cotton Mather would be the principal agent in her deliverance.[503] Five weeks later the angel reappeared to Margaret predicting her freedom from demonic torment on the third day of Mather's next fast.

Deliverance ministry, however, had its dangers as well as its victories. The next specters to appear to Margaret Rule were in Mather's own image, causing Rule to complain that Cotton Mather "threatened her and molested her," a charge that Mather's antagonist Robert Calef would later make. Mather worried about insults from Boston and New England "if such a lying Piece of a Story should fly abroad, that the Divels in my Shape tormented the Neighborhood."[504] Ironically, Cotton Mather had once written to judge John Foster that he himself would have no fear of being tried by the Court of Oyer if his own image should appear as a specter.[505] Now, in the aftermath of Salem, his reaction was not as certain. Cotton Mather was undoubtedly relieved that "his spectral appearances" ceased on the third day of his fast when "without any further noise, the possessed person [Margaret

Rule] . . . was delivered from her captivity."[506] Once again Mather's fasting and prayer had successfully liberated a victim of witchcraft.

The previous sections have revealed two of the three points of Cotton Mather's predictable response toward witchcraft. First, believing that Salem witchcraft was the equivalent of a judgement upon Salem and by extension New England, he summoned New England to repentance and reformation to avert the judgment of God upon his generation's spiritual decline. This act would deal with the witchcraft attack on a national level. Second, Cotton Mather's opinion was that Salem witchcraft was a retaliatory attack by demons due to the Puritan settlement of America. As such, he exercised a regimen of fasting and prayer to counteract this demonic incursion in both his personal life and deliverance ministry. These points now prepare this study for an explanation of Mather's third and final proposition about Salem witchcraft as found in *The Wonders of the Invisible World*: an end-time plot of Satan to destroy New England.

When Cotton Mather preached at the Old North Church on August 4, 1692, his message was alarming. He took Revelation 12:12 as his text: "Woe to the Inhabitants of the Earth, and of the Sea; for the Devil has come down unto you, having great wrath; because he knoweth, that he hath but a short time." Mather warned his congregation and all of New England that because of the immediacy of Christ's appearance, the Devil was presently carrying out a diabolical plot to destroy New England. This plot was none other than the recent invasion of devils, carried out by witches in covenant with Satan. Kenneth Silverman has suggested that this message was a "changed understanding of the outbreak at Salem."[507] One can validate this opinion by the fact that Mather was predisposed toward viewing the Salem affair as an end-time plot of Satan. Two influences led to this important interpretation: Mather's eschatological expectations, and the Andover witchcraft case.

Cotton Mather had been preaching and writing concerning the return of Christ which would result in the Millennium for some time before his August 4, 1692, fast-day sermon. Mather's understanding had been influenced by the works of two renowned eschatologists, England's Joseph Mede, and Pierre Jurieu, a Dutch professor of divinity in France.[508] In part, their combined research insisted that the Protestant Reformation of 1517 signaled the papal Antichrist's final 180-year reign would end in 1697, heralding Christ's appearance and the Antichrist's defeat.[509]

Cotton Mather and a large part of the New England's seventeenth-century clerics accepted at least some form of this eschatological interpretation. They had established an impressive catalogue of sermons and books maintaining that the American experiment was nothing less than an "end times" part of church history, in which the cosmic battle between God and Satan was being played out between the Church of England and the Antichrist papacy.

This eschatological positioning on the part of the New England Puritans was part of a broader compendium of belief common throughout seventeenth-century Europe in which millennialism and eschatology were being addressed by both Protestants and Catholics. These viewpoints were espoused and developed in a number of ways by early modern radical groups that Stuart Clark describes as "deviant religious sects [who] conceived of the complete transformation of their world by supernatural agency," and conservative academics and clerics such as Mede and Jurieu.[510] The composite of these groups, as Clark also points out, lent itself to apocalyptic expectations periodically manifested in dramatic pronouncements in which

> *there were many comments on the prevalence of social misrule—the rebelliousness of the young and the lower orders expected in the last times, whether involving the supplanting of social and moral values by their opposites, the disasters of famine, pestilence, persecution, and warfare, or violent upheavals in the environment.*[511]

In England, this expectation of universal upheaval and eschatological fulfillment seemed quite real with respect to such historical events as the English Civil War, the 1649 execution of Charles I, the Interregnum, and, perhaps most pointedly, the Glorious Revolution. These events saw the emergence of millenarian groups with their accompanying militant challenges, as embodied in groups such as the Fifth Monarchists, with their powerful influence on the New Model Army.[512] Beyond these, there were conservative and radical separatists such as the Quakers, Levellers, Diggers, and Ranters.[513]

Throughout the seventeenth century, New England had also experienced its share of what seemed to many, including Cotton Mather, to be stark indicators of eschatological upheaval. Cotton Mather's own contemporary preaching reflected an expectation of the imminent return of Christ, but also a belief in a renewed but brief end-time attack of Satan.

Mather makes this plain in *A Discourse on the Wonders of the Invisible World*, writing, "The Devils Eldest Son seems to be toward the End of his last Half-time; and if it be so, the Devils Whole-time cannot but be very near its end."[514] Two other examples of this pattern of thought, contemporary with the Salem witch episode, reflect Mather's beliefs at this time. The first example is a sermon Mather published, entitled "Things to be Look'd For." He first proclaimed this message on June 1, 1691, at the annual meeting of the Artillery Company of Massachusetts. In it, Mather rehearsed the recent Boston revolution, which ended with the deposition of Governor Andros, and the European situation involving the persecution of the French Protestants by Louis XIV. Balancing eschatological prophecies from the Bible with New England's recent troubles and world events, Mather led his hearers to one "glorious expectation," which he identified as "the speedy approaches of . . . the Latter Dayes."[515]

"A Midnight Cry," another of Cotton Mather's published sermons, is also a good example of Mather's chiliasm. It came about in the first part of 1692, as Mather twice preached at the Old North

Church on the text Romans 13:11: "And that knowing the time, that it is high time to awake out of sleep."

Similar to "Things to be Look'd For," it predicted that Christ's return was imminent. Following Mather's eschatological viewpoint, this pointed sermon maintained that the recent problems with the "serpentine" Quakers, Bloody Kirke, the Arminians, and the Indians were all acts of Satan's end-time diabolism and, therefore, precursors to Christ's Second Coming. Mather further insisted there might also be worse attacks of Satan yet to come, noting that New England was "doubtless very near the Last Hours of That Wicked One, whom our Lord shall Destroy with the Brightness of his Coming."[516]

Cotton Mather expected the imminent return of Christ, even going as far as to set a date of 1697 for that return. Although Mather's expectation remained unfulfilled, it remains profoundly significant for events at Salem. Cotton Mather placed the events of Europe and New England within his eschatological framework, and expected Christ's return to occur within only a few short years. Just before that event, the world would necessarily be plunged into convulsions because of God's judgment upon the world's sin. Mather was also convinced that Satan would attempt to take over the human race before Christ's Second Coming ushered in the millennium.

This belief created the premise upon which Cotton Mather established a pattern of interpreting diabolical events as portents of Satan's end-times assaults. This can be seen in Mather's sermon "A Discourse on the Wonders of the Invisible World," in which he outlined his anticipation of an end-time assault by Satan. He initiated this sermon by telling his seventeenthcentury audience to anticipate that "the Devil towards the end of his Time, will make a Descent upon a miserable World,"[517] and that in such a descent, "the dying Dragon, will bite more cruelly and sting more bloodily than ever he did before."[518]

Accordingly, Mather saw the "last days" as the great battleground between God and Satan. Because Satan knew his time on the earth was short, he would descend upon the nations in wrath attempting to destroy God's Kingdom. To Mather's thinking, New England might well be the subject of this end-time attack, since the Puritans had taken over Satan's former New World dominion, filling it with Evangelical churches.

It was because of Cotton Mather's expectation of an end-time attack by Satan that he was not completely surprised when in the summer of 1692 the next Salem-related event seemed to confirm a diabolical conspiracy within New England. That incident was the Andover witchcraft case. Although this episode has already been described, it is difficult to overstate its importance to Mather's interpretation of Salem witchcraft. Silverman's account of the initial story is telling:

> *Sometime in the early summer of 1692, an Andover man name Joseph Ballard sent to Salem for some of the possessed girls, hoping they could identify the specter afflicting his wife, who was ill and later died of a fever. . . . The girls acted in the Andover sickrooms as they had in the Salem court: they fell to fits and named the persons whose specters they saw tormenting the sick. Fifty persons in Andover were accused of witchcraft and thirty to forty sent to prison.*[519]

The result of the accusations was that a trial of the Andover suspects yielded information about a satanic plot against New England. During the prosecution of these alleged witches, their confessions were so similar that the judges suspected something more diabolical than previously imagined.

By this time, the conviction and, in most cases, execution of several witches had passed, including Tituba, Sarah Good, Goody Glover, Rose Cullender, and Ann Durent. Acting on individual instincts, the devils had, in Mather's view, tormented individual victims, but rarely multiple families. Additionally, their testimonies were largely individualistic and distinctive.

The Andover group did not fit this profile, as their confessions were too similar. To begin, they all agreed to the identity of the Devil and his method for ensnaring subjects. Silverman reports, "He got them to undo their allegiance to the Congregational Church . . . and had them seal their covenant with him by signing his book."[520] The Andover witches also testified to their participation in several specific acts of Devil worship including rebaptism and receiving a "hellish" communion, as well as being commissioned by Satan.

There was one further startling feature to this unified confession of the Andover witches—one that seemed to confirm Cotton Mather's eschatological expectations: the claim of a diabolical end-times plot by the Devil. The testimonies suggested that there were as many as five hundred confederates within New England. Only the Devil himself knew the exact number.

Beyond this testimony, at least eight of the suspects confided that former Salem minister George Burroughs and Martha Carrier, both accused of witchcraft, were the organizing human agents in the Andover plot. Salem defendant Deliverance Hobbs testified that George Burroughs had directed the Salem witches to "bewitch all in the Village . . . gradually and not all att once, assureing them they should prevail."[521] Mary Lacey would make a similar allegation at her trial, admitting the witches' unified task was to "afflict persons and over come the Kingdome of Christ, and set up the Divels Kingdome . . . throughout the whole country."[522]

For Cotton Mather this revelation confirmed that the Salem chapter was not only the judgment of God upon New England's spiritual degeneration and a demonic retaliation due to the Puritan settlement of America. The Salem affair had one more alarming feature; it had the marks of the end-time attack Mather had been anticipating and preaching about in recent years. Stuart Clark emphasizes the universality of this approach when he writes,

> *It is clear that, in so far as history was brought to bear on the problem of witchcraft, this was by virtue of an overwhelmingly eschatological account of events. The activities of demons and witches were apocalyptic both because they could be matched with description of the last times lying encoded in the prophetic texts of scripture, and because, in turn, they too were texts which, when suitably analyzed, might reveal truths about the nature and nearness of the world's end.*[523]

From the testimony of several of the Andover witches, it becomes apparent, whether advertently or inadvertently, that they too had come to believe in a plot to overthrow New England's religious and governmental structure. Andover witch William Barker outlined the intention of the joint Salem-Andover witches:

> *They mett there to destroy that place by reason of the peoples being divided and their differing with their ministers. Satan's desire was to set up his own worship, abolish all the churches in the land, to fall next upon Salem and soe goe through the countrey.*[524]

Beyond this, these confessed witches also foresaw a period in which Satan himself would be ruling America. Barker gave some insight into what a New England society would be like when the planned infiltration and overthrow of the colony was complete. He described it in terms of the Devil's offer in exchange for the allegiance of the witches:

> *The Devil promised that all his people should live bravely that all persones should be equall, that there should be no day of resurrection or of judgment, and neither punishment nor shame for sin.*[525]

Richard Gildrie points out the likely import of this latter language:

> *That "there should be no day of resurrection nor of judgement" removed the cosmological framework for the New England way, abolishing the orthodox meaning of history as expressed through providence and the jeremiad. That there be "neither punishment nor shame for sin" directly challenged the most common early modern rationale for government, as well as the urge to reform popular culture where "shame for sin" was a most potent weapon.*[526]

According to this testimony the Devil was planning to attack New England through a covert witch invasion. The Salem-Andover witches were therefore localized and organized, specific in their leadership and their adherents. Taken within the period, this revelation stood out to the court and the Boston clergy, since this group was far from a mythical and generalized threat. The Andover witches portrayed Salem witchcraft as more than an isolated event; it was the manifestation of a localized witch army preparing and launching a premeditated assault of Satan upon New England.

When the Salem judges heard this evidence they were greatly bolstered in their determination to deal with this alleged invasion of the colony. They obviously believed in the veracity of the accounts of the confessing witches and the dangers that such a plan suggested. One of the results of these revelations was that the number of indictments for witchcraft during the Salem episode would greatly increase. From February to April 1692, there would be some twenty-seven indictments, while the months of May and June would witness the issuance of some forty-eight more. After the Barker confession, some seventy-eight indictments were handed down, with more than half of them served upon residents of Andover. Additionally, many of the accused persons known for their exemplary Puritan piety had voluntarily confessed to the organized plot to overthrow New England and establish Satan's kingdom in America.[527]

As for Cotton Mather, he was predisposed to believing in this plot. As previously noted, Mather had already faced prior "plots" of the devil in his attempts to liberate bewitched persons. Mercy Short had revealed that the demons were planning to diabolically burn the city of Boston, Mather's newborn son had probably died due to a spectral appearance to his pregnant wife, and Margaret Rule's possession had included the Devil's plot to destroy Mather's reputation by an appearance of a specter in Mather's image. Cotton Mather was also aware of another plot. Some forty years before the Salem events, a condemned prisoner on his way to the gallows predicted

> *An Horrible PLOT against the Country by WITCHCRAFT, and a Foundation of WITCHCRAFT then laid, which if it were not seasonably discovered would probably Blow up, and pull down all the Churches in the Country.*[528]

This brings the present study back to Mather's August 4, 1692, sermon entitled "A Discourse on the Wonders of the Invisible World." On that momentous day when Mather stood to deliver his sermon at the Old North Church, he had in his hands a powerful manuscript, but in his heart he possessed a thorough belief that the end times were at hand. He therefore proclaimed that the Andover witch trials proved the existence of a final plot of Satan to overtake New England. Mather repeated the details of this plot in a personal letter to John Cotton, writing,

> *Five witches were lately executed, impudently demanding of God a miraculous vindication of their innocency. Immediately upon this, our God miraculously sent in five Andover witches, who made a most ample, surprising, amazing confession of all their villanies, and declared*

> *the five newly executed to have been of their company, discovering many more, but all agreeing in Burroughs being their ringleader.*[529]

The five witches convicted on August 5 and hanged on August 19 were John Proctor, George Jacobs Sr., John Willard of Salem Village, and then George Burroughs of Maine, and Martha Carrier of Andover: the secret "king and queen" of hell.[530]

To Mather, the import of these revelations was clear. The Salem-Andover invasion had been planned by Satan, encouraged by demons, and to this point carried out by human vassals. The Andover testimonies suggested that even if the previously convicted and executed Salem witches had been silent or uninformed, they had still been a part of Satan's overall plot to conquer New England.

As the final chapter of this study shows, in response to this perceived danger Cotton Mather would take his place alongside his New England clerical counterparts as they advised the Salem court about the witchcraft examinations. In that role, Cotton Mather articulated his personal opinion that the judges and ministers of New England needed to do something to stop Satan's assault against the colony. That "something" was a strategy for a careful but nonetheless deliberate adjudication process. After all, the colony was dealing with a "dreadful knot" of witches that Satan had placed in the land. In following a careful strategy, an eradication of the malicious witches would end the demonic siege, while clearing innocent persons of guilt.

As the historical evidence will demonstrate, although Mather was willing to offer his personal, considered opinions to the court, he was unwilling to propel himself to the forefront of the witchcraft trials even when the examinations went horribly amiss. Despite his ministerial prominence as a pastor of the Old North Church in Boston, Cotton Mather chose to limit his involvement in the Salem trials to advising the Salem court and the New England government. Out of a sense of personal paucity and respect for his colleagues, many who were his mentors and elders, Mather would not only refuse to confront their errors but unwittingly become their scapegoat.

Conclusion

THIS CHAPTER HAS DEMONSTRATED that Cotton Mather's interpretation and response to witchcraft, and especially Salem witchcraft, was predictable. When Cotton Mather's pre-Salem and Salem era preaching, publications, and activities are examined, it becomes clear that his cosmology was more than a set of theorems. Rather, it was the basis upon which he interpreted the events of his era and determined his responses.

Relative to the Salem episode, again, Mather's cosmology was met with corresponding actions as his three strongly held postulates about witchcraft and his world were accompanied by corresponding behavior. First, Cotton Mather saw Salem witchcraft as God's judgment upon New England's spiritual degeneration; he therefore called for national repentance and reformation. Second, Mather believed Salem witchcraft was a demonic retaliation due to the Puritan settlement of America, and he therefore proposed and employed a private and public practice of using fasting and prayer to counteract the demonic incursion. Last, Cotton Mather believed Salem witchcraft was an end-times plot of Satan to destroy New England, based upon his eschatological expectations and confirmed by the Andover witchcraft case. He responded by warning his community of its danger.

Having presented the consistent factors of Mather's cosmology and conduct in the Salem enigma, our study now turns to an exploration of Mather's role as an advisor to the Salem court and assesses his errors in connection with the Salem affair.

6

The Salem Trials: Cotton Mather's Dilemma

For my own part, I was alwayes afraid of proceeding to convict and condemn any Person, as a Confederate with afflicting Daemons, upon so feeble an Evidence, as a spectral Representation. Nevertheless, on the other side, I saw in most of the Judges, a most charming Instance of Prudence and Patience. . . . Though I could not allow the Principles, that some of the Judges had espoused, yett I could not but speak honourably of their Persons, on all Occasions.
Cotton Mather, *Diary* (May 1692)

The previous chapter revealed two lines of congruence between Cotton Mather's worldview and behavior during the Salem trials. The first was Cotton Mather's consistent overall pattern of interpreting contemporary international, local, and personal events within the parameters of his preconceived worldview as spiritual warfare and end-times indicators. The second focused on Mather's propositions about the meaning of the Salem witchcraft episode as detailed in several of his works. These showed a strong degree of consistency between Mather's stated beliefs and his responses to episodes of witchcraft in New England.

Taking up this second thread, this chapter begins with a sketch of the challenges the New England government and magistrates faced in prosecuting individuals accused of witchcraft. Following this, a fuller exploration of Mather's advice to the Court of Oyer and Terminer is given, outlining Mather's approach to the examinations and prosecutions of the accused. After tracing the progression of the Salem trials, the final section of this chapter addresses the dilemma the trials produced for Cotton Mather in relation to his continuing role as spiritual advisor to the Salem court. This dilemma is explored through an examination of Mather's personal relationship to the Salem court, his advice about spectral evidence, and his published account of the trials, *The Wonders of the Invisible World.*

Without underplaying Mather's responsibility in the tragedy, this chapter explores why Mather avoided openly opposing the Salem judges or the conduct of the trials. The evidence for this examination includes both Cotton Mather's personal and administrative writings, particularly letters written to John Richards and John Foster, both judges in the Salem trials, and the more public document "The Return of the Ministers." While representing the collective opinions of the Boston-area ministers, it was penned by Cotton Mather, and clearly reflects his beliefs and influence. When these are examined, a recognizable pattern of thinking and activity surfaces which allows a more nuanced and sophisticated understanding of Mather's role and motivations.

Cotton Mather's Proposals for the Salem Adjudications

WITH THE OUTBREAK OF witchcraft accusations in 1692, the New England courts faced several serious problems. And as the crisis began to expand significantly beyond the scope of earlier accusations and examinations, the Massachusetts government was forced to put in place a mechanism to deal with the situation. Strictly speaking, the Massachusetts legislature alone had the authority to create new courts, yet, as Koenig observes,

> *in the rush to prosecute, Phips yielded to pressure and established the special court [Oyer and Terminer] without waiting for the newly authorized legislature to convene. . . .*

Although it possessed broad powers of punishment, its jurisdiction was limited to witchcraft cases alone.[531]

The newly authorized court would face two specific challenges. First, neither the New England courts nor Chief Justice Stoughton, who supervised the initial investigations, had ever dealt with an outbreak of witchcraft on this scale. Second, the court struggled to find an appropriate methodology for the examination process itself. Although New England's standard guidelines for prosecutions embodied by England's *Laws and Liberties* contained general rules for capital crimes, as Peter Hoffer explains, witchcraft examinations brought with them a singular level of difficulty with respect to the use and assessment of evidence:

The best evidence of crime is probative: it proves to the jury that the facts are as alleged. Probative evidence may be direct, that is, eyewitness testimony, or indirect, re-created through a convincing sequence of circumstantial inferences. Witchcraft cases threw these precepts into confusion, for only perpetrators' or confederates' confessions could establish that a pact with the Devil existed, and indirect evidence—the causal chain—rested upon spectral evidence that only victims could see.[532]

Being cognizant of these difficulties, the Court of Oyer and Terminer chose as their prosecutor Anthony Checkley, an Essex County lawyer with a reputation for arguing strenuously for "legal precision against informality and uncertainty."[533]Additionally, the court addressed its problems over the use of evidence by consulting previous witchcraft trial guidelines drawn from English witch trials, and the advice of several eminent English witchcraft scholars.

Cotton Mather was aware of the great dangers that lay in store at Salem if the court did not balance the desire to reach a judgement with solid and appropriate procedures.[534] In several documents Mather admonished the Salem court to use rules for witchcraft prosecution based upon the works of three earlier English witchcraft scholars: William Perkins of Christ's College in Cambridge, who wrote *A Discourse of the Damned Art of Witchcraft*; John Gaule, author of *Select Cases of Conscience Touching Witches and Witchcrafts*; and Richard Bernard, a renowned minister in Somersetshire, who published *A Guide to Jurymen*.[535]

Describing them as a "triumvirate of as eminent persons as have ever handled it," Mather recommended these authors because he knew they largely agreed upon the examination process and were well respected throughout New England's legal and religious establishment.[536] Drawing primarily upon these sources, Mather gave the Salem court his opinion concerning the best way to approach the trials. He addressed three specific elements: evidentiary matters, the use of leniency in certain cases, and the prosecution and execution of malicious witches.

Mather's foremost concern was the use of spectral evidence as a basis for witchcraft convictions. Spectral evidence—the testimony of acts committed by the witch's familiar spirit, visible only to their victims—had been used in England as early as 1593. By the late seventeenth century, despite growing doubts about the validity of spectral evidence on the part of the English legal establishment, even the ardent skeptic Chief Justice Sir John Holt allowed its admission into evidence in cases in 1690, 1696, and 1701. In the 1701 case, Richard Hathaway was charged with falsely accusing a woman named Sarah Mordike of witchcraft.[537] Although Holt's influence over the court proceedings eventually led to the conviction of Hathaway and acquittal of Sarah Mordike, he had nonetheless allowed the jury to consider the weight of spectral evidence.[538] The New England courts had also allowed spectral evidence in some pre-Salem trials, although there was a divergence of opinion among the clergy about its use.[539]

Mather's concern about spectral evidence is apparent in a letter he wrote to Salem judge John Richards on 31 May 1692, three days before the trials started.[540] Mather's first request was that Richards would not "lay too much stress upon pure specter testimony," since the Devil might appear in the form of innocent persons. Mather therefore recommended that such testimonies should have a single purpose: to justify a search of a suspect's home for further material evidence such as puppets, images, or other objects used in witchcraft.[541] Three months later, as the scope of the trials expanded, Mather repeated this advice in a letter to John Foster, emphasizing that testimonies alleging that "a specter in their [the accused's] shape doth afflict a neighbor . . . is not enough to convict" a suspect.[542]

Mather then went on to raise the issue of the use of evidentiary experiments to confirm witchcraft allegations. As chapter three detailed, there were a number of such tests, including having the accused person look upon the victim, having the afflicted person touch the accused, or having the accused recite the Lord's Prayer. If the suspect's glances or their touch induced fresh torment in their accusers, it was considered a powerful sign of bewitchment. Similarly, if the suspect could not recite the Lord's Prayer flawlessly, their guilt was allegedly established.

Although Cotton Mather himself had used a modified version of the recitation test in his experiments with possession victim Martha Goodwin, he considered private experiments and public examinations to be very different. Mather told Richards that the court should be looking for "good, plain, legal evidence" to convict an alleged witch.[543] Urging the court to use evidentiary experiments only to elicit voluntary confessions, Mather wrote,

> *The danger of this experiment will be taken away if you make no evidence of it, but only put it to use . . . confounding the lisping witches to give a reason why they cannot . . . repeat those heavenly composures. The like I would say of some*

> *other experiments, only we may venture too far before we are aware.*[544]

In a final directive, Mather told Richards that a "satisfactory confession," devoid of any forms of torture, would be the best form of evidence. Torture had been practiced to a limited extent in English witch trials, but had been a consistent component of Scottish examinations.[545] James I had "warmly" recommended its use, as did William Perkins.[546] Cotton Mather, however, cautioned the court by expressing repugnance toward confessions by torture, insisting that a voluntary and "unexpected confession" by an accused witch would be the preferred type.[547]

The second part of Cotton Mather's plan regarding the Salem trials dealt with the use of leniency toward convicted witch suspects, under certain circumstances. For example, Mather proposed to Councilman John Foster that in cases where convictions lacked a solid determination by the judges, "it would certainly be for the glory of the whole transaction to give that person a reprieve."[548] Similarly, Mather recommended leniency for persons whom Mather called "lesser criminals." In a compassionate tone, he told Judge John Richards that he was concerned about the entrapment of some "poor mortals" into unintentional witchcraft. He suggested lesser punishments be applied, such as "some solemn, open, public, and explicit renunciation of the Devil" or even banishment, if it would spare the life of the accused while preventing further witchcraft allegations.[549]

Chief Justice Stoughton obviously did not agree with Mather's analysis, or, at least in the intensity of the examinations, he simply ignored it. Although seventeenth-century trials were not conducted in the climate or manner of modern English and North American courtrooms, the Salem transcripts indicate a harsh examination pattern even by seventeenth-century standards. A case in point is the questioning of Mary Easty of Topsfield, who was accused by the Salem girls Ann Putnam, Mercy Lewis, Mary Walcot, and Abigail

Williams of tormenting them through her spectral image. The transcripts of Easty's examination went along these lines:

> Court: *How can you say you know nothing, when you see these Tormented?*
> Easty: *Would you have me accuse my self?*
> Court: *Yes if you be guilty.*
> Easty: *Sir, I have no complyance with Satan in this. What would you have me do?*
> Court: *Confess if ye be guilty.*
> Easty: *I will say it, if it was my last time, I am clear of this sin.*[550]

Similarly, during the course of the trials Stoughton would also ignore Mather's advice about the rules of evidence. He not only failed to require strict adherence to the rules of evidence for the conviction of accused witches, but also lowered the standard of conviction by appealing to less specific grounds such as the mere intent to harm others. As Koenig describes it, the result of Stoughton's use of the punishment clauses of the 1604 Witchcraft Statute without requiring the strict evidentiary rulings was that for the purposes of conviction "no harm (maleficium) need be inflicted . . . it was only necessary to prove the girls were the objects of any type of magical actions that incidentally brought such pains and contortions with it."[551]

Mather's tone would not be so compassionate or understanding when it came to the last aspect of his advice to the court. He took a markedly different perspective on those witchcraft cases marked by several specific indications of purposeful diabolism: an explicit covenant with the Devil or obvious attempts to injure or murder others, or to overthrow Puritanism. Referring back to his own pre-Salem trial letter to Judge Richards, Mather equated Salem witchcraft with the crimes of treason and murder, insisting,

"Our dear neighbors are most really tormented, really murdered, and really acquainted with hidden things, which are afterwards proved plainly to have been realities."[552] In that same letter, Mather compared the Salem witchcraft trials to an outbreak of witchcraft in Mora, Sweden, that took place from 1669 to 1670. Mather wrote,

> *I cannot for once forbear minding the famous accidents at Mohra [sic] in Swedeland, where . . . a stupendous witchcraft, much like ours, making havoc of the kingdom, was immediately followed with a remarkable smile of God upon the endeavors of the judges to discover and extirpate the authors of that execrable witchcraft.*[553]

The witchcraft outbreak in Mora was part of a much larger witch hunt that had begun in 1668 in northern Dalarna and before its apex in 1675 had included Norrland, Uppland, and Stockholm. The situation was in some ways similar to the Salem events in that the trial testimonies included an inverted covenant and sabbath, mythically described as *Blakulla*; the supernatural transportation of witches; and maleficium primarily directed at the seduction (transvection) of children.[554] The Mora witch trials also had a specific parallel to the Salem and Andover situation in that the outbreak was primarily viewed as a threat to communal order, and in that evidentiary matters caused no small frustration to the cooperative efforts of the courts and clerics.[555] By the end of the outbreak some seventeen adults had been beheaded and their bodies burned.

Cotton Mather had described the Mora witchcraft events in his 1689 book, *Memorable Providences*, no doubt drawing his information from reports in Glanvil's *Sadducismus Triumphatus*. By the 1690s, in the aftermath of the Salem affair, Mather was making a qualitative comparison between the events at Mora and at Salem, noting the Swedish judges' eradication of the guilty witches and the consequent ending of "execrable witchcraft." In Salem, those witches proved by the court to be "obnoxious" and therefore unrepentant earned none of Mather's leniency, and gave him no hesitation in concurring with their speedy execution. By their own admission, these witches had willfully joined Satan's army to overthrow Christ's Kingdom on earth.

Consequently, in the course of the Salem trials, when Mather believed malicious witches had been discovered he gave his approvalfor their execution. To Mather, those who had intentionally aligned themselves with Satan in order to overthrow the government posed a genuine threat to New England's existence. In all such cases, to Mather's seventeenth-century mind, the execution of the accused was the only certain means of eliminating the overwhelming danger. Mather therefore went directly to the biblical injunction found in Exodus 22:18, which stated, "You shall not suffer a witch to live." It was an act of divine justice to execute such notable witches as Goody Glover, the tormentor of the Goodwin children; and, of course, George Burroughs and Martha Carrier, the ringleaders of the Andover plot.

The Stoughton Court and the Course of the Salem Trials

IN THE COURSE OF the Salem examinations, the judges apparently ignored the advice of Cotton Mather. When the new governor, Sir William Phips, arrived in Boston on May 14, 1692, he found the prisons full of people, and new accusations surfacing almost daily. He could not personally manage the affair due to the recent incursion of a combined French and Indian force into the colony. However, he did order that all those who had previously been examined and incarcerated in Boston should now be formally tried.

The first round of prosecutions began on June 2, 1692, under the auspices of a newly configured adjudication panel. William Stoughton was retained as the chief judge, assisted by Bartholomew Gedney, Nathaniel Saltonstall, John Richards, William Seargent, Samuel Sewell, and Wait Winthrop.

The reconfigured panel proved to be no more cautious than the original magistrates, since, as Silverman observes, "by the standard Cotton Mather set forth to John Richards, the new court on which Richards sat was reckless and severe."[556] The trials proceeded with a flurry of accusations and interrogations, followed by speedy convictions and executions. This approach is typified by the case of Bridget Bishop, a tavern owner with a disreputable reputation. On June 10, she was convicted and then expeditiously hanged on the west side of Salem Town: the first Salem witch to die.[557] Bishop's death greatly alarmed the populace and the governor's newly formed council, prompting Phips to halt the proceedings while he consulted the Boston clergy. Meanwhile, Judge Saltonstall resigned and was replaced by Jonathan Corwin of Salem.

It was June 28 before the judges reconvened, but when they did, the court tried five cases in one day, an amazing pace for any court, even a seventeenth-century one. On July 19, 1692, the first mass execution was carried out as Rebecca Nurse, Goody Good, Elizabeth How, Sarah Wild, and Susanna Martin were taken to Gallows Hill at Salem Town and hanged simultaneously. These were followed by another set of examinations and executions stemming from the Andover witch cases. Six witches were condemned on August 5, 1692, only one day after Cotton Mather delivered his sermon "A Discourse on the Wonders of the Invisible World." On August 19, five of the six, John Proctor, George Jacobs Sr., John Willard, George Burroughs, and Martha Carrier, were all executed in a second mass hanging. The number of deaths now stood at eleven.

Starting on September 9, 1692, the trials began anew in Salem, which had now become the focus of the accusations, trials, and executions. The court continued to work with remarkable speed: In less than two weeks nine more persons were condemned. On September 22, eight of the nine were taken to Gallows Hill. There, before a large gathering of spectators, Mary Easty, Alice Parker,

Ann Pudeator, Margaret Scott, Wilmott Reed, Samuel Wardwell, Mary Parker, and Martha Corey were simultaneously executed. Three days before Corey's execution, her husband, Giles, had been unintentionally "pressed to death" by the local magistrates. Salem's death toll now stood at twenty, the final number.

Meanwhile, after the last round of executions, Increase Mather wrote a stinging indictment of the trials, which he appropriately titled and subsequently published by the title *Cases of Conscience Concerning Evil Spirits Personating Men* (1693). As will be seen, the document clearly insisted that because of the Salem court's unwarranted use of spectral evidence, innocent people had been executed and that others were still in jeopardy.

Phips explicitly acknowledged the intent of the publication. On October 26, 1692, a bill was sent to the assembly calling for a fast day, as the ministers met privately to discuss the fate of the trials. Afterwards, Phips dismissed the Court of Oyer and Terminer, replacing it with the regular Superior Court of Judicature. Incredibly, when the new court convened, Stoughton was still in charge, but spectral evidence had become inadmissible. However, when Massachusetts' highest court, the Court of Assistants, met on January 3, 1693, it quickly acquitted forty-nine of the fifty-two suspects awaiting decisions, while Phips reprieved three persons for whom Stoughton and the Superior Court had signed execution warrants. Shortly thereafter, Stoughton resigned as chief justice. Governor Phips had effectively ended Salem's witchcraft episode.

With the exception of a small number of modern Salem scholars, most historians have credited Increase Mather with having the largest hand in ending the Salem trials by his straightforward contradiction of spectral evidence as presented in *Cases of Conscience*.[558] Conversely, for three hundred years Cotton Mather has been portrayed as the personification of the worst about the Salem trials. One question that historians continue to ask is this:

Why did Cotton Mather refuse to openly and directly confront the procedures used by Chief Justice Stoughton and the Salem court, as his father, Increase, had done so effectively?

Some answers to this question can be found in Mather's preconceived cosmology. To understand his reluctance to openly oppose the Salem judges and the trial procedures, or the reasons behind his decision to publish a half-baked and partisan account of the trials, his *Wonders of the Invisible World,* we need to recognize the meaning the trials had for Mather. By comparing Mather's stated worldview to his actions, it becomes evident that Mather found himself in perhaps the greatest dilemma of his ministerial career: how to support the battle against the witch invasion while disagreeing with some aspects of the way in which the trials were conducted.

Mather's Ambiguous Advice to the Salem Court about Spectral Evidence

ONE OF THE GREAT difficulties that Cotton Mather faced throughout the Salem affair was the contradiction between his own desire to give balanced advice and the pressures on him created by his personal relationship with the members of the Court of Oyer and Terminer. As Murdock observes, at those points in which Mather's advice appeared to contradict the court's procedure, Mather found himself

> *caught in a painful dilemma . . . his father, by virtue of his age, experience, and achievement, could afford to rebuke them, but Cotton . . . must preserve the good will of such local potentates as Stoughton and Sewell.*[559]

In truth, Cotton Mather did have personal reasons to be cautious about criticizing the Salem judges, since at least four of them were either friends of the Mather family or members of the Old North

Church. For example, Judge John Richards, a wealthy member of the Mathers' congregation, had backed Cotton Mather both politically and financially when he became Increase's assistant in the church. The young Mather turned to John Richards for advice and support in times of congregational problems. Similarly, John Foster, whom Mather advised during the Salem situation, was an influential member of the Old North Church, a member of the Governor's Council, and a confidant of Mather. Wait Winthrop, another court member and a friend of Cotton Mather, had intervened on Cotton's behalf during the 1689 Boston Revolt when Andros signed a warrant for Cotton's arrest. Likewise, Samuel Sewell, whose trial records Mather used in his book *Wonders*, frequently attended Mather's lectures.

The most troubling relationship, however, was between Cotton Mather and the chief justice of the special court, Lieutenant Governor William Stoughton. The Mather family's ties to him were clear: They had been largely responsible for Stoughton coming to power in New England's post-Andros government.

Unfortunately for Cotton Mather, the trials were not conducted on the basis of the type of evidence that Perkins, Bernard, and Gaule required, and as the General Court would follow from January of 1693. Instead, Stoughton became the main proponent of the use of spectral evidence, and the other members of the court followed his direction. As a result of these conflicts of interest and belief, Mather's interaction with Stoughton and the rest of the court would be notably bereft of criticism and, at times, contradictory. Mather's response to this dilemma was to provide the court with ambivalent advice about spectral evidence, and to pen a paradoxical account of the trials in *Wonders*.

As previously demonstrated, the clergy and the civil courts in New England shared responsibility for a wide range of moral and legal issues. As Peter Hoffer notes, "The close ties between ministerial roles and magisterial roles in New England made the judges' recourse to the ministers a natural step. . . . They expected to be consulted in the crisis."[560] This cooperation was nonetheless fraught with complications. The courts and the clerics would particularly struggle at those points at which evidentiary matters proved a stumbling block in the court's headlong rush to convict and punish accused witches. These issues would be faced by seventeenth-century New England courts and clerics by the application of the Old Testament code and contemporary legal statutes in several areas besides witchcraft, including accusations like adultery, fornication, infanticide, and homosexuality.

A particularly significant example of the variety of complications created by issues of evidence can be seen in the circumstances surrounding a trial in Massachusetts in 1641. By permanently relocating to England, Massachusetts magistrate John Humfrey apparently abandoned his two young daughters, leaving them in the care of some household servants. Unfortunately, over a period of two years, three of these male servants sexually abused the girls.[561] When the authorities were notified of these shocking events, their first instinct was to convict and execute all three men. However, complications arose with respect to both the evidence and the statutory authority upon which they wished to base their judgement. The local authorities attempted to apply a recent New England law against sodomy to the case, a law which allowed for the execution of the accused.

The court consulted a number of prominent New England clerics who offered conflicting advice on the biblical and legal nature of the application of the sodomy prohibition to this case of sexual abuse.[562] Lacking a consensus, the court finally sentenced the three men to severe physical punishment and confined them to specific geographical areas, threatening execution if they ever left these districts.[563] In the end, the difficulty in providing appropriate evidence to prove either rape or sodomy both complicated the judicial proceedings and prevented the Massachusetts General Court from executing the three defendants.

When the Salem events unfolded, the New England authorities would face similar problems in their use of evidence. Just as the General Court had done in the 1641 sexual abuse case, their response was to seek out the advice of the New England clergy. Accordingly, among the Boston ministers, Cotton and Increase Mather were a logical point of reference for the authorities. Both Mathers were well known for their compilations of supernatural wonder stories and involvement in prior witchcraft scares. Furthermore, Cotton Mather's account of the possession of the Goodwin children published in 1688 went a long ways toward accrediting him as a local Boston authority on the subject of witchcraft and spectral evidence.[564]

A chronological sampling of Mather's advice to the Salem court reveals that, without duplicitous intent, Cotton Mather failed to incontrovertibly state his strongly held view on the dubious value of spectral evidence. Yet, more than this, it demonstrates the nature of the twofold dilemma that Cotton Mather faced throughout the Salem period. The first of these dilemmas was how he could support the Salem judges while openly disagreeing with their deliberative methodology. The second dilemma was how to assert the reality of witchcraft as exhibited in spectral evidence without condoning convictions based exclusively upon such unstable evidence.

The results of these dilemmas are best viewed in Mather's letters to his contemporaries, the "Return of the Ministers," the debate about Increase Mather's *Cases of Conscience*, and Mather's use of spectral evidence within his book *The Wonders of the Invisible World.* Taken together, these sources and events show that although Mather did not change his view on spectral evidence during the Salem trials, he failed to openly oppose the Salem court's use of spectral evidence as the primary basis of the conviction and execution of witch suspects.

One of the most telling sources of Mather's unintentional ambivalence in relation to the validity of spectral evidence is found in his correspondence to John Richards and John Foster. For example, Mather's pre-trial letter to Richards suggested,

> *When you are satisfied . . . that the demons which molest our poor neighbors do indeed represent such and such people to the sufferers . . . I suppose you will not reckon it a conviction that the people so represented are witches to be immediately exterminated.*[565]

However, in an apparent contradiction, Mather blunted the impact of his cautionary statements by proceeding to include questionable evidence such as alleged prior threats reported by neighbors, apparent supernatural knowledge, and physical harm to victims caused by an accused witch's specter in his letter. Mather writes,

> *If therefore you can find that when the witches do anything easy, that is not needful . . . I say if you find the same thing, presently, and hurtfully, and more violently done by any unseen hand unto the bodies of the sufferers, hold them, for you have catched a witch.*[566]

Cotton Mather's confusing approach to spectral evidence is also apparent in his August 17, 1692, letter to John Foster. Again, although he warned Foster that the court should not hand down convictions based upon spectral appearances when "there is no further evidence against a person but only this," only two paragraphs later he wrote,

> *Nevertheless, a very great use is to be made of the spectral impressions upon the sufferers. They justly introduce, and determine, an inquiry into the circumstances of the person accused, and they strengthen other presumptions.*[567]

It is evident that on one hand Mather was warning Foster against convicting persons solely upon spectral evidence, while on the other he gave it credence as a basis for profound suspicion and further inquiry. However, by August 1692, the court had already used this unreliable and divisive evidence too often. Spectral evidence was simply too expedient a tool by which to prosecute the alleged witches. This pattern of using a "nevertheless" in relation to this issue invariably gave an ambivalent and ambiguous quality to Mather's advice.[568]

Perhaps it was because five more people were then awaiting execution that Mather pointed to a "way out" for the judges in those cases lacking in substance or primarily based on spectral evidence. In his letter to Foster, he went on to suggest several means of reducing or setting aside previous convictions. These included transportation to another part of the colony, asking the General Court to reduce the penalties for witchcraft, or even imploring the governor to "relax the judgments of death." It seems obvious that Mather was tactfully telling Richards that the court was executing persons upon the very spectral evidence he has previously warned against using. Yet, at the end of the same letter Mather returned to the pattern of avoiding an outright confrontation with the Salem judges. Noting the comparative simplicity of a 1645 New England witch trial, Mather wrote,

> *Our case is extraordinary . . . I entreat you that whatever you do, strengthen the hands of our honorable judges in the great work before them. They are persons for whom no man living has a greater veneration than Sir, Your Servant.*[569]

Finally, at the end of the trials, Mather's letter requesting Stoughton's endorsement of *Wonders* avoided any direct discussion of his differences with the court over the use of spectral evidence. Instead Mather praised Stoughton for the "weighty and worthy undertakings wherein almighty God has employed Your Honor as his instrument for the extinguishing of as wonderful a piece of devilism as has been seen in the world." [570] Mather had chosen to put any disagreements he had with Stoughton in the body of *The Wonders of the Invisible World.* There, and only there, after the chaos of the trials was past, would Mather give his first open indication that the Salem judges and Stoughton in particular had mismanaged the evidence against the alleged Salem witches.

Beyond his personal correspondence, Mather also faced difficulties in his role connected to the Boston ministers' advisement of Governor Phips. This is demonstrated in two critical documents from the Salem trials: "The Return of the Ministers," and *Cases of Conscience.*

The initial advice given by the Boston ministers resulted from the uproar over the June 10, 1692, execution of Bridget Bishop. This collective opinion of the Boston ministers, entitled "The Return of the Ministers," was penned by none other than Cotton Mather. In their response, the thirteen Boston clergymen used the bulk of their document to warn the court that the past use of spectral evidence had provided "no infallible proof" of guilt. However, using the "nevertheless" clause so common to Cotton Mather's advice, he and the Boston clergy included one last article in which they wrote,

> *Nevertheless, we cannot but humbly recommend unto the Government, the speedy and vigorous Prosecution of such as have rendered themselves obnoxious; according to the best directions given in the Laws of God, and the wholesome Statutes of the English nation for the Detection of Witchcraft.*[571]

While some historians have inferred that Mather included this last article without consulting the other clerics, Cotton Mather insisted in *Wonders* that "those very men of God most conscientiously subjoined this Article to that Advice."[572]

In retrospect, this was a serious error on the part of the Boston ministers and more particularly on the part of Cotton Mather.[573] As Frances Hill observes,

> *The effect was to give Stoughton and his court the ministers' seal of approval. The judges could not prosecute speedily and vigorously except by employing the methods they had already been using, including spectral evidence. The Return would not impede the course of events but encourage it.*[574]

In light of the clergy's knowledge of Stoughton's use of spectral evidence, their decision to encourage "speed" or "vigor" gave license to the worst features of the court's prior procedures.[575] By then, the Stoughton court's use of spectral evidence had taken on an increasingly predictable form as the allegedly tormented Salem girls along with John Indian widened their net of accusations.

Had Cotton Mather and the Boston clergy held fast to their stance against spectral evidence, control of the trials might have been reestablished. Instead, as Levin points out, "In May or June, when absolute condemnation of spectral evidence might have affected the court, neither Mather nor the other ministers could make the caution unequivocal."[576] Consequently, Stoughton took the eighth clause as a sign of approval for the unsound procedures of the court. Governor Phips verifies this when he notes in his records that Stoughton "persisted vigorously in the same method, to the great dissatisfaction and disturbance of the people."[577]

By September 22, the Salem trials had reached a second major crisis, with another mass execution of eight out of nine persons convicted earlier that month. Phips had been absent during most of the Salem episode, but upon his return from the French and Indian combat at Pemaquid, Maine, he faced a populace discontent with the growing number of executions. Realizing the potentially dangerous antipathy to the trials felt in Boston and throughout New England, Phips again sought the advice of the Boston clergy.

Much as in "The Return of the Ministers," the reply he received was their concerted opinion. However, Increase Mather penned this most recent document in order to leave little room for ambiguity. Refuting the Salem court's use of spectral evidence as a sole determinant for convicting and condemning suspects, Increase wrote:

> *This then I declare and testify, that to take away the life of anyone, merely because a Spectre or Devil, in a bewitched or possessed person does accuse them, will bring the Guilt of innocent Blood on the Land.*[578]

This brings this study to yet another point where Cotton Mather faced an apparent dilemma in which his actions seem to contradict his stated beliefs. Although fourteen other Boston ministers had signed the preface to *Cases of Conscience*, Cotton Mather refused to do so for reasons he stated in a letter to his uncle John Cotton dated October 20, 1692:

> *I did in my conscience, think that as the humours of this people now run, . . . such a discourse going alone would . . . everlastingly stifle any further proceedings of justice, and more than so, produce a publick and open contest with the judges . . . I did with all the modesty I could use, decline setting my hand unto the book, assigning this reason: that I had already a book in the press which would sufficiently declare my opinion.*[579]

Historians have debated the sincerity of this explanation, offering interpretations ranging from duplicity on Cotton's part to an insistence that he and his father did in fact disagree about the limits of spectral evidence.[580] Whether or not Cotton Mather's explanation is believed, one thing is certain: Increase Mather's *Cases of Conscience* and Cotton Mather's *The Wonders of the Invisible World* do not present a unified view of the use and importance of spectral evidence. Increase Mather's straightforward analysis of spectral evidence insisted it was "influenced by the Devil," making it utterly unreliable as a basis of lawful conviction, while Cotton's ambiguous language both cautioned against and encouraged its limited use.

A Paradoxical Account: The Wonders of the Invisible World

On September 2, 1692, while Increase Mather was writing *Cases of Conscience,* Cotton wrote a letter to Chief Justice William Stoughton offering to publish an account of the Salem trials. Mather indicated his intention to "vindicate the country, as well as the judges and juries" and "rectify the opinions of men" concerning the Salem trials and executions.[581]

Considering the political backlash against the trials spreading throughout New England, Stoughton gave his approval for the project. On September 20, just two days before the final Salem executions, Mather wrote to his friend Samuel Sewell, the court secretary, asking for a "narrative of the evidences" from the recent trials.[582] He needed these to arrange his account of a half dozen or more cases.

In a postscript to this letter, Mather relates that Governor Phips had specifically "commanded" him to prepare a record of the Salem trials. In truth, Phips, like Stoughton, also had political motivations for asking Mather to write the defense; his handling of the episode was being criticized to his London superiors. This is borne out by a letter written by Governor Phips on October 12, 1692, to William Blathwayt, the clerk of the Privy Council. Citing the enormous difficulties associated with the Salem trials, Phips reported,

> *I did before any application was made unto me about it put a stop to the proceedings of the Court and they are now stopt till their Majesties pleasure be known. Sir I beg pardon for giving you all this trouble, the reason is because I know my enemies are seeking to turn it all upon me and . . . [I] desire you will please to give a true understanding of the matter if any thing of this kind be urged or made use of against mee.*[583]

Having received permission from Phips and Stoughton, Cotton Mather began to arrange the materials he had gathered. The resulting book, *The Wonders of the Invisible World,* was probably his most dubious contribution to the Salem episode. Within this complicated compilation of his own sermons, historical sketches, theological conclusions and chronicle of five specific Salem cases, Mather flits from subject to subject, interjecting opinions, interpretations, and supposed proofs for his own conclusions. The entire composition has the feel of a manuscript inadvisably rushed to the printer. Yet beyond its failings as a piece of literature, *Wonders* reveals the personal and public dilemma which Cotton Mather faced with respect to how the entire Salem situation had evolved. In a way reminiscent of his advice to the court, Mather would attempt within *Wonders* to uphold the reality of witchcraft without directly censuring the Salem court.

Perhaps no single term more accurately describes the results of this effort than "paradoxical." Two elements of his paradox stand out in *Wonders*. First, although Mather purported to write *Wonders* as a historian, he more often wrote as an advocate for the court's behavior, selectively including and excluding material to bolster his case, than as an objective witness to the Salem episode. Second, faced with the errors of the Court of Oyer and Terminer, Mather tried to defend the Salem proceedings while simultaneously including a number of statements about the Salem court, Lieutenant Governor Stoughton, Governor Phips, and the trial accounts which on analysis appear to criticize and invalidate the court's actions.

Throughout the pages of *Wonders,* Mather's self-proclaimed intention for publishing his account was first "to countermine the whole PLOT of the Devil, against New England, in every Branch of it, as far as one of my darkness, can comprehend such a World of Darkness."[584] Mather did this fully. The first two-thirds of *Wonders* deals with Mather's cosmology as it related to witchcraft, detailing theological postulates, providences, previously published jeremiads, and calls for repentance and reformation. These were interspersed with his considered opinions about witchcraft covenants and spectral appearances.

Although *Wonders* is at times complicated and fraught with side issues, it is nevertheless Cotton Mather's single most important document on witchcraft. In terms of the sheer volume of theological consideration, *Wonders* provides a revealing picture of seventeenth-century witchcraft beliefs in colonial America. Had Mather stopped with the first division of his book, it may well have become a standard reference for seventeenth-century New England witchcraft studies, avoiding the ensuing vilification that vexed Mather.

It would be Mather's other primary purpose for writing *Wonders* that caused his historical stigmatization. At the beginning of the final third of the book, Mather purposed to relate

> *a brief account of the Tryals which have passed upon some of the Malefactors lately Executed at Salem, for the Witchcrafts whereof they stood convicted . . . For which cause I have only singled out Four or Five . . . and I report matter not as an Advocate, but as an Historian.*[585]

English concepts of historical reporting were being advanced throughout the seventeenth century. This is evidenced by such works as John Craige's *Mathematical Principles of Christian Theology*. Craige's attempts at explaining what appeared to be a declining belief in Christianity was placed within the context of his mathematical formulations of the truthfulness of reported events. As Richard Nash has summarized it,

> *Two premises underlie Craige's argument. The first is that belief is not fixed and compelled, but is subject to change; the second is that the further we are removed from an event through time and space, the greater are the suspicions we entertain concerning reports of that event.*[586]

By the end of the seventeenth century, English history models had also become largely defined by two genres, the "general or particular histories" and the "memoirs." General history related events either prior to the author's own era or in which the author had no participation. Its corollary, the particular history, predominantly dealt with the history of one's own era, often based upon personal observation and participation. Nonetheless, the latter still required an objective, impartial accounting of events. Philip Hicks describes this model:

> *The historian's proper tone was one of lofty impartiality. He kept enough distance from events and from his own self-interest . . . he avoided speaking in the first person, because that would call his objectivity into question and draw undignified attention to himself. . . . Since history was "merely narrative," the historian simply told his own story, rarely digressing to argue over disputed interpretations or adding self-justifying transcriptions of supporting documents.*[587]

The second seventeenth-century genre, the "memoir," entailed a less strict set of standards and was therefore considered to be a lesser model of historical writing. It was often punctuated with the author's own biased judgment and defense of arguments traceable to the memoirist's involvement in or first-person witness of the events being recorded. The memoir was often the preparatory document for a general or particular history in which, as Philip Hicks indicates,

> *unlike the historian, the writer of memoirs wrote from a patently personal perspective, often in the first person . . . [and] based his own account primarily on his own observations and interviews with other participants in events, rather than on research into public records or the account of other historians.*[588]

Contemporary to Cotton Mather's era are two notable works that reflect such standards of writing: Clarendon's *The History of the Rebellion and Civil Wars in England* and Bishop Gilbert Burnet's *History of His Own Time.*[589] Clarendon served as an advisor to King Charles I, and later worked to restore the Prince of Wales to the throne, but was banished in 1667 as a result of political fallout with the court and Parliament. Although an active participant in the events which he described, Clarendon's history was written in the model of a general and impartial history, "from a lofty impersonal perspective, in rolling, archaic periods."[590]

Burnet, the minister at Saltoun and professor of divinity at Glasgow University (1669), was appointed bishop of Salisbury by William III after the Glorious Revolution of 1688. His general history of England and Scotland under the later Stuarts, Charles II, James II, William III, Mary II and Anne, embodies elements of both general and particular history. The first section of Burnet's history, dealing with the pre-Restoration era and predating his own era, is a "proper," impartial history taken from the monarchical and public records. The remainder of Burnet's history deals with events in which he participated. In these records, Burnet acted in the role of a particular historian or memoirist, suggesting that "those who have been themselves engaged in affairs are the fittest to write history, as knowing best how matters were designed and carried on."[591]

It was against this backdrop of generally defined English histories that Cotton Mather proposed to write his account of the Salem trials. Yet serious complications arose. Mather had been involved in advising Governor Phips about the Salem trials, yet had attended none of the examinations he records in *Wonders*. Further, his historical rendering of the trials did not directly fit the model of general/particular history or memoir even though his objective seemed heavily weighted toward writing a "particular" yet impartial history of the trials.

Cotton Mather would find writing an objective, detached

account of the trials an elusive goal. The causes for this lack of objectivity can be traced to two defects.

The first is the fact that Mather wrote his book partly in a spirit of partisan defense of his friends on the Salem court. Cotton Mather had conceived the idea for *Wonders* during the height of the public outcry against the trial procedures and executions. The last witches executed would face Gallows Hill only weeks after Mather first dipped his pen in the inkwell to write *Wonders*. At that point, however, Mather knew the public mood was clearly becoming more critical, as his letters to Stoughton and Sewell demonstrate. In his request for Stoughton's permission, Mather describes his intended efforts to "divert the thoughts of my readers, even with something of a designed contrivance, unto those points which help very much to flatten that fury which we now so much turn upon one another."[592] Similarly, Mather's request to Samuel Sewell for the trial records demonstrates his dual intention of "lifting up an standard against the infernal enemy," and his willingness to "expose myself unto the utmost, for the defense of my friends with you."[593]

Given this self-acknowledged intention for writing *Wonders*, Cotton Mather could only try to convince himself that despite writing in defense of Lieutenant Governor Stoughton and for Governor Phips, his account could nevertheless be an accurate historical rendering of the Salem cases. Additionally, he could claim some comfort from the fact that his chronicle would be partially based on the trial transcripts obtained from Samuel Sewell. Unfortunately, the trial accounts were not accurate; nor was his rendering of them free from Mather's own determined bias.

The second feature that predisposed Mather to be a court advocate rather than a historian was the approach he took in writing the last third of *Wonders*. To begin, his selection of trials was largely unrepresentative. Mather insisted that if he had included more Salem trial accounts, *Wonders* would have "swollen too big."[594] In reality, Mather's silence on many of the cases limited his chronicle to the trials and executions of those whose guilt could be demonstrated without recourse to spectral evidence alone. This afforded him an arsenal against the attacks of an angry and confused populace, as well as providing Mather some level of comfort in reporting those cases his conscience could accept.

Mather includes the cases of Bridget Bishop, Susanna Martin, Elizabeth How, and Martha Carrier and George Burroughs. Of these, only George Burroughs's case raised the issue of spectral evidence. In effect, Mather only used those cases supported either by tangible witchcraft objects, the confession of the accused witch, or the testimonies of two other or more credible persons.[595] The remaining fourteen cases remained unreported. Yet, in his August 17, 1692, letter to John Foster, Mather had insisted that the Salem judges "had such an encouraging presence of God with them, as that scarce any, if at all any, have been tried before them, against whom God has not strangely sent in other, and more human and most convincing, testimonies."[596]

In addition to his problematic selection of cases, Mather's approach to the historical side of *Wonders* was also marred by personal annotations within this part of his book. While claiming to write strictly as a historian, a title which implied objectivity even and perhaps more especially in the seventeenth century, Mather punctuated his book with inflammatory statements about the convicted and executed suspects, making Cotton Mather appear even more a court advocate.

Several instances of this occur within *Wonders*. For example, speaking of George Burroughs, Mather wrote in the opening passage, "Glad should I have been, if I had never known the name of this man; or never had this occasion to mention so much as the first Letters of his name."[597] Mather would show another personal prejudice in detailing the story of Susanna Martin. After giving the case in full, Cotton Mather added another paragraph as a postscript in which he wrote that "this woman was one of the most impudent, scurrilous, wretched Creatures in the World; and she did now throughout her whole Tryal, discover herself to be such an one."[598] Finally, in a memorandum about Martha Carrier, George Burroughs's female counterpart in the Andover witchcraft case, Mather noted,

> *This Rampant Hag, Martha Carrier, was the person, of whom the confessions of the Witches, and of her own Children among these agreed, that the Devil had promised her, she should be Queen of Hell.*[599]

For a historian and not an advocate, Mather's account, largely taken from Sewell's records, is even by his own standards peppered with loaded and inappropriate asides about the victims of this tragedy. Consequently, Mather's account of the trials and executions belied his stated purpose to the degree that, as Chadwick Hansen has so aptly put it, "one of the most cogent critics of the court . . . became their chief apologist."[600]

Another major aspect of *Wonders* that is clearly paradoxical is Mather's presentation of the adjudication process used by the Court of Oyer and Terminer. The book vacillates between defending the court and stealthily suggesting that from the beginning errors accompanied the trials of the alleged Salem witches. The reader of *Wonders* could not help but notice Cotton Mather's presentation of contradictory opinions about the integrity of the adjudication process and some unnamed court members. The patterns found within these contradictions is centered on two opposed premises. In essence, Mather suggested to his readers that the court had erred in its deliberations without specifically saying so. On the one hand, Mather tactfully opposed the court's trial methodology, while on the other hand he did not purposely single out the erring judges. Illustrations of this are scattered throughout the pages of *Wonders.*

The initial hint of the court's mistakes comes only thirteen pages into Cotton Mather's manuscript, where he asks, "In fine,

Have there been any faults on any side fallen into? Surely, they have at worst been but the faults of a well meaning Ignorance."[601] Just a few pages later, noting the use of questionable tactics by the Salem judges, Mather makes yet another veiled assessment of the Salem trial failures as he says,

> *Have there been any disputed Methods used in discovering the Works of Darkness? It may be none but what have had great Precedents in other parts of the World; which may, though not altogether justifie, yet much alleviate a Mistake in us if there should happen to be found any such mistake in so dark a Matter.*[602]

Again, citing the Court of Oyer and Terminer's use of spectral evidence, Mather observes,

> *The whole business is become hereupon so Snarled, and the determination of the Question [validity of spectral evidence] one way or another, so dismal, that our Honourable Judges have a Room for Jehoshaphat's Exclamation, "We know not what to do!"*"[603]

Using this pattern, Cotton Mather implies, if not quietly confides to the New England populace, that the court had blundered, perhaps executing some innocent persons. Still, he left unnamed the judges responsible for those errors. He certainly could have named William Stoughton, who was not only the chief justice but also the chief proponent of spectral evidence. Mather's implications of wrongdoing were shadowed by his perfectly ambiguous criticism.

The second contradiction of opinions Cotton Mather demonstrates is his pattern of explaining the failures of the court by citing the confusion that reigned in the Salem adjudications. With each of Mather's subsequent illustrations, it becomes apparent he was attempting to distance himself from the errors of the Court of Oyer and Terminer, while protecting the judges from the backlash of the Salem trials and executions.

Cotton Mather began by describing the Salem affair as a part of an ongoing and unfinished war between the Devil and New England:

> *But I do not believe, that the progress of Witchcraft among us, is all the Plot which the Devil is managing in the Witchcraft now upon us. . . . And it may be feared that in the Horrible Tempest which is now upon ourselves, the design of the Devil is to sink that Happy Settlement of Government, wherewith Almighty God has graciously inclined Their Majesties to favour us. . . . The wretches have proceeded so far, as to concert and consult the methods of rooting out the Christian religion from this country, and setting up instead of it, perhaps a more gross diabolism, than ever the world saw before.*[604]

This was true to his cosmology of Salem witchcraft. However, his next statement centered the errors of the court within the confusion of the hour, as seen in the following statement:

> *But in the mean time, the Devil improves the Darkness of this Affair, to push us into a Blind Mans Buffet, and we are even ready to be sinfully, yea, hotly, and madly, mauling one another in the dark.*[605]

Placing the trials within the context of a war of Satan and the witches upon New England, through these assertions, Mather could point to the mistakes of the court while shielding them from total blame. Mather suggested that although the court's management may have been deficient, this was, after all, a war with the Devil. Clearly, the import was that just as times of physical warfare incurred "mistakes," a spiritual war against the Devil might also.

The description of the judges and people as participating in a "blind man's buffet" is particularly telling. The illustration lent itself to an explanation of how the court could have erred innocently, could have "blindly" fallen into error, led by the Devil himself. Emphasizing the difficulties inherent in reaching a judicial judgement in cases of witchcraft, Mather hoped to pacify the New England populace's anger toward the judges.

In assessing these examples, one might ask why Cotton Mather could not or did not plainly censure the court for its failures in the Salem trials. Why did he resort to contradictory statements instead of openly criticizing the court's use of spectral evidence and its erroneous procedures? Beyond his relationship to the Salem court,[606] other issues may have influenced Mather's choice. One difficulty arose from Mather's apprehension that challenging the prosecutions might lead the populace to believe as Robert Calef did: that witchcraft was spurious.[607] Here Calef and Mather were specifically and irrefutably on the opposite side of the debate. Calef would write with an air of stinging sarcasm, "It is rather a Wonder that no more blood was shed, for if that Advice of his Pastor's could still have prevail'd with the Governour, Witchcraft had not been so shammed off as it was."[608] To Mather, in comparison to the errors of the Salem court, a sweeping dismissal of the trial process would ultimately prove to be more destructive since it might invalidate the dangers of witchcraft itself. Mather alludes to this in *Wonders*:

> *[To] obstruct a Regular Detection of that Witchcraft, is what we may well with an holy fear avoid. Their Majesties good Subjects must not every day be torn to pieces by horrid Witches, and those bloody Felons, be left wholly unprosecuted. The Witchcraft is a business that will not be*

> *sham'd, without plunging us into sore plagues, and of long continuance.*[609]

Another explanation for Mather's hesitance in castigating the Salem court is the fact that he honestly believed that for the most part the judges had sought to faithfully discharge their duties. After all, the situation was truly perplexing. Mather stated in *Wonders* that although he "could not allow the principles" some of the judges had used, he still "could not but speak honourably" of them.

Finally, Mather's hesitance in confronting the Salem court can be traced to his view of their biblical obligation to prosecute malevolent witch suspects. In *Wonders*, Mather cites the court's dilemma:

> *What an Arduous Task, have those Worthy Personages now upon their Hands? To carry the knife so exactly, that on the one side, there may be no innocent blood shed by too unseeing a Zeal for the Children of Israel; and that on the other side, there may be no shelter given to those diabolical works of darkness without the Removal whereof we never shall have peace or to those furies whereof several have kill'd more people perhaps than would serve to make a Village.*[610]

Mather's statement returns to an earlier theme: the Salem trials as an end-times attack of Satan upon New England. To Mather, the judges had been thrust into an assignment requiring them to defeat the Devil's witch attack upon New England without blindly and zealously executing innocent persons. This view is repeated by William Stoughton's observation to Mather that by his publication of *Wonders*, "the Spirit of the Lord has thus enabled you to lift up a Standard against the Infernal Enemy, that hath been coming in like a Flood against us."[611] Mather could attest the need to punish any malevolent witches living in New England, but he also was taken with the plight of those who may have been innocently condemned by the court. His emotional ties to the court engendered compassion for the judges, while his conscience told him that he should attempt to quell the populace by ambiguously citing the errors of the court.

Unfortunately for Cotton Mather, his pattern of using ambiguous criticism put him squarely on the side of the Court of Oyer and Terminer. No matter how tactfully Mather may have couched his rebuttals, his later antagonists such as Perry Miller would describe such ambiguous criticisms as attempts to "make those killings legitimate when he knew they were murders."[612]

The final set of Mather's contradictory viewpoints within *Wonders* is seen in his attempts to cautiously disassociate himself from the Court of Oyer and Terminer, Chief Justice William Stoughton, Governor Phips, and the Salem executions. These attempts were not overt, but if one knew Cotton Mather and his disagreement with the Stoughton court, one could easily spot the carefully worded disavowals.

The first comes in Mather's much-needed Author's Defense where he says, "In fine; For the Dogmatical part of my Discourse, I want no Defense; for the Historical part of it, I have a very Great One; the Lieutenant-Governour of New-England."[613] The next disassociation appears at the very beginning of the book. In the first sentence of the text Cotton Mather wrote, "I live by Neighbors that force me to produce these undeserved lines."[614] Then, before Mather related the initial account of the Salem trials he included this statement: "But the Government requiring some Account of this trial to be inserted into his book, it becomes me with all Obedience to submit unto the Order."[615] Having finished the five selective chronicles of the Salem affair, Mather went on to say, "Having thus far done the Service imposed upon me: I will further pursue it."[616]

Taken within their context, the purpose of these statements is apparent. Cotton Mather wanted to indicate that what he was about to write was not entirely to his liking, or to be interpreted as a complete agreement with Stoughton's court or Phips's government.

As for the historical part, Stoughton had given Mather "a shield" and "umbrage" under which he dared to walk; therefore, Stoughton would be accountable for the trial accounts, not Cotton Mather. Something had obviously changed in Mather's mind leading to such a disclaimer, as Mather later wrote that Stoughton's shield had proven "too much."

Finally, with the "Government requiring some account" of Burroughs's trial and the others, Mather had "submitted to the order." He had been "commanded" by the governor to write the official Salem story. Of course, an informed observer would also have known that it was Cotton Mather who both convinced Governor Phips to authorize the publication of *Wonders* as the official Salem account and used Phips's command in obtaining the court transcripts.

Such statements were veiled contradictions of the original facts. It was not Cotton Mather's theology that had changed, but his feeling toward the writing of the manuscript, a change presumably caused by William Stoughton's persistent misapplication of spectral evidence. Added to this was Mather's fear about how the book would now be perceived. It appears that his original willingness to expose himself "to the utmost, for the defense" of his friends had melted into distress as Cotton Mather worried about his reputation after the release of *The Wonders of the Invisible World.*

Mather's fear proved to be well founded. Increase Mather's *Cases of Conscience* appeared as a bold attack on the premises of the Salem trials, chastising the Court of Oyer and Terminer for its use—worse yet, abuse—of spectral evidence. Conversely, Phips's delayed 1693 release of Cotton Mather's *Wonders* in New England made it appear as an ill-timed and badly written defense of the Salem trials. Speculation arose that Increase and Cotton Mather were at odds with one another over the Salem episode, prompting Cotton Mather to complain in his diary that some "besotted people" were contending that Increase's *Cases of Conscience* was "in opposition to it."[617] Although Increase and Cotton Mather refuted this idea in public and in print, this would become a lasting perception.[618]

At the end of the Salem nightmare, Increase Mather appeared to New England as the hero of the moment; he had addressed the main impropriety of the trials, and Governor Phips had ended the Salem proceedings.[619] As for Cotton Mather, *The Wonders of the Invisible World* and his subsequent battle with Robert Calef, as Rosenthal indicates, "has been instrumental in offering the popular view of Cotton Mather as a rabid witch-hunter."[620]

Conclusion

IN THE YEARS FOLLOWING the trials, Cotton Mather's personal assessment of *Wonders* and his conduct during the Salem episode is well documented. Long after Cotton Mather wrote *The Wonders of the Invisible World*, he entertained doubts as to the full meaning of the Salem episode, while questioning the advice he had himself given to the court, including "The Return of the Ministers." He was also bothered by the possibility that the Salem court had condemned and executed innocent people, while privately wondering if his failure to confront the judges had contributed to the tragedy.

Mather was not alone in his doubts. His friend Samuel Sewell had also wrestled with the outcome of the trials. Five years after the trials, while attending a service at the South Church in Boston, Sewell stood next to the Reverend Samuel Willard as he read this confession:

> *Samuel Sewall, sensible of the reiterated strokes of God upon himself and family; and being sensible, that as to the Guilt contracted upon the opening of the late Commission of Oyer and Terminer at Salem . . . Desires to take the Blame and shame of it, Asking pardon of men, And especially desiring prayers that God, who has an Unlimited Authority, would pardon that sin and all other his sins; personal and Relative.*[621]

Cotton Mather's continuing discomfort with the Salem events was evident in his book *Magnalia Christi Americana* (1702). Mather found it necessary or desirable to modify the "The Return of the Ministers" by excluding the document's paramount "eighth article" encouraging the "speedy and vigorous" prosecution of the Salem witches. Additionally, the worrisome doubts that Cotton Mather had concealed within his heart are fully recorded in his diary. An entry for January 15, 1696, relates Cotton Mather's fear that he had not entirely understood the Salem episode or acted properly at the time. Mather records it this way:

> *Being afflicted last Night, with discouraging Thoughts as if unavoidable Marks, of the Divine Displeasure must overtake my Family, for my not appearing with Vigor enough to stop the proceedings of the Judges, when the Inextricable Storm from the Invisible World, assaulted the Countrey, I did this morning, in prayer with my Family, putt my Family into the Merciful hands of the Lord.*[622]

What is notable about this journal entry is that Mather admitted that he had failed to stop the Salem trials before the deaths of twenty persons. It was now some four years after the last Salem execution, and Cotton Mather's heart troubled him about the situation. Had he now realized the error of supporting the flawed court, writing the trial accounts in *Wonders,* and including that fatal "eighth article" in "The Return of the Ministers"?

His only recourse was to pray that those errors might not bring judgment to his own family. Mather records in his *Diary,* "And, with Tears, I received Assurance of the Lord, that Marks of His Indignation should not follow my Family, but . . . Goodness and Mercy should follow us, and the signal Salvation of the Lord."[623] Despite any inconsistencies in his involvement in the Salem affair, he had acted with godly intentions. God knew this and had promised Cotton Mather's family a "signal salvation."

Sixteen years later, at age fifty, Mather would make one final entry in his daily journal about Salem's dark hour. He recorded that he was continuing to pray that he might understand the meaning of the "Descent from the Invisible World."[624] Although Cotton Mather still believed that Satan had been at the head of the witch invasion, even then he was not entirely certain about those tragic events. Perhaps he never did fully understand them. Even so, until his death in 1728 he continued to believe what he had held from the inception of the Salem trials: the events had been an "invasion from the invisible world."

In summary, this chapter has established that Cotton Mather faced a two-pronged dilemma with respect to his beliefs and his conduct during and after the Salem enigma. First, Mather allowed his relationship to the judges to prevent him from challenging their abuse of spectral evidence in the Salem trials. Instead of confronting the court, he acquiesced to their flawed decisions. Second, faced with a set of awkward situations, Mather presented ambiguous advice to the Salem court on the issue of spectral evidence by presenting both encouragement to and caution against its use. Last, this chapter has shown that *The Wonders of the Invisible World* inadvertently became a paradoxical and self-contradictory account of the Salem trials. Although he claimed to write as a historian, Mather's account of the Salem trials attempts to defend the special court, while at the same time suggesting that it had made serious errors of judgement. He also used his publication to distance himself, in a largely self-serving way, from the principal individuals involved and the trials themselves, by peppering his prose with disclaimers and appeals to higher authority.

CONCLUSION

I was concern'd, when I saw that no abler hand emitted any Essays to engage the Minds of this People, in such holy, pious, fruitful Improvements, as God would have to be made of his amazing Dispensations now upon us. THEREFORE it is, that One of the least among the Children of New-England, has here done, what is done. . . . My hitherto unvaried Thoughts are here published; and I believe, they will be owned by most of the Ministers of God in these Colonies; nor can amends be well made me, for the wrong done me, by other sorts of Representations.

Cotton Mather, *The Wonders of the Invisible World* (1693)

DESPITE THE PASSAGE OF three centuries, the Salem witchcraft trials and Cotton Mather's role in them continue to engage both the popular imagination and interest of historians. In their efforts to give meaning to the Salem episode, scholars have used a wide variety of social science approaches, including psychology, sociology, ethnography, anthropology, and economics. Yet, as this study has insisted, no single approach to the history of the Salem trials has been fully satisfactory. We are still left with no clear explanation of how this specific set of events was set in motion or why it concluded in the way it did. In parallel with many of the early modern European witch scares, the origin and course of the scare at Salem must be attributed to a number of disparate forces and personalities working in the specific and distinct context of late seventeenth-century New England. It is only by allowing a full and reasonable weight to be given each aspect of this complex set of events that we can begin to explain the basis of this deadly episode.

The evidence presented argues that the theological worldview of seventeenth-century New England offers an important lens through which to study these events, and that Cotton Mather provides an excellent exemplar for a historical-theological examination of the Salem trials. Mather produced a number of published and unpublished works dealing with witchcraft, in whole or in part, that typify seventeenth-century New England witchcraft beliefs. This study has therefore considered a number of facets of Cotton Mather's personal theology and compared them to his activities during the Salem episode. Additionally, Cotton Mather's cosmology provides a much-needed new emphasis upon what his contemporaries, especially the clergy, chose to identify as the underpinnings of the entire tragic episode: the work of Satan and demons, as well as the dangers of witchcraft.

The starting point for this book was a consideration of Cotton Mather's personal cosmology as it related to witchcraft. It was observed that Mather's cosmological perspective gave a full and important place to the roles of Satan, demons, and witchcraft. Furthermore, although Mather has been accused by critics of inventing a theology of witchcraft in the wake of the Salem events, and publishing it in *The Wonders of the Invisible World*, the historical evidence adduced leads to a different conclusion. This suggests that Cotton Mather gradually developed his own worldview, including its witchcraft dimension, between the years of 1678 and his 1689 publication of *Memorable Providences Relating to Witchcrafts and Possessions*. The theology of witchcraft found in *Wonders* bears no marks of being theologically innovative when compared to *Memorable Providences* or other works written by Mather prior to 1692 in terms of his specific articulation of Puritan clerical beliefs about the power of Satan and witches. Instead, both *Wonders* and Mather's other works dealing with witchcraft are largely consistent in their theological assertions and conclusions.

In brief, like most of his clerical contemporaries, Mather believed in the reality and power of Satan and demons. Together, they formed a vast and well-organized array of devils that sought to ruin humanity. To Mather, witchcraft was one of their greatest weapons, allowing them to seduce and destroy humanity. More than this, witchcraft was a weapon which entailed its own internally logical progression, equivalent to that contained in the process of salvation itself. Although this satanic progression often began with apparently innocent and simple forms of magic and beneficent witchcraft, it easily led to the darkest and most dangerous level of covenant witchcraft. As a result, to Mather and his contemporaries witchcraft became one of the most powerful tools Satan and the demons could utilize in their attempts to control humans and eventually destroy God's kingdom, and especially its crowning glory, New England.

As Cotton Mather saw it, when witch invasions occurred, the covenant people of New England were expected by God to react in specific ways. The first was spiritual in nature: repentance on the part of the covenant nation. To Cotton Mather, repentance was the first and most powerful act a covenant community could take, as it removed the source of both divine judgment and the Devil's power over the population. Second, Mather insisted upon a judicial response. He believed that during witchcraft episodes, New England's judicial code, based upon the Bible, needed to be strictly enforced in order to cleanse the land of people who by their allegiance to Satan were necessarily a grave threat to both individuals and the broader community.

Regardless of the judicial errors committed during the 1692 Salem trials, Mather's post-Salem writings on the nature of witchcraft and the power of Satan remained consistent. There is no evidence to suggest that Mather's personal cosmology as presented in his post-Salem works, including *Magnalia Christi Americana* (1702), *The Armour of Christianity* (1704), and *The Diary of Cotton Mather* (1681-1724), changed in any substantial way. These works attest to Mather's continuing defense of the Salem trials, his opposition to all forms of magic and witchcraft, and his lifelong belief that the late seventeenth century was witnessing a broader spiritual warfare and end-times scenario. It was this preconceived and consistent cosmology that formed the basis for Mather's response to the Salem witchcraft trials and other episodes of New England witchcraft.

Although Cotton Mather's well-developed personal theology included beliefs about the existence and work of Satan and demons, as well as the dangers of witchcraft, such a cosmology cannot be studied in isolation from its seventeenth-century historical context. This study therefore addressed how Mather's personal cosmology was related to, representative of, or incompatible with that of his own contemporaries.

The intellectual landscape of seventeenth-century New England with respect to beliefs in Satan, demons, and witchcraft provides such an evaluation. Looking at pre-Salem, Salem episode, and post-Salem journals, publications, and court records, what emerges is a broad "congruence" in elite and popular conceptions of the supernatural within early modern New England. In this context, witchcraft was understood to be an everyday reality of life, and categorized into four broad types: magic, counter-magic, maleficium, and covenant witchcraft. The first three of these categories of witchcraft involved the use of supernatural power to perform acts ranging from the beneficial to the malevolent. While magic and counter-magic were used to bring about healing and remedy adversity, maleficium involved disrupting the natural order, causing harm, effecting witchcraft possession, as well as inflicting injury or death upon animals or humans. The final category, covenant witchcraft, included the systematic progression of individuals into Satan's service involving the complete denouncing of the Christian faith and adherence to an inverted satanic church. The culmination of this process was manifested in attempts to conscript others for the eventual overthrow of society.

This is not to say that clerical and popular attitudes toward all forms of witchcraft were identical, or that Mather's views coincided with them entirely. Indeed, in seventeenth-century New England disagreements existed between the clerics and populace over the seriousness and validity of such practices. While the populace at large might use these arts to remedy ills and problems without attributing their effectiveness to diabolism, clerics insisted that the Bible prohibited all forms of magic and witchcraft. The clerics further warned that such practices constituted a departure from the Puritan faith, suggesting that these practices represented an attempt to manipulate or overturn God's will, creating a propensity toward more dangerous varieties of witchcraft.

Despite disagreements between clerics and the populace over the legitimacy of magic and witchcraft, the historical context of seventeenth-century Massachusetts suggests that Puritans as a whole perceived themselves to be facing both internal and external threats in the decades before the Salem episode. While some of these challenges took the form of political struggles and were acted out in the broader Atlantic and European world, local agricultural disasters and the influx of religious dissenters and military conflicts, particularly with Native Americans, represented threats specific to New England. The historical record from early modern New England is replete with popular, clerical, and historical accounts claiming malevolent witchcraft activities on the part of Native Americans as well as such radical dissenters as the Antinomians, Anabaptists, and Quakers. Witchcraft was seen as part of a real attempt to weaken New England's orthodoxy or destroy its covenant status.

In addition, if these palpable local threats were not enough to set the stage for the initial Salem accusations, they were exacerbated by yet another peril: Puritans practicing witchcraft. At a time when Puritan clerics already perceived New England to be falling away from its original spiritual errand, this added challenge seemed all the more insidious, as it emanated from within the ranks of the Puritan community itself.

In this milieu, Cotton Mather's theology of Satan, demons, and witchcraft was neither incompatible nor exaggerated compared to his contemporaries. It was the congruence of belief between clerics such as Mather and the New England populace that contributed to their collective willingness to accept witchcraft invasions as real events which needed real and dramatic reactions.

Having laid the groundwork of New England's conceptions of witchcraft, both elite and popular, this study examined Robert Calef's indictment of Cotton Mather within *More Wonders of the Invisible World* (1700). Calef insisted that Cotton Mather's preaching and publications about witchcraft were the catalyst for the Salem trials and executions. Calef's censure of Cotton Mather was considered in detail because it has formed the basis for many later analyses by a succession of authors from the eighteenth to the twentieth century. Two substantive issues arise in this scrutiny: the preaching and written works of Cotton Mather prior to the Salem trials, and the historical climate of New England in relation to witchcraft.

In the period between Mather's publication of *Memorable Providences* in 1689 and the aftermath of the Salem episode in 1693, Cotton Mather kept the concept of a malevolent spiritual world in front of his own congregation and of his broader New England audience. He did this through his published and unpublished works and sermons dealing with witchcraft. Nonetheless, when Mather's activities are weighed against the larger late seventeenth-century context, these were an indirect and general influence on a preexisting propensity toward the type of episode that descended upon Salem in 1692.

Far from Mather playing a fundamental role in the instigation of the episode, three historical and theological factors within New England's early history can be identified as more significant for the initiation and perpetuation of the Salem trials. The first of these is found in the prevalence of prior witchcraft publications. Beyond clerical witchcraft scholarship, publications commonly available to New Englanders during the late seventeenth-century included a wide range of texts which dealt with witchcraft, including the Bible and the "wonder pamphlets." The Bible, the unquestioned and ubiquitous authority on witchcraft, defined witchcraft by depicting the witch's activities, identifying both genders as potential practitioners, and categorizing maleficium as a capital crime under Old Testament law. Beyond the Bible, by the seventeenth century, the wonder pamphlets had proliferated on both sides of the Atlantic. These publications acted as an additional authority for what people in England and New England commonly believed about supernatural events, recording and popularizing a conception of an invisible world of angels, demons, and witches.

Preaching on witchcraft forms a second major historical influence on the events at Salem. Cotton Mather's critics have portrayed him as a lone voice in his Boston pulpit, castigating the practitioners of magic and witchcraft during the period before and after the Salem trials. However, a number of late seventeenth-century sermons and publications by Mather's clerical contemporaries can be identified which take a similar approach to the issue. In the period immediately preceding the Salem trials, Mather's colleagues insisted that one of the indications of New England's spiritual decline was the use of magic, counter-magic, and malevolent witchcraft among the Puritan populace. A growing crescendo of clerical voices in Boston and throughout Massachusetts warned of the dangers of witchcraft and the possibility of God's judgment upon New England for its use of these powers.

The final historical precedent impacting the Salem episode is the prevalence of earlier witch trials in New England, and the other American colonies. New England's clerical and court records reveal that from the 1620s to 1646, only a tiny number of witchcraft allegations reached the stage of an official examination. However, between 1647 and the 1692, a marked increase in witchcraft allegations, trials, and executions can be identified. Prior to Salem, a number of sites throughout New England and the American colonies became the setting for witchcraft trials. Common to the vast majority of these cases was the high propensity for women to be the subject of witchcraft allegations and prosecutions. As a result, and despite its greater magnitude, the Salem trials were not an isolated witchcraft episode. More than this, the Salem events were not the final capstone to New England's witchcraft troubles, since arrests and trials for witchcraft continued well into the eighteenth century.

Viewed within this larger context of New England's early modern period, Cotton Mather's historical reputation as the initiator of the Salem trials is eclipsed by these preexisting factors. Against the backdrop of seventeenth-century New England witchcraft beliefs, the Salem events were precipitated by the prevalence of prior witchcraft publications in New England, contemporaneous seventeenth-century preaching about witchcraft, and a legacy of prior witchcraft trials and executions.

Although Cotton Mather could not have initiated the Salem trials, he did have a limited role in the proceedings, derived primarily from New England's system of judicial cooperation between the judges and clergy and his personal ministerial prominence in Boston. However, the argument has been made for the importance of other factors. Because Mather's conduct in direct relation to the Salem trials still needs to be assessed, this study examined the extent to which Mather's preconceived, cohesive cosmology was acted out prior to and during the Salem trials.

This review of Mather's actions finds its basis within a range of documents written by Cotton Mather before, during, and after the Salem episode. These include his personal letters, his unpublished diary, and such tracts as *Remarkable Providences* and *Magnalia Christi Americana*. Used in a corroboratory and comparative manner, these materials add to the creation of a fuller portrait of Mather's cosmology and overall response to witchcraft events in New England and specifically the New England of the early 1690s.

This reading of Mather's works revealed a pattern, and suggested that he interpreted international, local, and personal events within a preconceived and well-articulated worldview. Within his specifically

Puritan biblical and eschatological cosmology, Mather consistently observed and understood his era's events and circumstances as both spiritual warfare and end-times indicators. Shoe-horned into this framework were seventeenthcentury international religious and political situations, national revolts, military conflicts, and natural disasters. Similar occurrences taking place within New England's own early modern era would also be interpreted by Mather as the marks of end-times conflicts in which New England faced external and internal challenges in its journey toward fulfilling its role in God's kingdom. This pattern of interpretation also extended to Mather's personal life, as he surveyed both positive and negative situations and phenomena within the parameters of his cosmology. Perceiving himself to be personally locked in a battle with the Devil, Mather often described reversals within his personal and family life in terms of spiritual oppression.

Cotton Mather's response toward all signs indicating spiritual warfare was to utilize fasting and prayer in both his personal life and public ministry. This is evident in Mather's pastoral ministry to persons whose situations indicated manifest elements of supernatural diabolism, including witchcraft. His response to cases that he deemed to involve genuine "diabolical possession" was to call for a season of prayer and fasting in order to break the grip of demons acting on behalf of their witch confederates. This pattern held true before, during, and after the Salem trials in such cases as those of Mercy Short, Margaret Rule and the Goodwin children. During the Salem episode, it was his only prescribed response to the crisis.

With these consistent patterns in focus, this undertaking outlined Mather's three major propositions about the meaning of the Salem witchcraft episode as detailed in *The Wonders of the Invisible World*. Using *Wonders* as a benchmark, Mather's other significant published and unpublished works were used to show the interrelationship between Mather's stated beliefs and his response to witchcraft episodes in New England, including that of Salem.

Three observable, broad areas of congruence between Mather's cosmology and conduct during the Salem events emerge from these documents. First, in a manner consistent with his clerical contemporaries, Mather deemed Salem witchcraft to be one of God's judgments upon New England's spiritual degeneration. Mather's response throughout the Salem trials and afterwards, in both his public lectures and publications, was to urge New Englanders to embark upon a new Reformation. He insisted that by true repentance, Satan's wrath would be turned back, and God's certain judgment averted.

Second, Mather saw Salem witchcraft as a demonic retaliation against the Puritan settlement of America. Believing, as many of his predecessors and contemporaries did, that America had been the long-held dominion of Satan and demonically controlled Indians, Mather saw the witchcraft outbreak as another attempt by the demons to seduce and torture humans. Cotton Mather therefore exhorted New Englanders to engage in a period of spiritual warfare against Satan through fasting and prayer. This would result in the defeat of the demons molesting the populace through witchcraft, effectively breaking their diabolical influence over the situation.

Finally, Cotton Mather interpreted the Salem trials to be a clear indication of an end-times assault by Satan upon New England. Mather's ardent millenarian expectations seemed more than justified by the Salem-Andover confessions and trials. In line with his recent eschatological pronouncements, he came to believe that the Salem-Andover invasion had been planned by Satan, encouraged by demons, and carried out by human vassals. Accordingly, Mather warned his New England community of the real dangers they faced from this end-times assault if they failed to take immediate and appropriate actions, including a careful strategy for the identification and examination of suspected witches.

Even though Mather's behavior was consistent with his ardent beliefs about the Salem situation, there remained a distance between these strongly held postulates and Mather's willingness to intentionally place himself at the forefront of the Salem adjudications. Despite his theological certainty, he adopted a limited course of action of a sort that was to be repeated throughout his life. Despite his sermons and published opinions about the events unfolding at Salem, he chose to take a secondary role, rather than acting as a prime mover.

While this is perplexing, it is typical of Cotton Mather. Whether out of personal insecurity or deference to those he believed were more capable or authorized, Mather would offer his advice but retreat from any direct conflict. This is true whether the situation involved having Robert Calef arrested for slander and then conspicuously avoiding a court appearance, or refusing to refute the Court of Oyer and Terminer's use of spectral evidence in "The Return of the Ministers." In similar fashion, Cotton Mather shrank from leading any attempts to discover, examine, or execute those suspected of witchcraft during the Salem trials.

Consequently, even though Mather was convinced that the Salem-Andover events were an end-times attack of Satan, he kept his distance from Salem. He remained in Boston, engaging in fasting and prayer, and acting as an advisor and chronicler of the trials, without becoming personally and directly involved in the proceedings.

Cotton Mather's stated cosmology and his overall conduct as it related directly to the Salem events were consistent, and demonstrably so. Unfortunately, the advice he subsequently gave to the Salem judges and his account of their proceedings found in *The Wonders of the Invisible World* failed to meet his own standards of rectitude and accuracy. This dissonance allowed for Mather's historical condemnation by Robert Calef and a long line of Salem historians and scholars to gain such credence in the popular and scholarly imagination.

Cotton Mather was aware of the dangers in the situation at Salem. If the court did not effectively deal with the witchcraft episode, New England would be lost, but at the same time, any prosecutions which led to the punishment of innocent people would likewise undermine the religious authority of the covenant community. The Salem-era records show that Mather admonished the Salem court to use rules for witchcraft prosecution based upon the works of earlier English witchcraft scholars, such as William Perkins, John Gaule, and Richard Bernard. He specifically recommended these works because of the fact that by the late seventeenth century they had become standard works in the area of witchcraft discovery and prosecution.

Beyond this, Mather gave three major guidelines. He suggested a careful detection of witchcraft that avoided reliance upon spectral evidence, evidentiary experiments, or the use of torture in the confirmation of witchcraft allegations. Instead, he insisted upon a voluntary or unexpected confession by an accused witch. Further, Cotton Mather proposed that the Salem judges apply leniency in those cases which lacked a solid determination of guilt, or in which those convicted were guilty of non-malevolent witchcraft. Mather's third suggestion was directed at the treatment of cases of provable diabolism involving an explicit covenant with the Devil and a purposeful attempt to injure or murder others, or to overthrow Puritanism. In these circumstances he insisted that such persons needed to be prosecuted to the full extent of New England's statutes and executed.

Despite Mather's efforts, the Salem court ignored these cautions, and plunged the trials into a confusing pattern of accepting evidence which lead to erroneous convictions and executions. In the process, Cotton Mather faced what was arguably the greatest dilemma of his ministerial career: how to support the battle against the witch invasion while criticizing the trial procedures being used by the Salem judicial panel. This dilemma manifested itself in at least three specific areas of Mather's behavior.

The first contradiction surfaced between Mather's desire to give balanced advice and the pressures on him created by his personal relationship with the members of the Court of Oyer and Terminer. While Mather privately confessed his dissent with the Salem trial process, he avoided directly criticizing or opposing either the Salem judges or their questionable methodologies. This weakness was directly linked to Mather's relationship with the various members of the court of Oyer and Terminer, many of whom were Mather's superiors in terms of position and authority within New England.

A second contradiction is seen in Mather's handling of his advice to the Salem court on the issue of spectral evidence. In his letters to his contemporaries, "The Return of the Ministers," the debate about Increase Mather's *Cases of Conscience,* and Mather's use of spectral evidence within his book *The Wonders of the Invisible World,* a basic contradiction is found. When these documents and events are compared, they show that Mather unintentionally presented ambidextrous advice to the Salem court on the issue of spectral evidence, both encouraging and cautioning the judges about its value and dependability. Even though Mather did not change his view on spectral evidence during the Salem trials, he failed to openly oppose the judges' use of spectral evidence as the primary basis of conviction and execution of witch suspects.

Mather's third major dilemma is seen in his account of the trials, *The Wonders of the Invisible World,* which created the lasting historical impression that he had fully agreed with and defended the Salem trials. Although this view is not entirely fair, Mather helped to create this legacy through his own failures, both in writing this clerical defense of the Salem trials, and by failing to be totally transparent about his disagreements with the procedures used by the court.

Although Mather intended to write *The Wonders of the Invisible World* as an objective, detached account of the trials, it failed on several points. First, because Mather wrote his book partly in a spirit of partisan defense of his friends on the Salem court, his approach lent itself to the creation of an account that was largely unrepresentative of the entire trials. Furthermore, Mather limited the volume to consideration of those cases in which the trials and executions were pursued without recourse to spectral evidence alone. Beyond this, *Wonders* was itself paradoxical. Mather presented contradictory opinions about certain unnamed court members and the integrity of the adjudication process. Last, Mather's contradictory viewpoints within *Wonders* is seen in his attempts to cautiously disassociate himself from the Court of Oyer and Terminer, Chief Justice William Stoughton, Governor Phips, and the Salem executions. He did this by interspersing within his text disclaimers and appeals to higher authority.

In the end, we must embrace certain conclusions about Cotton Mather that perhaps do not fully comprehend his personality or satisfy a desire to justify or condemn his actions relative to the Salem trials. While Mather certainly cannot be blamed for initiating the Salem events, or for causing the episode to turn out so horribly, he cannot entirely escape blame. He plainly refused to confront Chief Justice William Stoughton and the rest of the Court of Oyer and Terminer for, among other things, their poor handling of spectral evidence and willingness to execute persons based upon such ambiguous evidence.

Neither can Mather be absolved of his worst error connected to the Salem events: his subtle but ill-fated defense of the flawed proceedings and those officials who conducted them. Had Mather stopped at the theological defense of witchcraft itself, he no doubt would have escaped much of the historical condemnation his reputation has endured. It seems evident from *The Wonders of the Invisible World* that he both expected and was willing to pay a personal price for his defense of his colleagues who sat on the Salem court. In historical retrospect, perhaps the payment has proven too weighty. Cotton Mather was by all accounts a powerful Puritan preacher, a remarkable theologian and scholar, a thorough student of natural philosophy, and a voluminous writer. Yet, for all of this, he has been characterized by a succession of historians and scholars as a Puritan zealot and witch-hunter who cared more about his personal reputation than the lives of the twenty people taken during the Salem witch trials.

Of course, a comprehensive and fair reading of the Salem trials and Mather's actions during them refutes such a view. Nonetheless, one is forced to agree with a description of Mather's historical legacy written two decades ago: "In the public memory, however, he personifies the worst elements of Puritanism. Even among scholars, he has until recently been perceived as a disconcerting mixture of scarcely reconcilable opposing qualities, good and bad."[625] Mather's historical reputation is perhaps just beginning to improve, no doubt due to the willingness of some scholars to view Mather's person and actions within the broader seventeenth-century New England context. Here, the recent trends in scholarship in which events such as witch hunts are viewed from a multi-faceted perspective have allowed us to move away from the simplistic and prejudiced approach of assigning blame to individuals. The results of this shift have led to a more comprehensive understanding of events such as those at Salem.

This has been the overarching argument of this examination. While Cotton Mather has been made the enigmatic representative of the Salem witch hunt, a fuller evaluation of his cosmology within his own seventeenth-century setting provides a much clearer insight into Mather himself and the Salem trials. Using this approach, although Mather cannot be absolved of his personal errors connected to Salem, at least his actions can be assessed more equitably than has been done to date. How the historical reputation of both Cotton Mather and the Puritans of his era will eventually fare will unquestionably be linked to the continued willingness of future scholars to avoid judging him by modern standards. Instead, studying both Cotton Mather and the Salem episode in the light of their own seventeenth-century worldview will undoubtedly yield further valuable interpretive insights into what happened at Salem during that brief but infamous period of 1692 to 1693.

ACKNOWLEDGMENTS

IN THE PROCESS OF writing and publishing a book, there are so many people that contribute to the final work. This is especially true in my case.

A World of Wonders began its life as a PhD dissertation, written during my time at the University of North London, UK. I had the distinct privilege of being mentored by Dr. Tim Hitchcock (University of Sussex), a skilled professor and an accomplished author. Tim provided me the perfect balance of scholarly insight and excellent guidance throughout the process.

I also received a great deal of encouragement from Dr. Laura Gowing, professor of early modern history at King's College, London. Laura's insights into the role of women in the seventeenth century was invaluable to the study of witchcraft trials.

More recently, my dream of publishing the dissertation became a reality because of the people in my life. My family encouraged me take a "leap of faith" to publish this book. Many friends banded together and helped me financially throughout the process.

I am particularly indebted to the Ike Rigell family, and especially Scott Rigell, former US Representative for Virginia's second congressional district, for graciously making a connection for me with Koehler Books.

Finally, I want to acknowledge John Koehler of Koehler Books. John's guidance and encouragement has been invaluable. His team is second to none when it comes to taking a first-time author through the process of co-publishing. John and his team represent the very best in their field.

Notes

Endnotes

[1] Paul Boyer and Stephen Nissenbaum, (eds), *The Salem Witchcraft Papers: Verbatim Transcripts of the Legal Document of the Salem Witchcraft Outbreak of 1692* (3 vols.; New York, 1977), 1:164.

[2] Boyer and Nissenbaum, *The Salem Witchcraft Papers*, 1:164.

[3] Ibid, 1:166.

[4] See Larry Gragg, *The Salem Witch Crisis* (New York, 1992), p. 114.

[5] See George Lincoln Burr, *Narratives of the Witchcraft Cases*, 1648-1706 (New York, 1952), p. 361.

[6] Robert Calef, *More Wonders of the Invisible World*, (London, 1700), in Samuel Drake, (ed.), The Witchcraft Delusion in New England (3 vols.; New York, 1866), 3:38.

[7] Those executed with George Burroughs were John Willard, Martha Carrier, John Proctor, and George Jacobs. See Calef, *More Wonders of the Invisible World*, 3:360-61.

[8] David Levin, "Did the Mathers disagree about the Salem witchcraft trials?" *The Proceedings of the American Antiquarian Society*, 95, (1), (1985), pp. 19-37.

[9] Representative of the arguments against Puritan glorification of their New World errand, see Andrew Delbanco, "The Puritan errand re-viewed," *Journal of American Studies*, 18, (1984), pp. 343-60, and Theodore Dwight Bozeman, *To Live Ancient Lives: The Primitivist Dimension in* Puritanism (Chapel Hill, 1998).

[10] Mark A. Peterson, *The Price of Redemption: The Spiritual Economy of Puritan New England* (Stanford, 1997).

[11] Phillip H. Round, *By Nature and Custom Cursed: Transatlantic Civil Discourse and New England Cultural Production, 1620-1660* (Hanover, 1999).

[12] Emerson W. Baker, *A Storm of Witchcraft: The Salem Trials and the American Experience* (New York, 2014).

[13] Elaine Forman Crane, *Ebb Tide in New England: Women, Seaports, and Social Change 1630-1800* (Boston, 1998).

[14] The declining place of women in New England's seventeenth to eighteenth-century society is echoed in several women's studies. For examples, see Kathleen M. Brown, *Good Wives, Nasty Wenches, and Anxious Patriarchs: Gender, Race, and Power in Colonial Virginia* (Chapel Hill, 1996); Carol Karlsen, *The Devil in the Shape of a Woman, Witchcraft in Colonial New England* (New York, 1989); Suzanne Lebsock, *The Free Women of Petersburg: Status and Culture in a Southern Town* (New York, 1984).

[15] Jane Kamensky, *Governing the Tongue: The Politics of Speech in Early New England* (New York, 1997).

[16] Bethany Reid, "Unfit for light: Anne Bradstreet's monstrous birth," *The New England Quarterly*, 71, (December 1998), pp. 517-42.

[17] See Peter C. Mancall and James H. Merrell, (eds), *American Encounters: Natives and Newcomers from European Contact to Indian Removal, 1500-1850* (Boston, 1999).

[18] For a good example of spatial organization studies, see Joseph S. Wood, with a contribution by Michael P. Steinitz, *The New England Village* (Baltimore, 1997).

[19] Kathleen Bragdon, *Native People of Southern New England, 1500-1650* (Tulsa, 1996).

[20] James Sharpe, *Instruments of Darkness: Witchcraft in England 1550-1750* (New York, 1996), p. 5.

[21] Richard MacKenny, *Sixteenth Century Europe Expansion and Conflict* (Handsmill, 1993).

[22] Anthony Wright, *The Counter Reformation: Catholic Europe and the Non-Christian* World (London, 1982).

[23] See Mary Condren, *The Serpent and the Goddess* (San Francisco, 1989).

[24] Bob Scribner, "Witchcraft and Judgement in Reformation Germany," *History Today*, (April 1990),
pp. 34-47.

[25] Christina Larner, *Witchcraft and Religion: The Politics of Popular Belief* (Oxford, 1984),
(Published posthumously under the editorship of Alan Macfarlane).
[26] Brian Levack, *The Witch-hunt in Early Modern Europe* (New York, 1987), preface, ix.
[27] Rossell Robbins, *The Encyclopedia of Witchcraft and Demonology* (London, 1959). For a review of rationalism, see Leland L. Estes, "Incarnations of evil: Changing perspectives on the European witch-craze," Clio 13, (1984), pp. 136-9.
[28] Hugh Trevor-Roper, *The European Witch-craze of the 16th and 17th Centuries* (Harmondsworth, 1969).
[29] Peter Burke, "The Comparative Approach to European Witchcraft" in Bengt Anklaroo and Gustav Henningsen, (eds), *Early Modern European Witchcraft: Centres and* Peripheries (Oxford, 1990), p. 436.
[30] Alan Macfarlane, *Witchcraft in Tudor and Stuart England: A Regional and Comparative Study* (New York, 1970), and Keith Thomas, *Religion and the Decline of Magic* (New York, 1971).
[31] William E. Monter, *Witchcraft in France and Switzerland The Borderlands During the Reformation* (New York, 1976).
Midlefort, H.C. Erik, *Witch-Hunting in Southwestern Germany 1562-1684* (Stanford, 1972).
[32] Christina Larner, *The Enemies of God: The Witch-hunt in Scotland* (London, 1981).
[33] Lyndal Roper, *Oedipus and the Devil: Witchcraft, Sexuality and Religion in Early Modern Europe* (London, 1994). For additional women's studies on European witchcraft, see Anne Barstow, "On Studying Witchcraft as Women's History: A Historiography of the European Witch Persecutions," *Journal of Feminist Studies in Religion*, 4, (1988), pp. 7-19; Sigrid Brauner, *Fearless Wives and Frightened Shrews:The Construction of the Witch in Early Modern Germany* (Amherst, 1995); Marriane Hester, "Patriarchal Reconstruction and Witch Hunting" in Jonathan Barry, et al., (eds),

Witchcraft in Early Modern Europe: Studies in Culture and Belief (Cambridge, 1996), pp. 288-308.

[34] Stuart Clark reviews the acculturation model in greater depth in his book, *Thinking with Demons: The Idea of Witchcraft in Early Modern Europe* (New York, 1997), pp. 509-25.

[35] Robert Muchembled, *Popular Culture and Elite Culture in Early Modern France* (Baton Rouge, 1985); Peter Burke, "A Question of Acculturation?" in Paola Zambelli, (ed.), *Scienze, Credinze Oculte, Livellie di Cultura* (Florence, 1982), pp. 197-204. For Carlo Ginzburg, see the following: *Ecstasies: Deciphering the Witches Sabbat* (London, 1991); *The Night Battles: Witchcraft and Agrarian Cults in the 16th and 17th* Centuries (London, 1983); "The Witches Sabbat: Popular Culture or Inquisitorial Stereotype," in Stephen L. Kaplan (ed.), *Understanding Popular Culture Europe from the Middle Ages to the Nineteenth Century* (Berlin, 1984); for Gustav Henningsen, "The Ladies from Outside: An Archaic Pattern of the Witches' Sabbath" in Ankarloo and Henningsen, *Early Modern European Witchcraft: Centres and Peripheries*, pp. 191-215.

[36] Briggs, *Witches and Neighbors*, p. 8.

37 James Sharpe, *Instruments of Darkness: Witchcraft in England 1550-1750* (New York, 1996).

[38] Using this model, Sharpe has also written a study on the 1605 Jacobean English case of Anne Gunter. See: James Sharpe, *The Bewitching of Anne Gunter: A Horrible and True Story of Football, Witchcraft, Murder and the King of England* (London, 2000).

[39] Cotton Mather, *The Wonders of the Invisible World* (Boston, 1693); John Hale, "A Modest Inquiry into the Nature of Witchcraft" in George Lincoln Burr, (ed.), *Narratives of the Witchcraft Cases*, 1648-1706 (New York, 1914); Robert Calef, *More Wonders of the Invisible World* in Drake, Witchcraft Delusion.

[40] Thomas Hutchinson, *The History of the Colony and Province of Massachusetts-Bay* (ed.), Lawrence Shaw Mayo, (3 vols.; New York, 1970); Charles Upham, *Salem Witchcraft* (2 vols.; Boston, 1867);

George Bancroft, *History of the United States of America from the Discovery of The Continent* (Boston, 1879); Vernon Louis Parrington, *Main Currents in American Thought* (New York, 1954).

[41] Upham, *Salem Witchcraft*, 2:366-367.

[42] Bancroft, *History of the United States* p. 266.

[43] Parrington, *Main Currents in American Thought* p. 116.

[44] James Truslow Adams, *The Founding of New England* (Boston, 1921); Samuel Eliot Morse, *The Intellectual Life of Colonial New England*, 4th edn. (New York, 1970).

[45] George Lyman Kittredge, "Notes on Witchcraft," *Proceedings of the American Antiquarian Society*, XVIII, (April 1907), repeated in *Witchcraft in Old and New England* (Cambridge, 1929), p. 329.

[46] Kittredge, *Witchcraft in Old and New England*, p. 329.

[47] Perry Miller, *The New England Mind: From Colony to Province* (Cambridge, 1953).

[48] For additional studies presenting New England Puritanism as a homogenous culture, see Sacvan Bercovitch, *The Puritan Origins of the American Self* (New Haven, 1975); Charles E. Hambrick-Stowe, *The Practice of Piety: Puritan Devotional Disciplines in Seventeenth Century New England* (Chapel Hill, 1982); Robert Middlekauff, *The Mathers: Three Generations of Puritan Intellectuals* (New York, 1971); George Selement, "The meeting of elite and popular minds at Cambridge, New England, 1638-1645," *William and Mary Quarterly*, 3d series, 41, (1984), pp. 32-48.

[49] Later scholars would distance themselves from Miller's stance, emphasizing emotional piety and cultural plurality within seventeenth-century New England. For examples, see: Laura Ricard, "New England Puritan studies in the 1970s," *Fides et Historia*, 15, (1982): pp. 6-27; Charles Lloyd, *God's Caress: The Psychology of Puritan Religious Experience* (New York, 1986), pp. 275-89; Theodore Dwight Bozeman, *To Live Ancient Lives: The Primitivist Dimension in Puritanism* (Chapel Hill, 1988).

[50] Miller, p. 203.

[51] Ibid, p. 192.
[52] Ibid., p. 178. Kai T. Erikson would take a similar interpretive approach, insisting that the Salem trials were an attempt by New England's clergy to restore the sense of unity and purpose by exterminating those who modeled their own spiritual failure. See, Kai T. Erikson, *Wayward Puritans: A Study in the Sociology of Deviance* (New York, 1966).
[53] The jeremiad was used throughout early-modern England, but found particular development and contextual usage by the clerics of New England. See: Miller, *The New England Mind: From Colony to Province* pp. 27-39.
[54] Ibid, p. 197.
[55] Ernest Caulfield, "Pediatric aspects of the Salem witchcraft tragedy," *American Journal of Diseases of Children*, 65, (May 1943), pp. 788-802.
[56] Sigmund Freud, "A seventeenth-century demonological neurosis," in Standard Edition of the *Complete Psychological Works of Sigmund Freud* (London, 1961), Volume 4, preface, xix.
[57] Ibid, p. 6. See also, David Harley, "Explaining Salem: Calvinist psychology and the diagnosis of possession," American Historical Review, 101, (1996), pp. 307-330: Robert D. Anderson, "The history of witchcraft: A review with some psychiatric comments," *American Journal of Psychiatry*, 126, (1970), pp. 1727-35.
[58] Ibid, p. 277.
[59] Marilynne K. Roach, *Six Women of Salem: The Untold Story of the Accused and Their Accusers in the Salem Witch Trials* (Boston, 2013).
[60] Stacy Schiff, *The Witches: Suspicion, Betrayal and Hysteria in 1692 Salem* (New York, 2015)
[61] Chadwick Hansen, *Witchcraft at Salem* (New York, 1969). Hansen used psychology, but also insisted Cotton Mather attempted to restrain the excesses of the witchcraft crisis, see: preface, x.
[62] Hansen, *Witchcraft at Salem*, pp. 10-11.

[63] Ibid, p. 10.

[64] For example, see Sally Hickey, (Parkin) "Fatal feeds? Plants, livestock losses and witchcraft accusations in Tudor and Stuart Britain," *British Journal of Folklore*, 101, (1990), pp. 131-42; Geoffrey Quaife, *Godly Zeal and Furious Rage* (London, 1987), pp. 201-204; Carolyn Merchant, *The Death of Nature: Women, Ecology, and the Scientific Revolution* (San Francisco, 1980); Michael J. Harner, *Hallucinogens and Shamanism* (New York, 1974).

[65] Linnda R. Caporael, "Ergotism: The Satan loosed in Salem?" *Science*, 192, (April 1976), pp. 21-26. Ergot, a fungus which hosts cereal grains, but especially rye, has a form of sclerotia containing a large number of potent alkaloid pharmacologie agents including LSD (lysergic acid diethylamide), capable of producing mental disturbances.

[66] Caporael, "Ergotism: The Satan loosed in Salem?" p. 23. The manifestations included crawling sensations in the skin, tingling in the fingers, vertigo, tinnitus aurium, headaches, disturbance in sensation, hallucinations, painful muscle contractions, epileptiform convulsions, vomiting and diarrhea.

[67] Nicholas Spanos and Jack Gotlieb, "Ergotism and the Salem village witch trials," *Science*, 194, pp. 1390-4.

[68] Spanos and Gotlieb, "Ergotism and the Salem village witch trials," p. 1390.

[69] Ibid, p. 1391.

[70] Ibid, p. 1394. Spanos also details psychological aspects at Salem in "Witchcraft and social history: An essay review," *Journal of the History of the Behavioral Sciences*, 21, (1985), pp. 60-66.

[71] Mary Matossian, "Ergotism and the Salem Witchcraft Affair," *American Scientist* 70, no. 4 (1982).

[72] Paul Boyer and Stephen Nissenbaum, *Salem Possessed: The Social Origins of Witchcraft* (Cambridge, 1974), p. 65. Tracing this conflict, Boyer and Nissenbaum showed that by 1691, the year the Salem Village church committee hired Samuel Parris to become their pastor,

an important power shift had occurred in which the Putnams and Porters constituted a serious breach within the Salem church.

[73] Boyer and Nissenbaum note that Salem Town saw extensive mercantile expansion in the 1660s and was named (along with Boston) by the Massachusetts General Court as the principal port for both import and export taxable products. Taxation records reveal that from 1661 to 1681 the Salem townspeople averaged one-third greater wealth than the Salem villagers. See Boyer and Nissenbaum, *Salem Possessed*, p. 86.

[74] Ibid, pp. 81-85.

[75] Ibid, p. 181.

[76] Ibid, p. 181.

[77] John Demos, *Entertaining Satan: Witchcraft and the Culture of Early New England* (New York, 1982), See also, Patricia Henry Davis, "Siding with the Judges: A Psychohistorical Analysis of Cotton Mather's Role in the Salem Witch Trials," (Princeton Theological Seminary PhD thesis, 1992).

[78] For witch hunts as societal persecution of non-conforming persons, see: Nachman Ben-Yehuda, "Deviance and Moral Boundaries: Witchcraft, the Occult, Science Fiction, Deviant Science and Scientists" (Chicago, 1985) and "The witch craze of the fourteenth to seventeenth centuries: A sociologist's perspective," *American Sociological Journal*, 86, (1980), pp. 1-31; Robert Moore, *The Formation of a Persecuting Society: Power and Deviance in Western Europe*, 950-1250 (Oxford, 1987).

[79] Demos, *Entertaining Satan*, p. 309.

[80] A variety of gender studies have been written as explanations for witch hunts. For examples, see, Marianne Hester, *Lewd Women and Wicked Witches: A Study of the Dynamics of Male Domination* (London, 1992); Janet A. Thompson, *Wives, Widows, Witches, and Bitches: Women in Seventeenth Century Devon* (New York, 1993); Francis E. Dolan, *Dangerous Familiars: Representations of Domestic Crime in England 1550-1700* (New York, 1995); Merry Weisner,

Women and Gender in Early Modern Europe (Cambridge, 1993); Lyndal Roper, *Oedipus and the Devil: Witchcraft, Sexuality and Religion in Early Modern Europe* (London, 1994); Deborah Willis, *Malevolent Nurture: Witch-Hunting and Maternal Power in Early Modern England* (New York, 1995).

[81] Karlsen, *The Devil in the Shape of a Woman*, preface, xiii.

[82] Ibid, pp. 75-76. Karlsen notes that in the late seventeenth-century New England, "Men worried especially about masterlessness—insubordination in women, children, servants, vagabonds, beggars, and even in themselves."

[83] Ibid, pp. 144-5. According to Karlsen, local healers and midwives placed themselves in competition with male doctors who attempted to establish their own "professional" superiority by barring women from "professional training," and, it seems, by accusing women practitioners of witchcraft. This view is also held by a number of feminist writers. For examples, see: Anne Barstow, "Women as healers, women as witches," *Old Westbury Review*, 2, (1986), pp. 121-33; Barbara Ehrenreich and Deirdre English, *Witches, Midwives, and Nurses: A History of Women Healers* (Old Westbury, 1973); Thomas Rodgers Forbes, *The Midwife and the Witch* (New Haven, 1966).

[84] Peter Burke, "A Question of Acculturation?" in Paola Zambelli, (ed.), *Scienze, Credinze Oculte, Livellie di Cultura* (Florence, 1982), pp. 197-204; Mary O'Neil, "Magical Healing, Love Magic and the Inquisition in late Sixteenth-Century Modena," in Stephen Haliczer (ed.), *Inquisition and Society in Early Modern Europe* (London, 1986), pp. 88-114; Ruth Martin, *Witchcraft and the Inquisition in Venice*, 1550-1650 (Oxford, 1989).

[85] Richard Weisman, *Witchcraft, Magic, and Religion in 17th-Century Massachusetts* (Amherst, 1984).

[86] Weisman, *Witchcraft, Magic, and Religion*, p. 184.

[87] Ibid, p. 187.

[88] Ibid, p. 185.

[89] Ibid, p. 183.

[90] David D. Hall, *Worlds of Wonder, Days of Judgment: Popular Religious Belief in Early New England* (New York, 1989), p. 245.
[91] Hall, *Worlds of Wonder*, p. 245.
[92] Ibid, p. 192.
[93] Richard Godbeer, *The Devil's Dominion: Magic and Religion in Early New England* (New York, 1992), p. 5. Godbeer insisted that, from the Puritan's initial days in New England, "alongside Protestant Christianity there coexisted a tangled skein of magical beliefs and practices that the colonists brought with them from England."
[94] Godbeer, *The Devil's Dominion*, p. 31.
[95] Ibid, p. 60.
[96] Ibid, p. 217. Godbeer's view of the coexistence of Puritan pietistic and magical approaches has been discussed by a number of scholars. See: Laurence Veysey, "Intellectual History and the New Social History," in John Higham and Paul Conkin, (eds), *New Directions in American Intellectual History* (Baltimore, 1979), p. 16; William A. Lessa and Evon Z. Vogt, (eds), *Reader in Comparative Religion: An Anthropological Approach*, 3d edn. (New York, 1972); John Middleton, (ed.), *Magic, Witchcraft, and Curing* (Austin, 1967); Stanley Jeyaraja Tambiah, *Magic, Science, Religion, and the Scope of Rationality* (New York, 1999).
[97] Elizabeth Reis, *Damned Women, Sinners and Witches in Puritan New England* (New York, 1997). Reis's discussion in many ways complements the works of Ann Kibbey, who has also addressed the critical relationship between religious ideology and gender studies in Puritan New England. See, Kibbey's "Mutations of the supernatural: witchcraft, remarkable providences, and the power of Puritan men" *American Quarterly*, 34, (1982), pp. 125-48; Patricia Caldwell, *The Puritan Conversion Narrative: The Beginnings of American Expression* (Cambridge, 1983); Cornelia Hughes Dayton, "Taking the trade: Abortion and gender relations in an eighteenth-century New England village," *William and Mary Quarterly*, 3rd series, 48:1, (January 1991), pp. 19-50.

[98] Reis, Damned Women, preface, xvi.

[99] Ibid, 43. For discussions of women and the "sin" of witchcraft, see also, Allison Coudert, "The Myth of the Improved Status of Protestant Women: The Case of the Witchcraze," in Jean Brink et al., (eds), The Politics of Gender in Early Modern Europe (Kirkville, 1989); Louise Jackson, "Witches, wives, and mothers: Witchcraft persecution and women's confessions in seventeenth-century England," *Women's History Review*, 4, (1995), pp. 63-83.

[100] Ibid, p. 115. For women's acceptance of their own susceptibility, see also Michael MacDonald, *Mystical Bedlam: Madness, Anxiety and healing in Seventeenth-Century England* (Cambridge, 1981).

[101] Ibid, p. 124.

[102] Ibid, p. 139.

[103] Peter Lockwood Rumsey, *Acts of God and of the People, 1620-1730* (Ann Arbor, 1986). Michael P. Winship has also done a convincing study of Puritan providentialism in his book, *Seers of God: Puritan Providentialism in the Restoration and Early Enlightenment* (Baltimore, 1996).

[104] Rumsey, *Acts of God and of the People*, p. 65.

[105] Ibid, p. 62.

[106] Michele Tarter Lise, *Clio*, 28:1, (Fall 1998), pp. 93-97.

[107] Ralph Boas, *Cotton Mather* (New York, 1928), p. 98.

[108] Upham, Charles W., *Salem Witchcraft* (2 vols.; Boston, 1867).

[109] Cotton Mather, *The Wonders of the Invisible World* (Boston, 1693), in Samuel Drake, (ed.), *The Witchcraft Delusion in New England* (3 vols.; New York, 1866; repr. 1970).

[110] David Levin, Cotton Mather, *The Young Life of the Lord's Remembrancer, 1663-1703* (Cambridge, 1978), p. 216. Mather records that "some revered persons" had sent him encouraging letters about the release of *Wonders*, including William Stoughton. See, *Diary of Cotton Mather*, 1681-1709, 1709-1724 (2 vols.; New York, 1957), 1:153.

[111] Robert Calef, *More Wonders of the Invisible World in Drake*, (ed.), *The Witchcraft Delusion.*

[112] Perry Miller, *The New England Mind: From Colony to Province* (Cambridge, 1953), pp. 200-04.
[113] Richard Weisman, *Witchcraft, Magic, and Religion in Seventeenth-Century Massachusetts* (Amherst, 1984), p. 24.
[114] Kenneth Silverman, *The Life and Times of Cotton Mather* (New York, 1984), p. 14.
[115] Silverman, *Life and Times of Cotton Mather*, p. 31.
[116] For a thorough bibliography of Cotton Mather's works, see Thomas James Holmes, *Cotton Mather: A Bibliography of His Works* (3 vols.; Newton, 1974).
[117] Cotton Mather, *Memorable Providences Relating to Witchcrafts and Possessions* (Boston, 1689; 2nd edn. London, 1691) in *American Antiquarian Society Early American Imprints*, 1639-1800, Microcard no. 486, (Worcester, 1967), p. 123.
[118] Cotton Mather, *Diary*, 1:489.
[119] Cotton Mather, *Magnalia Christi Americana* (2 vols.; London, 1702; repr. Hartford, 1853), 2:445.
[120] Cotton Mather, *Wonders*, 1:55.
[121] Edward Taylor, *Harmony of the Gospels* in Thomas M. and Virginia L. Davis (eds), (3 vols.; New York, 1983), 1:67.
[122] Elizabeth Reis, *Damned Women*, p. 65. For an in-depth examination of the role of Satan in seventeenth-century ministerial discourse, see Edward K. Trefz, "A Study of Satan with Particular Emphasis upon the Preaching of Certain New England Puritans," (Union Theological Seminary, D.D. thesis, 1952).
[123] Cotton Mather, *The Armour Of Christianity* (Boston, 1704), in *American Antiquarian Society, Early American Imprints*, 1639-1819, Micro-card no.1171, (Worcester, 1967). See also, Cotton Mather's Speedy Repentance Urged (Boston, 1690), p. 10.
[124] See Jonathan Mitchell, *Continuation of Sermons Concerning Man's Misery*, 15 August 1655, Massachusetts Historical Society; Samuel Willard, *A Compleat Body of Divinity in Two Hundred and Fifty Expository Lectures* . . . (Boston, 1726), pp. 180-81.

125 Mitchell, "Continuation of Sermons"; This narration of the "Fall of Satan" is also given in Deodat Lawson's book, *Christ's Fidelity the Only Shield against Satan's Malignity* (Boston, 1692), pp. 1-2.

126 Cotton Mather, *Wonders*, 1:55.

127 Richard Godbeer, *The Devil's Dominion: Magic and Religion in Early New England* (New York, 1992), p. 87. Puritan clerics described Satan, demons, and persons aligned with Satan or his works as "devils." In one sermon, during the Salem trials, Salem minister Samuel Parris described humans in collusion with Satan as "devils." See, "Sermon on 6.John.70, 27 March 1691/2" in James F. Cooper, Jr. and Kenneth P. Minkema, (eds), *The Sermon Notebook of Samuel Parris*, 1689-1694 (Boston, 1993), pp. 194-8.

128 Cotton Mather, *Wonders of the Invisible World*, 1:55-7.

129 Henry Smith, in Thomas Fuller, (ed.), *The Works of Henry Smith: Including Sermons, Treatises, Prayers, and Poems* (2 vols.; Edinburgh, 1867), 2:19.

130 Jonathan Mitchell, "Continuation of Sermons, 15 August 1655."

131 Samuel Willard, *The Child's Portion* (Boston, 1684), pp. 29-30.

132 Mather, *Wonders*, 1:58.

133 Ibid, 1:211.

134 Cotton Mather, *The Armour Of Christianity* (Boston, 1704), *American Antiquarian Society, Early American Imprints*, 1639-1819, Microcard no.1171, (Worcester, 1967), p. 59.

135 Mather, *Armour of Christianity*, p. 141.

136 Ibid, p. 10.

137 William Perkins, *A Fruitful Dialogue Concerning the End of the World*, in *The Workes of William Perkins* (3 vols.; London 1616-18), 3:465-477.

138 Cotton Mather, *The Gospel of Justification by the Righteousness of God* (Boston, 1700), p. 21; for other examples of this explanation, see Increase Mather, *The Folly of Sinning* (Boston, 1699), p. 50; John Williams, *Warning to the Unclean* (Boston, 1699), p. 53.

139 Cotton Mather, *Wonders*, 1:239-40.

[140] Paul Boyer and Stephen Nissenbaum, (eds), *The Salem Witchcraft Papers: Verbatim Transcripts of the Legal Documents of the Salem Witchcraft Outbreak of 1692* (3 vols.; New York, 1977), 1:67.
[141] Cotton Mather, *Wonders*, 1:63.
[142] Cotton Mather, *The Armour Of Christianity*, p. 13.
[143] Cotton Mather, *Wonders*, 1:63.
[144] Ibid, 1:63.
[145] Ibid, 1:65.
[146] Cotton Mather, *The Armour Of Christianity*, p. 6.
[147] Mather, *Wonders*, 1:80.
[148] Peter Thatcher, *The Saint's Victory and Triumph over Sin and Death* (Boston, 1696), p. 19.
[149] Mather, Wonders, 1:230-31. The sermon, The Wonders of the Invisible World was first preached at the Old North Church in Boston, before it became part of the printed manuscript which bears the same title.
[150] Ibid, 1:58.
[151] Ibid, 1:59.
[152] Mather, *Armour Of Christianity*, p. 3.
[153] Mather, *Wonders*, 1:58.
[154] Ibid, 1:11.
[155] See Deodat Lawson, *Christ's Fidelity*, pp. 1-2.
[156] For examples of the attacks of Satan and demons upon humanity, see Daniel Russell, "Sermon notes, 1677," in Collections of the Massachusetts Historical Society, p. 23; Joshua Moodey, *Soldiery Spiritualized* (Cambridge, 1673), p. 36; "Benjamin Wadsworth, Good Souldiers a Great Blessing" (Boston, 1700), p. 28.
[157] Mather, *Armour Of Christianity*, p. 2.
[158] John Norton, "Notes on sermons of Jonathan Mitchell, 1654-5," (1 February 1654), in the *Collections of the Massachusetts Historical Society.*
[159] Mather, *Wonders*, 1:220.
[160] William Hubbard, *The Happiness of a People in the Wisdom*

of Their Rulers Directing and in the Obedience of their Brethren Attending (Boston, 1676), p. 17.

[161] Cotton Mather, *Wonders,* 1:235.

[162] Cotton Mather, *Wonders,* 1:69-70.

[163] Weisman, *Witchcraft, Magic, and Religion, p. 89.* For Mather's insistence of this, see *Cotton Mather, A Good Man Making a Good End* (Boston, 1698), p. 36.

[164] Cotton Mather, *Wonders,* 1:20.

[165] Cotton Mather, *A Brand Pluck'd Out of the Burning* (Boston, 1689), in George Lincoln Burr, (ed.), *Narratives of the Witchcraft Cases, 1648-1706* (New York, 1914), p. 263.

[166] Cotton Mather, *Wonders,* 1:102.

[167] Ibid, 1:131.

[168] Ibid, 1:164.

[169] Ibid, 1:24.

[170] Ibid, 1:158-59.

[171] Weisman, *Witchcraft, Magic, and Religion,* p. 19.

[172] Mather, *Wonders,* 1:4.

[173] Cotton Mather, *A Discourse on Witchcraft* (Boston, 1689), in *American Antiquarian Society, Early American Imprints,* 1639-1800, Microcard no. 486, p. 4, (Worcester, 1967).

[174] Mather, *A Discourse on Witchcraft,* p. 9.

[175] See Weisman, *Witchcraft, Magic, and Religion,* p. 35.

[176] See: Richard Weisman, *Witchcraft, Magic, and Religion*; David D. Hall, *Worlds of Wonder, Days of Judgment* (New York, 1989).

[177] Mather, Wonders, 1:23.

[178] Ibid, 1:24.

[179] Ibid, 1:111.

[180] Peter Charles Hoffer, *The Devil's Disciples* (Baltimore, 1996), p. 79.

[181] Cotton Mather, *Diary,* 1:155. Note: This and other descriptions are repeatedly put forth as evidence of witchcraft afflictions. This is not unique to Mather or seventeenth-century New England beliefs. See George Kittredge, *Witchcraft in Old and New England,* chapter 18.

[182] Carol Karlsen, *The Devil in the Shape of a Woman: Witchcraft in Colonial New England* (New York, 1989), p. 2.
[183] Mather, *Wonders,* 1:109.
[184] Ibid, 1:18.
[185] Ibid, 1:123.
[186] Ibid, 1:129.
[187] Silverman, *Life and Times of Cotton Mather,* p. 59. For a well-written narrative of Cotton Mather's own view of New England as a church-state, see Sacvan Bercovitch, *The Puritan Origins of the American Self* (New Haven, 1975), pp. 35-71.
[188] Hoffer, *The Devil's Disciples,* p. 139.
[189] Samuel Drake, *The Witchcraft Delusion,* p. 24
[190] Robin Briggs, *Witches and Neighbors: The Social and Cultural Context of European Witchcraft* (New York, 1996), p. 8. Similarly, James Sharpe puts the total of executions resulting from the European witch trials at less than 50,000. He indicates this total was less than one half of the casualties during the Civil Wars. James Sharpe, *Instruments of Darkness: Witchcraft in England,* 1550-1750 (London, 1996), p. 5.
[191] Mather, *Magnalia,* 2:449.
[192] Ibid, 2:472-3.
[193] Silverman, *Life and Times of Cotton Mather,* p. 111.
[194] *Wonders,* 1:126.
[195] Richard Chamberlain, *Lithobolia, or the Stone-Throwing Devil* in George Lincoln Burr, (ed.), *Narratives of the Witchcraft Cases,* 1648-1706 (New York, 1914), pp. 58-77; Increase Mather, *An Essay for the Recording of Illustrious Providences* (Boston, 1684), pp. 142-55.
[196] John Winthrop, "History of New England, 1630-1649," in James Kendall Hosmer, (ed.), *Original Narratives of Early American History* (2 vols.; New York, 1908), 2:346.
[197] Paul Boyer and Stephen Nissenbaum, (eds), *The Salem Witchcraft Papers: Verbatim Transcripts of the Legal Documents of the Salem Witchcraft Outbreak of 1692* (3 vols.; New York, 1977), 3:851.

[198] David D. Hall, *Worlds of Wonder, Days of Judgment: Popular Religious Belief in Early New England* (New York, 1989), p. 71.
[199] Richard Godbeer, *The Devil's Dominion: Magic and Religion in Early New England* (New York, 1992),
p. 177. The quote was taken from Jasper Danckaerts, *Journal of a Voyge to New York and a Tur of Several of the American Colonies* in 1679-1680 trans. Henry C. Murphy, *Memoirs of the Long Island Historical Society*, 1, (1867), p. 419.
[200] James A. Sharpe, *Instruments of Darkness: Witchcraft in England, 1550-1750* (London, 1996), p. 7.
[201] Keith Thomas, *Religion and the Decline of Magic* (New York, 1971), p. 449.
[202] Godbeer, *The Devil's Dominion:Magic and Religion in Early New England* (New York, 1992), p. 31.
[203] Ibid, p. 60.
[204] John Hale, "A Modest Inquiry into the Nature of Witchcraft in Burr," *Narratives of the Witchcraft Cases*, p. 430.
[205] For various views regarding the degree of seventeenth-century magic and witchcraft practices, see: Godbeer, *The Devil's Dominion* (New York, 1992) and Richard Weisman, *Witchcraft, Magic, and Religion in Seventeenth-Century New England* (Amherst, 1984); Hall, *Worlds of Wonder* (New York, 1989); Timothy Breen and Stephen Foster, "The Puritans' greatest achievement: a study of social cohesion in seventeenth-century Massachusetts," *Journal of American History* 60, (1973), pp. 5-22.
[206] Stuart Clark, "Protestant Demonology: Sin, Superstition, and Society (c.1520-c.1630)," in Bengt Anklaroo and Gustav Henningsen, (eds), *Early Modern European Witchcraft: Centres and Peripheries* (Oxford, 1990), p. 458.
[207] Alfred A. Cave, "Indian shamans and English witches in seventeenth-century New England," in *Essex Institute of Historical Collections*, 128 (October 1992), p. 41.
[208] Cave, "Indian Shamans and English Witches," p. 41. See also:

Increase Mather, *A Brief History of the War with the Indians in New-England* 2nd edn. (London, 1676), p. 1.

[209] Cotton Mather, *A Brand Pluck'd Out of the Burning* in Burr, *Narratives of the Witchcraft Cases*, p. 99.

[210] Increase Mather, *Angelographia*, (1694), quoted in Chadwick Hansen, *Witchcraft at Salem* (New York, 1969), p. 198. During the Salem trials Sarah Osborne's defense included claims of bewitchment, after having been assaulted by "a thing like an Indian all black." See: Boyer and Nissenbaum, *Salem Witchcraft Papers*, 2:610-11.

[211] John Winthrop, "History of New England, 1630-1649," in Hosmer, *Original Narratives of Early American History*, 1:268.

[212] This adaptation of heresy and monstrous conceptions was commensurate with the popular views of covenant witchcraft, in which witches were impregnated by Satan or demons. For the claims that Anne Hutchinson and Mary Dyer had produced demonic offspring, see: Winthrop, "History of New England, 1630-1649," 1:214, 1:268.

[213] In this vein, heresiographers such as Daniel Featley would write of the Anabaptists that "in one Anabaptist you have many heretics, and in this one Sect as it were one stock, many erroneous and schismaticall positions and practices ingraffed." See Daniel Featley, *The Dippers Dipt, or Then Anabaptists Ducked and Plung'd Over Head and Eares* 3rd edn. (London, 1645), sig. B2.

[214] Carla Gardina Pestana, "The city upon a hill under siege: The Puritan perception of the Quaker threat to Massachusetts Bay, 1656-1661," *The New England Quarterly*, 56, (September 1983), pp. 323-53.

[215] Pestana, "The city upon a hill under siege," p. 337. For the association of Quakers with witchcraft, also see: William C. Braithewaite, *The Beginnings of Quakerism* (New York, 1923); *Thomas, Religion and the Decline of Magic* (New York, 1971); Amelia Mott Gummere, *Witchcraft and Quakerism: As Study of Social History* (Philadelphia, 1908).

[216] Increase Mather, *Illustrious Providences*, pp. 341-56.
[217] George Francis Dow, (ed.), Records and Files of the Quarterly Court of Essex County, Massachusetts, 1636-1683, (8 vols.; Salem, Essex Institute, 1911-1921), 2:219.
[218] Godbeer, *The Devil's Dominion*, pp. 6, 10-11. Godbeer defines the major theological difference between magic and religion: that the Puritan devotional ritual was supplicative, whereas popular magic was coercive in nature. In general, the Puritan Protestants were reacting to the prior centuries in which the Catholics had attribute some powers to humans in the form of ritual, while the English culture had blended an amount of folk beliefs with Christianity. The results were that Catholics believed in ritual to prevent or relieve misfortune, while Protestants attributed misfortune to sin or to the will of God; either way, submission to providence was the only recourse for Puritans.
[219] Carol Karlsen, *The Devil in the Shape of a Woman* (New York, 1987), p. 35.
[220] For English examples of cunning folk, see Sharpe, *Instruments of Darkness*, pp. 66-70. For the New England cunning folk see Godbeer, *The Devil's Dominion*, pp. 20-22, and chapter 2.
[221] Cotton Mather, "Paper on Witchcraft," *Proceedings of the Massachusetts Historical Society*, 47, (1914), pp. 265-66.
[222] Cotton Mather, *The Wonders of the Invisible World* (Boston, 1693), in Samuel G. Drake, (ed.), *The Witchcraft Delusion in New England* (3 vols.; New York, 1866; repr. 1970), 1:123.
[223] Records of the Town of Easthampton (5 vols.; New York, 1887-1892), 1:134.
[224] John Winthrop, "History of New England," 2:344.
[225] George Lyman Kittredge, *Witchcraft in Old and New England*, 187-188.
[226] John Winthrop, "History of New England," 2:156.
[227] Cotton Mather, "Paper on Witchcraft," p. 265.
[228] Mather, *Wonders*, 1:124.

[229] For a further detailed study of the use of astrology in seventeenth-century New England see: Godbeer, *The Devil's Dominion*, pp. 122-52; Hall, *Worlds of Wonder*, pp. 58-60.
[230] Boyer and Nissenbaum, *Salem Witchcraft Papers*, 2:398.
[231] Ibid, 3:769.
[232] Ibid, 2:397-398. In another part of his deposition Hale noted other Beverly residents who practiced palmistry "to tell persons their Fortunes [as they call it] or future Condition by looking into their hands." See John Hale, *A Modest Inquiry*, quoted in Godbeer, *The Devil's Dominion*, p. 35.
[233] Ibid, 3:787.
[234] Ibid, 3:783.
[235] Ibid, 3:784.
[236] Ibid, 1:228.
[237] Ibid, 1:328.
[238] Ibid, 2:507.
[239] Ibid, 1:271-72.
[240] Ibid, 2:626.
[241] Attempts at determining the future would be a problem in the post-Salem days in New England as well. In 1695 Cotton Mather would record in his diary that two young women had been guilty of consulting 'and ungodly fortune teller, in the Neighborhood, with desire to be informed of some secret and future things'. Upon their confession of sin, Mather notes, "the Church was reconciled to them as such." See: *Diary of Cotton Mather*, 1681-1709, 1709-1724, (2 vols.; New York, 1957), 1:181.
[242] There is some debate as to whether or not the practitioners of malevolent witchcraft actually believed that they were doing real harm. Godbeer believes so, but Demos and Karlsen doubt this. For this discussion see: Godbeer, *The Devil's Dominion*, p. 40; Demos, *Entertaining Satan* (New York, 1982), pp. 80-84; Carol Karlsen, *The Devil in the Shape of a Woman*, (New York, 1987) p. 132, n. 50.
I would concur with Godbeer that some of the participants did in

fact believe in their own powers to cause harm through the diabolical arts. The Salem court records abound with such statements, although at times it is difficult to determine the voluntary nature of such confessions.

[243] Jane Kamensky, "Words, witches, and woman trouble: Witchcraft, disorderly speech, and gender boundaries in Puritan New England," Essex Institute Historical Collections, 128, (October 1992), p. 299.

[244] This perhaps explains why accused witches tended to have, as John Demos demonstrates, a higher rate of charges against them for both assaultive speech and crimes. See: Demos, *Entertaining Satan*, pp. 77-78.

[245] Laura Gowing, "Gender and the language of insult in early modern London," History Workshop, 35, (Spring 1993), pp. 1-21. For more on the history of sexual defamation cases see: Martin Ingram, *Church Courts, Sex and Marriage in England, 1570-1640* (Cambridge, 1987).

[246] Jane Kamensky, "Words, witches, and woman trouble: witchcraft, disorderly speech, and gender boundaries in Puritan New England," pp. 270-85.

[247] William Perkins, *A Discourse of the Damned Art of Witchcraft*, 1608) found in Ian Breward, (ed.), *The Works of William Perkins* (Abingdon, 1970), pp. 596-600.

[248] The *Salem Witchcraft Papers*, 1:190.

[249] Ibid, 1:103.

[250] Ibid, 3:741.

[251] Ibid, 3:762.

[252] Cotton Mather, "Paper on Witchcraft," 265.

[253] Cotton Mather, *Memorable Providences relating to Witchrafts and Possessions* (Boston, 1691), in *American Antiquarian Society, Early American Imprints*, 1639-1800, Microcard no. 486, (Worcester, 1967), p. 12.

[254] Richard Godbeer, *The Devil's Dominion*, p. 106.

[255] Sir Thomas Browne, *Religio Medici* (Oxford, 1642), p. 32.

[256] "The Chronicle of the English Augustinian Canonesses Regular of the Lateran, at St. Monica's, Louvain," (ed.), A. Hamilton (1904), pp. 251-252.

[257] Clarke Garrett, *Spirit Possession and Popular Religion: From the Camisards to the* Shakers (Baltimore, 1987), p. 10.

[258] Stuart Clark, *Thinking with Demons: The Idea of Witchcraft in Early Modern* Europe (New York, 1997), p. 413.

[259] See Michael MacDonald, *Mystical Bedlam: Madness, Anxiety and Healing in Seventeenth-Century England* (Cambridge, 1981), pp. 198-217.

[260] For an excellent example of possession by witchcraft, taken from the English annals, see *The Most Strange and Admirable Discoverie of the three Witches at Warboys arraigned, convicted and executed at the last Assizes at Huntingdon* (London, 1593).

[261] Godbeer, *The Devil's Dominion*, p. 106.

262 Karlsen, *The Devil in the Shape of a Woman*, p. 232.

[263] Increase Mather, *Remarkable Providences* in Burr, *Narratives of the Witchcraft Cases*, pp. 18-19.

[264] Mather, *Remarkable Providences*, pp. 21-23. Also, see John Demos, *Entertaining Satan*, pp. 99-111.

[265] Holland, Henry, *Spiritual Preservatives against the Pestilence . . . chiefly collected out the 91.Psalme* (London, 1593), pp. 69-70. Henry Holland was the Vicar of St. Bride's church in London.

[266] Deodat Lawson, *Christ's Fidelity the Only Shield against Satan's Malignity* in Charles Upham (ed.), *Salem Witchcraft* (2 vols.; Boston, 1867), 2:78-87.

[267] George Gifford, *Two Sermons upon I Peter 5, verses 8 and* 9 (London, 1597), p. 66.

[268] See Godbeer, *The Devil's Dominion*, p. 42.

[269] John Hale, *A Modest Inquiry*, in Burr, *Narratives of the Witchcraft Cases*, p. 411.

[270] *Salem Witchcraft Papers*, 2:635.

[271] Suffolk County Court Files: Original Depositions and other

Materials in *Proceedings of the Quarterly Courts of Suffolk County, Massachusetts*, 24, (1972).

[272] John Taylor, *The Witchcraft Delusion in Colonial Connecticut* 1647-1697 (New York, 1908), p. 41.

[273] As Richard Godbeer has noted, archaeologists have discovered twenty such bottles in Great Britain, though none have survived from New England. See Ralph Merrifield, "Witch bottles and magical jugs," *British Journal of Folklore*, 66 (1955), pp. 195-207, id, *The Archaeology of Ritual and Magic*, (London, 1988).

[274] Cotton Mather, *Memorable Providences*, p. 59.

[275] *Salem Witchcraft Papers*, 3:745-57.

[276] For two considerable works on the idea of witchcraft covenants see: Elizabeth Reis, "Witches, sinners, and the underside of covenant theology," Essex Institute Historical Collections 129 (1993), pp. 103-18; Ian Bostridge, "Debates about witchcraft in England, 1650-1736," (Oxford University PhD thesis, 1990), pp. 27-31.

[277] *Salem Witchcraft Papers*, 2:423.

[278] Thomas, *Religion and the Decline of Magic*, p. 439.

[279] Kittredge, *Witchcraft in Old and New England*, p. 265.

[280] Thomas, *Religion and Magic*, p. 444.

[281] Mather, *Illustrious Providences*, p. 21. Although two other alleged accomplices fled before they could be examined and convicted, both of the Greensmiths were subsequently convicted and executed for malefic witchcraft, despite Nathaniel's protests that he was not involved in these activities.

[282] Ibid, pp. 20-21.

[283] Robert Rowland, "Fantasticall and Devilshe Persons: European Witch-Beliefs in Comparative Perspective," in Bengt Ankarloo and Gustav Henningsen, (eds), *Early Modern European Witchcraft: Centres and Peripheries* (Oxford, 1990), p. 169.

[284] Richard Gildrie, "The Salem witchcraft trials as a crisis of popular imagination," *Essex Institute Historical Collections*, 128:4, (October 1992), pp. 270-85.

[285] The Gospel According to Luke, chapter four.
[286] John Rogers, *Some Account of the Life and Opinions of a Fifth-Monarchy-Man* (London, 1867), pp. 474-5.
[287] *Salem Witchcraft Papers*, 3:748.
[288] Ibid, William Barker: 1:65; Stephen Johnson: 2:509; Mary Bridges Jr: 1:135; Andrew Carrier: 2:528.
[289] Ibid, 3:767.
[290] Richard Baxter, *The Certainty of the World of Spirits* (London, 1691), preface.
[291] For a discussion of sexuality related to New England witchcraft, see: Robert Masters, *Eros and Evil: The Sexual Psychopathology of Witchcraft* (New York, 1962).
[292] Sharpe, *Instruments of Darkness*, p. 74.
[293] Cotton Mather, *Memorable Providences*, p. 62.
[294] *Salem Witchcraft Papers*, 1:112.
[295] Ibid, 1:140.
[296] Ibid, 2:643.
[297] Ibid, 1:168-9.
[298] Cotton Mather, *Wonders*, 1:60.
[299] John Davies, *A History of Southampton* (Southampton, 1883), p. 236.
[300] Sharpe, *Instruments of Darkness*, p. 73.
[301] Karlsen, *The Devil in the Shape of a Woman*, pp. 12-13.
[302] Laura Gowing has written a thorough article dealing with the aspects of secret births and infanticide, including the female world's formal and informal surveillance of suspects, and how such measures reflected social boundaries between a woman's privacy and community relationships. See Laura Gowing, *"Secret births and infanticide in seventeenth-century England,"* Past and Present Journal, 156, (August 1997), p. 91. Gowing notes that "since at least some people expected milk to be present in the breasts from around the fourth month of pregnancy, the test served to check for a current pregnancy as well as a recent birth or miscarriage." For

additional studies of this subject, see: Regina Schulte, *The Village in Court: Arson, Infanticide and Poaching in the Court Records of Upper Bavaria, 1848-1910* trans. Barrie Selman, (Cambridge, 1994); Robert Malcomson, 'Infanticide in the Eighteenth Century', in James Cockburn (ed.), Crime in England, 1500-1800 (Princeton, 1977).

[303] Gowing, *"Secret births and infanticide,"* p. 98.

[304] *Salem Witchcraft Papers*, 1:105. The allegation of Susannah Sheldon that Giles Corey suckled an imp is significant, for most Salem scholarship tends to focus upon the female gender in the discussion of the witch's imp.

[305] Ibid, 3:951. When Thomas Manning presented his 1692 "accounts tally" to the Boston magistrates he included, among other costs, a bill for "providing a Jury to make search upon Cori and his wife, and Clenton Easty Hoare, Cloisss and Mrs. Bradbury."

[306] Ibid, 1:159. On a similar note, on 2 June 1692 a panel including Dr. Barton, a local physician, searched John Proctor Sr. and John Willard for witch's marks or teats but without finding anything to "farther suspect them." Ibid, 2:681.

[307] Ibid, 2:423; 2:529.

[308] Ibid, 1:140.

[309] Keith Thomas, *Religion and the Decline of Magic*, p.445. Cecil L. Ewen notes the singular usage of witch transportation in English withcraft trials in his book, *Witchcraft and Demonaniam: A Concise Account Derived From Sworn Depositions And Confessions Obtained In The Courts Of England And Wales* (London, 1933), p. 337.

[310] *Salem Witchcraft Papers*, 3:748.

[311] Ibid, 2:615.

[312] Ibid, 1:135.

[313] Phillip F. Gura, *A Glimpse of Sion's Glory: Puritan Radicalism in New England, 1620-1660* (Middletown, 1984), p. 95.

[314] Gura, *A Glimpse of Sion's Glory*, p. 100. Gura notes that heresiographers noted Anabaptist meetings in open spaces, in which such baptisms were often supplemented by "love feasts" at which

they washed each other's feet, imposed hands on the new convert, and then offered a "kiss of charity."

[315] *Salem Witchcraft Papers*, 1:59.

[316] Ibid, 2:388.

[317] Joshua Scottow, *A Narrative of the Planting of the Massachusetts Colony Anno 1628* (Boston, 1694), pp. 46-48.

[318] *Salem Witchcraft Papers*, 2:659.

[319] Ibid, 2:423.

[320] Gildrie, "The Salem witchcraft trials," p. 283.

[321] Cotton Mather, *Diary*, 1:155.

[322] Gildrie, "The Salem witchcraft trials," p. 278.

[323] *Salem Witchcraft Papers*, 1:325.

[324] Ibid, 2:423.

[325] Ibid, 2:529.

[326] Ibid, 1:166.

[327] Ibid, 1:165.

[328] R. Boulton, *An Account of the First Rise of Magicians and Witches* (London, 1715), cover.

[329] Gura, *A Glimpse of Sion's Glory*, p. 233.

[330] Robert Calef, *More Wonders of the Invisible World in Samuel Drake*, (ed.), *The Witchcraft Delusion in New England* (3 vols.; New York, 1866; repr. 1970).

[331] Charles Upham, *Salem Witchcraft* (2 vols.; Boston, 1867).

[332] Upham, *Salem Witchcraft*, 2:366-67.

[333] Marc Mappen, *Witches and Historians: Interpretations of Salem* (Malabar, 1996), p. 36.

[334] Nathaniel Hawthorne, *Alice Doane's Appeal* (1843), quoted in Kenneth Silverman, *The Life and Times of Cotton Mather* (New York, 1984), p. 53.

[335] Hugh Trevor-Roper, *The European Witch-craze of the Sixteenth and Seventeenth Centuries* (Harmondsworth, 1969).

[336] George Malcolm Yool, *The 1692 Witch Hunt: The Layman's Guide to the Salem Witchcraft Trials* (Bowie, 1992), pp. 4, 74.

[337] Samuel Drake, *The Witchcraft Delusion in New England* (New York, 1866; repr. 1970), preface, xxi. According to Drake, Calef was born in 1648 and died in 1719. Drake has compiled what little relevant biographical history of Robert Calef is available, including his genealogical records, in his introduction of *More Wonders.*

[338] Drake, *The Witchcraft Delusion in New England,* preface, xii.

[339] This first letter was written on 11 January 1693, see *More Wonders,* 2:48.

[340] For a complete transcript of the accusation see Drake, *Witchcraft Delusion,* 2:49.

[341] Calef, *More Wonders,* 2:50.

[342] Mather, *The Wonders of the Invisible World* (Boston, 1693), in Samuel Drake, (ed.), *The Witchcraft Delusion in New England* (3 vols.; New York, 1866; repr. 1970), 2:65.

[343] Cotton Mather, *Diary of Cotton Mather,* 1681-1709, 1709-1724 (2 vols.; New York, 1957), 1:264, (June 1698).

[344] Richard Lovelace notes that this was the "traditional way of stigmatizing a libelous book." See: Richard E. Lovelace, *The American Pietism of Cotton Mather* (Grand Rapids, 1979), p. 22.

[345] Upham, *Salem Witchcraft,* p. 462; Lovelace, *American Pietism of Cotton Mather,* p. 23.

[346] Robert Calef, *More Wonders,* 2:6-7.

[347] Ibid, 2:92.

[348] Ibid, 2:152.

[349] Peter Hoffer, *The Devil's Disciples: Makers of the Salem Witchcraft Trials* (Baltimore, 1996), p. 139.

[350] Sacvan Bercovitch, *The American Jeremiad* (Madison, 1978), p. 7. Bercovitch's book is a thorough study in the formulation and modification of the jeremiad within colonial New England.

[351] Emory Elliot, in Sacvan Bercovitch, (ed.), *The Cambridge History of American Literature* (3 vols.; Cambridge, 1994), 1:257.

[352] Cotton Mather, *The Present State of New England* (Boston, 1690), p. 38.

[353] For a depiction of these circumstances and the Metacomet War, see: Alden T. Vaughan and Edward W. Clark, (eds), *Puritans among the Indians: Accounts of Captivity and Redemption, 1676-1724* (Cambridge,1981), p. 9.
[354] Cotton Mather, *Things to be Look'd For* (Cambridge, 1691), pp. 18-19.
[355] George Keith was born in Aberdeen, Scotland, in 1639. He became a member of the Society of Friends in his early years. He was well known for his debates with the Boston ministerium through a number of tracts on behalf of the Quakers. Eventually Keith came into disagreement with the Society of Friends over certain theological issues and was disowned by the Yearly Meeting in 1694. Ironically, Keith became an Anglican Minister in 1700 and published several works against the Quakers before his death in 1716.
[356] Cotton Mather, *Little Flocks guarded against Grievous Wolves* (Boston, 1691), p. 9.
[357] Cotton Mather, *Fair Weather* (Boston, 1692), p. 50.
[358] Cotton Mather, *A Midnight Cry (Boston,* 1692), p. 24.
[359] Cotton Mather's preaching and publications can be plotted to show that he continued this pattern beyond Salem. See, Cotton Mather, *Batteries Upon the Kingdom of the Devil* (London, 1695), pp. 21, 26. See also, Cotton Mather, *Another Brand Pluck't from the Burning,* originally circulated in manuscript form, and preserved by the Massachusetts Historical Society. The first printing was done without Mather's permission by Robert Calef in his book *More Wonders of the Invisible World.*
[360] William Frederick Poole notes, "One who has never examined this point would be surprised at the number of witch books." See Poole, *Cotton Mather and Salem Witchcraft* (Cambridge, 1689) p. 13.
[361] This is not to ignore the fact that by the end of the seventeenth century, witchcraft beliefs were also reflected by an extensive witchcraft bibliography available from English, Continental, and American colonial sources. Written by the clergy, monarchs, and legal

advisors, these had a broader appeal to and influence upon the learned classes of New England. A partial list of these works includes: Jacob Sprenger and Heinrich Kramer, *Malleus Maleficarum* (1487); Jean Bodin *De la Demonomanie des Sorciers*, (Paris, 1580); Martin Del Rio's *Disquisitionum Magicarum Librie Sex*, (Lyons, 1608); James VI and I, *Daemonologie* (Edinburgh, 1597); John Gaule, *Select Cases of Conscience Touching Witches and Witchcraft* (London, 1646); William Perkins, *A Discourse of the Damned Art of Witchcraft* (London, 1608); Richard Bernard, *Guide to Grand Jury Men* 2nd edn. (London, 1630); Michael Dalton, *Countrey Justice* 4th edn. (London 1630); Richard Baxter, *Certainty of the World of Spirits* (London, 1691); Joseph Keble, *An Assistance to Justice of the Peace* (London, 1689); Matthew Hale, *A Tryal of Witches at the Assizes Held at Bury St.* Edmunds (London, 1682). Many of these works were utilized by the Salem court: See thesis chapters five and six for the Salem court's use of seventeenth-century witchcraft scholarship.

[362] This assertion of the Bible's infallibility also represented the Puritans' (and all Protestants') doctrinal stand against the Roman Catholic Church's tradition and ceremonies. As William Ames would declare in his book, *Fresh Suit against Ceremonies*, "The word of God, and nothing else, is the only standard in matters of religion." See: William Ames, in Ralph Bronkema, *The Essence of Puritanism* (Rotterdam, 1929), p. 84.

[363] David Hall, *Worlds of Wonder, Days of Judgment: Popular Religious Belief in Early New England* (New York, 1989), p. 37. For example, John Barnard could remember that before age six he had read the entire Bible through three times. See: John Barnard, *Massachusetts Historical Society Collections* 3rd Series, 5 (1836). Barnard may not have been all that unusual, since the *Young Child's Catechism* by Isaac Watts was a standard of the day, usually taught to children of ages three and four. See Clifton Johnson, *Old-Time Schools and School-Books* (New York, 1963), p. 13.

[364] Hall, *Worlds of Wonder*, p. 32. Hall notes that these estimates are

based upon "a careful count of signatures as against simple marks on wills" sampled from 1660.

[365] Stuart Clark, *Thinking with Demons: The Idea of Witchcraft in Early Modern Europe* (New York, 1997), p. 529.

[366] Hyder Edward Rollins, (ed.), *The Pack of Autolycus* 2nd edn. (Cambridge, 1969), preface, x. During the same era, both German and French publications were listing the same types of "wonders" included in the English variety. There is little difference in the general makeup of such stories. For further reading on the European "wonder publications" see Miriam Chrisman, *Lay Culture, Learned Culture: Books and Social Change in Strausberg 1480-1599* (New Haven, 1982). Also see Jean Ceard, *La Nature et les Prodiges: L'insolite au XVI siecle en France* (Geneva, 1977).

[367] See William P. Upham, "Remarks," in Proceedings of the Massachusetts Historical Society, 2nd Series, 13, (1900), pp. 126-7. Increase Mather, *Wo to Drunkards* (Cambridge, 1673), p. 28; *The Diary of Increase Mather*, Proceedings of the Massachusetts Historical Society, 2nd Series, 13, (1900), p. 345.

[368] See Worthington C. Ford, *The Boston Book Market, 1679-1700* (Boston, 1917), p. 149.

[369] Richard Godbeer, *The Devil's Dominion: Magic and Religion in Early New England* (New York, 1992), p. 56.

[370] Peter Lake, "Deeds against Nature: Cheap Print, Protestantism and Murder in Early Seventeenth-Century England," in Kevin Sharpe and Peter Lake, (eds), *Culture and Politics in Early Stuart England* (London, 1994), p. 270.

[371] John Trundle, *A Miracle of Miracles*, (London, 1614), in David Hall, *World of Wonders*, p. 72.

[372] Paul Boyer and Stephen Nissenbaum, (eds), *The Salem Witchcraft Papers: Verbatim Transcripts of the Legal Documents of the Salem Witchcraft Outbreak of 1692* (3 vols.; New York, 1977), 2:578.

[373] For examples of this tendency refer to Herschel Baker, *The Race of*

Time, (Toronto, 1965), pp. 57-63 and Joseph J. Morgan Jr., *Chaucer and the Theme of Mutability* (The Hague, 1961).

[374] Hall, *Worlds of Wonders*, p. 52. For further reading on these types of books, see Roger Thompson, *Unfit for Modest Ears: A Study of Pornographic, Obscene, and Bawdy Works Written or Published in England in the Second Half of the Seventeenth Century* (London, 1979) and J.L. Gaunt, "Popular fiction and the ballad market in the second half of the seventeenth century," Papers of the Bibliographical Society of America 72, (1978), pp. 1-14.

[375] Rollins, *Pack of Autolycus*, for Margery Perry, p. 146; Gabriel Harding pp. 163, 221.

[376] Benjamin Keach, *The Progress of Sin* (Boston, 1744), pp. 10, 19.

[377] John Bunyon, *Some Sighs from Hell: or The Groans of a Damned Soul* (London, 1658).

[378] Stephen Batman, *The Doome warning all men to Judgemente* (London, 1581).

[379] Thomas Beard, *The Theatre of God's Judgment* (London, 1648). Beard, who was a schoolteacher and ordained minister under Queen Elizabeth, described divine providences and demonic witchcraft within the same volume. It was so popular it eventually saw three more editions, the last being in 1648.

[380] John Downame, *The Christians Warfare Against the Devill, the World, and Flesh* (London, 1604).

[381] William Gurnall, *The Christian in Compleat Armour* (London, 1665; 1662).

[382] Michael Wigglesworth, *The Day of Doom* (Boston, 1662).

[383] John Hart's inexpensive chapbooks also found a large audience. Hart dwelt on such themes as the powers of Satan, the "threats of atheism," and the judgment of God upon sinners. See C. John Sommerville, "Popular religion in Restoration England," *University of Florida Social Science Monographs*, 59 (Gainesville, 1977), p. 45.

[384] Samuel Clarke, *A Mirrour or Looking Glasse for both Saints, and*

Sinners, held forth in some thousands of examples, 2nd edn. (London, 1654). Clarke's *Examples* was so popular that five editions of it were published, with the last one in 1671, just seventeen years before *Memorable Providences.*

[385] For a good survey of the belief in Satan's appearances as a black dog, etc., see Katharine M. Briggs, *British Folk Tales and Legends: A Sampler* (London, 1977), pp. 115-20.

386 Well after the Salem trials and Increase Mather's *Remarkable Providences*, William Turner would produce a book entitled *Compleat History of the Most Remarkable Providences, both of Judgement and Mercy, which have hapned* [sic] *in this Present Age* (London, 1697).

[387] David Hall insists that Increase and Cotton Mather both borrowed heavily from medieval to contemporary sources in their own "wonder books" on providences. See Hall, *Worlds of Wonders*, p. 88.

[388] Michael Wigglesworth, "God's controversy with New England," in *Proceedings of the Massachusetts Historical Society*, 12, (1871-3), p. 88.

[389] Godbeer, *The Devil's Dominion*, p. 75. Godbeer notes of this growing opinion of the clergy, writing, "Throughout the 1670s and 1680s, an overwhelming majority of sermons addressed the issued of spiritual decline . . . and urged new Englanders to repent."

[390] Ibid, p. 60. For an excellent treatment on this subject see: Stuart Clark, "Protestant Demonology: Sin, Superstition, and Society" in Bengt Ankarloo and Gustav Henningsen, (eds), *Early Modern European Witchcraft: Centres and Peripheries* (Oxford, 1990), pp. 45-81.

[391] Jonathan Mitchell, "Continuation of Sermons upon the Body of Divinity," (Cambridge, 1656).

[392] Increase Mather, *Essay for the Recording of Illustrious Providences* (Boston, 1684), p. 261.

[393] Increase Mather, *Angelographia* (Boston, 1696), p. 25.

[394] Kenneth Silverman, *The Life and Times of Cotton Mather* (New York, 1984), p. 88. Like Lawson, the minister at Andover, Francis Dane, also found it necessary to preach to his congregation about the dangers of the use of magic, and particularly divination, as his testimony to the Salem judges indicates. See: *Salem Witchcraft Papers*, 3:881. The manuscript has not survived. Godbeer suggests that this may indeed be the fate of a number of sermons that were preached against witchcraft during this period. See Godbeer, *Devil's Dominion*, p. 74.
[395] Godbeer, *Devil's Dominion*, p. 88.
[396] Lawson, *Christ's Fidelity the Only Shield against Satan's Malignity* (Boston, 1692), p. 65.
[397] Lawson's sermon is found in *Charles Upham's Salem Witchcraft*, 2:78-87.
[398] James F. Cooper, Jr. and Kenneth P. Minkema, (eds), *The Sermon Notebook of Samuel Parris, 1689-1694* (Boston, 1993), p. 3.
[399] Parris discovered that a member of his congregation, Mary Sibley, had instructed Tituba to make the now famous "witch-cake" for the purpose of discovering the source of the Parris family possession. For this sermon, see: "Records of the Salem-village Church," in *Danvers First Church Records*, (Microfilm Copy: Essex Institute, Salem, Massachusetts, 27 March 1692).
[400] Peter Hoffer, *The Devil's Disciples: Makers of the Salem Witchcraft Trials* (Baltimore, 1996), p. 18.
[401] David Levin, Cotton Mather, *The Young Life of the Lord's Remembrancer* (Cambridge, 1978),
p. 201.
[402] Robert Oaks, *"Perceptions of homosexuality by Justices of the Peace in Colonial Virginia,"* in The Journal of Homosexuality, 5, (1& 2), (Fall-Winter 1979/80), pp. 35-41, see p. 35.
[403] Frances Hill, *A Delusion of Satan: The Full Story of the Salem Witch Trials*, (London, 1995), p. 15.
[404] Louis Crompton explains this process as a Puritan attempt to

"form a Bible Commonwealth and to bring their laws into line with the Old Testament." See: Louis Crompton, "Homosexuals and the death penalty in colonial America," *Journal of Homosexuality*, 1, (3), (Spring 1976), pp. 277-293, see p. 279.

[405] The first list of "Capitall offences lyable to death" established in Plymouth Colony included treason, murder, witchcraft, arson, sodomy, rape, and adultery. The "Body of Laws and Liberties," adopted by the New England authorities, authorized capital punishment for twelve crimes as well. For these laws, see William Bradford's *Of Plymouth Plantation*, 1620-1647, Samuel E. Morrison, (ed.), (New York, 1975); *Records of the Governor and Company of Massachusetts Bay in New England*, (ed.), Nathaniel B. Shurtleff, (2 vols.; Boston, 1853-54); Max Farrand, (ed.), The *Laws and Liberties of Massachusetts*, (1648 edn.; repr. Cambridge, 1929).

[406] Shurtleff, *Records of the Governor and Company of Massachusetts Bay*, 2:21-22.

[407] See: William Whitmore, *The Colonial Laws of Massachusetts reprinted from the edition of 1672 . . . together with the Body of Liberties of 1641* (Boston, 1890); *Acts and Laws Passed by the Great And General Council or Assembly of the Province Of Massachusetts Bay in New-England from 1692 to 1719* (London, 1724) in British Library General Collections, ASM 79/2.

[408] Crompton, "Homosexuals and the death penalty in Colonial America," p. 288.

[409] This list is largely drawn from David D. Hall's *Witch-Hunting in Seventeenth-Century New England*, See: "Appendix: Statutes Relating to Witchcraft in New England," pp. 315-16.

[410] There are no extant records descriptive of the charges or examinations for either woman. Windsor, Connecticut, town clerk Matthew Grant, and Massachusetts governor John Winthrop's journals indicate the conviction and execution of the accused. See: John Winthrop, "History of New England, 1630-1649," in James Kendall Hosmer (ed.), *Original Narratives of Early American History*

(2 vols.; New York, 1908), 2:323 and Matthew Grant, "Diary, 1637-1654" in Archives, History and Genealogy Unit, Connecticut State Library, verso of front cover.

[411] Winthrop, *History of New England,* 1630-1649, 1:268.

[412] See Samuel Drake, (ed.), *Annals of Witchcraft, Woodward's Historical Series* (8 vols.; New York, 1869) 8:62.

[413] Poole, *Cotton Mather and Salem Witchcraft,* p. 12.

[414] Silverman, *Cotton Mather,* p. 89.

[415] Sharpe, *Instruments of Darkness,* p. 169.

[416] Nicolas Remy, *Demonolatry,* (Lyon, 1595), (ed.), Montague Summers, (New York, 1974), Book 1, chapter 15.

[417] Henri Boguet, *An Examen of Witches* (N.p. 1929), chapter 13.

[418] Perkins, *The Damned Art,* quoted in Gragg, *The Salem Witch Crisis,* p. 12.

[419] Alexander Roberts, *A Treatise of Witchcraft: Wherein Sundry Propositions are Laid Down, Plainely Discovering the Witnesse of that Damnable Art* (London, 1616), pp. 40-47.

[420] Christian Larner, *Witchcraft and Religion: The Politics of Popular Belief* (Oxford, 1984), (Published posthumously under the editorship of Alan Macfarlane). See chapter eight on "Who Were the Witches."

[421] Sharpe, *Instruments of Darkness,* p. 171.

[422] Carol Karlsen, *The Devil in the Shape of a Woman: Witchcraft in Colonial New England* (New York, 1989), p. 256. On the issue of the midwife as the common subject of witchcraft accusations, Robin Briggs challenges this notion:

The idea that midwives were commonly accused of witchcraft has proved quite untenable. . . . [S]urviving European records show very few such cases. A painstaking check of all known British cases reveals precisely two rather dubious instances in England, and fourteen out of some 3,000 accused in Scotland. In both countries midwives, far from being prime targets, are under-represented among the suspects. See Robin Briggs, *Witches and Neighbors: The Social and Cultural Context of European Witchcraft* (New York, 1996), p. 279.

[423] Elizabeth Reis, *Damned Women, Sinners and Witches in Puritan New England* (New York, 1997), preface, xvi.
[424] Ibid, pp. 5, 94. Reis specifically notes the correlation between the Devil's pact and episodes involving the demonic possession of a witch.
[425] Carol Karlsen estimates that in New England's overall history of witch prosecutions some sixty-seven out of seventy-eight accusations were brought against women by allegedly possessed women. See: Karlsen, *The Devil in the Shape of a Woman*, p. 223.
[426] Briggs, *Witches and Neighbors*, p. 259.
[427] William E. Monter notes that during the fifteenth century the number of men executed far outweighed females in the Jura region during the Waldensian Heresy. See his book, *Witchcraft in France and Switzerland: The Borderlands during the Reformation* (New York, 1976), pp. 23-24. In a similar situation, some seventy-two percent of all witches were male in the Aragonese Inquisition.
[428] Levack, *The Witch-Hunt in Early Modern Europe*, p. 125.
[429] Sharpe, *Instruments of Darkness*, p. 188.
[430] Salem *Witchcraft Papers*, 3:885.
[431] Ibid, p. 90.
[432] Peter Hoffer, *The Devil's Disciples: Makers of the Salem Witchcraft* Trials (Boston, 1996), p. 157.
[433] See Kenneth Silverman, *Selected Letters of Cotton Mather* (Baton Rouge, 1971), p. 41.
[434] Cotton Mather, *Diary of Cotton Mather*, 1681-1703, 1709-1724 (2 vols.; New York, 1957), 1:257.
[435] This passage is quoted and further described in *Cotton Mather's Diary*, 1:135.
[436] Phillip Guru, *A Glimpse of Sion's Glory: Puritan Radicalism in New England, 1620-1660* (Middletown, 1984), p. 151.
[437] Carol F. Karlsen, *The Devil in the Shape of a Woman, Witchcraft in Colonial New England* (New York, 1997), p. 123. Primary source reading on this event can be found in Humphrey Norton's account entitled *New England's Ensign: Being the Account of Cruelty, the*

Professors' Pride, and the Articles of Faith (London, 1659), pp. 5-11.
[438] Cotton Mather, *Magnalia Christi Americana* (2 vols.; London, 1702; repr. Hartford, 1853), 2:528.
[439] Mather, *Magnalia,* 2:528. Near the end of his life, Cotton Mather displayed a recurring pattern of ambidextrous reasoning by accepting the Quakers as "spiritual Friends." This occurred as Mather shifted his viewpoint in an attempt to create an ecumenical spirit in New England. See: Thomas J. Holmes, *Cotton Mather: A Bibliography of his Works,* (3 vols.; Newton, 1974), 2:564-69.
[440] Cotton Mather, *Diary,* 1:330.
[441] Ibid, 2:632.
[442] Mather's claim was that an angel he called the "Angel of Bethesda" had appeared which promised him he would accomplish great things for God in his ministry in New England. For more on this, see Kenneth Silverman's *The Life and Times of Cotton Mather,* (New York, 1984), p. 128.
[443] Mather, *Diary,* 1:585.
[444] Ibid, 1:164.
[445] Ibid, 1:164.
[446] Ibid, 1:172.
[447] Ibid, 1:172-3.
[448] Ibid, 1:155-56.
[449] Ibid, 2:99.
[450] Cotton Mather, *The Wonders of the Invisible World* (Boston, 1693), in Samuel Drake, (ed.), *The Witchcraft Delusion in New England* (3 vols.; New York, 1866; repr. 1970), 1:6.
[451] Mather, *Wonders,* 1:6.
[452] Ibid, 1:13-14.
[453] Perry Miller, *The New England Mind, Colony to Province* (Cambridge, 1953), p. 282.
[454] Mather, *Wonders,* 1:282. Perry Miller described the first part of Wonders as "reconstituted jeremiads" and the "epitome of all the pronouncements since 1689." Miller, *New England Mind,* p. 282.

[455] Ibid, 1:15.

[456] See notes on this in Cotton Mather's *Magnalia Christi Americana*, (ed.), Kenneth B. Murdock, (2 vols.; Cambridge, 1977), 2:443, n220:90.

[457] Peter Hoffer, *The Devil's Disciples* (Boston, 1996) p. 140.

[458] Cotton Mather, *Wonders*, 1:20.

[459] Barrett Wendell points out that Mather believed that Salem witchcraft was "a real attack of the Devil, permitted . . . as punishment for dabbling in sorcery and magical tricks which people had begun to allow themselves." Barrett Wendell, *Cotton Mather* (New York, 1980) p. 160.

[460] Mather, *Wonders*, 1:59.

[461] Ibid, 1:108.

[462] Kenneth Silverman, *Life and Times of Cotton Mather*, p. 47.

[463] Holmes, *Cotton Mather: A Bibliography*, 2:846.

[464] Ibid, 2:848.

[465] Ibid, 2:682.

[466] Cotton Mather, *Magnalia*, 1:95.

[467] Ibid, 1:41-2.

[468] William Bradford, *Of Plymouth Plantation, 1620-1647* (ed.), Samuel Eliot Morrison, (New York, 1952), p. 84.

[469] Roger Williams, *The Complete Writings of Roger Williams* (7 vols.; New York, 1963), 1:152.

[470] Cotton Mather, *Memorable Providences Relating to Witchcrafts and Possessions* (Boston, 1689;

2nd edn. 1691), American Antiquarian Society, Early American Imprints, 1639-1819, Microcard no.486, preface, ii, (Worcester, 1967).

[471] This would be true in spite of the fact that Cotton Mather made a diligent attempt to evangelize the Native American population for a great part of his ministerial career including translating the scriptures and his sermons for various tribes. For an excellent review of this, see Silverman, *Life and Times of Cotton Mather*, pp. 237, ff.

[472] Cotton Mather, *Wonders*, 1:95.

[473] Cotton Mather, *Magnalia*, 2:597-8.

[474] Frances Hill, *A Delusion of Satan* (London, 1995), p. 40. Hill writes,

The New Englanders' fear of the Devil was in turn rendered more concrete and powerful by their terror of the flesh-and-blood enemies with whom he was linked. Devils and spirits were not abstract ideas but creatures dwelling all around them.

[475] James E. Kences, "Some unexplored relationships of Essex County witchcraft to the Indians wars of 1675 and 1689," *Essex Institute Historical Collections*, 120, (1984), p. 191.

[476] Cotton Mather, *Magnalia*, 1:206.

[477] Paul Boyer and Steven Nissenbaum, (eds), *The Salem Witchcraft Papers: Verbatim Transcripts of the Legal Documents of the Salem Witchcraft Outbreak of 1692* (3 vols.; New York, 1977), 2:610-11.

[478] Cotton Mather, *A Brand Pluck'd Out of the Burning*, in George Lincoln Burr, (ed.), *Narratives of the Witchcraft Cases*, 1648-1706 (New York, 1914), p. 99.

[479] Found in Robert Calef's *More Wonders of the Invisible World*, in Samuel Drake, (ed.), *The Witchcraft Delusion in New England* (3 vols.; New York, 1866; repr. 1970), 3:27.

[480] Alfred A. Cave, "Indian Shamans and English Witches in Seventeenth-Century New England" in Essex Institute Historical Collections, 128, (October 1992), pp. 239-54.

[481] Mather, *Diary*, 1:150.

[482] Mather, *Diary*, 1:147.

[483] Ibid, 1:114.

[484] Ibid, 1:147.

[485] Ibid, 1:152.

[486] Silverman, *Life and Times of Cotton Mather*, p. 94.

[487] Cotton Mather, *Magnalia Christi Americana*, 1:210.

[488] Mather, *Memorable Providences*, p. 3.

[489] Ibid, p. 12.

[490] Ibid, p. 3.

[491] Ibid, p. 21.

[492] Ibid, preface, vii.

[493] Ibid, p. 44.

[494] Sarah Good was incarcerated at Boston, March 7, 1692. She was condemned by the Salem Court of Oyer and Terminer, on June 30 and executed there on July 19, 1692.

[495] Cotton Mather, *A Brand Pluck'd Out of the Burning,* in Burr, *Narratives of the Witchcraft Cases.* This
quote and the Mercy Short account, pp. 259-87.

[496] Cotton Mather, *A Brand Pluck'd Out of the Burning,* p. 261.

[497] Ibid, p. 262.

[498] Ibid, p. 273.

[499] Ibid, p. 276.

[500] Mather, Diary, 1:161.

[501] Cotton Mather never published *A Brand Pluck'd Out of the Burning,* because the backlash from the Salem trials was too great at that time. Mather explained this in the following quote taken from the above title, page 286: "No man in his wits would fully expose his thoughts unto them till the charms which enrage the people are a little better dissipated."

[502] Cotton Mather, *Another Brand Pluck'd out of the Burning,* p. 315.

[503] Ibid, p. 317.

[504] Ibid, p. 178.

[505] See Kenneth Silverman's *Selected Letters of Cotton Mather,* p. 41.

[506] Mather, *Diary,* 1:179.

[507] Silverman, *Life and Times of Cotton Mather,* p. 107.

[508] For a very thorough explanation of Jurieu and Mede's theories, see Robert Middlekauf's *The Mathers, Three Generations of Puritan Intellectuals, 1596-1728* (New York, 1971), pp. 333-50.

[509] Mede's system of prophetic interpretation centered upon the millennial expectation was first introduced in 1627 in his book,

Clavis Apocalyptica. The popularity of this first work would eventually lead to its translation into English in 1642. Mede followed this with two more forays into this realm, entitled *The Apostasy of the Latter Times* (1641) and *The Key to the Revelation* (1643). The latter did much to establish Mede as one of the foremost prophetic interpreters of his era.

[510] Stuart Clark, *Thinking with Demons: The Idea of Witchcraft in Early Modern Europe* (New York, 1997) pp. 336-37.

[511] Clark, *Thinking with Demons,* p. 349.

[512] Bernard Capp, *The Fifth Monarchy Men: A Study in Seventeenth-Century English Millenarianism* (London, 1972); Leo Solt, "The Fifth Monarch men: Politics and the Millennium," *Church History,* 30, (1961), pp. 314-24; See Also: Michael Adas, *Prophets of Rebellion: Millenarian Protest Movements against the European Colonial Order* (Chapel Hill, 1979).

[513] For a discussion of the relationship of the various separatists and millennial expectations, see Frederic J. Baumgartner, *Longing for the End: A History of Millennialism in Western Civilization* (New York, 1999), pp. 100-17.

[514] Mather, *Wonders,* 1:89.

[515] See: Holmes, *Cotton Mather: A Bibliography*, 3:84. Holmes described this attempt well:

He interpreted the history of Europe and the Christian Church to determine the probable and approximate time of the inception of the great day of peace, to which he pointed . . . "It is possible that many of Us, may Live to see the Peace of the Latter Dayes."

[516] Cotton Mather, "A Midnight Cry" (Boston, 1692), p. 24. When Cotton Mather finished this sermon, he called the Old North Church to a day of fasting held on 10 April 1692. On that day he presented the members with an instrument of repentance for their ratification, calling his church and New England to repentance and a renewed preparation for the Second Coming of Christ.

[517] Mather, *Wonders,* 1:54.

[518] Ibid, 1:72.

[519] Silverman, *Life and Times of Cotton Mather*, p. 105.

[520] Ibid, p. 105.

[521] Boyer and Nissenbaum, *Salem Witchcraft Papers*, 2:423.

[522] Ibid, 2:529.

[523] Clark, *Thinking with Demons*, p. 335.

[524] *Salem Witchcraft Papers*, 1:67.

[525] Ibid, 1:66.

[526] Richard Gildrie, "The Salem witchcraft trials as a Crisis of Popular Imagination," *Essex Institute Historical Collections*, 128, (October 1992), pp. 270-85.

[527] Ibid, 284. Gildrie gives an excellent breakdown of three phases of the Salem adjudication based upon the dates of the indictments levied against the residents of Salem and the region.

[528] Ibid, p. 16.

[529] Cotton Mather, in Silverman, *Selected Letters*, p. 40.

[530] Cotton Mather, *Wonders*, 1:200.

[531] David Koenig, *Law and Society in Puritan Massachusetts, Essex County, 1629-1692* (Chapel Hill, 1979), p. 170.

[532] Peter Hoffer, *The Devil's Disciples: Makers of the Salem Witchcraft Trials* (Baltimore, 1996), p. 133. Christina Larner convincingly describes the issues related to the "Crimen Exceptum" model of witchcraft trial procedures in her volume on Scottish witch trials. See: Christina Larner, *Enemies of God, The Witchhunt in Scotland* (Baltimore, 1981), p. 68.

[533] Koenig, *Law and Society*, p. 171.

[534] Mather had once intended to write his own manual on this subject, as indicated in *Wonders*:

I was going to make one Venture more; that is, to offer some safe Rules for the finding out of the Witches . . . but this were a Venture too Presumptuous and Icarian for me to make; I leave that unto those Excellent and Judicious Persons, with whom I am not worthy to be numbered.

See: Cotton Mather, *The Wonders of the Invisible World* (Boston, 1693), in Samuel Drake, (ed.), *The Witchcraft Delusion in New England* (New York, 1866; repr. 1970), 1:36.

[535] William Perkins, *A Discourse of the Damned Art of Witchcraft* (Cambridge, 1613); John Gaule, *Select Cases of Conscience Touching Witches and Witchcrafts* (London, 1646); Richard Bernard, *A Guide to Jurymen* (London, 1630). These discourses, where dealing with witchcraft trials, are all printed in full in Cotton Mather's *Wonders,* 1:37-48.

[536] Mather, *Wonders,* 1:36.

[537] *The Tryal of Richard Hathaway upon an Information for being a Cheat and Imposter, for endeavouring to take away the Life of Sarah Morduck [Mordike], for being a Witch* (London, 1702).

[538] Sir John Holt tried witchcraft cases in 1690, 1693, 1696, 1701, and seven others. For a discussion of the Hathaway case and Holt's supervision of the trial, see James Sharpe, *Instruments of Darkness, Witchcraft in England 1550-1750* (London, 1996), pp. 227-228.

[539] Kittredge cites the use of this evidence in trials in England and its colonies when he writes, "The fact is, and it should never be lost sight of, there was noting strange in their admitting such evidence. It was a matter of course that they should admit it." See: George Lyman Kittredge, *Witchcraft in Old and New England* (Cambridge, 1929), p. 363.

[540] This letter in its entirety is reproduced in Kenneth Silverman's *Selected Letters of Cotton Mather* (Baton Rouge, 1971), pp. 35-36.

[541] This concern is repeated in the sixth article of "The Return of the Ministers," which states,

Presumptions whereupon persons may be . . . condemned as guilty of witchcrafts, ought certainly to be more considerable than barely the accused person being represented by a Spectre unto the afflicted.

See William Frederick Poole, *Cotton Mather and Salem Witchcraft* (Cambridge, 1689), p. 32.

[542] See Kenneth Silverman, *Selected Letters of Cotton Mather,* p. 41.

[543] This advice was repeated in "The Return of Several Ministers," in article six, stating, "Nor can we esteem altercations made in the sufferers by a look or a touch of the accused to be infallible evidence of guilt, but frequently liable to be abused by the Devil's legerdemains." See: Poole, *Cotton Mather*, p. 32.

[544] Silverman, *Selected Letters of Cotton Mather*, p. 38.

[545] Larner, *Enemies of God*, pp. 107-109.

[546] As it would turn out, one clear incident of torture being used to exact a confession took place during the Salem trials. In a July 23, 1692, legal petition, John Proctor complained that his son William, as well as Richard and Andrew Carrier, had all been "tyed neck and heels till the Blood was ready to come out their noses" during their prison examinations. See: Paul Boyer and Stephen Nissenbaum, (eds), *The Salem Witchcraft Papers, Verbatim Transcripts of the Legal Documents of the Salem Witchcraft Outbreak of 1692* (3 vols.; New York, 1977), 2:689-690.

[547] Silverman, *Selected Letters*, p. 38.

[548] Ibid, p. 42.

[549] Ibid, p. 40.

[550] Boyer and Nissenbaum, *Salem Witchcraft Papers*, 1:288·

[551] Koenig, *Law and Society*, p. 173.

[552] Kenneth Silverman, *The Life And Times of Cotton Mather (*New York, 1984), p. 37.

[553] Silverman, *Selected Letters of Cotton Mather*, p. 36.

[554] For a detailed description of medieval and early modern witchcraft beliefs in Sweden, see Bengt Anklaroo, "Sweden: The Mass Burnings (1688-1676)" in Bengt Ankarloo and Gustav Henningsen, (eds), *Early Modern European Witchcraft: Centres and Peripheries* (Oxford, 1990), pp. 285-317. See also, Stuart Clark, *Thinking with Demons: The Idea of Witchcraft in Early Modern Europe* (New York, 1997), p. 185.

[555] Anklaroo, "Sweden: The Mass Burnings," p. 292.

[556] Silverman, *The Life and Times of Cotton Mather*, p. 99.

[557] For an excellent review of the case of Bridget Bishop's ordeal, see Marion Starkey's *The Devil in Massachusetts* (New York, 1950), pp. 146-57.

[558] Certainly, this was not the only factor since the accusation against Phips's wife must have provided some incentive for the governor to control the situation. Further, the growing criticism of the populace had its own impact. Phips was sensitive to the ramifications of another mob like the one that had deposed Andros in the recent past. All these must have had some part in ending the trials.

[559] Kenneth B. Murdock, in Murdock, (ed.), *Magnalia Christi Americana* (2 vols.; Cambridge, 1977), 1:11.

[560] Hoffer, *The Devil's Disciples*, p. 139.

[561] This case is given in its entirety in an article by Robert F. Oaks entitled, "Defining sodomy in seventeenth-century Massachusetts," *The Journal of Homosexuality*, 6, (1-2), (Fall/Winter 1980/81), pp. 79-83.

[562] As Robert Oaks details this situation, it was the inability of the prosecutors to prove that sexual penetration had occurred that prevented the court from being able to execute the three defendants for rape. See Oaks, "Defining Sodomy," p. 80.

[563] Two of the men had their nostrils slit upwards, and were forced to wear a rope about their necks signifying their punishment if they ever left their restricted districts. See: Oaks, "Defining Sodomy," p. 81.

[564] Cotton Mather, *Memorable Providences Related to Witchcraft Possessions* (Boston, 1691), in *American Antiquarian Society, Early American Imprints*, 1639-1800, Microcard no. 486, (Worchester, 1967).

[565] Silverman, *Selected Letters*, p. 36.

[566] Ibid, pp. 38-39.

[567] Ibid, p. 41.

[568] Ibid, p. 42. Within the same letter, Cotton Mather, sensing that at least a part of the judges were becoming worried about Stoughton's

insistence upon using spectral evidence, suggested to Foster, "It would make all matters easier if at least bail were taken for people accused only by the invisible tormentors of the poor sufferers and not blemished by any further grounds of suspicion against them."

[569] Ibid, p. 43.

[570] Ibid, p. 43.

[571] Mather, *Wonders,* 1:31.

[572] Ibid, 1:31. Francis Hill has suggested that Cotton Mather may have written this last article encouraging "Speed and Vigor" without consulting the other Boston clergy. See, Frances Hill, *A Delusion of Satan* (London, 1995), p. 165.

[573] Bernard Rosenthal points out that the only mitigating factor that may be viewed with respect to the outcome of the eighth article in "The Return" is that regardless of whatever advice Cotton Mather and the other ministers had given the court, it was the court after all, and the not the clergy, that was empowered to convict and execute the accused witches. See, Bernard Rosenthal, *Salem Story: Reading the Witch Trials of* 1692 (Cambridge, 1995), p. 70.

[574] Frances Hill, *A Delusion of Satan*, p. 165.

[575] Paul Boyer and Stephen Nissenbaum, *Salem Possessed: The Social Origins of Witchcraft* (Cambridge, 1974), p. 10.

[576] David Levin, *Cotton Mather, The Young Life of the Lord's Remembrancer* (Cambridge, 1978), p. 205.

[577] Silverman, *Life and Times of Cotton Mather*, p. 104.

[578] Ibid, p. 113. Kenneth Silverman, reflecting on the nature of the document, further notes that "Cases of Conscience" refers to works of casuistry—that is, resolutions of moral dilemmas by skilled theologians.

[579] Silverman, Sel*ected Letters*, p. 46.

[580] Perry Miller and Kenneth Silverman have taken Mather's protestations and excuse as insincere. They would insist that Increase and Cotton Mather did in fact disagree about the use of spectral evidence. Levin takes the approach that Mather's statement bears out his true views.

[581] Cotton Mather's letter to William Stoughton is reproduced in its entirety in Silverman's *Selected Letters,* pp. 43-44.

[582] Ibid, p. 44.

[583] *Letter of Sir William Phips to the Privy Council dated 12, October 1692,* in Boyer and Nissenbaum, *The Salem Witchcraft Papers,* 3:861-2.

[584] Mather, *Wonders,* preface, vi.

[585] Ibid, 1:139.

[586] Richard Nash, John Craige's *Mathematical Principles of Christian Theology* (Carbondale, 1991), introduction, xv.

[587] Philip Hicks, *Neoclassical History and English Culture: From Clarendon to Hume* (New York, 1996), p. 10.

[588] Hicks, *Neoclassical History and English Culture,* p. 11.

[589] Edward Hyde Clarendon, *The History of the Rebellion and Civil Wars in England* (ed.), W. Dunn Macray, (6 vols.; Oxford, 1849); Bishop Gilbert Burnet, *History of His Own Time,* (London, 1724; repr. 1979).

[590] Hicks, *Neoclassical History and English Culture,* p. 46.

[591] David Allen, *History of His Own Time,* introduction, vii-ix.

[592] Silverman, *Selected Letters,* pp. 43-44.

[593] Ibid, p. 45.

[594] Mather, *Wonders,* 1:139.

[595] Just the opposite was true of those cases that Mather chose not to explicate in his book. Two specific examples come to mind in this regard. Cotton Mather spent but a brief moment in the end of *Wonders* mentioning the execution of Giles Corey without admitting that spectral evidence was the main condition upon which "poor Giles Corey" was "Lately Prest to Death." See: *Salem Witchcraft Papers* 1:244. Mather also did not mention the case of Rebecca Nurse in *Wonders.* Such an example would have been contradictory, since the main reason for prosecuting Nurse was based upon evidentiary tests, including an examination of physical manifestations upon the afflicted when Nurse moved her hands or

leaned on the witness chair. For the complete account of Rebecca Nurse's trial, see Robert Calef, *More Wonders of the Invisible World* in Drake, *Witchcraft Delusion*, 3:7-33 as well as *Salem Witchcraft Papers*, 2:604.

[596] Silverman, *Selected Letters*, p. 42.

[597] Mather, *Wonders*, 1:152.

[598] Ibid, 1:187.

[599] Ibid, 1:200.

[600] Chadwick Hansen, *Witchcraft at Salem* (New York, 1969), p. 171.

[601] Mather, *Wonders*, 1:33. [Page 13 of the original manuscript].

[602] Ibid, 1:29-30.

[603] Ibid, 1:106.

[604] Ibid, 1:8. Mather is referring to the anticipated New Charter, promised by William and Mary, which was granted and received in Boston on May 14, 1692. Sir William Phips arrived with the charter and assumed his role as governor of Massachusetts.

[605] Ibid, 1:107.

[606] A statement by Silverman echoes this contention: "In writing to and about the Salem court, Cotton Mather was addressing not only judges whom he felt were abusing evidence, but simultaneously neighbors, old friends, [and] members of his church." See: Silverman, *Life and Times of Cotton Mather*, p. 102.

[607] David Levin contends that Mather's *Wonders*, in part, attempted to show "why one should still believe in the Devil's power to set witches loose on human victims, and how a well-meaning, though fallible court could have justly convicted and condemned guilty defendants." See: David Levin, "Did the Mathers disagree about the Salem witchcraft trials?," *Proceedings of the American Antiquarian Society*, 95 (I), (1985), pp. 19-37.

[608] Calef, *More Wonders the Invisible World*, 3:157.

[609] Cotton Mather, *Wonders*, 1:34.

[610] Ibid, 1:50.

[611] Ibid, preface, p. vi.

[612] Perry Miller, *The New England Mind, Colony to Province* (Cambridge, 1953), p. 294.

[613] Mather, *Wonders*, Preface, vi.

[614] Ibid, viii.

[615] Ibid, 1:152.

[616] Ibid, 1:200.

[617] As David Levin points out, the two books were taken to be opposed on the issue of spectral evidence and the trials:

Increase Mather, the father, presents a thorough argument, scriptural and rational, for excluding all evidence that is any way influenced by the Devil. Increase's son, Cotton published . . . a narrative to show how the people became perplexed . . . and how a well-meaning, though fallible court could have justly convicted and condemned guilty defendants.

See: Levin, "Did the Mathers disagree about the Salem witchcraft trials?," p. 24.

[618] See, Mather, *Diary of Cotton Mather*, 1681-1709, 1709-1724 (2 vols.; New York, 1957), 1:153.

[619] Those presenting this view are Perry Miller, Kenneth Silverman, and Kenneth Murdock, all eminent New England and Salem scholars. David Levin rejects this particular view, suggesting both Mathers cooperated in every attempt to clarify the issue of spectral evidence.

[620] Rosenthal, *Salem Story*, p. 144.

[621] *Collections of the Massachusetts Historical Society*, Vol. 5, Series 5, 1878, pages 358 - 464. For an excellent study of Samuel Sewall's role in the Salem trials, see: Ricard Francis's *Judge Sewall's Apology: The Salem Witch Trials and the Forming of an American Conscience*, (New York, 2005)

[622] Cotton Mather, *Diary*, 2:216.

[623] Ibid, 2:216.

[624] Ibid, 2:200.

[625.] Richard Lovelace. *The American Pietism of Cotton Mather*, (Grand Rapids, 1979), 290.

BIBLIOGRAPHY

Manuscripts

"A Bill Against Conjurations, Witchcraft, and Dealing with Evil and Wicked Spirits," December

1692, Massachusetts State Archives, 135 (78).

"Acts and Laws passed by the Great and General Council or Assembly of the province of Massachusetts Bay in New England from 1692 to 1719," (London, 1724), in *British Library General Collections*, ASM 79/2.

Calef, Robert, Letter to Cotton Mather dated 11 January 1693, in Samuel Drake, (ed.), *The Witchcraft Delusion in New England* (New York, 1866; repr.1970).

_____. *Letter to Cotton Mather dated 24 November 1693*, in Samuel Drake, (ed.), *The Witchcraft Delusion in New England* (New York, 1866; repr. 1970).

_____ . *Letter to Thomas Brattle dated 1 March 1694*, in Samuel Drake, (ed.), *The Witchcraft Delusion in New England* (New York, 1866; repr. 1970).

"Chronicle of the English Augustinian Canonesses Regular of the Lateran, at St. Monica's, Louvain," (ed.), A. Hamilton (1904).

Cler, Jona, "Officials' Expense Accounts for 1692, Superior Court of Judicature," in Essex County Archives, 2:82

Danckaerts, Jasper, "Journal of a Voyge to New York and a Tur of Several of the American Colonies in 1679-1680," trans. Henry C. Murphy, Memoirs of the Long Island Historical Society, 1, (1867).

Dane, Francis, "Statement on the Andover Massachusetts Witchcraft Outbreak," in Essex County Archives, 1:142.

Gifford, George, *Two Sermons upon I Peter 5, verses 8 and 9* (London, 1597).

Mather, Cotton, *A Discourse on Witchcraft* (Boston, 1689), *Collections of the Massachusetts Historical Society.*

_____. "An Account of the Method and Success of Inoculating the Small Pox," (Boston, 1721), Massachus*etts Historical Society, Early American Imprints*, 1639-1819, Evans Microfiche No. 2206, (Worcester, 1967).

_____. "Paper on Witchcraft," *Proceedings of the Massachusetts Historical Society*, 47, (1914).

_____. *The Angel of Bethesda*, (New London, 1722), *Massachusetts Historical Society, Early American Imprints*, 1639-1819, Evans Microfiche No. 2352, (Worcester, 1967).

Newton, Thomas, *Letter to Isaac Addington for Preparation of the Court of Oyer and Terminer*, 31 May 1692, *Massachusetts Archives* 1135, (25).

Norton, John, "Notes on sermons of Jonathan Mitchell, 1654-5," (1 February 1654), in the *Collections of the Massachusetts Historical Society.*

Phips, Sir William, *Letter to the Privy Council dated 12 October 1692*, in Paul Boyer and Stephen Nissenbaum, (eds), *The Salem Witchcraft Papers: Verbatim Transcripts of the Legal Document of the Salem Witchcraft Outbreak of 1692* (3 vols.; New York, 1977).

_____. *Letter to the Earl of Nottingham dated 24 May 1693*, in Paul Boyer and Stephen Nissenbaum, (eds), *The Salem Witchcraft Papers: Verbatim Transcripts of the Legal Document of the Salem Witchcraft Outbreak of 1692* (3 vols.; New York, 1977).

Records of the Governor and Company of Massachusetts Bay in New England (ed.), Nathaniel B. Shurtleff, (2 vols.; Boston, 1853-54).

"Records of the Salem-village Church, 27 March 1692," in *Danvers First Church Records*, (Microfilm Copy: Essex Institute, Salem, Massachusetts).

"Records of the Town of Easthampton," (5 vols.; New York 1887-1892).

Russell, Daniel, "Sermon Notes, 1677," in Collections of the Massachusetts Historical Society.

Suffolk County Court Files: *Original Depositions and other Materials in Proceedings of the Quarterly Courts of Suffolk County, Massachusetts*, 24, (1972).

Wigglesworth, Michael, "God's Controversy with New England," (Boston, 1662), in *Proceedings of the Massachusetts Historical Society*, 12, (3), (1871).

Unpublished Doctoral Theses

Bostridge, Ian, "Debates about Witchcraft in England, 1650-*1736*," (Oxford University Ph.D. thesis, 1990).

Davis, Patricia Henry, "Siding with the Judges: A Psychohistorical Analysis of Cotton Mather's Role in the Salem Witch Trials," (Princeton Theological Seminary Ph.D. thesis, 1992).

Trefz, Edward K., "A Study of Satan with Particular Emphasis upon the Preaching of Certain New England Puritans," (Union Theological Seminary DD thesis, 1952).

Primary Sources

Ames, William, *Fresh Suit against Ceremonies* in Ralph Bronkema, *The Essence of Puritanism*, (Rotterdam, 1929).

Bateman, Stephen, *The Doome Warning all men to Judgemente* (London, 1581).

Baxter, Richard, *The Certainty of the World of Spirits* (London, 1691).

Beard, Thomas, *The Theatre of God's Judgment* (London, 1648).

Bernard, Richard, *A Guide to Jurymen* (London, 1630).

Boulton, Richard, *An Account of the First Rise of Magicians and Witches* (London, 1715).

Bradford, William, *Of Plymouth Plantation, 1620-1647* (ed.), Samuel E. Morrison, (New York, 1975).

Browne, Sir Thomas, *Religio Medici* (Oxford, 1642).

Bunyon, John, Some *Sighs from Hell: or The Groans of a Damned Soul* (London, 1658).

Burnett, Bishop Gilbert, *History of His Own Time*, (London, 1724; repr. 1979).

Calef, Robert, *More Wonders of the Invisible World*, in Samuel Drake, (ed.), *The Witchcraft Delusion in New England* (3 vols.; New York, 1866; repr. 1970).

Clarke, Samuel, *A Mirrour or Looking Glasse for both Saints, and Sinners* 2nd edn. (London, 1654).

Craige, John, *Mathematical Principles of Christian Theology* (ed.), Richard Nash, (Carbondale, 1991).

Dalton, Michael, *Countrey Justice* 4th edn. (London, 1630).

Downame, John, *The Christians Warfare Against the Devill, the World, and Flesh* (London, 1604).

Featley, Daniel, *The Dippers Dipt, or Then Anabaptists Ducked and Plung'd Over Head and* Eares 3rd edn. (London, 1645).

Gaule, John, *Select Cases of Conscience touching Witches and Witchcraft* (London, 1646).

Grant, Matthew, *"Diary, 1637-1654"* Archives, History and Genealogy Unit, Connecticut State Library.

Gurnall, William, *The Christian in Compleat Armour* (London, 1665; 1662).

Hale, John, *A Modest Inquiry into the Nature of Witchcraft* in George Lincoln Burr, (ed.), *Narratives of the Witchcraft Cases, 1648-1706* (New York, 1914).

Holland, Henry, *Spiritual Preservatives against the Pestilence . . . chiefly collected out the 91.Psalme* (London, 1593).

Hubbard, William, *The Happiness of a People in the Wisdom of Their Rulers Directing and in the Obedience of their Brethren Attending* (Boston, 1676).

Hutchinson, Thomas, *The History of the Colony and Province of Massachusetts-Bay*, (ed.), Lawrence Shaw Mayo, (3 vols.; New York, 1970).

Keach, Benjamin, *The Progress of Sin* (Boston, 1744).

Kramer, Heinrich and Sprenger, Jacob, *Malleus Maleficarum* (1487) in Montague Summers, (ed.) *A History of Witchcraft* (New York, 1928).

Lawson, Deodat, *Christ's Fidelity the Only Shield against Satan's Malignity* (Boston, 1692).

Mather Cotton, *Diary of Cotton Mather*, 1681-1709, 1709-1724 (2 vols., New York, 1957).

_____ . *Eleutheria: or, An Idea of Reformation in England, and a History of Non-Conformity in and since that Reformation . . .* (London, 1698).

_____ . *Memorable Providences Relating to Witchcrafts and Possessions* (Boston, 1689; 2nd edn. London, 1691), in *American Antiquarian Society, Early American Imprints*, 1639-1800, Microcard no. 486, (Worcester, 1967).

_____ . *A Brand Pluck'd Out of the Burning* (Boston, 1689), in George Lincoln Burr, (ed.), *Narratives of the Witchcraft Cases*, 1648-1706 (New York, 1914).

_____ . *Speedy Repentance Urged* (Boston, 1690).

_____ . *The Present State of New England* (Boston, 1690).

_____ . *Little Flocks guarded against Grievous* Wolves (Boston, 1691).

_____ . *Things to be Look'd For* (Cambridge, 1691).

_____ . *A Midnight Cry* (Boston, 1692).

_____ . *Fair Weather* (Boston, 1692).

_____ . *Another Brand Pluck'd out of the Burning* (1693), in George Lincoln Burr, (ed.), *Narratives of the Witchcraft Cases* (New York, 1946).

_____ . *The Wonders of the Invisible World* (Boston, 1693), in Samuel Drake, (ed.), *The Witchcraft Delusion in New England* (3 vols.; New York, 1866; repr. 1970).

_____. *Batteries Upon the Kingdom of the Devil* (London, 1695).

_____. *A Good Man Making a Good End* (Boston, 1698).

_____. *The Gospel of Justification by the Righteousness of God* (Boston, 1700).

_____. *Magnalia Christi Americana* (2 vols.; London, 1702; repr. Hartford, 1853).

_____. *The Armour Of Christianity*, (Boston, 1704), in *American Antiquarian Society, Early American Imprints*, 1639-1819, Microcard no.1171, (Worcester, 1967).

Mather Increase, *Wo to Drunkards* (Cambridge, 1673).

_____. *A Brief History of the War with the Indians in New-England* (London, 1676).

_____. *An Essay for the Recording of Illustrious Providences* (Boston, 1684).

_____. *Angelographia* (1694).

_____. *The Folly of Sinning* (Boston, 1699).

_____. *The Diary of Increase Mather*, in *Proceedings of the Massachusetts Historical Society*, 2nd Series, 13, (1900).

Mede, Joseph, *Clavis Apocalyptica* (English trans. 1642).

_____. *The Apostasy of the Latter Times* (1641).

_____. *The Key to the Revelation* (1643).

Mitchell, Jonathan, *"Continuation of Sermons upon the Body of Divinity,"* (Cambridge, 1656).

Moodey, Joshua, *Soldiery Spiritualized* (Cambridge, 1673).

Norton, Humphrey, *New England's Ensign: It Being the Account of Cruelty, the Professors' Pride, and the Articles of Faith* (London, 1659).

Perkins, William, *A Discourse of the Damned Art of Witchcraft* (London, 1608) in Ian Breward (ed.), *The Works of William Perkins* (Abingdon, 1970).

_____. *A Treatise of Witchcraft: Wherein Sundry Propositions are Laid Down, Plainely Discovering the Witnesse of that Damnable Art* (London, 1616).

_____ . *A Fruitful Dialogue Concerning the End of the World in The Workes of . . . William Perkins* (3 vols.; London 1616-18), iii.

Remy, Nicolas, *Demonolatry* (Lyon, 1595), (ed.), Montague Summers (New York, 1974).

Rogers, John, *Some Account of the Life and Opinions of a Fifth-Monarchy-Man*, (ed.), Edward Rogers, (London, 1867).

Scottow, Joshua, *A Narrative of the Planting of the Massachusetts Colony Anno 1628* (Boston, 1694).

Thatcher, Peter, *The Saint's Victory and Triumph over Sin and Death* (Boston, 1696).

The Most Strange and Admirable Discoverie of the three Witches at Warboys arraigned, convicted and executed at the last Assizes at Huntingdon (London, 1593).

The Tryal of Richard Hathaway upon an Information for being a Cheat and Imposter, for endeavouring to take away the Life of Sarah Morduck [Mordike], for being a Witch (London, 1702).

Trundle, John, *A Miracle of Miracles* (London, 1614).

Turner, William, *Compleat History of the Most Remarkable Providences, both of Judgement and Mercy, which have hapned [sic] in this Present Age* (London, 1697).

Wadsworth, Benjamin, *Good Souldiers a Great Blessing* (Boston, 1700).

Wigglesworth, Michael, *The Day of Doom* (Boston, 1662; 2nd edn. Cambridge, 1666), in *American Antiquarian Society, Early American Imprints*, 1639-1800, Evans Microfiche no. 112, (Worcester, 1967).

_____ . "God's Controversy with New England," (Boston, 1662), in *Proceedings of the Massachusetts Historical Society* 1871-3, (88).

Willard, Samuel, *The Child's Portion* (Boston, 1684).

_____ . *A Compleat Body of Divinity in Two Hundred and Fifty Expository Lectures . . .* (Boston, 1726).

Williams, John, *Warning to the Unclean* (Boston, 1699).

Williams, Roger, *The Complete Writings of Roger Williams* (7 vols.; New York, 1963).

Winthrop, John, "History of New England, 1630-1649," in James Hosmer, (ed.), *Original Narratives of Early American History* (2 vols.; New York, 1908).

Secondary Sources

Adams, James Truslow, *The Founding of New England* (Boston, 1921).

Adas, Michael, *Prophets of Rebellion: Millenarian protest Movements against the European Colonial Order* (Chapel Hill, 1979).

Anderson, Robert D., "The history of witchcraft: A review with some psychiatric comments," *American Journal of Psychiatry*, 126, (1970).

Anklaroo, Bengt, "Sweden: The Mass Burnings (1668-1676)," in Bengt Ankarloo and Gustav Henningsen, (eds), *Early Modern European Witchcraft: Centres and Peripheries* (Oxford, 1990).

Baker, Emerson W., *A Storm of Witchcraft: The Salem Trials and the American* Experience (New York, 2014).

Baker, Herschel, *The Race of Time* (Toronto, 1965).

Bancroft, George, *History of the United States of America from the Discovery of The Continent* (Boston, 1879).

Barstow, Anne, "Women as healers, women as witches," *Old Westbury Review*, 2, (1986).

_____. "On studying witchcraft as women's history: A historiography of the European witch persecutions," *Journal of Feminist Studies in Religion* 4, (1988).

Baumgartner, Frederick J., *Longing for the End: A History of Millennialism in Western Civilization* (New York, 1999).

Ben-Yehuda, Nachman, "The witch-craze of the fourteenth to seventeenth centuries: A sociologist's perspective," *American Sociological Journal*, 86, (1980).

_____ . *Deviance and Moral Boundaries: Witchcraft, the Occult, Science Fiction, Deviant Science and Scientists* (Chicago, 1985).

Bercovitch, Sacvan, *The Puritan Origins of the American Self* (New Haven, 1975).

_____ . *The American Jeremiad* (Madison, 1978).

Boas, Ralph, *Cotton Mather* (New York, 1928).

Boguet, Henri, *An Examen of Witches* (N.p. 1929).

Boyer, Paul, and Nissenbaum, Stephen, *Salem Possessed: The Social Origins of Witchcraft* (Cambridge, 1974).

_____ . (eds), *The Salem Witchcraft Papers: Verbatim Transcripts of the Legal Document of the Salem Witchcraft Outbreak of 1692* (3 vols.; New York, 1977).

Bozeman, Theodore Dwight, *To Live Ancient Lives: The Primitivist Dimension in Puritanism* (Chapel Hill, 1998).

Bragdon, Kathleen, *Native People of Southern New England, 1500-1650* (Norman, 1996).

Braithewaite, William C., *The Beginnings of Quakerism* (New York, 1923).

Brauner, Sigrid, *Fearless Wives and Frightened Shrews: The Construction of the Witch in Early Modern Germany* (Amherst, 1995).

Breen, Timothy, and Foster, Stephen, "The Puritans' greatest achievement: A study of social cohesion in seventeenth-century Massachusetts," *Journal of American History*, 60, (1973).

Briggs, Katharine M., *British Folk Tales and Legends: A Sampler* (London, 1977).

Briggs, Robin, *Witches and Neighbors, The Social and Cultural Context of European Witchcraft* (New York, 1996).

Brown, Kathleen M., *Good Wives, Nasty Wenches, and Anxious Patriarchs: Gender, Race, and Power in Colonial Virginia* (Chapel Hill, 1996).

Burke, Peter, "A Question of Acculturation?," in Paola Zambelli, (ed.), *Scienze, Credinze Oculte, Livellie Di Cultura* (Florence, 1982).

_____ . "The Comparative Approach to European Witchcraft," in Bengt Ankarloo and Gustav Henningsen, (eds), *Early Modern European Witchcraft: Centres and Peripheries* (Oxford, 1990).

Burr, George Lincoln, *Narratives of the Witchcraft Cases, 1648-1706* (New York, 1952).

Capp, Bernard, *The Fifth Monarchy Men: A Study in Seventeenth-Century English Millenarianism* (London, 1972).

Caporael, Linnda R., "Ergotism: The Satan loosed in Salem?" *Science*, 192, (April 1976).

Caldwell, Patricia, *The Puritan Conversion Narrative: The Beginnings of American Expression* (Cambridge, 1983).

Caulfield, Ernest, "Pediatric aspects of the Salem witchcraft tragedy," *American Journal of Diseases of Children*, 65, (May 1943).

Cave, Alfred A., "Indian shamans and English witches in seventeenth-century New England," in Essex Institute of Historical Collections, 128, (4), (October 1992).

Chamberlain, Richard, *Lithobolia*, (London, 1698), in George Lincoln Burr, (ed.), *Narratives of the Witchcraft Cases, 1648-1706* (New York, 1914).

Clark, Stuart, *Thinking with Demons: The Idea of Witchcraft in Early Modern Europe* (New York, 1997).

_____ . "Protestant Demonology: Sin Superstition, and Society (c. 1520-c.1630)," in Bengt Ankarloo and Gustav Henningsen, (eds), *Early Modern European Witchcraft: Centres and Peripheries* (Oxford, 1990).

Clarendon, Edward Hyde, *The History of the Rebellion and Civil Wars in England* (ed.), W. Dunn Macray, (6 vols.; Oxford, 1849).

Cohen, Charles Lloyd, *God's Caress: The Psychology of Puritan Religious Experience* (New York, 1986).

Condren, Mary, *The Serpent and the Goddess: Women, Religion, and Power in Celtic Ireland* (San Francisco, 1989).

Cooper, James F. Jr., and Minkema, Kenneth P., (eds), *The Sermon Notebook of Samuel Parris, 1689-1694* (Boston, 1993).

Coudert, Allison, "They Myth of the Improved Status of Protestant Women: The Case of the Witchcraze," in Jean Brink et al., (eds), *The Politics of Gender in Early Modern Europe* (Kirkville, 1989).

Crane, Elaine Forman, *Ebb Tide in New England: Women, Seaports, and Social Change 1630-1800* (Boston, 1998).

Crompton, Louis, "Homosexuals and the death penalty in Colonial America," *Journal of Homosexuality, 1*, (3), (Spring, 1976).

Chrisman, Miriam, *Lay Culture, Learned Culture: Books and Social Change in Strausberg 1480-1599* (New Haven, 1982).

Ceard, Jean, *La Nature et les Prodiges: L'insolite au XVI siecle en France* (Geneva, 1977).

Davies, John, *A History of Southampton* (Southampton, 1883).

Dayton, Cornelia Hughes, "Taking the trade: abortion and gender relations in an eighteenth-century New England village," *William and Mary Quarterly*, 3rd series, 48:1 (January 1991).

Delbanco, Andrew, "The Puritan Errand Re-viewed," *Journal of American Studies*, 18, (1984).

Demos, John, *Entertaining Satan: Witchcraft and the Culture of Early New England* (New York, 1982).

Dolan, Francis E., *Dangerous Familiars: Representations of Domestic Crime in England 1550-1700* (New York, 1995).

Dow, George Francis, (ed.), *Records and Files of the Quarterly Court of Essex County, Massachusetts*, 1636-1683, (8 vols.; Essex Institute, 1911-1921).

Drake, Samuel, *The Witchcraft Delusion in New England* (New York, 1866; reprint, 1970).

_____ . *Annals of Witchcraft* (New York, 1869).

Ehrenreich, Barbara, and English, Deirdre, Witches, *Midwives, and Nurses: A History of Women Healers* (Old Westbury, 1973).

Elliot, Emory, in Sacvan Bercovitch, (ed.), *The Cambridge History of American Literature* (3 vols.; Cambridge, 1994).

Erikson, Kai T., *Wayward Puritans: A Study in the Sociology of Deviance (*New York, 1966).

Estes, Leland T., "The medical origins of the European witch-craze: A hypothesis," *Journal of Social History*, (Winter, 1983).

_____ . "Incarnations of evil: Changing perspectives on the European witch-craze," *Clio*, 13, (1984).

Ewen, Cecil L., *Witchcraft and Demonaniam: A Concise Account Derived From Sworn Depositions and Confessions Obtained in the Courts of England and Wales* (London, 1933).

Farrand, Max, (ed.), *The Laws and Liberties of Massachusetts* (1648 edn.; repr. Cambridge, 1929).

Forbes, Thomas Rodgers, *The Midwife and the Witch* (New Haven, 1966).

Ford, Worthington C., *The Boston Book Market, 1679-1700* (Boston, 1917).

Francis, Richard, *Judge Sewall's Apology: The Salem Witch Trials and the Forming of an American Conscience*, (New York, 2005)

Freud, Sigmund, "A Seventeenth-century Demonological Neurosis," in *Standard Edition of the Complete Psychological Works of Sigmund Freud* (4 vols.; London, 1961), preface, xix.

Fuller, Thomas, (ed.), *The Works of Henry Smith: Including Sermons, Treatises, Prayers, and Poems*, (2 vols.; Edinburgh, 1867).

Garrett, Clarke, *Spirit Possession and Popular Religion: From the Camisards to the Shakers* (Baltimore, 1987).

Gaunt, J.L., "Popular Fiction and the Ballad Market in the Second half of the Seventeenth Century," Papers of the Bibliographical Society of America, 72, (1978).

Gildrie, Richard, "The Salem witchcraft trials as a crisis of popular imagination," in *Essex Institute Historical Collections*, 128, (4), (October, 1992).

Ginzburg, Carlo, Ecstasies: *Deciphering the Witches Sabbat* (London, 1991).

_____ . The Night Battles: *Witchcraft and Agrarian Cults in the 16th and 17th Centuries* (London, 1983).

_____ . "The Witches Sabbat: Popular Culture or Inquisitorial Stereotype," in Stephen L. Kaplan (ed.), *Understanding Popular Culture Europe from the Middle Ages to the Nineteenth Century* (Berlin, 1984).

Godbeer, Richard, *The Devil's Dominion: Magic and Religion in Early New England* (New York, 1992).

Gowing, Laura, "Gender and the language of insult in early modern London, " in *History Workshop*, 35, (Spring 1993).

_____ . "Secret births and infanticide in seventeenth-century England," *Past and Present*, 156, (August 1997).

Gragg, Larry, *The Salem Witch Crisis* (New York, 1992).

Gummere, Amelia Mott, *Witchcraft and Quakerism: As Study of Social History* (Philadelphia, 1908).

Gura, Phillip F., *A Glimpse of Sion's Glory: Puritan Radicalism in New England*, 1620-1660 (Middletown, 1984).

Hall, David D., *Worlds of Wonder, Days of Judgment: Popular Religious Belief in Early New England* (New York, 1989).

Hansen, Chadwick, *Witchcraft at Salem* (New York, 1969).

Harley, David, "Explaining Salem: Calvinist psychology and the diagnosis of possession, " *American Historical Review*, 101, (1996).

Harner, Michael J., *Hallucinogens and Shamanism* (New York, 1974).

Hawthorne, Nathaniel, *Alice Doane's Appeal*, (1843), in Kenneth Silverman, *The Life and Times of Cotton Mather* (New York, 1984).

Henningsen, Gustav, "The Ladies from Outside: An Archaic Pattern of the Witches' Sabbath," in Bengt Ankarloo and Gustav Henningsen, (eds), *Early Modern European Witchcraft: Centres and Peripheries* (Oxford, 1990).

Hester, Marianne, *Lewd Women and Wicked Witches: A Study of the Dynamics of Male Domination* (London, 1992).

_____. "Patriarchal Reconstruction and Witch Hunting," in Jonathan Barry, et al., (eds), *Witchcraft in Early Modern Europe: Studies in Culture and Belief* (Cambridge, 1996).

Hickey, Sally, (Parkin) "Fatal feeds? Plants, livestock losses and witchcraft accusations in Tudor and Stuart Britain," *British Journal of Folklore*, 101, (ii), (1990).

Hicks, Philip, *Neoclassical History and English Culture: From Clarendon to Hume* (New York, 1996).

Hill, Frances, *A Delusion of Satan* (London, 1995).

Hoffer, Peter, *The Devil's Disciples: Makers of the Salem Witchcraft Trials* (Baltimore, 1996).

Holmes, Thomas J., *Cotton Mather: A Bibliography of His Works* (3 vols.; Newton, 1974).

Ingram, Martin, *Church Courts, Sex and Marriage in England, 1570-1640* (Cambridge, 1987).

Jackson, Louise, "Witches, wives, and mothers: Witchcraft persecution and women's confessions in seventeenth-century England," *Women's History Review*, 4, (1995).

Johnson, Clifton, *Old-Time Schools and School-Books* (New York, 1963).

Kamensky, Jane, *Governing the Tongue: The Politics of Speech in Early New England* (New York, 1997).

_____. "*Words, witches, and woman trouble: Witchcraft, disorderly speech, and gender boundaries in Puritan New England*," in Essex Institute of Historical Collections, 128, (4), (October 1992).

Karlsen, Carol, *The Devil in the Shape of a Woman, Witchcraft in Colonial New England* (New York, 1989).

Kences, James E., "*Some unexplored relationships of Essex County witchcraft to the Indians wars of 1675 and 1689*," *Essex Institute Historical Collections*, 120, (1984).

Kibbey Ann "Mutations of the supernatural: Witchcraft, remarkable providences, and the power of Puritan men," *American Quarterly*, 34, (1982).

Kittredge, George L., "Notes on witchcraft," in *Proceedings of the American Antiquarian Society*, XVIII, (April 1907).

_____. *Witchcraft in Old and New England* (Cambridge, 1929).

Koenig, David, *Law and Society in Puritan Massachusetts, Essex County, 1629-1692* (Chapel Hill, 1979).

Lake, Peter, "Deeds against Nature: Cheap Print, Protestantism and Murder in Early Seventeenth-Century England," in Kevin Sharpe and Peter Lake, (eds), *Culture and Politics in Early Stuart England* (London, 1994).

Larner, Christina, *The Enemies of God: The Witch-hunt in Scotland* (London, 1981).

_____. *Witchcraft and Religion: The Politics of Popular Belief* (ed.), Alan MacFarlane, (Oxford, 1984).

Lebsock, Suzanne, *The Free Women of Petersburg: Status and Culture in a Southern Town* (New York, 1984).

Lessa, William A., and Vogt, Evon Z., (eds), *Reader in Comparative Religion: An Anthropological Approach* 3d edn. (New York, 1972).

Levack, Brian P., *The Witch-hunt in Early Modern Europe* (New York, 1987), preface, ix.

Levin, David, Cotton Mather, *The Young Life of the Lord's Remembrancer* (Cambridge, 1978).

_____. "Did the Mathers disagree about the Salem witchcraft trials?" *Proceedings of the American Antiquarian Society*, 95, (1), (1985).

Lise, Michele Tarter, *Clio*, 28, (1), (Fall '98).

Lovelace, Richard E., *The American Pietism of Cotton Mather* (Grand Rapids, 1979).

Lowell, Robert, "New England and Further," in Kenneth Silverman, *The Life and Times of Cotton Mather* (New York, 1984).

MacDonald, Michael, *Mystical Bedlam: Madness, Anxiety and Healing in Seventeenth-Century England* (Cambridge, 1981).

MacFarlane, Alan, *Witchcraft in Tudor and Stuart England: A Regional and Comparative* Study (New York, 1970).

MacKenney, Richard, *Sixteenth Century Europe Expansion and Conflict* (Handsmill, 1993).

Malcomson, Robert, "Infanticide in the Eighteenth Century," in James Cockburn (ed.), *Crime in England, 1500-1800* (Princeton, 1977).

Mancall, Peter C. and Merrell, James H., (eds), *American Encounters: Natives and Newcomers from European Contact to Indian Removal, 1500-1850* (Boston, 1999).

Mappen, Marc, *Witches and Historians: Interpretations of Salem* (Malabar, 1996).

Martin, Ruth, *Witchcraft and the Inquisition in Venice, 1550-1650* (Oxford, 1989).

Masters, Robert, *Eros and Evil: The Sexual Psychopathology of Witchcraft* (New York, 1962).

Merchant, Carolyn, *The Death of Nature: Women, Ecology, and the Scientific* Revolution (San Francisco, 1980).

Merrifield, Ralph, "Witch bottles and magical jugs," *British Journal of Folklore*, 66, (1955).

_____. *The Archaeology of Ritual and Magic* (London, 1988).

Midlefort, H.C. Erik, Witch-*Hunting in Southwestern Germany 1562-1684* (Stanford, 1972).

Middlekauff, Robert, *The Mathers: Three Generations of Puritan Intellectuals* (New York, 1971).

Middleton, John, (ed.), *Magic, Witchcraft, and Curing* (Austin, 1967).

Miller, Perry, *The New England Mind: From Colony to Province* (Cambridge, 1953).

Morse, Samuel Eliot, *The Intellectual Life of Colonial New England* 4th edn. (New York, 1970).

Monter, William E., *Witchcraft in France and Switzerland The Borderlands During the Reformation* (New York, 1976).

Moore, Robert, *The Formation of a Persecuting Society: Power and Deviance in Western Europe, 950-1250* (Oxford, 1987).

Morgan, Joseph J. Jr, *Chaucer and the Theme of Mutability* (The Hague, 1961).

Muchembled, Robert, *Popular Culture and Elite Culture in Early Modern France* (Baton Rouge, 1985).

Murray, Margaret, *The Witch-Cult in Western Europe: A Study in Anthropology* (Oxford, 1921).

Murdock, Kenneth B., (ed.), *Magnalia Christi Americana* (2 vols.; Cambridge, 1977).

Norton, John, "Notes on Sermons of Jonathan Mitchell, 1654-5," Massachusetts Historical Society, (1 February 1654).

Oaks, Robert, F., "Perceptions of homosexuality by Justices of the Peace in Colonial Virginia," *Journal of Homosexuality*, 5, (1-2), (Fall-Winter, 1979/80).

_____ . "Defining sodomy in seventeenth-century Massachusetts," *Journal of Homosexuality*, 6, (1-2), (Fall/Winter, 1980/81).

O'Neil, Mary, "Magical Healing, Love Magic and the Inquisition in Late Sixteenth-Century Modena," in Stephen Haliczer (ed.), *Inquisition and Society in Early Modern Europe* (London, 1986).

Parrington, Vernon Louis, *Main Currents in American Thought* (New York, 1954).

Pestana, Carla Gardina, "The city upon a hill under siege: The Puritan perception of the Quaker threat to Massachusetts Bay, 1656-1661," *The New England Quarterly*, 56, (September 1983).

Peterson, Mark A., *The Price of Redemption: The Spiritual Economy of Puritan New England* (Stanford, 1997).

Poole, William Frederick, *Cotton Mather and Salem Witchcraft* (Cambridge, 1689).

Quaife, Geoffrey, *Godly Zeal and Furious Rage* (London, 1987).

Reid, Bethany, "Unfit for light: Anne Bradstreet's monstrous birth," *The New England Quarterly*, 71, (December, 1998).

Reis, Elizabeth, *Damned Women, Sinners and Witches in Puritan New England* (New York, 1997).

_____. "Witches, Sinners, and the Underside of Covenant Theology," *Essex Institute Historical Collections*, 129, (1993).

Ricard, Laura, "New England Puritan studies in the 1970s," *Fides et Historia*, 15, (1982).

Roach, Marilynne, *Six Women of Salem: The Untold Story of the Accused and Their Accusers in the Salem Witch Trials*, (Boston, 2013)

Round, Phillip H., *By Nature and Custom Cursed: Transatlantic Civil Discourse and New England Cultural Production, 1620-1660* (Hanover, 1999).

Robbins, Rossell, *The Encyclopedia of Witchcraft and Demonology* (London, 1959).

Rollins, Hyder Edward, (ed.), *The Pack of Autolycus* (Cambridge, 1969).

Roper, Hugh-Trevor, *The European Witch-craze of the 16th and 17th Centuries* (Harmondsworth, 1969).

Roper, Lyndal, *Oedipus and the Devil: Witchcraft, Sexuality and Religion in Early Modern Europe* (London, 1994).

Rosenthal, Bernard, *Salem Story: Reading the Witch Trials of 1692* (Cambridge, 1995).

Rowland, Robert, "Fantasticall and Devilshe Persons: European Witch-beliefs in Comparative Perspective," in Bengt Ankarloo and Gustav Henningsen, (eds), *Early Modern European Witchcraft: Centres and Peripheries* (Oxford, 1990).

Rumsey, Peter Lockwood, *Acts of God and of the People, 1620-1730* (Ann Arbor, 1986).

Schoenenman, Thomas, J., "The role of mental illness in the European witch-hunts of the 16th and 17th centuries: An assessment," *Journal of Behavioral Sciences*, 13, (1977).

Schiff, Stacy, *The Witches: Suspicion, Betrayal and Hysteria in 1692 Salem* (New York, 2015)

Schulte, Regina, *The Village in Court: Arson, Infanticide and Poaching in the Court Records of Upper Bavaria, 1848-1910* trans. Barrie Selman, (Cambridge, 1994).

Scribner, Bob, "Witchcraft and judgment in Reformation Germany," *History Today*, (April 1990).

Selement, George, "The meeting of elite and popular minds at Cambridge, New England, 1638-1645," *William and Mary Quarterly*, 3d series, 41, (1984).

Sharpe, James, *Instruments of Darkness: Witchcraft in England, 1550-1750* (London, 1996).

Silverman, Kenneth, *Selected Letters of Cotton Mather* (Baton Rouge, 1971).

_____. *The Life and Times of Cotton Mather* (New York, 1984).

Solt, Leo, "The Fifth Monarch men: Politics and the Millennium," Church History, 30, (1961).

Sommerville, C. John, "Popular religion in Restoration England," *University of Florida Social Science Monographs*, 59, (Gainesville, 1977).

Spanos, Nicholas, and Gotlieb, Jack, "Ergotism and the Salem village witch trials," *Science*, 194, (24 December 1976).

Spanos, Nicholas, "Witchcraft and social history: An essay review," *Journal of the History of the Behavioral Sciences*, 21, (1985).

Starkey, Marion L., *The Devil in Massachusetts, A Modern Inquiry into the Salem Witch Trials* (New York, 1949).

Hambrick-Stowe, Charles E., *The Practice of Piety: Puritan Devotional Disciplines in Seventeenth- Century New England* (Chapel Hill, 1982).

Tambiah, Stanley Jeyaraja, *Magic, Science, Religion, and the Scope of Rationality* (New York, 1999).

Taylor, Edward, *Harmony of the Gospels*, (eds), Thomas M. and Virginia L. Davis, (3 vols.; Delmar, 1983).

Taylor, John, *The Witchcraft Delusion in Colonial Connecticut 1647-1697* (New York, 1908).

Thomas, Keith, *Religion and the Decline of Magic* (New York, 1971).

Thompson, Janet, *Wives, Widows, Witches, and Bitches: Women in Seventeenth Century Devon* (New York, 1993).

Thompson, Roger, *Unfit for Modest Ears: A Study of Pornographic, Obscene, and Bawdy Works Written or Published in England in the Second Half of the Seventeenth Century* (London, 1979).

Upham, William P., "Remarks," *Proceedings of the Massachusetts Historical Society*, 2nd Series, (13), (1900).

Upham, Charles, *Salem Witchcraft* (2 vols.; Boston, 1867).

Vaughan, Alden T., and Clark, Edward W., (eds), *Puritans among the Indians: Accounts of Captivity and Redemption, 1676-1724* (Cambridge, 1981).

Veysey, Laurence, "Intellectual History and the New Social History," in John Higham and Paul Conkin, (eds), *New Directions in American Intellectual History* (Baltimore, 1979).

Weisner, Merry, *Women and Gender in Early Modern Europe* (Cambridge, 1993).

Weisman, Richard, *Witchcraft, Magic, and Religion in Seventeenth-Century Massachusetts* (Amherst, 1984).

Wendell, Barrett, *Cotton Mather* (New York, 1980).

Whitmore, William, *The Colonial Laws of Massachusetts reprinted from the edition of 1672 . . . together with the Body of Liberties of 1641* (Boston, 1890).

Willis, Deborah, *Malevolent Nurture: Witch-Hunting and Maternal Power in Early Modern England* (New York, 1995).

Winship, Michael P., *Seers of God: Puritan Providentialism in the Restoration and Early Enlightenment* (Baltimore, 1996).

Wood, Joseph S., *The New England Village* (Baltimore, 1997).

Wright, Anthony, *The Counter Reformation: Catholic Europe and the Non-Christian World* (London, 1982).

Yool, George Malcolm, *The 1692 Witch Hunt: The Layman's Guide to the Salem Witchcraft Trials* (Bowie, 1992).

Zilboorg, Gregory, *The Medical Man and the Witch During the Renaissance* (New York, 1969).

Lightning Source UK Ltd.
Milton Keynes UK
UKHW011348050620
364504UK00002B/370

Fact And Fiction: A Collection Of Stories

Lydia Maria Francis Child

Entered, according to Act of Congress, in the year 1846,
BY C. S. FRANCIS & CO.
In the Clerk's Office of the District Court for the Southern District of New-York.

Printed by
MUNROE & FRANCIS,
BOSTON.

TO

ANNA LORING,

THE CHILD OF MY HEART,

This Volume

IS AFFECTIONATELY INSCRIBED.

Printing Statement:

Due to the very old age and scarcity of this book, many of the pages may be hard to read due to the blurring of the original text, possible missing pages, missing text, dark backgrounds and other issues beyond our control.

Because this is such an important and rare work, we believe it is best to reproduce this book regardless of its original condition.

Thank you for your understanding.

CONTENTS.

The Children of Mount Ida, ... 9
The Youthful Emigrant, ... 40
The Quadroons, ... 61
The Irish Heart, ... 77
A Legend of the Apostle John, ... 91
The Beloved Tune, ... 116
Elizabeth Wilson, ... 126
The Neighbour-in-Law, . : 149
She waits in the Spirit-Land, ... 163
A Poet's Dream of the Soul, ... 177
The Black Saxons, ... 199
Hilda Silfverling, ... 205
Rosenglory, ... 241
A Legend of the Falls of St. Anthony, ... 261
The Brothers, ... 275

THE CHILDREN OF MOUNT IDA.

"Spirit, who waftest me where'er I will,
And seest, with finer eyes, what infants see,
Feeling all lovely truth,
With the wise health of everlasting youth,
Beyond the motes of bigotry's sick eye,
Or the blind feel of false philosophy—
O Spirit, O Muse of mine,
Frank, and quick-dimpled to all social glee,
And yet most sylvan of the earnest Nine—
O take me now, and let me stand
On some such lovely land,
Where I may feel me as I please,
In dells among the trees."

In very ancient times there dwelt, among the Phrygian hills, an old shepherd and shepherdess, named Mygdomus and Arisba. From youth they had tended flocks and herds on the Idean mountains. Their only child, a blooming boy of six years, had been killed by falling from a precipice. Arisba's heart overflowed with maternal instinct, which she yearned inexpressibly to lavish on some object; but though they laid many offerings on the altars of the gods, with fervent supplications, there came to them no other child.

Thus years passed in loneliness, until one day, when Mygdomus searched for his scattered flock among the hills, he found a babe sleeping under the shadow of a plane tree. The grass bore no marks of footsteps, and how long he had lain there it was impossible to conjecture. The shepherd shouted aloud, but heard only echoes in the solitude of the mountains. He took the child tenderly in his arms, and conveyed it to Arisba, who received it gladly, as an answer to her prayers. They nurtured him with goat's milk, and brought him up among the breezes of the hills, and the boy grew in strength and beauty. Arisba cherished him with exceeding love, but still her heart was not quite satisfied.

"If he had but a sister to play with him," said she, "it would be so pleasant here under the trees."

The boy was three years old, and beautiful as a morning in spring, when his foster-parents carried him down to the plains, to a great festival of Bacchus, held during the vintage. It was a scene of riot and confusion; but the shepherd loved thus to vary the loneliness of his mountain life, and Arisba fondly desired to show her handsome boy, with his profusion of dark glossy curls bound in a fillet of ivy and grape leaves. Her pride was abundantly satisfied; for everywhere among the crowd the child attracted attention. When the story was told of his being found in the mountain forest, the women said he must have been born of Apollo and Aurora, for only they could produce such beauty. This gossip reached the ears of an old woman, who came hobbling on her crutch, to look at the infant prodigy.

"By the Adorable! he *is* a handsome boy," said she; "but come with me, and I too will show you something for the Mother of Love to smile upon."

She led the way to her daughter, who, seated under a tree, apart from the multitude, tended a sleeping babe.

"By the honey sweet! isn't *she* pretty, too?" exclaimed the old woman, pointing to the lovely infant, whose rosy lips were slowly moving, as if she suckled in her dreams. "My son, who hunts among the hills, found her on the banks of the Cebrenus, with one little foot dipped in the stream. Methinks the good Mountain Mother scatters children on our Phrygian hills, as abundant as the hyacinths."

"Then she is not your own?" eagerly inquired Arisba.

"No; and, pretty as she is, I do not want her, for I have ten. But what can I do? One must not leave babes to be devoured by wild beasts."

"Oh, give her to me," cried Arisba: "My boy so needs a playmate."

The transfer was readily made; and the child-loving matron, rejoicing in her new treasure, soon after left the revellers, and slowly wended her way back to the silent hills.

A cradle of bark and lichen, suspended between two young olive trees, held the babe, while Arisba, seated on a rock, sung as she plied the distaff. The boy at her side built small altars of stones, or lay at full length on the grass, listening to the gurgling brook, or watching the shadows at their play. Thus peacefully grew these little ones, amid all harmonies of sight and sound; and the undisturbed beauty of nature, like a pervading soul, fashioned their outward growth into fair proportions and a gliding grace.

For a long time they had no names. They were like unrecorded wild flowers, known at sight, on which the heart heaps all sweet epithets. Their foster-parents spoke of them to strangers as the Forest-found, and the River-child. A lovelier picture could not be imagined, than these fair children, wreathing their favourite kid with garlands, under the shadow of the trees, or splashing about, like infant Naiades, in the mountain brook. On the hill side, near their rustic home, was a goat's head and horns, bleached by sun and winds. It had been placed on a pole to scare the crows; and as it stood there many a year, the myrtle had grown round it, and the clematis wreathed it with flowery festoons, like the architectural ornaments of a temple. A thrush had built her nest between the horns; and a little rill gushed from the rock, in a cleft of which the pole was fastened. Here the boy loved to scoop up water for his little playmate to drink from his hand; and as they stood thus under the vines, they seemed like children of the gods. But the most beautiful sight was to see them kneeling hand in hand before the altar of Cybele, in the grove, with wreaths about their heads and garlands in their hands, while the setting sun sprinkled gold among the shadow-foliage on the pure white marble. Always they were together. When the boy was strong enough to bend a bow, the girl ran ever by his side to carry his arrows; and then she had a smaller arrow for herself, with which she would shoot the flowers from their stems, as skilfully as Cupid himself.

As they grew older, they came under the law of utility; but this likewise received a poetic charm from their free and simple mode of life. While the lad tended the flocks, the maiden sat on a rock at his feet, spinning busily while she sang summer melodies to the warblings of his flute. Sometimes, when each tended flocks on separate hills, they relieved the weary hours by love messages sent through the air on the wings of music. His Phrygian flute questioned her with bold bright voice, and sweetly answered her Lydian pipe, in mellow tones, taking their rest in plaintive cadences. Sometimes they jested sportively with each other; asking mischievous questions in fragments of musical phrases, the language of which could be interpreted only by themselves. But more frequently they spoke to each other deeper things than either of them comprehended; struggling aspirations towards the infinite, rising and lowering like tongues of flame; half uttered, impassioned prophecies of emotions not yet born; and the wailing voice of sorrows as yet unknown.

In the maiden especially was the vague but intense expression of music observable. In fact, her whole being was vivacious and impressible in the extreme; and so transparent were her senses, that the separation between earthly and spiritual existence seemed to be of the thinnest and clearest crystal. All noises were louder to her than to others, and images invisible to them were often painted before her on the air, with a most perfect distinctness of outline and brilliancy of colouring. This kind of spirit-life was indicated in her face and form. Her exquisitely beautiful countenance was remarkably lucid, and her deep blue eyes, shaded with very long dark fringes, had an intense expression, as if some spirit from the inner shrine looked through them. Her voice was wonderfully full of melodious inflexions, but even in its happiest utterance had a constant tendency to slide into sad modulations. The outline of her slight figure swayed gracefully to every motion, like a young birch tree to the breath of gentle winds ; and its undulations might easily suggest the idea of beauty born of the waves.

Her companion had the perfection of physical beauty. A figure slender but vigorous ; a free, proud carriage of the head, glowing complexion ; sparkling eyes, voluptuous mouth, and a pervading expression of self-satisfaction and joy in his own existence. A nature thus strong and ardent, of course exercised a powerful influence over her higher but more ethereal and susceptible life. Then, too, the constant communion of glances and sounds, and the subtle influence of atmosphere and scenery, had so intertwined their souls, that emotions in the stronger were felt by the weaker, in vibrations audible as a voice. Near or distant, the maiden felt whether her companion's mood were gay or sad ; and she divined his thoughts with a clearness that sometimes made him more than half afraid.

Of course they loved each other long before they knew what love was ; and with them innocence had no need of virtue. Placed in outward circumstances so harmonious with nature, they were drawn toward each other by an attraction as pure and unconscious as the flowers. They had no secrets from their good foster-mother ; and she, being reverent towards the gods, told them that their union must be preceded by offerings to Juno, and solemnized by mutual promises. She made a marriage feast for them, in her humble way, and crowned the door-posts with garlands. Life passed blissfully there, in the bosom of the deeply wooded hills. Two souls that are sufficient to each other; sentiments, affections, passions, thoughts, all blending in love's harmony, are earth's most perfect medium of heaven. Through them the angels come and go continually, on missions of love to all the lower forms of creation. It is the halo of these heavenly visitors that veils the earth in such a golden glory, and makes every little flower smile its blessing upon lovers. And these innocent ones were in such harmony with nature in her peaceful spring time! The young kids, browsing on the almond blossoms, stopped and listened to their flutes, and came ever nearer, till they looked in the eyes of the wedded ones. And when the sweet sounds died away into silence, the birds took up the strain and sang *their* salutation to the marriage principle of the universe.

Thus months passed on, and neither heart felt an unsatisfied want. They were known to each other by many endearing names, but the foster-parents usually called them Corythus and Œnone. These names were everywhere cut into the rocks, and carved upon the trees. Sometimes, the child-like girl would ask, nothing doubting of the answer, "Will you love me thus when I am as old as our good Arisba?" And he would twine flowers in the rich braids of her golden hair, as he fondly answered, "May the Scamander flow back to its source, if ever I cease to love my Œnone." That there were other passions in the world than love, they neither of them dreamed. But one day Corythus went down into the plains in search of a milk-white bull, that had strayed from the herd.

He was returning with the animal, when he encountered a troop of hunters, from the city on the other side of the river. The tramp of their horses and the glitter of their spears frightened the bull, and he plunged madly into the waves of the Scamander. The uncommon beauty of the powerful beast, and his fiery strength, attracted attention. Some of the hunters dismounted to assist in bringing him out of the river, and with many praises, inquired to whom he belonged. The shepherd answered their questions with a graceful diffidence, that drew some admiration upon himself. As the troop rode away, he heard one of them say, "By Apollo's quiver! that magnificent bull must be the one in which Jupiter disguised himself to carry off Europa."

"Yes," replied another, "and that handsome rustic might be Ganymede in disguise."

A glow of pleasure mantled the cheeks of Corythus. He stood for a moment proudly caressing the neck and head of the superb animal, and gazed earnestly after the hunters. The adventure made a strong impression on his mind; for by the brazen helmets and shields, richly embossed with silver, he rightly conjectured that they who had spoken thus of him were princes of Ilium. From that day he dressed himself more carefully, and often looked at the reflection of himself in the mountain pool. Instead of hastening to Œnone, when they had by any chance been separated for a few hours, he often lingered long, to gaze at the distant towers of Ilium, glittering in the setting sun. The scene was indeed surpassingly fair. The Scamander flowed silverly through a verdant valley girdled by an amphitheatre of richly wooded mountains. Europe and Asia smiled at each other across the bright waters of the Ægean, while the lovely islands of Imbros and Tenedos slept at their feet. But it was not the beauty of the scene which chiefly attracted his youthful imagination. The spark of ambition had fallen into his breast, and his shepherd life now seemed unmanly and dull. Œnone soon felt this; for the usually quick perception of love was rendered still more keen by her peculiar impressibility to spiritual influence. For the first time, in her innocent and happy life, came conscious sadness without a defined reason, and unsatisfied feelings that took no name. She gave out the whole of her soul, and not being all received, the backward stroke of unabsorbed affection struck on her heart with mournful echoes. It made her uneasy, she knew not why, to hear Corythus talk of the princes of Ilium, with their dazzling crests and richly embroidered girdles. It seemed as if these princes, somehow or other, came between her and her love. She had always been remarkable for the dreaming power, and in her present state of mind this mysterious gift increased. Her senses, too, became more acute. A nerve seemed to be thrust out at every pore. She started at the slightest sound, and often, when others saw nothing, she would exclaim—

"Look at that beautiful bird, with feathers like the rainbow!"

The kind foster-mother laid all these things to her heart. Something of reverence, tinged with fear mixed with her love for this dear child of her adoption. She said to her husband—

"Perhaps she is the daughter of Apollo, and he will endow her with the gift of prophecy, as they say he has the beautiful princess Cassandra, in the royal halls of Ilium."

The attention of Corythus was quite otherwise employed. All his leisure moments were spent in making clubs and arrows. He often went down into the plains, to join the young men in wrestling matches, running, leaping, throwing of quoits. In all games of agility or strength, he soon proved his superiority so decidedly that they ceased to excite him. Then he joined hunting parties, and in contests with wild beasts he signalized himself by such extraordinary boldness and skill, that in all the country round he came to be known by the name of Alexander, or the Defender.

The echo of his fame flattered the pride of his foster-father, who often predicted for him a career of greatness; but poor Œnone wept at these periods of absence, which became more and more frequent. She concealed her tears from him, however, and eagerly seized every little moment of sunshine to renew their old happiness. But of all the sad tasks of poor humanity, it is the most sorrowful to welcome ghosts of those living joys that once embraced us with the warmest welcome. To an earnest and passionate nature it seems almost better to be hated, than to be less beloved. Œnone would not believe that the sympathy between them was less perfect than it had been; but the anxious inquiry and the struggling hope were gradually weakening her delicate frame; and an event occurred which completely deranged her nervous organization. One day they had both been tending flocks on the hills, and had fallen asleep in the shade of a gigantic oak. When they awoke, the flock had wandered away, and they went in search of them. Twilight drew her cloud-curtain earlier than usual, and only a solitary star was here and there visible. Bewildered by the uncertain light, they lost their way, and were obliged to trust to the sagacity of their dog. The sky, through the thickly interlacing boughs of gigantic trees, looked down upon them solemnly; bushes here and there started forth, like spectral shadows, across their path; and their faithful dog now and then uttered a long howl, as if he felt the vicinity of some evil beast. Œnone was overcome with exceeding fear. The wind among the trees distressed her with its wailing song; and her acute senses detected other sounds in the distance, long before they reached the ear of her companion.

"Ha! what is that?" she exclaimed, clinging more closely to his arm.

"'Tis only the evening wind," he replied.

"Don't you hear it?" she said: "It is a horrible noise, like the roar of lions. Ah, dear Corythus, the wild beasts will devour us."

He stood and listened intently.

"I hear nothing," said he, "but the Dryads whispering among the trees, and pulling green garlands from the boughs. Your ears deceive you, dearest."

There was silence for a few moments; and then, with a faint shriek, she exclaimed:

"Oh, did'nt you hear that frightful clash? The dog heard it. Hark! how he growls."

For some time, Corythus insisted that there were no other sounds than those common to evening. But at last a deep roar, mingled with howls, came through the air too distinctly to be mistaken. Œnone trembled in every joint, and the perspiration stood in large drops on her lips and forehead. The sounds grew louder and louder. Booming timbrels were answered with the sharp clash of cymbals, and at every pause of the rolling drums the Phrygian pipe moaned on the winds. The roars, shrieks and howls of a furious multitude rent the air with fierce discords, and the earth shook as with the tramp of an army. As they passed by, the glare of their torches came up from below, and cast fantastic gleams on the dark foliage of the firs.

"The gods be praised," said Corythus, "these are no wild beasts; but the Corybantes on their way to the temple of Cybele. The sounds are awful indeed; but the Mountain Mother has been kind to us, dear Œnone; for by the route they have taken I see that the good dog has guided us right, and we are not far from our home."

He received no answer and could hear no breathing. He felt the arm that clutched him so convulsively, and found it cold and rigid. Fitful flashes of lurid light gleamed ever and anon in the distance; the hills echoed the roar of Cybele's lions, and the passionate clang of cymbals pierced into the ear of night. There was no hope of making his voice heard through the uproar; so he tenderly lifted his fair burthen and bore it vigorously down the steep hill, pausing now and then to take breath. At last, his eyes were greeted by the welcome sight of Mygdomus with a torch, anxiously looking out for them. Œnone's terror, and its consequences, were briefly explained, and quickly as possible they carried her into the dwelling.

The swoon continued so long, that it seemed like death; but at last she opened her eyes, gazed around with an unconscious stare, and soon fell into a deep sleep. The next morning she appeared exceedingly weak, and there was a strange expression about her eyes. She so earnestly besought Corythus not to leave her, that the old shepherd and his wife proposed to go forth with the flocks; and it was agreed to call them, in case of need, by a shrill summons on the pipe. But Œnone, though much exhausted, and nervously sensitive to light and sound, slept most of the time quietly. Corythus had in his hand a branch of laurel; and to amuse her waking moments, he wove a garland of the leaves and playfully wreathed it round her head. Her eyes lighted up with a singular inward radiance, and she exclaimed joyfully, "I like that. It makes me feel strong."

Corythus gazed anxiously into her eyes, and a superstitious fear crossed his mind that she had in some way offended the dread goddess Cybele, and been punished with insanity. But she smiled so sweetly on him, and spoke so coherently, that he soon dismissed the fear. An insect buzzed about her head, and he moved his hand slowly up and down, to keep it away. When he paused, she said:

'Do that again. It is soothing and pleasant."

He continued the motion, and with a delighted smile, she said:

"Ah, the laurel bough has golden edges, and there are rays about your head, like a shining crown."

The smile was still on her lips, when she sunk into a profound slumber. But when he rose and attempted to go out, she said, imploringly:

"Oh, don't leave me!"

Yet she still seemed in the deepest possible sleep.

"Œnone, do you see me?" he asked.

"Yes, I see you on a hill where there is a marble temple. There are three very beautiful women, and they all beckon to you."

"What do they ask of me?" said he.

"They ask of you to say which is the fairest. One offers you a king's crown if you decide for her; another holds forth a glittering spear, and says she will make you the most renowned warrior in the world; the other offers a myrtle wreath, and says, 'Decide in my favour, and you shall marry the most beautiful princess in the world.' "

"I choose the myrtle," said Corythus; "but this is an odd dream."

"It is not a dream," replied Œnone.

"Are you not asleep, then?"

"Yes, I am asleep; the motion of your hands put me to sleep, and if you move that hazel twig over my face, it will wake me."

He waved the twig, and her eyes opened immediately; but when questioned, she said she had seen no marble temple, and no beautiful women.

This incident made an indelible impression on the mind of Corythus. He merely told the foster-parents that she had talked in her sleep, and had at times looked very strangely. But, within himself, he pondered much upon what she had said concerning the beautiful princess. Some days after, when he and Œnone were out on the hill-side, he told her what she had said of the motion of his hands, and the effect of the hazel twig; but an undefined feeling led him to forbear mentioning her prophecy that he would marry the most beautiful princess in the world.

She answered, playfully:

"Move your hands over my head again, and see if I shall fall asleep."

He did so, and in a few minutes, she said:

"Ah, all the leaves on the trees now wear a golden edge, the flowers radiate light, there is a shining crown around your head, and from your fingers dart lines of fire. Dear Corythus, this is like what the minstrel sung of the Argonauts, when they were benighted, and Apollo's bow cast bright gleams along the shore, and sparkled on the waves."

She continued to talk of the beautiful appearance more and more drowsily, and in a few minutes sunk into slumber. Corythus watched the statue-like stillness of her features, and the singularly impressive beauty of their expression. It was unlike anything he had ever seen. A glorious light beamed from the countenance, but it shone *through*, not *on* it; like a rose-coloured lamp within a vase of alabaster. For a few moments, he was too much awed to interrupt the silence. There was something divine in her loveliness, as she lay there peacefully under the whispering foliage, while the breezes gently raised her golden ringlets. But curiosity was too powerful to be long subdued by reverence; and Corythus at last asked:

"Œnone, where *is* the beautiful princess whom I shall marry?"

After a pause, she replied:

"In a fair city girdled by verdant hills, far south from here, toward the setting sun."

"Do you see her?" he asked.

"Yes. She is in a magnificent palace, the walls of which are ivory inlaid with golden vines, and grapes of amber. Beneath her feet is spread a rich green cloth, embroidered with flowers. A handmaid is kneeling before her, with a shining silver vase, twined round with golden serpents, and heaped with fine purple wool. Another sits at her feet, with the infant princess in her arms."

"She is married, then?"

"She is the famous Helena, of whose many lovers the minstrels sing, and who was married to Menelaus, king of Laconia."

"How does she look?"

"Majestic as Juno, and beautiful as Venus. She has large dark glowing eyes, a proud but very beautiful mouth, and neck and shoulders as white as ivory. Her glossy brown hair is bound round the forehead with a golden fillet, and falls in waves almost to her feet. She is very beautiful, and very vain of her beauty."

"How then is it that she will consent to marry me, a poor shepherd?"

"You are the son of a king; and when she sees you, she will think you the most beautiful of men."

"*I* the son of a king! Dearest Œnone, tell me of what king?"

"Of Priam, king of Troy."

"How then came I on Mount Ida?"

"The night you were born, your mother dreamed of a torch that set all Ilium on fire. The dream troubled her, and she told it to the king, her husband. He summoned the soothsayers, and they told him that the babe which was born would cause the destruction of the city. While your mother slept, the king gave you to his favourite slave, Archelaus, with orders to strangle you. But he had not the heart to do it, and so he left you under a plane tree on Mount Ida, and prayed the gods to send some one to save you."

"Shall I be happy with the beautiful princess?"

"You shall have joy, but much, much more sorrow. She will bring destruction on you; and you will come to Œnone to die."

Being further questioned, she said she knew the healing virtues of all herbs, and the antidotes for all poisons.

Corythus walked slowly back and forth, with folded arms, revolving all that had been uttered. Could it be that those handsome princes of Ilium were his brothers? And the lovely Helena, the renown of whose beauty had even reached the ears of shepherds on these distant hills, could she ever be *his* wife?

He paused and gazed on Œnone, and compared in his mind her innocent spiritual beauty with the voluptuous picture she had given of Helena; and there arose within him a vague longing for the unknown one.

"Wake me! wake me!" exclaimed the sleeper: "there is a strange pain in my heart."

Marvelling much, and blushing at his own thoughts, he hastily woke her. He felt an unwillingness to reveal what she had uttered; and she was satisfied when told that she had talked incoherently of the splendours of a palace. From that day he often tried the experiment, and was never satisfied with hearing of her visions.

It was a sad task of this fair prophetess, thus unconsciously to paint the image of a rival in the heart of him she loved. And though there remained in the waking state no remembrance of the revelations made, yet the effect of them gave a more plaintive tone to her whole existence. The angelic depth of expression increased in her beautiful eyes, and evermore looked out through a transparent veil of melancholy; for she *felt* the estrangement of her beloved Corythus, though she *knew* it not. In fact, his wayward behaviour attracted the attention of even good old Arisba. Moody and silent, or irritable and impetuous, he no longer seemed like the loving and happy youth, whom she had doated on from his infancy. Sometimes he would hurl the heaviest stones, with might and main, down the sides of the mountain, or wrench the smaller trees up by the roots. He was consumed by a feverish restlessness, that could find no sufficient outward expression; a fiery energy that knew not how to expend itself. Into the smallest occasions of play or labour he threw such vehemence and volcanic force, that Arisba jestingly said, "We will call you no more Corythus, but Cœculus, who is said to have been born of a spark from Vulcan's forge."

To Œnone, his conduct was wayward in the extreme. Sometimes he seemed to forget that she was in existence; and then, as if reproaching himself, he treated her with a lavishness of love that laid her weeping on his bosom. Then she would look up, smiling through her tears, and say, "You *do* love me, still? I know not what to make of you, dear Corythus. Your love seems like the Scamander, that has two sources, one warm and the other cold. But you *do* love me; do you not?"

The allusion to two sources brought a faint flush to his cheek; and when he kissed her, and said "I do," her listening spirit heard a broken echo in the answer.

Thus was life passing with them, when a messenger from king Priam came to obtain the white bull, which had been so much admired by the hunters. There was to be a gladiatorial contest in Ilium, and the king had promised to the victor the most beautiful bull that could be found on Mount Ida. Corythus proudly replied that he would not give up the noble animal, unless he were allowed to enter the lists for the prize. Mygdomus, fearing the royal displeasure, remonstrated with him, and reminded him that the contest was for princes and great men, and not for shepherds and rustics. But Corythus persisted that on such terms only would he send away the pride of their herds. The courier departed, and returned next day with a message from the king, saying he liked the bold spirit of the youth, and would gladly admit into the lists one so famous for courage and skill.

Poor Œnone could not overcome her reluctance to have him go. There had always been in her mind an uncomfortable feeling with regard to those princes of Ilium; and now it returned with redoubled force. But, alas, in those mysterious sleeps she prophesied victory and glory, and thus kindled higher than ever the flame of ambition within his breast.

At last the important day arrived; and with throbbing hearts the shepherd-family saw their young gladiator depart for the contest. He drew Œnone to his heart and kissed her affectionately; but when they parted, he did not stop to look back, as he used to do in those blissful days when their souls were fused into one. With vigorous, joyful leaps, he went bounding down the sides of the mountain. Œnone watched his graceful figure as he swung lightly from the trunk of a young olive tree, down into the plain below. When she could no longer see even a moving speck in the distance, she retired tearfully, to tend the flocks alone. All that day her eyes were fixed sadly on the towers of Ilium, and the thought ever present was, "He did not look back upon me, when we parted."

He promised to return on the third day; but the fourth, and the fifth, and the sixth passed, and still he came not. Mournfully, mournfully, wailed Œnone's pipe, and there came no answer now, but sad echoes from the hills.

"What can have become of him?" said Arisba,

when the evening of the fourth day closed. "Surely, if harm had happened to him, they would send a messenger."

"He is either dead, or he has tasted the waters of Argyra, which make people forget those they love," said Œnone; and as she spoke, hot tears fell on the thread she spun.

* * * * * * * *

How had it fared meanwhile with Corythus? Victor in all the games, his beauty and his strength called forth shouts of applause. One after another of the king's sons were obliged to yield to his superior vigour and skill. At last came the athletic and hitherto unconquered Hector. After a fierce protracted struggle, the shepherd of Ida overthrew him also. Enraged at being conquered by a youth of such inferior birth, he started on his feet and rushed after him, in a paroxysm of wrath. Corythus, to elude his fury, passed through a gate which led into the inner court of the palace. It chanced that queen Hecuba and her daughter Cassandra were there, when he rushed in, and panting threw himself upon the altar of Jupiter for protection. Hecuba flung her mantle over him, and summoned a slave to bring him water. Cassandra, gazing earnestly at the youthful stranger, exclaimed,

"How like he is to my mother, as I first remember her!"

The queen inquired his age, and Cassandra, listening to his answer, said,

"If my brother Paris had lived, such also would have been his years."

"Fair Princess," replied Corythus, "an oracle has

told me that I am he. Is Archelaus yet alive? If so, I pray you let him be summoned, and inquire of him whether he destroyed the infant Paris."

The old slave, being questioned, fell on his knees and confessed that he had left the babe under a plane tree, on Mount Ida, and that he had afterward seen him in the hut of Mygdomus. With a cry of joy, Hecuba threw herself into the arms of her beautiful, her long-lost son. Slaves brought water for his feet and spread rich carpets before him. They clothed him in royal robes, and there was feasting and rejoicing, and magnificent processions to the temples, and costly sacrifices to the gods. Brothers and sisters caressed him, and he was attended by beautiful bondwomen, whose duty it was to obey his every wish. Electra, a handsome Greek girl, with glowing cheeks and eyes of fire, brought water for his hands in vases of silver; while Artaynta, a graceful Persian, with kiss-inviting lips, and sleepy oriental eyes, always half-veiled by their long silken fringes, knelt to pour perfumes on his feet. Thus surrounded by love and splendour, the dazzled youth forgot Œnone. It was not until the fourth day of his residence in the palace, that the new prince began to think how anxious must be the humble hearts that loved him on Mount Ida. Should he raise Œnone to his own royal rank? She was unquestionably lovely enough to grace a throne; but the famous Spartan queen had taken possession of his imagination, and he was already devising some excuse to visit the court of Menelaus. He had not courage to reveal these feelings to Œnone; and a selfish wish to screen himself from embarrassment and pain induced him to send Archelaus to convey the news, with munificent presents to his foster-parents and his wife, and a promise that he would come hereafter.

When Œnone heard the unexpected tidings, she fell into a swoon more deadly than the one she had experienced on the night of Cybele's procession. She knew that her feelings could not have changed toward Corythus, had the Fates offered her the throne of the world; but she felt that it might be otherwise with him. Weary weeks passed, and still he came not. Œnone, wakeful and nervous, at last asked the foster-mother to try to soothe her into sleep, as Corythus had formerly done. Under this influence all the objects around her again radiated light; and when the mysterious slumber veiled her senses, she entered the royal palace of Priam, and saw her beloved. Sometimes she described him as reclining on a crimson couch, while Electra brought him wine in golden goblets. At other times, Artaynta knelt before him and played on her harp, while he twined the long ringlets of her glossy hair. At last she said he was fitting out a fleet, and would soon sail away.

When Arisba asked where he would go, she answered:

"He says he is going to Salamis to redeem the Princess Hesione, who was carried away prisoner by the Greeks; but his real object is to visit the beautiful queen of Sparta, whom I told him he would marry."

"Poor child," thought Arisba, "then it was thou thyself that kindled strange fires in his bosom. What wrong hast thou done, in thy innocent life, that the gods should thus punish thee?"

In her waking hours, Œnone asked eager questions concerning all she had said in her state of inner consciousness.

"Oh, if I could only see him again!" she would exclaim with mournful impatience. "To have these painted visions, and to retain no memory of them—this is worse than the doom of Tantalus. Oh, how *could* he forget me so easily? We who have slept in the same cradle, and so often folded each other in mutual love. I could not thus have forgotten *him*."

She invented many projects of going to Ilium in disguise, that she might at least look upon him once more. But timidity and pride restrained her.

"The haughty ones will scorn a poor shepherd girl," she said; "and he will be ashamed to call me his wife. I will not follow him who wishes to leave me. It would break my heart to see him caressing another's beauty. Yet if I could only *see* him, even with another folded to his heart! Oh, ye gods, if I could only *see* him again!"

Arisba listened to these ravings with deep compassion.

"Poor child," she would say, "when thou wert born, the Loves sneezed to thee from the unlucky side."

Œnone would fain have been in her mysterious sleep half the time; so eager was she to receive tidings from Corythus. But Arisba had not the leisure to spare, nor did she think such constant excitement favourable to the health of her darling child. Already her thin form was much attenuated, and her complexion had the pale transparency of a spirit. But the restlessness, induced by hearing no news of her beloved, had a worse effect upon her nerves than the excitement caused by her visions. So day by day, Arisba tried to soothe her wretchedness, by producing the sleep, and afterward repeating to her what she had said. In this strange way, all that occurred at the palace in Ilium was known in the hut on Mount Ida. The departure of the young prince for Salamis, the gorgeous fleet, with gay streamers and gilded prows, the crowd about the shores waving garlands, were all described in the liveliest manner. But Œnone's sadness was not deepened by this event. Corythus had been previously separated from her, more completely than if he had already passed into the world of spirits. One only hope consoled her misery; her own prophecy that he would come to her to die.

Arisba was rejoiced to discover that her darling would soon become a mother. She trusted this would resuscitate withering affections, by creating a visible link between her desolate heart and the being she so fondly loved. And the first glance of the young mother upon her innocent babe did seem to renew the fountains of her life. She named the boy Corythus, and eagerly watched his growing beauty, to catch some likeness of his father. But the child had been born under influences too sad to inherit his father's vigorous frame, or his bounding, joyous, volatile spirit. His nature was deep and loving, like his mother's, and he had her plaintive, prophetic eyes. But his rosy mouth, the very bow of Cupid, was the image of his father's. And oh, with what a passionate mixture of maternal fondness and early romantic love, did poor Œnone press it to her own pale lips!

Less frequently now she sought the relief of supernatural sleep; and when she did, it was not always followed by visions. But at various times she saw her beloved in Sparta, weaving garlands for the beautiful queen, or playing upon his flute while he reclined at her feet.

"She loves him not," said the sleeper; "but his beauty and his flattery please her, and she will return with him. It will prove a fatal day for him, and for Ilium."

When little Corythus was a year old, the fleet returned from Greece, bearing Paris and his beautiful Spartan queen. Œnone was, of course, aware of this event, long before the rumour was reported to Mygdomus by neighbouring shepherds. A feverish excitement returned upon her; the old intense desire to see the loved one. But still she was restrained by fear and womanly pride. She made unseen visits to the palace, as before, and told of Paris forever at the feet of his queenly bride, playing upon his silver lyre, while she decorated his curling tresses with garlands.

Again and again, the question rose in Œnone's mind, whether the forgetful one would love her fair child, if he could see him; and month by month, the wish grew stronger to show him this son of their love. Little Corythus was about two years old, when she foretold immediate war with the Grecian states, enraged at the abduction of queen Helena. When this was repeated to her, she said to herself,

"If I go not soon, the plain will be filled with warriors, and it will be dangerous to venture there."

She kept her purpose secret; but one morning,

when she and the little one were out alone upon the hills, she disguised herself in some of Arisba's old robes, and went forth to Ilium, hoping to gain entrance to the palace under the pretence of having herbs to sell. But when she came within sight of the stately edifice, her resolution almost failed. A slave, who was harnessing two superb white horses to a glittering chariot, demanded what she wanted; and when she timidly told her errand, he showed her an inner quadrangular court, and pointed out the apartments of the women. As she stood hesitating, gazing on the magnificent marble columns and gilded lattices, Paris himself came down the steps, encircling Helen with his arm. It was the first time she had looked upon him since he left her, in rustic garb, without pausing to look back upon her. Now, he wore sparkling sandals, and a mantle of Tyrian purple, with large clasps of gold. His bride was clothed in embroidered Sidonian garments, of the richest fashion, and a long flowing veil, of shining texture, was fastened about her head by a broad band of embossed gold. Poor Œnone slunk away, abashed and confounded in the presence of their regal beauty; and her heart sank within her, when she saw those well-remembered eyes gazing so fondly upon her splendid rival. But when the slave brought the chariot to the gate, she tried to rouse her courage and come forward with the child. Paris carefully lifted his bride into the chariot, and leaped in, to seat himself by her side. In the agony of her feelings, the suffering mother made a convulsive movement, and with a shrill hysteric shriek, exclaimed,

"Oh Corythus, do look once upon our child!"

The frightened horses reared and plunged. The chariot, turning rapidly, struck Œnone and she fell. The wheels merely grazed her garments, but passed over the body of the child. Paris being occupied with soothing Helen's alarm, was not aware of this dreadful accident. The slave reined in the startled horses with a strong hand, and drove rapidly forward. Œnone was left alone outside the gates, with the lifeless body of her babe.

It was evening when she returned weary and heart-broken to Arisba. A compassionate rustic accompanied her, bearing her melancholy burden. The sad story was told in a few wild words; and the old shepherds bowed down their heads and sobbed in agony. Œnone's grief was the more fearful, because it was so still. It seemed as if the fountains of feeling were dried up within her heart.

There was a painfully intense glare about her eyes, and she remained wakeful late into the night. At last, the good foster-mother composed her into an artificial sleep. She talked less than usual in such slumbers, and evinced an unwillingness to be disturbed. But, in answer to Arisba's question, she said,

"He did not know a child was killed, nor did he see us. In the confusion he thought only of Helen, and did not recognise Œnone's voice. His sister Cassandra, who sees hidden things by the same light that I do, has told him that the child killed at the gates was his own. But Helen and her handmaids are dancing round him, laughing and throwing perfumes as they go, and he thinks not of us. He would have loved our little Corythus, if he had known him."

"Thank the gods for that," said Arisba within herself; "for I would not like to hate the nursling I reared so fondly."

They buried the child in the shade of a gigantic oak, on which, in happier days, had been carved, with the point of an arrow, the united names of Corythus and Œnone. A beautiful Arum lily held its large white cup over the grave; and the sorrowing mother covered the broken soil with anemonies and the delicate blossoms of the crocus. There she would sit hours together, gazing on the towers of Ilium. But her desire to visit the palace, visibly or invisibly, seemed to have subsided entirely. No feeling of resentment against Corythus came into her gentle heart; but her patient love seemed to have sunk into utter hopelessness. Sometimes, indeed, she would look up in Arisba's face, with a heart-touching expression in her deep mournful eyes, and say, in tones of the saddest resignation,

"He will come to me to die."

Thus years passed on. War raged in all its fury in the plains below. Their flocks and herds were all seized by the rapacious soldiery, and the rushing of many chariots echoed like thunder among the hills. The nervous wakefulness of Œnone was still occasionally soothed by supernatural sleep; though she never sought it now from curiosity. At such times, she often gave graphic accounts of the two contending armies; but these violent scenes pained her in her sleep, and left her waking strength extremely exhausted. Sometimes she described Paris in the battle-field, in shining armour, over which a panther's skin was gracefully thrown, with a quiver of arrows at his shoulder, and a glittering spear balanced in his hand, brave and beautiful as the god of day. But more frequently she saw him at Helen's feet, playing on harp or flute, while she wove her gay embroidery. In the latter time, she often spoke of his handsome brother Deiphobus, standing near them, exchanging stolen amorous glances with the vain and treacherous Spartan.

"She is false to him," murmured the sleeper, mournfully. "But he will come to Œnone to die."

At last, the predicted hour arrived. The towers of Ilium were all in flames, and the whole atmosphere was filled with lurid light, as the magnificent city sank into her fiery grave. The wretched inhabitants were flying in all directions, pursued by the avenging foe. In the confusion, Paris was wounded by a poisoned arrow. In this hour of agony, he remembered the faithful, the long-forgotten one, and what she had said of her skill in medicine. In gasping tones, he cried out,

"Carry me to Œnone!"

His terrified slaves lifted him on a litter of boughs, and hastened to obey his orders.

Œnone sat by the grave of her child, watching the blazing towers of Ilium, when they laid Corythus at her feet. She sprang forward, exclaiming,

"Dear, dear Corythus, you have come to me at last!"

Bending over him, she kissed the lips, which, cold

as marble, returned no answer to the fond caress. She gazed wildly on the pale countenance for an instant—placed her trembling hand upon his heart—and then springing upward convulsively, as if shot by an arrow, she uttered one long shrill shriek, that startled all the echoes, and fell lifeless on the body of him she loved so well.

The weeping foster-parents dug a wide grave by the side of little Corythus, and placed them in each other's arms, under the shadow of the great oak, whose Dryad had so often heard the pure whisperings of their early love.

THE YOUTHFUL EMIGRANT.

A True Story of the Early Settlement of New Jersey.

A being breathing thoughtful breath;
A traveller betwixt life and death;
The reason firm, the temperate will,
Endurance, foresight, strength and skill.
A perfect woman, nobly planned,
To warn, to comfort, and command;
And yet a spirit still, and bright
With something of an angel light.—WORDSWORTH.

THE latter part of the seventeenth century saw rapid accessions to the Society of Friends, called Quakers. The strong humility, the indwelling life, which then characterised that peculiar sect, attracted large numbers, even of the wealthy, to its unworldly doctrines. Among these were John Haddon and his wife Elizabeth, well-educated and genteel people, in the city of London. Like William Penn, and other proselytes from the higher classes, they encountered much ridicule and opposition from relatives, and the grossest misrepresentations from the public. But this, as usual, only made the unpopular faith more dear to those who had embraced it for conscience' sake.

The three daughters of John Haddon received the best education then bestowed on gentlewomen, with the exception of ornamental accomplishments. The spinnet and mandolin, on which their mother had played with considerable skill, were of course banished; and her gay embroidery was burned, lest it should tempt others to a like expenditure of time. The house was amply furnished, but with the simplest patterns and the plainest colours. An atmosphere of kindness pervaded the whole establishment, from father and mother down to the little errand-boy; a spirit of perfect gentleness, unbroken by any freaks of temper, or outbursts of glee; as mild and placid as perpetual moonlight.

The children, in their daily habits, reflected an image of home, as children always do. They were quiet, demure, and orderly, with a touch of quaintness in dress and behaviour. Their playthings were so well preserved, that they might pass in good condition to the third generation; no dogs' ears were turned in their books, and the moment they came from school, they carefully covered their little plain bonnets from dust and flies. To these subduing influences, was added the early consciousness of being pointed at as peculiar; of having a cross to bear, a sacred cause to sustain.

Elizabeth, the oldest daughter, was by nature strong, earnest, and energetic, with warm affections, uncommon powers of intellect, and a lively imagination. The exact equal pressure on all sides, in strict Quaker families, is apt to produce too much uniformity of character; as the equal pressure of the air makes one globule of shot just like another. But in this rich young soul, the full stream, which under other circumstances might have overleaped safe barriers, being gently hemmed in by high banks, quietly made for itself a deeper and wider channel, and flowed on in all its fulness. Her countenance in some measure indicated this. Her large clear blue eye "looked out honest and friendly into the world," and there was an earnest seriousness about her mouth, very unusual in childhood. She was not handsome; but there was something extremely pleasing in her fresh healthy complexion, her bright intelligent expression, and her firm elastic motions.

She early attracted attention, as a very peculiar child. In her usual proceedings, her remarks, and even in her play, there was a certain individuality. It was evident that she never *intended* to do anything strange. She was original merely because she unconsciously acted out her own noble nature, in her own free and quiet way. It was a spontaneous impulse with her to relieve all manner of distress. One day, she brought home a little half-blind kitten in her bosom, which her gentle eloquence rescued from cruel boys, who had cut off a portion of its ears. At another time, she asked to have a large cake baked for her, because she wanted to invite some little girls. All her small funds were expended for oranges and candy on this occasion. When the time arrived, her father and mother were much surprised to see her lead in six little ragged beggars. They were, however, too sincerely humble and religious to *express* any surprise. They treated the forlorn little ones very tenderly, and freely granted their daughter's request to give them some of her books and playthings at parting. When they had gone, the good mother quietly said, "Elizabeth, why didst thou invite strangers, instead of thy schoolmates?"

There was a heavenly expression in her eye, as she looked up earnestly, and answered, "Mother, I wanted to invite *them*, they looked *so* poor."

The judicious parents made no circumstance of it, lest it should create a diseased love of being praised for kindness. But they gave each other an expressive glance, and their eyes filled with tears; for this simple and natural action of their child seemed to them full of Christian beauty.

Under such an education, all good principles and genial impulses grew freely and took vigorous root; but the only opening for her active imagination to spread its wings, was in the marvellous accounts she heard of America and the Indians. When she was five or six years old, William Penn visited her father's house, and described some of his adventures in the wilderness, and his interviews with red men. The intelligent child eagerly devoured every word, and kept drawing nearer and nearer, till she laid her head upon his knees, and gazed into his face. Amused by her intense curiosity, the good man took her in his lap, and told her how the squaws made baskets and embroidered moccasons; how they called a baby a pappoos, and put him in a birch-bark cradle, which they swung on the boughs of trees. The little girl's eyes sparkled, as she inquired, "And didst thou ever see a pappoos-baby thyself? And hast thou got a moccason-shoe?"

"I have seen them myself, and I will send thee a moccason," he replied; "but thou mayst go to thy mother now, for I have other things to speak of."

That night, the usually sedate child scampered

across the bed-room with but one sleeve of her night-gown on, and tossed up her shoe, shouting, "Ho, ho! Friend Penn is going to send me an Indian moccason! Mother, art thou glad? Hannah, art thou glad?"

This unwonted ebullition was not rebuked in words, but it soon subsided under the invisible influence of unvarying calmness.

From that time, a new character was given to all her plays. Her doll was named Pocahontas, and she swung her kitten in a bit of leather, and called it a pappoos. If she could find a green bough, she stuck it in the ground for a tree, placed an earthen image under it for William Penn, and sticks with feathers on them for Indian chiefs. Then, with amusing gravity of manner, she would unfold a bit of newspaper and read what she called Friend Penn's treaty with the red men. Her sisters, who were a of far less adventurous spirit, often said, "We are tired of always playing Indian. Why not play keep school, or go to see grandfather?"

But Elizabeth would answer, "No; let us play that we all go settle in America. Well, now suppose we are in the woods, with great, great, big trees all round us, and squirrels running up and down, and wolves growling."

"I don't like wolves," said little Hannah, "they will bite thee. Father says they will bite."

"I shouldn't be afraid," replied the elder sister; "I would run into the house and shut the door, when they came near enough for me to see their eyes. Here are plenty of sticks. Let us build a house; a wigwam, I mean. Oh, dear me, how I should love to go to America! There must be such grand great woods to run about in; and I should love to swing the little pappooses in the trees."

When Elizabeth was eleven years old, she went with her parents to Yearly Meeting, and heard, among other preachers, a young man seventeen years of age, named John Estaugh. He was a new proselyte, come from Essex county, to join the annual assembly of the Friends. Something in his preaching arrested the child's attention, and made a strong impression on her active mind. She often quoted his words afterwards, and began to read religious books with great diligence. John Haddon invited the youth home to dine, but as there was no room at the table for the children, Elizabeth did not see him. Her father afterward showed her an ear of Indian corn, which John Estaugh had given him. He had received several from an uncle settled in New England, and he brought some with him to London as curiosities. When the little girl was informed that the magnificent plant grew taller than herself, and had very large waving green leaves, and long silken tassels, she exclaimed, with renewed eagerness, "Oh, how I do wish I could go to America!"

Years passed on, and as the child had been, so was the maiden; modest, gentle and kind, but always earnest and full of life. Surrounding influences naturally guided her busy intellect into inquiries concerning the right principles of human action, and the rationality of customary usages. At seventeen, she professed to have adopted, from her own serious conviction, the religious opinions in which she had been educated. There was little observable change in outward manner; for the fresh spontaneousness of her character had been early chastened by habitual calmness and sobriety. But her views of life gradually became tinged with a larger and deeper thoughtfulness. She often spoke of the freedom of life away from cities, and alone with nature; of mutual helpfulness in such a state of society, and increased means of doing good.

Perhaps her influence, more than anything else, induced her father to purchase a tract of land in New Jersey, with the view of removing thither. Mechanics were sent out to build a suitable house and barns, and the family were to be transplanted to the New World as soon as the necessary arrangements were completed. In the meantime, however, circumstances occurred which led the good man to consider it his duty to remain in England. The younger daughters were well pleased to have it so; but Elizabeth, though she acquiesced cheerfully in her father's decision, evidently had a weight upon her mind. She was more silent than usual, and more frequently retired to her chamber for hours of quiet communion with herself. Sometimes, when asked what she had upon her mind, she replied, in the concise solemn manner of Friends, "It is a great thing to be a humble waiter upon the Lord; to stand in readiness to follow wheresoever He leads the way."

One day, some friends, who were at the house, spoke of the New Jersey tract, and of the reasons which had prevented a removal to America. Her father replied, that he was unwilling to have any property lying useless, and he believed he should offer the tract to any of his relatives who would go and settle upon it. His friends answered, "Thy relatives are too comfortably established in England, to wish to emigrate to the wilds of America."

That evening, when the family were about to separate for the night, Elizabeth begged them to remain a while, as she had something of importance to say. "Dear parents and sisters," said she, "it is now a long time since I have had a strong impression on my mind that it is my duty to go to America. My feelings have been greatly drawn toward the poor brethren and sisters there. It has even been clearly pointed out to me what I am to do. It has been lately signified that a sign would be given when the way was opened; and to-night when I heard thy proposition to give the house and land to whoever would occupy it, I felt at once that thy words were the promised sign."

Her parents, having always taught their children to attend to inward revealings, were afraid to oppose what she so strongly felt to be a duty. Her mother, with a slight trembling in her voice, asked if she had reflected well on all the difficulties of the undertaking, and how arduous a task it was for a young woman to manage a farm of unbroken land in a new country.

Elizabeth replied, "Young women have governed kingdoms; and surely it requires less wisdom to manage a farm. But let not that trouble us, dear mother. He that feedeth the ravens will guide me in the work whereunto he has called me. It is not to cultivate the farm, but to be a friend and physician to the people in that region, that I am called."

Her father answered, "Doubt not, my child, that we shall be willing to give thee up to the Lord's disposings, however hard the trial may be. But when thou wert a very little girl, thy imagination was much excited concerning America ; therefore, thou must be very careful that no desire for new adventures, founded in the will of the creature, mislead thee from the true light in this matter. I advise thee for three months to make it a subject of solid meditation and prayer. Then, if our lives be spared, we will talk further concerning it."

During the prescribed time, no allusion was made to the subject, though it was in the thoughts of all ; for this highly conscientious family were unwilling to confuse inward perceptions by any expression of feeling or opinion. With simple undoubting faith, they sought merely to ascertain whether the Lord required this sacrifice. That their daughter's views remained the same, they partly judged by her increased tenderness toward all the family. She was not sad, but thoughtful and ever-wakeful, as toward friends from whom she was about to separate. It was likewise observable that she redoubled her diligence in obtaining knowledge of household affairs, of agriculture, and the cure of common diseases. When the three months had expired, she declared that the light shone with undiminished clearness, and she felt, more strongly than ever, that it was her appointed mission to comfort and strengthen the Lord's people in the New World.

Accordingly, early in the spring of 1700, arrangements were made for her departure, and all things were provided that the abundance of wealth, or the ingenuity of affection, could devise. A poor widow of good sense and discretion accompanied her, as friend and housekeeper, and two trusty men servants, members of the Society of Friends. Among the many singular manifestations of strong faith and religious zeal, connected with the settlement of this country, few are more remarkable than the voluntary separation of this girl of eighteen years old from a wealthy home and all the pleasant associations of childhood, to go to a distant and thinly inhabited country, to fulfil what she considered a religious duty. And the humble, self-sacrificing faith of the parents, in giving up their beloved child, with such reverend tenderness for the promptings of her own conscience, has in it something sublimely beautiful, if we look at it in its own pure light. The parting took place with more love than words can express, and yet without a tear on either side. Even during the long and tedious voyage, Elizabeth never wept. She preserved a martyr-like cheerfulness and serenity to the end.

The house prepared for her reception stood in a clearing of the forest, three miles from any other dwelling. She arrived in June, when the landscape was smiling in youthful beauty; and it seemed to her as if the arch of heaven was never before so clear and bright, the carpet of the earth never so verdant. As she sat at her window and saw evening close in upon her in that broad forest home, and heard, for the first time, the mournful notes of the whippo-wil and the harsh scream of the jay in the distant woods, she was oppressed with a sense of vastness, of infinity, which she never before experienced, not even on the ocean. She remained long in prayer, and when she lay down to sleep beside her matron friend, no words were spoken between them. The elder, overcome with fatigue, soon sank into a peaceful slumber; but the young enthusiastic spirit lay long awake, listening to the lone voice of the whippo-wil complaining to the night. Yet notwithstanding this prolonged wakefulness, she rose early and looked out upon the lovely landscape. The rising sun pointed to the tallest trees with his golden finger, and was welcomed with a gush of song from a thousand warblers. The poetry in Elizabeth's soul, repressed by the severe plainness of her education, gushed up like a fountain. She dropped on her knees, and with an outburst of prayer exclaimed fervently, "Oh, Father, very beautiful hast thou made this earth! How bountiful are thy gifts, O Lord!"

To a spirit less meek and brave, the darker shades of the picture would have obscured these cheerful gleams; for the situation was lonely and the inconveniences innumerable. But Elizabeth easily triumphed over all obstacles, by her practical good sense and the quick promptings of her ingenuity. She was one of those clear strong natures, who always have a definite aim in view, and who see at once the means best suited to the end. Her first inquiry was, what grain was best adapted to the soil of her farm; and being informed that rye would yield best, "Then I shall eat rye bread," was her answer. The ear of Indian corn, so long treasured in her juvenile museum, had travelled with her across the Atlantic, to be planted in American soil. When she saw fields of this superb plant, she acknowledged that it more than realized the picture of her childish imagination.

But when winter came, and the gleaming snow spread its unbroken silence over hill and plain, was it not dreary then? It would have been dreary indeed to one who entered upon this mode of life from mere love of novelty, or a vain desire to do something extraordinary. But the idea of extended usefulness, which had first lured this remarkable girl into a path so unusual, sustained her through all its trials. She was too busy to be sad, and she leaned too trustingly on her Father's hand to be doubtful of her way. The neighbouring Indians soon loved her as a friend, for they found her always truthful, just, and kind. From their teachings, she added much to her knowledge of simple medicines. So efficient was her skill and so prompt her sympathy, that for many miles round, if man, woman, or child were alarmingly ill, they were sure to send for Elizabeth Haddon; and wherever she went, her observing mind gathered some new hint for the improvement of farm or dairy. Her house and heart were both large; and as her residence was on the way to the Quaker meeting-house in Newtown, it became a place of universal resort to Friends from all parts of the country travelling that road, as well as an asylum for benighted wanderers. When Elizabeth was asked if she were not sometimes afraid of wayfarers, she quietly replied, "Perfect love casteth out fear." And true it was that she, who was so bountiful and kind to all, found none to injure her.

The winter was drawing to a close, when late one evening, the sound of sleigh-bells was heard, and the crunching of snow beneath the hoofs of horses, as they passed into the barn-yard gate. The arrival of travellers was too common an occurrence to excite or disturb the well-ordered family. Elizabeth quietly continued her knitting, merely saying to one of the men, "Joseph, wilt thou put more wood on the fire? These friends, whoever they may be, will doubtless be cold; for I observed at nightfall a chilly feeling, as of more snow in the air."

Great logs were piled in the capacious chimney, and the flames blazed up with a crackling warmth, when two strangers entered. In the younger, Elizabeth instantly recognised John Estaugh, whose preaching had so deeply impressed her at eleven years of age. This was almost like a glimpse of home—her dear old English home! She stepped forward with more than usual cordiality, saying:

"Thou art welcome, Friend Estaugh; the more so for being entirely unexpected."

"And I am glad to see thee, Elizabeth," he replied, with a friendly shake of the hand. "It was not until after I landed in America, that I heard the Lord had called thee hither before me; but I remember thy father told me how often thou hadst played the settler in the woods, when thou wast quite a little girl."

"I am but a child still," she replied, smiling.

"I trust thou art," he rejoined; "and as for these strong impressions in childhood, I have heard of many cases where they seemed to be prophecies sent of the Lord. When I saw thy father in London, I had even then an indistinct idea that I might sometime be sent to America on a religious visit."

"And hast thou forgotten, Friend John, the ear of Indian corn which my father begged of thee for me? I can show it to thee now. Since then I have seen this grain in perfect growth; and a goodly plant it is, I assure thee. See," she continued, pointing to many bunches of ripe corn, which hung in their braided husks against the walls of the ample kitchen: "all that, and more, came from a single ear, no bigger than the one thou didst give my father. May the seed sown by thy ministry be as fruitful!"

"Amen," replied both the guests; and for a few moments no one interrupted the silence. Then they talked much of England. John Estaugh had not seen any of the Haddon family for several years; but he brought letters from them, which came by the same ship, and he had information to give of many whose names were familiar as household words.

The next morning, it was discovered that snow had fallen during the night in heavy drifts, and the roads were impassable. Elizabeth, according to her usual custom, sent out men, oxen and sledges, to open pathways for several poor families, and for households whose inmates were visited by illness. In this duty, John Estaugh and his friend joined heartily, and none of the labourers worked harder than they. When he returned, glowing from this exercise, she could not but observe that the excellent youth had a goodly countenance. It was not physical beauty; for of that he had little. It was that cheerful, child-like, out-beaming honesty of expression, which we not unfrequently see in Germans, who, above all nations, look as if they carried a crystal heart within their manly bosoms.

Two days after, when Elizabeth went to visit her patients, with a sled-load of medicines and provisions, John asked permission to accompany her. There, by the bedside of the aged and the suffering, she saw the clear sincerity of his countenance warmed up with rays of love, while he spoke to them words of kindness and consolation ; and there she heard his pleasant voice modulate itself into deeper tenderness of expression, when he took little children in his arms.

The next First Day, which we call the Sabbath, the whole family, as usual, attended Newtown meeting; and there John Estaugh was gifted with an outpouring of the spirit in his ministry, which sank deep into the hearts of those who listened to him. Elizabeth found it so marvellously applicable to the trials and temptations of her own soul, that she almost deemed it was spoken on purpose for her. She said nothing of this, but she pondered upon it deeply. Thus did a few days of united duties make them more thoroughly acquainted with each other, than they could have been by years of fashionable intercourse.

The young preacher soon after bade farewell, to visit other meetings in Pennsylvania and New Jersey. Elizabeth saw him no more until the May following, when he stopped at her house to lodge, with numerous other Friends, on their way to the Quarterly Meeting at Salem. In the morning, quite a cavalcade started from her hospitable door, on horseback; for wagons were then unknown in Jersey. John Estaugh, always kindly in his impulses, busied himself with helping a lame and very ugly old woman, and left his hostess to mount her horse as she could. Most young women would have felt slighted; but in Elizabeth's noble soul the quiet deep tide of feeling rippled with an inward joy. "He is always kindest to the poor and the neglected," thought she; "verily he *is* a good youth." She was leaning over the side of her horse, to adjust the buckle of the girth, when he came up on horseback, and inquired if anything was out of order. She thanked him, with slight confusion of manner, and a voice less calm than her usual utterance. He assisted her to mount, and they trotted along leisurely behind the procession of guests, speaking of the soil and climate of this new country, and how wonderfully the Lord had here provided a home for his chosen people. Presently the girth began to slip, and the saddle turned so much on one side, that Elizabeth was obliged to dismount. It took some time to re-adjust it, and when they again started, the company were out of sight. There was brighter colour than usual in the maiden's cheeks, and unwonted radiance in her mild deep eyes. After a short silence, she said, in a voice slightly tremulous, "Friend John, I have a subject of great importance on my mind, and one which nearly interests thee. I am strongly impressed that the Lord has sent thee to me as a partner for life. I tell thee my impression frankly, but not without calm and deep reflection; for matrimony is a holy relation, and should be entered into with all sobriety. If thou hast no light on the subject, wilt thou gather into the stillness, and reverently listen to thy own inward revealings? Thou art to leave this part of the country to-morrow, and not knowing when I should see thee again, I felt moved to tell thee what lay upon my mind."

The young man was taken by surprise. Though accustomed to that suppression of emotion, which characterizes his religious sect, the colour went and came rapidly in his face, for a moment; but he soon became calmer, and replied, "This thought is new to me, Elizabeth; and I have no light thereon. Thy company has been right pleasant to me, and thy countenance ever reminds me of William Penn's title-page, 'Innocency with her open face.' I have seen thy kindness to the poor, and the wise management of thy household. I have observed, too, that thy warm-heartedness is tempered by a most excellent discretion, and that thy speech is ever sincere. Assuredly, such is the maiden I would ask of the Lord, as a most precious gift; but I never thought of this connexion with thee. I came to this country solely on a religious visit, and it might distract my mind to entertain this subject at present. When I have discharged the duties of my mission, we will speak further."

"It is best so," rejoined the maiden; "but there is one thing disturbs my conscience. Thou hast spoken of my true speech; and yet, Friend John, I have deceived thee a little, even now, while we conferred together on a subject so serious. I know not from what weakness the temptation came; but I will not hide it from thee. I allowed thee to suppose, just now, that I was fastening the girth of my horse securely ; but, in plain truth, I was loosening the girth, John, that the saddle might slip, and give me an excuse to fall behind our friends; for I thought thou wouldst be kind enough to come and ask if I needed thy services."

This pure transparency of motive seemed less wonderful to John Estaugh, than it would to a man more accustomed to worldly ways, or less familiar with the simplicity of primitive Quakers. Nevertheless, the perfect guilelessness of the maiden endeared her to his honest heart, and he found it difficult to banish from his thoughts the important subject she had suggested. It was observable in this singular courtship, that no mention was made of wordly substance. John did not say, " I am poor, and thou art rich ;" he did not even think of it. And it had entered Elizabeth's mind only in the form of thankfulness to God that she was provided with a home large enough for both.

They spoke no further concerning their union ; but when he returned to England, in July, he pressed her hand affectionately, as he said, " Farewell, Elizabeth. If it be the Lord's will, I shall return to thee soon." He lingered, and their hands trembled in each other's clasp ; then drawing her gently toward him, he imprinted a kiss on her open innocent forehead. She looked modestly into his clear honest eyes, and replied in the kindest tones, " Farewell, Friend John ; may the Lord bless thee and guide thee."

In October, he returned to America, and they were soon after married, at Newtown meeting, according to the simple form of the Society of Friends. Neither of them made any change of dress for the occasion, and there was no wedding feast. Without the aid of priest or magistrate, they took each other by the hand, and, in the presence of witnesses, calmly and solemnly promised to be kind and faithful to each other. Their mutual promises were recorded in the church books, and the wedded pair quietly returned to their happy home, with none to intrude upon those sacred hours of human life, when the heart most needs to be left alone with its own deep emotions.

During the long period of their union, she three times crossed the Atlantic, to visit her aged parents, and he occasionally left her for a season, when called abroad to preach. These temporary separations were felt as a cross, but the strong-hearted woman always cheerfully gave him up to follow his own convictions of duty. In 1742, he parted from her, to go on a religious visit to Tortola, in the West Indies. He died there, in the sixty-seventh year of his age. A friend, in a letter informing her of the event, says: "A shivering fit, followed by fever, seized him on the first day of the tenth month. He took great notice that it ended forty years since his marriage with thee; that during that time you had lived in much love, and had parted in the same; and that leaving thee was his greatest concern of all outward enjoyments. On the sixth day of the tenth month, about six o'clock at night, he went away like a lamb." She published a religious tract of his, to which is prefixed a preface, entitled "Elizabeth Estaugh's testimony concerning her beloved husband, John Estaugh." In this preface, she says, "Since it pleased Divine Providence so high ly to favour me, with being the near companion of this dear worthy, I must give some small account of him. Few, if any, in a married state, ever lived in sweeter harmony than we did. He was a pattern of moderation in all things; not lifted up with any enjoyments, nor cast down at disappointments. A man endowed with many good gifts, which rendered him very agreeable to his friends, and much more to me, his wife, to whom his memory is most dear and precious."

Elizabeth survived her excellent husband twenty years, useful and honoured to the last. The Monthly Meeting of Haddonfield, in a published testimonial, speak of her thus: "She was endowed with great natural abilities, which, being sanctified by the spirit of Christ, were much improved; whereby she became qualified to act in the affairs of the church, and was a serviceable member, having been clerk to the women's meeting nearly fifty years, greatly to their satisfaction. She was a sincere sympathiser with the afflicted, of a benevolent disposition, and in distributing to the poor, was desirous to do it in a way most profitable and durable to them, and if possible not to let the right hand know what the left did. Though in a state of affluence as to this world's wealth, she was an example of plainness and moderation. Her heart and house were open to her friends, whom to entertain seemed one of her greatest pleasures. Prudently cheerful, and well knowing the value of friendship, she was careful not to wound it herself, nor to encourage others in whispering supposed failings or weaknesses. Her last illness brought great bodily pain, which she bore with much calmness of mind and sweetness of spirit. She departed this life as one falling asleep, full of days, like unto a shock of corn, fully ripe."

The town of Haddonfield, in New-Jersey, took its name from her; and the tradition concerning her courtship is often repeated by some patriarch among the Quakers. She laid out an extensive garden in rear of the house, which during her day was much celebrated for its herbs, vegetables and fruits, liberally distributed all round the neighbourhood. The house was burned down years ago; but some fine old yew trees, which she brought from England, are still pointed out on the site where the noble garden once flourished. Her medical skill is so well remembered, that the old nurses of New-Jersey still recommend Elizabeth Estaugh's salve as the "sovereignest thing on earth."

The brick tomb in which John Estaugh was buried at Tortola, is still pointed out to Quaker travellers; one of whom recently writes, "By a circuitous path, through a dense thicket, we came to the spot where Friends once had a meeting-house, and where are buried the remains of several of our valued ministers, who visited this island about a century ago, from a sense of gospel love. Time has made his ravages upon these mansions of the dead. The acacia spreads thickly its thorny branches over them, and near them the century-blooming aloe is luxuriantly growing."

THE QUADROONS.

"I promised thee a sister tale,
Of man's perfidious cruelty:
Come then and hear what cruel wrong
Befell the dark Ladie." COLERIDGE.

NOT far from Augusta, Georgia, there is a pleasant place called Sand-Hills, appropriated almost exclusively to summer residences for the wealthy inhabitants of the neighbouring city. Among the beautiful cottages that adorn it was one far retired from the public roads, and almost hidden among the trees. It was a perfect model of rural beauty. The piazzas that surrounded it were wreathed with Clematis and Passion Flower. Magnificent Magnolias, and the superb Pride of India, threw shadows around it, and filled the air with fragrance. Flowers peeped out from every nook, and nodded to you in bye-places, with a most unexpected welcome. The tasteful hand of Art had not learned to *imitate* the lavish beauty and harmonious disorder of Nature, but they lived together in loving unity, and spoke in according tones. The gateway rose in a Gothic arch, with graceful tracery in iron-work, surmounted by a Cross, around which fluttered and played the Mountain Fringe, that lightest and most fragile of vines.

The inhabitants of this cottage remained in it all

the year round, and peculiarly enjoyed the season that left them without neighbours. To one of the parties, indeed, the fashionable summer residents, that came and went with the butterflies, were merely neighbours-in-law. The edicts of society had built up a wall of separation between her and them; for she was a quadroon. Conventional laws could not be reversed in her favour, though she was the daughter of a wealthy merchant, was highly cultivated in mind and manners, graceful as an antelope, and beautiful as the evening star. She had early attracted the attention of a handsome and wealthy young Georgian; and as their acquaintance increased, the purity and bright intelligence of her mind, inspired him with far deeper interest than is ever excited by mere passion. It was genuine love; that mysterious union of soul and sense, in which the lowliest dew-drop reflects the image of the highest star.

The tenderness of Rosalie's conscience required an outward form of marriage; though she well knew that a union with her proscribed race was unrecognised by law, and therefore the ceremony gave her no legal hold on Edward's constancy. But her high poetic nature regarded the reality, rather than the semblance of things; and when he playfully asked how she could keep him if he wished to run away, she replied, "Let the church that my mother loved sanction our union, and my own soul will be satisfied, without the protection of the state. If your affections fall from me, I would not, if I could, hold you by a legal fetter."

It was a marriage sanctioned by Heaven, though

unrecognised on earth. The picturesque cottage at Sand-Hills was built for the young bride under her own direction; and there they passed ten as happy years as ever blessed the heart of mortals. It was Edward's fancy to name their eldest child Xarifa; in commemoration of a quaint old Spanish ballad, which had first conveyed to his ears the sweet tones of her mother's voice. Her flexile form and nimble motions were in harmony with the breezy sound of the name; and its Moorish origin was most appropriate to one so emphatically "a child of the sun." Her complexion, of a still lighter brown than Rosalie's, was rich and glowing as an autumnal leaf. The iris of her large, dark eye had the melting, mezzotinto outline, which remains the last vestige of African ancestry, and gives that plaintive expression, so often observed, and so appropriate to that docile and injured race.

Xarifa learned no lessons of humility or shame, within her own happy home; for she grew up in the warm atmosphere of father's and mother's love, like a flower open to the sunshine, and sheltered from the winds. But in summer walks with her beautiful mother, her young cheek often mantled at the rude gaze of the young men, and her dark eye flashed fire, when some contemptuous epithet met her ear, as white ladies passed them by, in scornful pride and ill-concealed envy.

Happy as Rosalie was in Edward's love, and surrounded by an outward environment of beauty, so well adapted to her poetic spirit, she felt these incidents with inexpressible pain. For herself, she cared but little; for she had found a sheltered home in Edward's heart, which the world might ridicule, but had no power to profane. But when she looked at her beloved Xarifa, and reflected upon the unavoidable and dangerous position which the tyranny of society had awarded her, her soul was filled with anguish. The rare loveliness of the child increased daily, and was evidently ripening into most marvellous beauty. The father rejoiced in it with unmingled pride; but in the deep tenderness of the mother's eye there was an indwelling sadness, that spoke of anxious thoughts and fearful forebodings.

When Xarifa entered her ninth year, these uneasy feelings found utterance in earnest solicitations that Edward would remove to France, or England. This request excited but little opposition, and was so attractive to his imagination, that he might have overcome all intervening obstacles, had not "a change come o'er the spirit of his dream." He still loved Rosalie; but he was now twenty-eight years old, and, unconsciously to himself, ambition had for some time been slowly gaining an ascendency over his other feelings. The contagion of example had led him into the arena where so much American strength is wasted; he had thrown himself into political excitement, with all the honest fervour of youthful feeling. His motives had been unmixed with selfishness, nor could he ever define to himself when or how sincere patriotism took the form of personal ambition. But so it was, that at twenty-eight years old, he found himself an ambitious man, involved in movements which his frank nature would have once abhorred, and watching the doubtful game of mutual cunning with all the fierce excitement of a gambler.

Among those on whom his political success most depended, was a very popular and wealthy man, who had an only daughter. His visits to the house were at first of a purely political nature; but the young lady was pleasing, and he fancied he discovered in her a sort of timid preference for himself. This excited his vanity, and awakened thoughts of the great worldly advantages connected with a union. Reminiscences of his first love kept these vague ideas in check for several months; but Rosalie's image at last became an unwelcome intruder; for with it was associated the idea of restraint. Moreover Charlotte, though inferior in beauty, was yet a pretty contrast to her rival. Her light hair fell in silken profusion, her blue eyes were gentle, though inexpressive, and her delicate cheeks were like blush-rose-buds.

He had already become accustomed to the dangerous experiment of resisting his own inward convictions; and this new impulse to ambition, combined with the strong temptation of variety in love, met the ardent young man weakened in moral principle, and unfettered by laws of the land. The change wrought upon him was soon noticed by Rosalie.

> "In many ways does the full heart reveal
> The presence of the love it would conceal;
> But in far more the estranged heart lets know
> The absence of the love, which yet it fain would show."

At length the news of his approaching marriage met her ear. Her head grew dizzy, and her heart fainted within her; but, with a strong effort at composure, she inquired all the particulars; and her pure mind at once took its resolution. Edward came that evening, and though she would have fain met him as usual, her heart was too full not to throw a deep sadness over her looks and tones. She had never complained of his decreasing tenderness, or of her own lonely hours; but he felt that the mute appeal of her heart-broken looks was more terrible than words. He kissed the hand she offered, and with a countenance almost as sad as her own, led her to a window in the recess, shadowed by a luxuriant Passion Flower. It was the same seat where they had spent the first evening in this beautiful cottage, consecrated to their youthful loves. The same calm, clear moonlight looked in through the trellis. The vine then planted had now a luxuriant growth; and many a time had Edward fondly twined its sacred blossoms with the glossy ringlets of her raven hair. The rush of memory almost overpowered poor Rosalie; and Edward felt too much oppressed and ashamed to break the long, deep silence. At length, in words scarcely audible, Rosalie said, "Tell me, dear Edward, are you to be married next week?" He dropped her hand, as if a rifle-ball had struck him; and it was not until after long hesitation, that he began to make some reply about the necessity of circumstances. Mildly, but earnestly, the poor girl begged him to spare apologies. It was enough that he no longer loved her, and that they must bid farewell. Trusting to the yielding tenderness of her character, he ventured, in the most soothing accents, to suggest that as he still loved her better than all the world, she would ever be his real wife, and they might see each other frequently. He was not prepared for the storm of indignant emotion his words excited. Hers was a passion too absorbing to admit of partnership; and her spirit was too pure and kind to enter into a selfish league against the happiness of the innocent young bride.

At length this painful interview came to an end. They stood together by the Gothic gate, where they had so often met and parted in the moonlight. Old remembrances melted their souls. "Farewell, dearest Edward," said Rosalie. "Give me a parting kiss." Her voice was choked for utterance, and the tears flowed freely, as she bent her lips toward him. He folded her convulsively in his arms, and imprinted a long, impassioned kiss on that mouth, which had never spoken to him but in love and blessing.

With effort like a death-pang, she at length raised her head from his heaving bosom, and turning from him with bitter sobs, she said, "It is our *last*. God bless you. I would not have you so miserable as I am. Farewell. A *last* farewell." "The *last!*" exclaimed he, with a wild shriek. "Oh, Rosalie, do not say that!" and covering his face with his hands, he wept like a child.

Recovering from his emotion, he found himself alone. The moon looked down upon him mild, but very sorrowful; as the Madonna seems to gaze on her worshipping children, bowed down with consciousness of sin. At that moment he would have given worlds to have disengaged himself from Charlotte; but he had gone so far, that blame, disgrace, and duels with angry relatives, would now attend any effort to obtain his freedom. Oh, how the moonlight oppressed him with its friendly sadness! It was like the plaintive eye of his forsaken one; like the music of sorrow echoed from an unseen world.

Long and earnestly he gazed at that dwelling, where he had so long known earth's purest foretaste of heavenly bliss. Slowly he walked away; then turned again to look on that charmed spot, the nestling-place of his young affections. He caught a glimpse of Rosalie, weeping beside a magnolia, which commanded a long view of the path leading to the public road. He would have sprung toward her, but she darted from him, and entered the cottage. That graceful figure, weeping in the moonlight, haunted him for years. It stood before his closing eyes, and greeted him with the morning dawn.

Poor Charlotte! had she known all, what a dreary lot would hers have been; but fortunately, she could not miss the impassioned tenderness she had never experienced; and Edward was the more careful in his kindness, because he was deficient in love. Once or twice she heard him murmur, "dear Rosalie," in his sleep; but the playful charge she brought was playfully answered, and the incident gave her : o real uneasiness. The summer after their marriage, she proposed a residence at Sand-Hills; little aware what a whirlwind of emotion she excited in her husband's heart. The reasons he gave for rejecting the proposition appeared satisfactory; but she could not quite understand why he was never willing that their afternoon drives should be in the direction of those plea sant rural residences, which she had heard him praise so much. One day, as their barouche rolled along a winding road that skirted Sand-Hills, her attention was suddenly attracted by two figures among the trees by the way-side; and touching Edward's arm, she exclaimed, "Do look at that beautiful child!" He turned, and saw Rosalie and Xarifa. His lips quivered, and his face became deadly pale. His young wife looked at him intently, but said nothing. There were points of resemblance in the child, that seemed to account for his sudden emotion. Suspicion was awakened, and she soon learned that the mother of that lovely girl bore the name of Rosalie; with this information came recollections of the "dear Rosalie," murmured in uneasy slumbers. From gossiping tongues she soon learned more than she wished to know. She wept, but not as poor Rosalie had done; for she never had loved, and been beloved, like her, and her nature was more proud. Henceforth a change came over her feelings and her manners; and Edward had no further occasion to assume a tenderness in return for hers. Changed as he was by ambition, he felt the wintry chill of her polite propriety, and sometimes in agony of heart, compared it with the gushing love of her who was indeed his wife.

But these, and all his emotions, were a sealed book to Rosalie, of which she could only guess the contents. With remittances for her and her child's support, there sometimes came earnest pleadings that she would consent to see him again; but these she never answered, though her heart yearned to do so. She pitied his fair young bride, and would not be tempted to bring sorrow into their household by any fault of hers. Her earnest prayer was that she might never know of her existence. She had not looked on Edward since she watched him under the shadow of the magnolia, until his barouche passed her in her rambles some months after. She saw the deadly paleness of his countenance, and had he dared to look back, he would have seen her tottering with faintness. Xarifa brought water from a little rivulet, and sprinkled her face. When she revived, she clasped the beloved child to her heart with a vehemence that made her scream. Soothingly she kissed away her fears, and gazed into her beautiful eyes with a deep, deep sadness of expression, which Xarifa never forgot. Wild were the thoughts that pressed around her aching heart, and almost maddened her poor brain; thoughts which had almost driven her to suicide the night of that last farewell. For her child's sake she conquered the fierce temptation then; and for her sake, she struggled with it now. But the gloomy atmosphere of their once happy home overclouded the morning of Xarifa's life.

> "She from her mother learnt the trick of grief,
> And sighed among her playthings."

Rosalie perceived this; and it gave her gentle heart unutterable pain. At last, the conflicts of her spirit proved too strong for the beautiful frame in which it dwelt. About a year after Edward's marriage, she was found dead in her bed, one bright autumnal morning. She had often expressed to her daughter a wish to be buried under a spreading oak, that shaded a rustic garden-chair, in which she and Edward had spent many happy evenings. And there she was buried; with a small white cross at her head, twined with the cypress vine. Edward came to the funeral, and wept long, very long, at the grave. Hours after midnight, he sat in the recess-window, with Xarifa folded to his heart. The poor child sobbed herself to sleep on his bosom; and the convicted murderer had small reason to envy that wretched man, as he gazed on the lovely countenance, which so strongly reminded him of his early and his only love.

From that time, Xarifa was the central point of all his warmest affections. He hired an excellent old negress to take charge of the cottage, from which he promised his darling child that she should never be removed. He employed a music master, and dancing master, to attend upon her; and a week never passed without a visit from him, and a present of books, pictures, or flowers. To hear her play upon the harp, or repeat some favourite poem in her mother's earnest accents and melodious tones, or to see her pliant figure float in the garland-dance, seemed to be the highest enjoyment of his life. Yet was the pleasure mixed with bitter thoughts. What would be the destiny of this fascinating young creature, so radiant with life and beauty? She belonged to a proscribed race; and though the brown colour on her soft cheek was scarcely deeper than the sunny side of a golden pear, yet was it sufficient to exclude her from virtuous society. He thought of Rosalie's wish to carry her to France: and he would have fulfilled it, had he been unmarried. As it was, he inwardly resolved to make some arrangement to effect it in a few years, even if it involved separation from his darling child.

But alas for the calculations of man! From the time of Rosalie's death, Edward had sought relief for his wretched feelings in the free use of wine. Xarifa was scarcely fifteen, when her father was found dead by the road-side; having fallen from his horse, on his way to visit her. He left no will; but his wife, with kindness of heart worthy of a happier domestic fate, expressed a decided reluctance to change any of the plans he had made for the beautiful child at Sand-Hills.

Xarifa mourned her indulgent father; but not as one utterly desolate. True, she had lived "like a flower deep hid in rocky cleft;" but the sunshine of love had already peeped in upon her. Her teacher on the harp was a handsome and agreeable young man of twenty, the only son of an English widow. Perhaps Edward had not been altogether unmindful of the result, when he first invited him to the flowery cottage. Certain it is, he had more than once thought what a pleasant thing it would be, if English freedom from prejudice should lead him to offer legal protection to his graceful and winning child. Being thus encouraged, rather than checked, in his admiration, George Elliot could not be otherwise than strongly attracted toward his beautiful pupil. The lonely and unprotected state in which her father's death left her, deepened this feeling into tenderness. And lucky was it for her enthusiastic and affectionate nature; for she could not live without an atmosphere of love. In her innocence, she knew nothing of the dangers in her path; and she trusted George with an undoubting simplicity, that rendered her sacred to his noble and generous soul. It seemed as if that flower-embosomed nest was consecrated by the Fates to Love. The French have well named it *La Belle Passion;* for without it life were "a year without spring, or a spring without roses." Except the loveliness of infancy, what does earth offer so much like Heaven, as the happiness of two young, pure, and beautiful beings, living in each other's hearts?

Xarifa inherited her mother's poetic and impassioned temperament; and to her, above others, the first consciousness of these sweet emotions was like a golden sunrise on the sleeping flowers.

> "Thus stood she at the threshold of the scene
> Of busy life. * * * *
> How fair it lay in solemn shade and sheen!
> And he beside her, like some angel, posted
> To lead her out of childhood's fairy land,
> On to life's glancing summit, hand in hand."

Alas, the tempest was brooding over their young heads. Rosalie, though she knew it not, had been the daughter of a slave, whose wealthy master, though he remained attached to her to the end of her days, yet carelessly omitted to have papers of manumission recorded. His heirs had lately failed, under circumstances which greatly exasperated their creditors; and in an unlucky hour, they discovered their claim on Angelique's grand-child.

The gentle girl, happy as the birds in spring-time, accustomed to the fondest indulgence, surrounded by all the refinements of life, timid as a fawn, and with

7

a soul full of romance, was ruthlessly seized by a sheriff, and placed on the public auction-stand in Savannah. There she stood, trembling, blushing, and weeping; compelled to listen to the grossest language, and shrinking from the rude hands that examined the graceful proportions of her beautiful frame. "Stop that!" exclaimed a stern voice. "I bid two thousand dollars for her, without asking any of their d—d questions." The speaker was probably about forty years of age, with handsome features, but a fierce and proud expression. An older man, who stood behind him, bid two thousand five hundred. The first bid higher; then a third, a dashing young man, bid three thousand; and thus they went on, with the keen excitement of gamblers, until the first speaker obtained the prize, for the moderate sum of five thousand dollars.

And where was George, during this dreadful scene? He was absent on a visit to his mother, at Mobile. But, had he been at Sand-Hills, he could not have saved his beloved from the wealthy profligate, who was determined to obtain her at any price. A letter of agonized entreaty from her brought him home on the wings of the wind. But what could he do? How could he ever obtain a sight of her, locked up as she was in the princely mansion of her master? At last, by bribing one of the slaves, he conveyed a letter to her, and received one in return. As yet, her purchaser treated her with respectful gentleness, and sought to win her favour, by flattery and presents; but she dreaded every moment, lest the scene should change, and trembled at the sound of every footfall. A plan was laid for escape. The slave agreed to drug his master's wine; a ladder of ropes was prepared, and a swift boat was in readiness. But the slave, to obtain a double reward, was treacherous. Xarifa had scarcely given an answering signal to the low cautious whistle of her lover, when the sharp sound of a rifle was followed by a deep groan, and a heavy fall on the pavement of the court-yard. With frenzied eagerness she swung herself down by the ladder of ropes, and, by the glancing light of lanthorns, saw George, bleeding and lifeless at her feet. One wild shriek, that pierced the brains of those who heard it, and she fell senseless by his side.

For many days she had a confused consciousness of some great agony, but knew not where she was, or by whom she was surrounded. The slow recovery of her reason settled into the most intense melancholy, which moved the compassion even of her cruel purchaser. The beautiful eyes, always pensive in expression, were now so heart-piercing in their sadness, that he could not endure to look upon them. For some months, he sought to win her smiles by lavish presents, and delicate attentions. He bought glittering chains of gold, and costly bands of pearl. His victim scarcely glanced at them, and her attendant slave laid them away, unheeded and forgotten. He purchased the furniture of the Cottage at Sand-Hills, and one morning Xarifa found her harp at the bedside, and the room filled with her own books, pictures, and flowers. She gazed upon them with a pang unutterable, and burst into an agony of tears; but she gave her master no thanks, and her gloom deepened.

At last his patience was exhausted. He grew

weary of her obstinacy, as he was pleased to term it; and threats took the place of persuasion.

* * * * * * *

In a few months more, poor Xarifa was a raving maniac. That pure temple was desecrated; that loving heart was broken; and that beautiful head fractured against the wall in the frenzy of despair. Her master cursed the useless expense she had cost him; the slaves buried her; and no one wept at the grave of her who had been so carefully cherished, and so tenderly beloved.

THE IRISH HEART.

A True Story.

It was a pleasant sight to look on James and Nora in their early childhood; their cheeks were so rosy, their hair so sunny, and their clear blue eyes so mild and innocent. They were the youngest of a cabin-full of children; and though they did now and then get a cuff from the elder ones, with the hasty words, "Get out of the way, you spalpeen," they were the pets and playmates of them all. Their love for each other was extreme; and though James, early in his boyhood, evinced the Irish predilection for giving knocks, he was never known to raise his hand against his little sister. When she could first toddle about, it was his delight to gather the Maygowans that grew about the well, and put them in Nora's curly hair; and then he would sit before her, with his little hands resting on his knees, contemplating her with the greatest satisfaction. When they were older, they might be seen weeding the "pathies"* side by side, or hand in hand gathering berries among the hawthorn bushes. The greatest difference between them seemed to be, that James was all fun and frolic, while Nora was ever serious and earnest.

When the young maiden was milking the cows, her

* Potatoes.

soft low voice might usually be heard, warbling some of the mournful melodies of Ireland. But plaintive tones were rarely heard from James. He came home from his daily labour whistling like a black-bird, mocking the cuckoo, or singing, at the top of his clear ringing voice, the merry jingle of St. Patrick's Day in the Morning, or the facetious air of Paudeen O'Rafferty. At dancing, too, he excelled all the lads of the neighbourhood. He could dance Irish jigs, three-part reel, four-part reel, or rowly-powly, to the tune of The Dusty Miller, or The Rakes of Bally-shanny, with such a quick ear for the music, that all the lassies declared they could "see the tune upon his feet." He was a comely lad, too, and at weddings and Christmas carousals, none of the rustic dandies looked more genteel than he, with his buff-coloured vest, his knot of ribbons at each knee, and his *caubeen*,* set jauntily on one side of his head. Being good-natured and mirthful, he was a great favourite at wakes and dances, and festivities of all sorts; and he might have been in danger of becoming dissipated, had it not been for the happy consciousness of belonging to an honest industrious family, and being the pride and darling of Nora's heart.

Notwithstanding the natural gayety of his disposition, he had a spirit of enterprise, and a love of earning money. This tendency led him early to think of emigrating to America, the Eldorado of Irish imagination. Nora resisted the first suggestion with many tears. But James drew fine pictures of a farm of his own in the new country, and cows and horses, and a

* Cap.

pleasant jaunting car; and in the farm-house and the jaunting car, Nora was ever by his side; for with the very first guineas that crossed his hand, sure he would send for *her*. Tho affectionate sister, accustomed to sympathise with all his plans, soon began to help him to build his castles in America; and every penny that she could earn at her spinning-wheel was laid away for passage money. But when the time actually arrived for him to go to Dublin, it was a day of sorrow. All the married sisters, with their little ones, and neighbours from far and near, came to bid him farewell, and give their parting blessing. The good mother was busy to the last, storing away some little comfort in his sea-box. Nora, with the big tears in her eyes, repeated, for the thousandth time, "And Jimmy, *mavourneen*,* if you grow grand there in the new country, you'll not be after forgetting *me?* You *will* send for your own Nora soon?"

"Forget *you!*" exclaimed James, while he pressed her warmly to his bosom: "When the blessed sun forgets to rise over the green earth, maybe I'll forget you, *mavourneen dheelish*."†

Amid oft repeated words of love and blessing, he parted from them. Their mutual sorrow was a little softened by distant visions of a final reunion of them *all* in America. But there was a fearful uncertainty about this. The big sea might swallow him up, he might sicken and die among strangers, or bad examples might lead him into evil paths worse than death.

To this last suggestion, made by an elder sister, Nora replied with indignant earnestness. "Led into

* Darling. † Sweet darling.

evil coorses, indade!" she exclaimed; "Shame be on you for spaking that same! and he the dacentest and best behaved boy in all the county Longford. You don't know the heart of him, as I do, or you'd never be after spaking of him in that fashion. It's a shame on you, and indade it is. But och, *wurrah dheelish*,* let him not sicken and die there in the strange country, and the sister not there to do for him!" And, overcome by the picture her own imagination had drawn, she burst into a passionate flood of tears.

In a few weeks, came a brief letter from James, written on board the ship in which he sailed from Dublin. About seven months later, came a letter, dated New York, saying he had obtained work at good wages, and, by God's blessing, should soon be enabled to send for his dear sister. He added a hint that one of these days, when he had a house of his own, perhaps the father and mother would be after coming over. Proud were they in the Irish cabin, when this letter was read aloud to all who came to inquire after the young emigrant. All his old cronies answered, "Throth, and *he'd* do well anywhere. He was always a dacent, clane, spirited boy, as there was widin a great ways of him. Divil a man in the ten parishes could dance the Baltihorum jig wid him, any how."

Time passed on, and no other letter came from James. Month after month, poor Nora watched with feverish anxiety to catch sight of her father when he returned from the distant post-office; for he promised, if he found a letter, to wave his hand high above his head, as soon as he came to the top of the hill front-

* Sweet Virgin.

ing the house. But no letter came; and at last Nora fully believed that her darling brother was dead. After writing again and again, and receiving no answer, she at last wrote to the son of a neighbour, who had emigrated to America, and begged of him, for the love of heaven, to ascertain whether James was dead or alive, and send them word as soon as possible. The Irishman to whom this urgent epistle was addressed, was at work on a distant rail-road, and had no fixed place of residence; and so it happened that Nora received no answer to her anxious inquiries, for more than a year and a half after they were written. At last, there came a crumpled square of soiled paper, containing these words:

"*Dear Frinds:*—Black and hevy is my hart for the news I have to tell you. James is in prison, concarnin a bit of paper, that he passed for money. Sorra a one of the nabors but will be lettin down the tears, when they hear o' the same. I don't know the rights of the case; but I will never believe he was a boy to disgrace an honest family. Perhaps some other man's sin is upon him. It may be some comfort to you to know that his time will be out in a year and a half, any how. I have not seen James sense I come to Ameriky; but I heern tell of what I have writ. The blessed Mother of Heaven keep your harts from sinkin down with this hevy sorrow. Your friud and nabor, MIKE MURPHY."

Deep indeed was the grief in that honest family, when these sad tidings were read. Poor Nora buried her face in her hands, and sobbed aloud. The old mother rocked violently to and fro, with her apron at her eyes; and the father, though he tried hard to conceal his emotion, could not restrain the big tears from rolling down his weather-beaten face. "Och, wo is the day," said he, "that ever we let him go from us. Such a dacent lad, and belonging to a family that never did a dishonest action. And sure all hearts were upon him, and we all so proud out of him."

"Father," said the weeping Nora, "I know the heart of him better nor any of you does; and I know he never had intintion to do anything that would bring to the blush the mother that bore him, and the sister that slept in his arms, when we were both weeny things. I'll go to Ameriky, and find out all about it, and write you word."

"*You* go to Ameriky!" exclaimed her mother. "Sure you're crazed with the big grief that's upon you, *coleen macree*,* or you'd niver spake thim words."

"And wouldn't he follow *me* to the ends of the earth, if the black trouble was on me?" replied Nora, with passionate earnestness. "There was always kindness in him for all human crathurs; but he loved me better nor all the world. Never a one had a bad word agin him, but nobody knew the heart of him as I did. Proud was I out of him, and lonesome is my heart widout him. And is it I will lave him alone wid his trouble? Troth, not if there was ten oceans atween us."

This vehemence subsided after awhile, and they talked more calmly of how they should hide their

* Pet of my heart.

disgrace from the neighbourhood. That their hearts were sad they could not conceal. Day after day, their frugal meals were removed almost untasted, and every one stepped about silently, as after a funeral. The very cows came slowly and disconsolately, as if they heard grief in the voice of their young mistress, when she called them to be milked. And the good old mother no longer crooned at her spinning wheel the song she had sung over the cradle of her darling boy. Nora at first persisted in her plan of crossing the Atlantic ; but her father forbade it, and she said no more. But her heart grew more and more impatient. She spoke less and less of James, but she sighed heavily at her work, and her eyes were often red with weeping. At last, she resolved to depart unknown to any one. She rose stealthily at midnight, tied up a small bundle of clothing, placed a little bag of money in her bosom, paused and gazed lovingly on her sleeping parents, hastily brushed away the gathering tears, and stept out into the moonlight. She stood for a few moments and gazed on the old familiar hills and fields, on the potato patch, where she and James had worked together many a day, on the old well, by the side of which the Maygowans grew, and on the clear white cabin, where the dear old ones slept. She passed into the little shed, that served as a stable for the animals, and threw her arms about the donkey's neck, and kissed the cow, that knew her voice as well as her own mother did. She came forth weeping, and gazed on the old homestead, as she would gaze on the face of a dying friend. The clustering memories were too much for her loving heart. Dropping on her knees, she prayed, in agony of sorrow: "If it be a sin to go away from the good old father and mother, perhaps niver to see them agin, till the judgment day, thou oh! Father in heaven, wilt forgive me; for thou seest I *can* not lave him alone wid his great trouble."

Then crossing herself, and looking toward the beloved home of her childhood, she said, in a stifled voice, "The Mother of Glory be wid ye, and bless and keep ye all."

Half blinded with tears, she wended her way over the moonlighted hills, and when her favourite cow called as usual for her milking pail, in the first blush of the morning, she was already far on her way to Dublin.

* * * * * * * *

And had James been criminal? In the eye of the law he had been; but his sister was right, when she said he had no intention to do a wicked thing. Not long after his arrival in America, he was one day walking along the street, in a respectable suit of Sunday clothes, when a stranger came up, and entered into conversation with him. After asking some indifferent questions, he inquired what his coat cost.

"Sixteen dollars," was the answer.

"I will give you twenty for it," said the stranger; "for I am going away in a hurry, and have no time to get one made."

James was as unsuspecting as a child. He thought this was an excellent opportunity to make four dollars, to send to his darling sister; so he readily agreed to the bargain.

"I want a watch, too," said the stranger; "but

perhaps you would not be willing to sell yours for ten dollars ?"

James frankly confessed that it was two dollars more than he gave for it, and very willingly consented to the transfer. Some weeks after, when he attempted to pass the money the stranger had given him, he found, to his dismay, that it was counterfeit. After brooding over his disappointment for some time, he came to a conclusion at which better educated men than himself have sometimes arrived. He thought to himself—"It is hard for a poor man to lose so much, by no fault of his own. Since it was put off upon me, I will just put it off upon somebody else. May-be it will keep going the rounds, or somebody will lose it that can better afford it than I can."

It certainly was a wrong conclusion; but it was a bewilderment of the reasoning powers in the mind of an ignorant man, and did not involve wickedness of intention. He passed the money, and was soon after arrested for forgery. He told his story plainly; but, as he admitted that he knew the money was counterfeit when he passed it, the legal construction of his crime was forgery in the second degree. He had passed three bills, and had the penalty of the law been enforced with its utmost rigour, he might have been sentenced to the state-prison for fifteen years; but appearances were so much in his favour, that the court sentenced him but for five years.

Five years taken away from the young life of a labouring man, spent in silent toil, in shame and sorrow for a blighted reputation, was, indeed, a heavy penalty for confused notions of right and wrong, concerning bits of paper, stamped with a nominal value. But law, in its wisest and kindest administration, cannot always make nice distinctions between thoughtless errors and wilful crimes.

It is probable James never felt the degree of compunction, that it is supposed every convict ought to feel; for the idea was ever with him, that if he had sinned against government, he did not mean to sin against God. That he had disgraced himself, he knew full well and felt keenly. The thoughts of what Nora and his good mother would suffer, if they could see him driven to hard labour with thieves and murderers, tore his soul with anguish. He could not bring his mind to write to them, or send them any tidings of his fate. He thought it was better that they should suppose him dead, than know of his disgrace. Thus the weary months passed silently away. The laugh of his eye and the bound of his step were gone. Day by day he grew more disconsolate and stupid.

He had been in prison about four years, when one of the keepers told him that a young woman had come to visit him, and he had received permission to see her. He followed silently, wondering who it could be; and a moment after, he was locked in his sister's arms. For some time, nothing but sobs were audible. They looked mournfully in each other's faces; then fell on each other's necks, and wept again.

"And so you know me, *mavourneen?*" said Nora, at last, trying to smile through her tears.

"Know you!" he replied, folding her more closely to his breast. "*A cushla machree*,* and wouldn't I

* Pulse of my heart.

know your shadow on the wall, in the darkest cellar they could put me in? But who came wid you, *mavourneen?*"

"Troth, and it was alone I come. I run away in the night. I hope it wasn't wrong to lave the good father and mother, when they had spoke agin my coming. I wouldn't like to do any thing displasing to God. But Jimmy, *machree*, my heart was breakin' widout you; and I couldn't lave you alone wid your great trouble. Sure it's long ago I would have been wid you, if you had let us know of your misfortin."

The poor fellow wept afresh at these assurances of his sister's affection. When he was calmer, he told her circumstantially how the great trouble had come upon him.

"God be praised for the words you spake," replied Nora. "It will take a load off of hearts at home, when they hear of the same. I always said there was no sin in your heart; for who should know that better nor me, who slept in the same cradle? A blessing be wid you, *mavourneen*. The music's in my heart to hear the sound of your voice agin. And proud will I be out of you, as I used to be when all eyes, young and old, brightened on you in warm old Ireland."

"But Nora, *dheelish*, the disgrace is on me," said the young man, looking down. "They will say I am a convict."

"Sorra a fig I care for what they say," replied the warm-hearted girl. "Don't I know the heart that is in you? Didn't I say there was no sin in your intintions, though you *was* shut up in this bad place? And if there had been—if the black murder had been widin you, is it Nora would be after laving you alone wid your sin and your shame? Troth, I would weary the saints in heaven wid prayers, till they made you a better man, for the sake of your sister's love. But there *was* no sin in your heart; and proud I am out of you, *a suillish machree;** and bad luck to the rogue that brought you into this trouble."

The keeper reminded them that the time allowed for their interview was nearly spent.

"You will come agin?" said James, imploringly. "You will come to me agin, *acushla machree?*"

"I had to beg hard to see you once," replied Nora. "They said it was agin the rules. But when I told them how I come alone across the big ocean to be wid you in your trouble, because I knew the heart that was in you, they said I might come in. It is a heavy sorrow that we cannot spake together. But it will be a comfort, *mavourneen,* to be where I can look on these stone walls. The kind man here they call the chaplain says I may stay wid his family; and sure not an hour in the day but I will think of you, *a villish.*† The same moon shines here, that used to shine on us when we had our May dances on the green, in dear old Ireland; and when they let you get a glimpse of her bright face, you can think maybe Nora is looking up at it, as she used to do when she was your own weeny darlint, wid the shamrock and gowan in her hair. I will work, and lay by money for you; and when you come out of this bad place, it's Nora will stand by you; and proud will I be out of you, *a suillish machree.*"

The young man smiled as he had not smiled for

* Light of my heart. † Dear.

years. He kissed his sister tenderly, as he answered, "Ah, Nora, *mavourneen*, it's yourself that was always too good to me. God's blessing be wid you, *acushla machree*. It will go hard wid me, but I will make some return for such goodness."

"And sure it's no goodness at all," replied Nora. "Is it yourself would be after laving *me* alone, and I in the great trouble? Hut, tut, Jimmy, avick. Sure it's nothing at all. Any body would do it. You're as dacent and clever a lad as iver you was. Sing that to your heart, *mavourneen*. It's Nora will stand by you, all the world over."

With a smile that she meant should be a brave one, but with eyes streaming with tears, she bade her beloved brother farewell. He embraced her with vehement tenderness, and, with a deep sigh, returned to his silent labour. But the weight was taken off his heart, and his step was lighter; for

> "*Hope's* sunshine lingered on his prison wall,
> And *Love* looked in upon his solitude."

Nora remained with the kind-hearted chaplain, ever watching the gloomy walls of Sing Sing. When her brother's term expired, she was at the prison door to welcome him, and lead him forth into the blessed sunshine and free air. The chaplain received them into his house, cheered and strengthened their hearts by kind words and judicious counsel, and sent them to the office of the Prison Association, No. 13 Pine-street, New-York. As James brought certificates of good conduct while in prison, the Association lent him tools, to be paid for if he should ever be able to do so, and recommended him to a worthy mechanic.

At this place he would have remained, had not his employer needed a journeyman thoroughly versed in his trade. It is the policy at Sing Sing not to allow the prisoners to learn all branches of any business, lest they should come into competition with mechanics out of the prison. What James had been accustomed to do, he did with great industry and expertness; but he could not do all his employer required, and was therefore kindly and honourably dismissed.

Had he been dishonest, he might have gone off with the tools; but he went to the office of the Association, to ask whether they were willing he should keep them till he could obtain work elsewhere, and earn enough to pay for them. They consented very cordially, and told him to remember them as friends in need, so long as he behaved well. His sister was with him, like his shadow, and their earnest expressions of gratitude were truly affecting.

Her good-natured honest countenance, and industrious habits, attracted the attention of a thriving young farmer, who succeeded in obtaining the treasure of her warm and generous heart. She who made so good a sister, can scarcely fail to be an excellent wife. James continues to do well, and loves her with superabounding love. The blessing of our Father be with them! They are two of the kindest hearts, and most transparent souls, among that reverent, loving, confiding, and impulsive people, who, in their virtues and their defects, deserve to be called the little children of the nations.

A LEGEND OF THE APOSTLE JOHN.

Suggested by a well known Anecdote in the Ecclesiastical History of Eusebius.

MORNING rose bright and clear on Ephesus, that beautiful city of the Ancients, which Pliny calls the Light of Asia. From the jutting points of lofty rocks on the mountain sides rose the massive and majestic pillars of Doric temples, embowered in verdant foliage, while the lighter and more elegant Ionian shafts shot up from the plain below, like graceful architectural flowers. Brilliant sunbeams streamed tremulously through the porticos, and reflected themselves in golden gleams on a forest of marble columns. The airy summits of the mountains smiled in serene glory beneath the lucid firmament. Troops of graceful swans and beautiful white sea-doves floated on the sparkling waters of the Cayster, running joyfully into the bright bosom of the Ægean. Maidens bearing Etruscan vases on their heads, went and came from the fountains, gliding majestically erect among the crowd of merchants, or the long processions of priests and worshippers. Here and there, a Roman soldier rode through the busy streets, his steel trappings and glittering harness shining in the distance like points of fire.

Strong and deep rolled the sonorous chant of bass voices from a Jewish synagogue, mingled with the sound of sackbut and harp. From the magnificent temple of Diana came up a plaintive strain, a modulated murmur, as of distant waves rippling to music; slowly swelling, slowly falling away, floating off in sweet echoes among the hills. There was a farewell sadness in this choral hymn, as of a religion passing away in its calm intellectual beauty, conscious that it had no adequate voice for the yearnings and aspirations of the human heart.

And then, as ever, when the want of a more spiritual faith began to be widely felt, it was already in existence. From the solemn shadows of Judaism, the mild form of Christianity had risen, and the Grecian mind was already preparing to encircle it with the mystic halo of a golden Platonism.

In the court of an artificer of Ephesus, there met that day an assembly of converts to the new and despised faith. Under the shadow of an awning, made by Paul the tent-maker, they talked together of Jesus, the holiness of his example, and the wide significance of his doctrines. It was a season of peculiar interest to the infant Church; for John, the disciple whom Jesus especially loved, had just returned from banishment. He was a man of ninety years, with hair and beard of silvery whiteness. His serious countenance beamed with resignation and love; but his high forehead, earnest eye, and energetic motions, showed plainly enough that his was not the serenity of a languid and quiet temperament. Through conflict he had attained humility and peace. His voice told the same story; for it was strong, deep, and restrained, though sweetly toned, and full of musical inflections.

His once erect figure was slightly bent; the effect of digging in the mines of Patmos. Many eyes were moistened with tears, as they gazed on his beloved and venerated countenance; for it brought sad memories of the hardships he had endured by the cruel orders of Domitian. He made no allusion to privations or sufferings, but spoke only of the heavenly visions, and the indwelling glory, that had been with him in the Isle of Patmos; how in the darkest mines the heavens opened, and in the narrowest prisons angels came and moved the stone walls afar off, so that he saw them not; and this he urged as proof how little power man has over a spirit at peace with God.

Of those who hung upon his words, the emotions of two were especially visible. One was a young maiden, who sat on a divan at his feet, and leaning on one arm gazed upwards in his face. She was closely veiled, but the outlines of her figure, imperfectly revealed through the ample folds of her rich dress, gave indication of personal grace. As she bent earnestly forward, her drapery had fallen back, and showed an arm of exquisite proportions, its clear soft olive tint beautifully contrasted by a broad bracelet of gold. She reclined partially on the shoulder of her old nurse, who was seated behind her on the same divan. Both ran great risk in visiting that Christian assembly; for Miriam's father was the wealthiest Jew in Ephesus; his was the highest place in the synagogue, and few of her thousand merchants could count so many ships. Narrow and bigoted in his own adherence to forms and traditions, he was the last man on earth to permit a woman to question them. But the earnest and truthful soul of his daughter early felt how little life there was in his solemn observances. Her nurse, a Galilean by birth, had told marvellous stories of the holy Nazarene, who had cured her father of blindness. With strict injunctions of secrecy, she lent her a copy of St. John's Gospel; and in this the young enthusiastic girl at once recognised the deeper and more spiritual teachings for which her soul had yearned. And so it came that the daughter of a wealthy house in Ephesus sat at the feet of the apostle, in the despised assembly of the Christians.

The other person who seemed most remarkably moved by the inspired eloquence of John, was a young Greek of superb beauty. His form was vigorous and finely proportioned. The carriage of his head was free and proud, and there was intense light in his large dark eyes, indicating a soul of fire. Indeed his whole countenance was remarkable for transparency and mobility of expression. When indignant at tyranny or insult, he looked like a young war-horse rushing to battle; but at the voice of tenderness, the dilated nostril subsided, and the flashing eye was dimmed with tears.

This constant revelation of soul particularly attracted the attention of the venerable apostle; for he saw in it a nature liable to the greatest dangers, and capable of the highest good. After he had dismissed the assembly, with his usual paternal benediction, "Little children, love one another," he stepped forward, and laying his hand affectionately on the head of the young Greek, said, "And thou, my son, art thou too a Christian?" With emphasis full of feeling, the young man replied, "I would I *were* a Christian." Pleased with the earnest humility of this answer, the apostle drew his arm within his own, and they retired to an inner apartment to converse together. During this confidential conversation, the young man made a full and free revelation of his soul, in all its strength and weakness. At times, his daring and fiery words startled the more subdued nature of the meek disciple; but at the same moment, the crystalline frankness of his heart excited the warmest and most confiding affection. From that time, it was observable that the apostle treated him with more marked tenderness than he evinced toward any other of his converts. A few months after, feeling that duty required him to take a long journey to comfort and strengthen the surrounding churches of Asia, he called his flock together, and bade them an affectionate farewell. At parting, he placed the hand of the young Greek within the hand of the presiding elder, and said solemnly, "To thy care I consign my precious, my beloved son, Antiorus. In the Epicurean gardens he has learned that pleasure is the only good; from Christians let him learn that good is the only pleasure. Be to him a father; for at my return I shall require his soul at thy hands." The bishop promised, and the young man wept as he kissed his venerable friend.

The apostle was gathering his robe about him, and fastening his girdle, preparing to walk forth, when Miriam glided timidly before him, saying in a tremulous tone, "My father, bless me before you go." She removed her veil, and stooped to kiss his hand. The veil dropped again instantly, but the sudden action had revealed to Antiorus a countenance of surpassing beauty. He had no time to analyze the features; but he saw that her contour was noble, and that her large almond-shaped eyes, of the darkest brown, were singularly brilliant, yet deep and serene in their expression. The tones of her voice, too, thrilled through his soul; for they were like a silver bell, softening language into music. For an instant, she caught the beaming glance of his eye, and an electric spark fell from it into her heart. Henceforth, each observed the other's motions, and each was indistinctly conscious of pervading the other's being. The customs of the times, combined with her maidenly reserve, rendered it difficult to form a personal acquaintance. But Antiorus had a Greek friend, whose dwelling adjoined the gardens of Miriam's father; and the house of this friend became singularly attractive to him. Here he could sometimes catch the sound of her voice, accompanied by her harp, as she sang to her father the psalms of David. At last, he ventured to speak to her, as they left the assembly of the Christians. He timidly asked her if she would play, on the next Sabbath evening, the same psalm he had heard on the preceding Sabbath. She started, and made no answer. The crimson suffusion of her face he could not see. But when the Sabbath came, softly on the evening air arose his favourite psalm, with a deeper expression, a more sweet solemnity than ever. While the strings yet vibrated, his Phrygian flute gently answered, in a simple Grecian air, the utterance of a soul tender and sad. Tear-drops fell slowly on the strings of Miriam's harp; but she alone knew that the spirit of the beautiful Greek had thus entered invisibly into the sanctuary of the Jewish maiden. How dear was now her harp, since his soul had kissed the winged messengers it sent from hers! Again and again, harp and flute responded to each other. Their young hearts were overflowing with new and heavenly emotions, which music alone could utter. For music is among the arts what love is among the passions; a divine mediator between spirit and matter; a flowery spiral, descending from the highest sanctuary of the soul into the outer court of the senses, returning again from the senses to the soul, twining them together in perpetual bloom and fragrance.

But music has the vagueness of all things infinite; and they who talked together in tones, earnestly desired to speak in words. At the Christian assemblies too strict decorum was observed, to admit of conversation between them. Into her father's house he could not gain entrance; or if he did, she would be carefully secluded from the gaze of a Gentile. And so at last, by help of the over-indulgent nurse, there came meetings in the garden, while all the household slept. Under the dim light of the stars, they talked of the new faith, which had brought them together. He loved to disclose to her mind the moonlight glory of Plato, showing a world of marvelous beautv in shadowy outline, but fully revealing nothing. While she, in soft serious tones, spoke of the Hebrew prophets, complaining that they seemed like an infinite glow, forever expressing a want they never satisfied. Beautiful and majestic was their utterance, but it was not high and deep enough to satisfy the aspirations of her soul; therefore she clung to the sublime all-embracing doctrines of Christ. From these high themes, they came gradually to speak of their affection for each other. There was no desecration in this mingling of emotions; for genuine love is as holy as religion; and all round the circling horizon of our mysterious being, heaven and earth do kiss each other.

One night, their stolen interview in the garden was interrupted by a noise on the house-top; and fearing they were suspected or observed, they resolved to be more prudent. Weeks passed, therefore, and they saw each other only at the meetings of the Christians, rendered doubly precious by the obstacles which elsewhere separated them. There was another reason why they thought more of each other's presence, than they would have done had the good apostle John been with them. As a deep rich musical voice will sometimes join itself to a company of timid and wavering singers, and gradually raise the whole chorus to its own power and clearness, so the influence of his holy and living soul elevated the character of every assembly he joined. With him, something of unction and fervour had departed from the Christian meetings, and still more of calm assured faith. More fear of the world was visible, more anxiety to build up a respectable name. The lovers felt this, though they had not distinctly defined it; and being less elevated by the religious services, their thoughts were more consciously occupied with each other. But their mutual absorption passed unobserved; for Miriam was always closely veiled, and if she dropped a rose, or Antiorus a sprig of myrtle, it seemed mere accident to all but the watchful and sympathizing nurse. These silent manifestations of course made the concealed flame burn all the more fervently. Perpetual separation was so wearisome, that at last Miriam, in the plenitude of her love and confidence, granted his urgent entreaty to walk with him once, only once, in disguise, when all were sleeping. He had a proposition to make, he said, and he *must* have an opportunity to talk freely with her. In the garb of Greek peasants they joined each other, and passing through the least frequented streets, sought the mountains by a solitary path. In a concealed nook of rock, under the shadow of broad-leaved trees, they spoke together in agitation and tears. Love is ever a troubled joy; a semi-tone changes its brightest strains into plaintive modulations. Miriam wept, as she told her beloved that they must part forever. She had come only to tell him so, and bid him farewell. As yet she had not courage to confess that she was promised to a wealthy kinsman, a stern old Pharisee; but her father had told her, that day, that immediate preparations must be made for the wedding. The enamoured Greek spoke with fiery indignation, that her father should dare thus to seal up the treasures of her large warm gushing heart, for the sake of preserving wealth in the family. To her timid suggestion that obedience was due to parents, he insisted upon a higher obedience to the divine law in the soul. In such a union as she spoke of, he said there was positive pollution, which no law or custom could cleanse; for the heart alone could sanctify the senses. The maiden bent her head, and felt her cheeks burning; for she was conscious of a painful sense of degradation whenever the odious marriage was forced upon her thoughts. He took her hand, and it trembled within his, while he spoke to her of flight, of secret marriage, and a hidden home of love in some far-off Grecian isle. He drew her gently toward him, and for the first time her lovely head rested on his bosom. As she looked up fondly and tearfully in his face, he stooped to kiss her beautiful lips, which trembling gave an almost imperceptible pressure in return. Faint and timid as was this first maiden kiss, it rushed through his system like a stream of fire. The earthly portion of love proclaimed ascendency over the soul, and tried him with a fierce temptation. She loved him, and they were alone in the midnight. Should he ever be able to marry her? Might not this stolen and troubled interview be, as she said, the last? He breathed with difficulty, his whole frame shook like a tree in the storm; but she lay on his bosom, as ignorant of the struggle, as if she had been a sleeping babe. Rebuked by her unconscious innocence, he said inwardly to the tempting spirit, "Get thee behind me! Why strivest thou to lead me into evil?" But the spirit answered, "The sin is wholly of man's making. These Christians are too ascetic. The Epicurean philosophy better agrees with nature."

The scene seemed to have entered into a league with the tempting spirit. Nothing interrupted the drowsy moon-stillness, save the pattering of a little rill that trickled from the rocks, the amorous cooing of two ring-doves awake in their nests among the shrubbery above, and the flute of some distant lover conversing passionately with the moon. The maiden herself, saddened by a presentiment, that this bliss was too perfect to last, and melted into unusual tenderness by the silent beauty of the night, and the presence of the beloved one, folded her arm more caressingly about his waist, till he felt the beating of her heart. With frantic energy, he pressed his hand against his throbbing brow, and gazed earnestly into the clear arch of heaven, as if imploring strength to aid his higher nature. Again the tempter said, "Thy Epicurean philosophy was more in harmony with nature. Pleasure is the only good." Then he remembered the parting words of St. John, "Good is the only pleasure." A better influence glided into his soul, and a still small voice within him whispered, "Thou hast no need to compare philosophies and creeds, to know whether it be good to dishonour her who trusts thee, or by thy selfishness to bring a stain on the pure and persecuted faith of the Christians. Restore the maiden to her home." The tempter veiled his face and turned away, for he felt that the young man was listening to an angel.

With a calm sad voice, spoke the tempted one, as he gently and reverently removed the beloved head from his breast. Taking Miriam by the hand, he led her out from the deep shadow of the trees, to the little rill that gurgled near by, and gathering water in his hands, he offered her to drink. As she stood there in the moonlight, drinking from his hand, the shadow of the vines danced across her face, and fluttered gracefully over the folds of her white dress. At that moment, when the thought of danger was far from them both, an arrow whizzed throgh the air, and with a groan the maiden fell backward on the arm that was hastily extended to save her from falling.

They were standing near a portion of Mt. Prion, whence marble had been dug for the numerous edifices of the city. It was full of grottoes, with winding mazes blocked up with fragments of stone. The first thought of Antiorus was to retreat hastily from the moonlight that had made them visible, and the next was to conceal his senseless burden within the recesses of the grotto, here and there made luminous by fissures in the rocks. Carefully he drew the arrow from the wound, and bound it tightly with his mantle. He gathered water from the dripping cavern, and dashed it in her face. But his efforts to restore life were unavailing. Regardless of his own safety, he would have rushed back to the city and roused his friends, but he dared not thus compromise the fair fame of her who had loved him so purely, though so tenderly. Perhaps the person who aimed the arrow might have mistaken them for others; at all events, they could not have been positively known. In a state of agonized indecision, he stepped to the entrance of the grotto, and looked and listened. All was still, save the pattering of water-drops. Presently he heard a sound, as of feet descending the path from the mountains. With long strides, he bounded up to meet the advancing stranger, and with energetic brevity begged for assistance to convey a wounded maiden to some place of safety, away from the city. The stranger said he had companions, who would bring a litter from the mountains, and he turned back to summon them. The minutes seemed hours to Antiorus, till his return; for though all hope of restoring the precious life was well nigh extinct, he felt continual dread of being discovered by the unseen foe, who had aimed the fatal arrow. At last, the promised assistance came, and they slowly ascended the mountain with their mournful burden. After pursuing a winding rugged path for some distance, they entered a spacious cavern. A lamp was burning on a table of rock, and several men were stretched on the ground sleeping. The litter was gently lowered, and Antiorus bent in agony over the senseless form so lately full of life and love. Not until every means had been tried that ingenuity could devise, would he believe that her pure and gentle spirit had passed from its beautiful earthly frame forever. But when the last ray of hope departed, he gave himself up to grief so frightfully stormy, that the rude dwellers in the cave covered their eyes, that they might not witness the terrible anguish of his sensitive and powerful soul. In his desperate grief, he heaped upon himself all manner of reproaches. Why had he sought her love, when it was almost sure to end unhappily? Why had he so selfishly availed himself of her tenderness, when the world would judge so harshly of the concessions she had made to love? Then, in the bitterness of his heart, he cursed the world for its false relations, its barriers built on selfishness and pride. But soon, in the prostration of deep humility, he forgave all men, and blamed only his own over-leaping nature. Through all his changes of mood, ran the intensely mournful strain, "Oh, my beloved, would to God I had died for thee!"

But it is kindly ordered that human nature cannot long remain under the influence of extreme anguish; its very intensity stupifies the soul. When Antiorus became calm from exhaustion, the man who had guided him to the mountain spoke in low tones of the necessity of burial. The mourner listened with a visible shudder. While he could gaze on her beautiful face, so placid in the sleep of death, it seemed as if something remained to him; but when that should be covered from his gaze forever, oh how fearfully lonely the earth would seem! By degrees, however, he was brought to admit the necessity of separation. He himself gathered green branches for the litter, and covered it with the fairest flowers. He cut a braid of her glossy hair, and his tears fell on it like the spring rain. In a green level space among the trees, they dug a deep grave, and reverently laid her within it, in her peasant robes. The doves cooed in the branches, and a pleasant sound of murmuring waters came up from the dell below. The mourner fashioned a large cross, and planted it strongly at the head of the grave. He sought for the most beautiful vines, and removing them in large sods, twined them about the cross. He sobbed himself to sleep on the mound, and when his companions brought him food, he ate as though he tasted it not.

The strong ardent nature of the young Greek, his noble beauty and majestic figure, commanded their involuntary respect, while the intensity of his sorrow moved even their slow sympathies. But when several days had elapsed, their leader began to question him concerning his future prospects and intentions. The subject thus forced upon his reluctant thoughts was a painful one. He dared not return openly to Ephesus; for whether his secret interviews with Miriam had been suspected by her family, or not, her sudden disappearance, connected with his own, must of course have given rise to the most unfavourable rumours. Of the effect on the little community of Christians, already so unpopular, he thought with exceeding pain. And these dark suspicious-looking men, that dwelt in caverns, who were they?

They soon resolved his doubts on this subject; for their leader said boldly, "We are robbers. You are in some way implicated in the death of this young woman, and you dare not return to Ephesus. Remain with us. We have seen your strength, and we like your temper. Stay with us, and you shall be our leader."

The proposition startled him with its strangeness, and filled his soul with loathing. He, on whose fair integrity no stain had ever rested, *he* become a robber! He, who had so lately sat at the feet of the holy apostle, and felt in his inmost heart the blessed influence of the words, "Love your enemies, do good to them that hate you"—was it proposed to *him* to arm himself against unoffending brethren? Concealing his abhorrence, by a strong effort, he thanked the robber for the kindness he had shown him in his great distress, and promised to repay him for it; but he told him mildly that his habits and his feelings alike unfitted him for a life like theirs. He would return to

Ephesus, and consult with friends concerning his future plans. The men seemed dissatisfied with their leader's courtesy to the stranger, and grumbled something about his going to guide the magistrates to their cavern in the mountains. Antiorus turned proudly toward them, and with strong convincing earnestness replied, "You cannot deem me base enough thus to recompense your kindness." His voice became lower and deeper with emotion, as he added, "Reverently and tenderly you have treated her who sleeps; and the secret that thus came to my knowledge shall never be revealed. I would die rather than divulge it." The men stood silent, awed by the dignity of his bearing and the clear truthfulness of his words. After a slight pause, their leader said, "We believe you; but there are doubtless those in Ephesus who would pay a handsome sum to gain tidings from you. You may keep your secret, if you like; but it cannot be concealed that you and the beautiful maiden were no peasants. What if we put the magistrates on *your* track?"

Looking him openly and fearlessly in the eye, Antiorus replied, "Because you have not so lost your manly nature. A voice within you would forbid you to persecute one already so crushed and heart-broken. You will not do it, because I am in your power, and because I trust you." This appeal to the manliness that remained within them, controlled their rough natures, and the bold frankness of his eyes kindled their admiration. Clasping his hand with rough cordiality, the leader said, "We will not inform against you, and we will trust you to go to Ephesus." "Let him seal his promise by an oath to Hecate and the Furies," murmured several voices. The leader folded his arms across his breast, and answered slowly and proudly, "The simple word of such a man is more sacred to him than the most terrible oaths." The countenance of the impetuous young Greek became at once illuminated. Seizing the hand of the robber-captain, he said, "My friend, you are worthy of a better occupation." "Perhaps so," replied the other, with a deep sigh; "at least, I thought so once."

* * * * * * *

Under the shadow of evening, and disguised in dress, Antiorus ventured to return to Ephesus. The first house he entered was the one adjoining the gardens, where he had so often listened to Miriam's harp. The moment he was recognised, all eyes looked coldly on him. "Why hast thou come hither?" said his once friendly host. "Already my house has been searched for thee, and I am suspected of aiding thy designs by bringing thee within hearing of the gardens. Curse on thy imprudence! Were there not women enough in the streets of Ephesus, that thou must needs dishonour one of its wealthiest families?"

In former times, the sensitive young man would have flashed fire at these insulting words; but now he meekly replied, "You judge me wrongfully. I loved her purely and reverently." His friend answered sarcastically, "Perhaps you learned this smooth hypocrisy at the meetings of the Christians; for there, I understand, to my great surprise, it has been your habit to attend. What name *they* give to such transactions I do not care to know. It is enough to say that you are no longer a welcome guest in my house." For a moment a deep flush went over the young man's expressive countenance, and his eye kindled; but he turned away, and silently departed; lingering for a moment with fond reluctance, on the steps of the terrace he had so often mounted rapidly, buoyant with love and hope.

With a sorrowful heart, he sought the dwelling of the Christian elder, to whom St. John had so affectionately confided him, at parting. As soon as he made himself known, a severe frown clouded the face of the bishop. "What impudence has brought thee hither?" he exclaimed. "Hast thou not sufficiently disgraced the Church by thy wickedness, without presuming to disgrace it further by thy presence?" "You judge me too harshly," replied the young man, meekly. "Imprudent I have been, but not wicked." "Where hast thou hidden thy paramour?" said the bishop impatiently. The eyes of the young Greek glowed like coals of fire, his nostrils expanded, his lips quivered, his breast heaved, and his hand strongly clenched the staff on which he leaned. But he constrained himself, and answered with mournful calmness, "I have no paramour. She on whose innocent name you have breathed an epithet so undeserved, has passed from earth to heaven, pure as the angels who received her."

In answer to further inquiries, he frankly repeated the whole story, not concealing the temptation, which had so nearly conquered him. In reply, the bishop informed him that suspicion had been awakened previous to their imprudent midnight ramble. The attendance of Miriam and her nurse at the Christian meetings had been discovered; her absence on that fatal night had been detected; the nurse fled in terror; the betrothed husband of Miriam went forth madly into the streets, vowing revenge; her father believed he had traced the fugitives on board a ship bound to Athens, whither he had sent spies to discover them. Whether the Jewish lover had fired the arrow or not, it was impossible to tell; but should it be known that Miriam was dead, her death would unquestionably be charged on Antiorus, and the effect would be to renew the popular hatred against the Christians, with redoubled vigour. At present, believing her to be in Athens, it was the policy of her family to keep the affair from the public, as much as possible.

Antiorus expressed the utmost contrition for his imprudence, but averred most solemnly that he had in no way violated his conscience, or his Christian obligations. He begged the bishop for credentials to some distant Christian Church, where by a life of humility and prayer, he might make himself ready to rejoin his beloved Miriam.

The bishop, vexed at an affair so likely to bring discredit on his own watchfulness, listened coldly, and replied, "For the prosperity of the Church, it is very necessary to obtain and preserve a good name. We must avoid the appearance of evil. Appearances are very much against you. You are young and of fiery blood. You have been an Epicurean, whose doctrines favour unbridled pleasure. You *say* that your love for this maiden was pure; but what proof have we, save your own word?" Antiorus raised his head proudly, and with a clear bold glance replied, "What more is needed? Have I ever spoken falsely to friend or foe?" "I know not," answered the bishop. "Young men do not usually decoy maidens into hidden grottoes, at midnight, for purposes as pure as the angels."

Alas, for his less noble nature! He knew not the value of the warm heart he was thus turning to gall. The young man bent upon him a most intense and searching gaze. He thought of that fearfully strong temptation in the lonely midnight hour; of his extreme reluctance to bring suspicion on the character of the Christian Church; of his conquest over himself; of his reverential love for the pure maiden; of his virtuous resolutions, and his holy aspirations. He had opened his whole heart to this father of the Church, and *thus* it had been received! Would Christ have thus weighed the respectability of the Church against the salvation of a human soul? Were these beautiful doctrines of love and forgiveness mere idle theories? Mere texts for fine speeches and eloquent epistles? A disbelief in all principles, a distrust of all men, took possession of him. With a deep sigh, he gathered his robe about him and departed. He walked hastily, as if to run away from his own mad thoughts. Ascending an eminence, he paused and looked back on the city, its white columns dimly visible in the starlight. "There is no one there to love me," said he. "I am an orphan; no mother or sister to comfort my aching heart. I have had great projects, great hopes, sublime aspirations; but that is all over now. No matter what becomes of me. I will go to the robbers. I have no other friends; and they at least believed me."

He was received in the mountain cavern with an uproarious burst of joy. They drank wine and caroused, and with loud acclamations proclaimed him king of their band. His heart was sick within him, but with wild desperation, he drank to their pledge. That night, when all the riotous crew were sleeping, he stole forth into the midnight, and stood alone on the mountain side, gazing mournfully upon the stars, that looked down upon him with solemn love. Then tossing his arms wildly above his head, he threw himself on the ground with a mighty sob, exclaiming, "Oh, if *she* had but lived, her pure and gentle spirit would have saved me!"

Hark! Is that a faint whispering of music in the air? Or is it memory's echo of Miriam's psalm? Now it dies away in so sad a cadence—and now it rises, full of victory. It has passed into his heart; and spite of recklessness and sin, it will keep there a nestling-place for holiness and love.

* * * * *

When the apostle John returned to Ephesus, his first inquiry of the bishop was, "Where is the beloved son I committed to thy charge?" The elder, looking down, replied, with some embarrassment, "He is dead!" "Dead!" exclaimed the apostle, "How did he die?" The elder answered with a sigh, "He is dead in trespasses and sins. He became dissolute, was led away by evil companions, and it is said he is now captain of a band of robbers in yonder mountains." With a voice full of sorrowful reproach, the apostle said, "And is it thus, my brother, thou hast cared for the precious soul that Christ and I committed to thy charge? Bring me a horse and a guide to the mountains. I will go to my erring son." "I pray you do not attempt it," exclaimed the elder. "You will be seized by the robbers and perhaps murdered." "Hinder me not," replied the venerable man. "If need be, I will gladly die to save his soul, even as Christ died for us. I will go to my son; perchance he will listen to me."

They brought him a horse, and he rode to the mountains. While searching for the cavern, one of the robbers came up and seized him rudely, exclaiming, "Who art thou, old man? Come before our captain, and declare thy business."

"For that purpose I came hither," replied the apostle. "Bring me to your captain."

Antiorus, hearing the sound of voices, stepped forth from the mouth of the cavern; but when he saw John, he covered his face and turned quickly away. The apostle ran toward him with outstretched arms, exclaiming, "Why dost thou fly from me, my son? From me, an old unarmed man? Thou art dear to me, my son. I will pray for thee. If need be, I will die for thee. Oh, trust to me; for Christ has sent me to thee, to speak of hope, forgiveness, and salvation."

Antiorus stood with his face covered, and his strong frame shook in his armour. But when he heard the words forgiveness and hope, he fell on the ground, embraced the old man's knees, and wept like a child. The apostle laid his hand affectionately on that noble head, and said, with a heavenly smile, "Ah, now thou art baptized again, my dear son—baptized in thy tears. The Lord bless thee and keep thee. The Lord lift up his countenance upon thee, and give thee peace."

After speaking together for a few moments, they retired to Miriam's grave, and there the young man laid open all his sinning and suffering heart. In conclusion, he said, "There seems ever to be within me two natures; one for good, and one for evil." "It is even thus with us all," replied the apostle. "But thou, my father," rejoined Antiorus, "thou canst not imagine how I have sinned, or what I have resisted. Thy blood flows so calmly. Thou art too pure and holy to be tempted as I have been."

"Hush, hush, I pray thee, my son," replied the apostle. "How I have struggled is known only to *Him* who seeth all the secrets of the heart. Because my blood has *not* always flowed so calmly, therefore, my son, have I been peculiarly drawn toward thee in the bonds of pity and of sympathy. Thy wild ambition, thy impetuous anger, are no strangers in my own experience; and that midnight temptation so brought back a scene of my youth, that it seemed almost like a page of my own history." "Of *thine!*" exclaimed the young man, with an accent of strong surprise. In a voice low and tender, he added, "Then thou hast loved?" The white-haired man bowed his head upon his hands, and with strong emotion answered, "Oh, how deeply, how tenderly."

There was silence for some moments, interrupted only by the quiet lullaby of the waters, rippling in the dell below. Pressing the apostle's hand, Antiorus said, in a low reverential tone, "Does love end here, my father? Shall we know our loved ones among the angels of heaven? Do they witness our conflicts? Do they rejoice over our victories?"

Hark! Is that music in the air? Or is it a memory of the psalm? How distinctly it swells forth in joy, how sweetly it breathes of love and peace! The listener smiles; for he seems to hear a harp in the heavens.

The two beautiful ones, the young and the old, stand with clasped hands, looking upward into the sky. The countenance of the apostle was radiant with spiritual light, as he said, "Let us believe and hope." They knelt down, embracing each other, and offered a silent prayer, in the name of him who had brought immortality to light.

Antiorus bade his wild comrades farewell, with exhortations, to which the apostle added words that were blessed in their gentleness; for the former leader of the band turned from the evil of his ways, and became a zealous Christian. The young Greek went to the church in Corinth, bearing affectionate credentials from the beloved apostle. Many years after, hearing that the family of Miriam had gone to a Syrian city, he returned to Ephesus. The cross had been removed from the mountain, but he planted another on the well-remembered spot. Near by, he built a little cabin of boughs, where an opening in the thick groves gave glimpses of the marble columns of Ephesus, and the harbour of Panormous sparkling in the sun. Many came to talk with him concerning the doctrines of Plato, and the new truths taught by Jesus. He received them all with humility and love; but otherwise he mixed not with the world, except to visit the sick and suffering, or to meet with the increasing band of Christians in the plain below. He was an old man when he died. The name of Miriam had not passed his lips for many years; but when they buried him beside the mountain cross, they found a ringlet of black hair in a little ivory casement next his heart.

THE BELOVED TUNE.

Fragments of a Life, in Small Pictures

A child, a friend, a wife, whose soft heart sings
In unison with ours, breeding its future wings.—LEIGH HUNT.

IN a pleasant English garden, on a rustic chair of intertwisted boughs, are seated two happy human beings. Beds of violets perfume the air, and the verdant hedge-rows stand sleepily in the moonlight. A guitar lies on the greensward, but it is silent now, for all is hushed in the deep stillness of the heart. That youthful pair are whispering their first acknowledgment of mutual love. With them is now unfolding life's best and brightest blossom, so beautiful and so transient, but leaving, as it passes into fruit, a fragrance through all the paths of memory.

And now the garden is alone in the moonlight. The rustic bench, and the whispering foliage of the tree, tell each other no tales of those still kisses, those gentle claspings, and all the fervent language of the heart. But the young man has carried them away in his soul; and as he sits alone at his chamber window, gazing in the mild face of the moon, he feels, as all do who love and are beloved, that he is a better man, and will henceforth be a wiser and a purer one. The worlds within and without are veiled in transfigured glory, and breathe together in perfect harmony.

For all these high aspirations, this deep tide of tenderness, this fulness of beauty, there is but one utterance; the yearning heart must overflow in music. Faint and uncertain come the first tones of the guitar, breathing as softly as if they responded to the mere touch of the moonbeams. But now the rich manly voice has united with them, and a clear spiritual melody flows forth, plaintive and impassioned, the modulated breath of indwelling life and love. All the secrets of the garden, secrets that painting and poetry had no power to reveal, have passed into the song.

At first, the young musician scarcely noticed the exceeding beauty of the air he was composing. But a passage that came from the deepest of the heart, returned to the heart again, and filled it with its own sweet echoes. He lighted a lamp, and rapidly transferred the sounds to paper. Thus has he embodied the floating essence of his soul, and life's brightest inspiration cannot pass away with the moonlight and the violet-fragrance that veiled its birth.

But obstacles arise in the path of love. Dora's father has an aversion to foreigners, and Alessandro is of mingled Italian and German parentage. He thinks of worldly substance, as fathers are wont to do; and Alessandro is simply leader of an orchestra, and a popular composer of guitar music. There is a richer lover in question, and the poor musician is sad with hope deferred, though he leans ever trustfully on Dora's true heart. He labours diligently in his vocation, gives lessons day by day, and listens with all patience to the learner's trip-hammer measurement of time, while the soul within him yearns to pour itself forth in floods of improvised melody. He composes music industriously, too; but it is for the market, and slowly and reluctantly the offended tones take their places per order. Not thus came they in that inspired song, where love first breathed its bright but timid joy over vanished doubts and fears. The manuscript of that melody is laid away, and seldom can the anxious lover bear its voice.

But two years of patient effort secures his prize. The loved one has come to his humble home, with her bridal wreath of jessamine and orange-buds. He sits at the same window, and the same moon shines on him; but he is no longer alone. A beautiful head leans on his breast, and a loving voice says, "Dearest Alessandro, sing me a song of thine own composing." He was at that moment thinking of the rustic seat in her father's garden, of violets breathing to the moonlight, of Dora's first bashful confession of love; and smiling with a happy consciousness, he sought for the written voice of that blissful hour. But he will not tell her when it was composed, lest it should not say so much to her heart, as it does to his. He begins by singing other songs, which drawing-room misses love for their tinkling sweetness. Dora listens well pleased, and sometimes says, "That is pretty, Alessandro; play it again." But now comes the voice of melting, mingling souls. That melody, so like sunshine, and rainbows, and bird-warbling, after a summer shower, with rain drops from the guitar at intervals, and all subsiding into blissful, dreamy moonlight. Dora leans forward, gazing earnestly in his face, and with beaming tearful eyes, exclaims, "Oh, that is very beautiful! That is *my* tune." "Yes, it is indeed thy tune," replied the happy husband; and when she had heard its history, she knew why it had seemed so like echoes of her own deepest heart.

Time has passed, and Alessandro sits by Dora's bed-side, their eyes looking into each other through happy tears. Their love is crowned with life's deepest, purest joy, its most heavenly emotion. Their united lives have re-appeared in a new existence; and they feel that without this rich experience the human heart can never know one half its wealth of love. Long sat the father in that happy stillness, and wist not that angels near by smiled when he touched the soft down of the infant's arm, or twined its little finger over his, and looked his joyful tenderness into the mother's eyes. The tear-dew glistened on those long dark fringes, when he took up his guitar and played the beloved tune. He had spoken no word to his child. These tones were the first sounds with which he welcomed her into the world.

A few months glide away, and the little Fioretta knows the tune for herself. She claps her hands and crows at sight of the guitar, and all changing emotions show themselves in her dark melancholy eyes, and on her little tremulous lips. Play not too sadly, thou fond musician; for this little soul is a portion of thine own sensitive being, more delicately tuned. Ah, see now the grieved lip, and the eyes swimming in tears! Change, change to a gayer measure! for the little heart is swelling too big for its bosom. There, now she laughs and crows again! Yet plaintive music is her choice, and especially the beloved tune. As soon as she can toddle across the room, she welcomes papa with a shout, and runs to bring the guitar, which mother must help her carry, lest she break it in her zeal. If father mischievously tries other tunes than her favourites, she shakes her little curly head, and trots her feet impatiently. But when he touches the first notes he ever played to her, she smiles and listens seriously, as if she heard her own being prophesied in music. As she grows older, the little lady evinces a taste right royal; for she must needs eat her supper to the accompaniment of sweet sounds. It is beautiful to see her in her night-gown, seated demurely in her small arm-chair, one little naked foot unconsciously beating time to the tune. But if the music speaks too plaintively, the big tears roll silently down, and the porringer of milk, all unheeded, pours its treasures on the floor. Then come smothering kisses from the happy father and mother, and love-claspings with her little soft arms. As the three sit thus intertwined, the musician says playfully, "Ah, this is the perfect chord!"

Three years pass away, and the scene is changed. There is discord now where such sweet harmony prevailed. The light of Dora's eyes is dim with weeping, and Fioretta "has caught the trick of grief, and sighs amid her playthings." Once, when she had waited long for the beloved father, she ran to him with the guitar, and he pushed her away, saying angrily, "Go to bed; why did your mother keep you up so long?" The sensitive little being, so easily repulsed, went to her pillow in tears; and after that, she no more ran to him with music in her hand, in her eye, and in her voice. Hushed now is the beloved tune. To the unhappy wife it seems a mockery to ask for it; and Alessandro seldom touches his guitar; he says he is obliged to play enough for his bread, without playing for his family at home. At the glee-club the bright wine has tempted him, and he is slowly burying heart and soul in the sepulchre of the body. Is there no way to save this beautiful son of genius and feeling? Dora at first pleads with him tenderly; but made nervous with anxiety and sorrow, she at last speaks words that would have seemed impossible to her when she was so happy, seated on the rustic chair, in the moonlighted garden; and then comes the sharp sorrow, which a generous heart always feels when it *has* so spoken to a cherished friend. In such moments of contrition, memory turns with fond sadness to the beloved tune. Fioretta, whose little fingers must stretch wide to reach an octave, is taught to play it on the piano, while mother sings to her accompaniment, in their lonely hours. After such seasons, a tenderer reception always greets the wayward husband; but his eyes, dulled by dissipation, no longer perceive the delicate shadings of love in those home pictures, once so dear to him. The child is afraid of her father, and this vexes him; so a strangeness has grown up between the two playmates, and casts a shadow over all their attempts at joy. One day Alessandro came home as twilight was passing into evening. Fioretta had eaten her supper, and sat on her mother's lap, chatting merrily; but the little clear voice hushed, as soon as father's step was heard approaching. He entered with flushed cheek and unsteady motions, and threw himself full length on the sofa, grumbling that it was devilish dismal there. Dora answered hastily, "When a man has made his home dismal, if he don't like it, he had better stay where he finds more pleasure." The next moment she would have given worlds if she had not spoken such words. Her impulse was to go and fall on his neck, and ask forgiveness; but he kicked over Fioretta's little chair with such violence, that the kindly impulse turned back, and hid itself in her widowed heart. There sat they silently in the twilight, and Dora's tears fell on the little head that rested on her bosom. I know not what spirit guided the child; perhaps in her busy little heart she remembered how her favourite sounds used to heighten all love, and cheer all sorrow: perhaps angels came and took her by the hand. But so it was, she slipped down from mother's lap, and scrambling up on the music-stool, began to play the tune which had been taught her in private hours, and which the father had not heard for many months. Wonderfully the little creature touched the keys with her tiny fingers, and ever and anon her weak but flexible voice chimed in with a pleasant harmony. Alessandro raised his head, and looked and listened. "God bless her dear little soul!" he exclaimed; "can *she* play it? God bless her! God bless her!" He clasped the darling to his breast, and kissed her again and again. Then seeing the little overturned chair, once so sacred to his heart, he caught it up, kissed it vehemently, and burst into a flood of tears. Dora threw her arms round him, and said softly, " Dear Alessandro, forgive me that I spoke so unkindly." He pressed her hand, and answered in a stifled voice, " Forgive *me*, Dora. God bless the little angel! Never again will father push away her little chair." As they stand weeping on each other's necks, two little soft arms encircle their knees, and a small voice says, " Kiss Fietta." They raise her up, and fold her in long embraces. Alessandro carries her to her bed, as in times of old, and says cheerfully, " No more wine, dear Dora; no more wine. Our child has saved me."

But when discord once enters a domestic paradise, it is not easily dispelled. Alessandro occasionally feels the want of the stimulus to which he has become accustomed, and the corroding appetite sometimes makes him gloomy and petulant. Dora does not make sufficient allowance for this, and her own nature being quick and sensitive, she sometimes gives abrupt answers, or betrays impatience by hasty motions. Meanwhile Alessandro is busy, with some secret work. The door of his room is often locked, and Dora is half displeased that he will not tell her why; but all her questions he answers only with a kiss and a smile. And now the Christmas morning comes, and Fioretta rises bright and early to see what Santa Claus has put in her stocking. She comes running with her apron full, and gives mother a package, on which is written, " A merry Christmas and a Happy New Year to my beloved wife." She opens it, and reads " Dearest Dora, I have made thee a music-box. When I speak hastily to my loved ones, I pray thee wind it up; and when I see the spark kindling in thy eyes, I will do the same. Thus, dearest, let memory teach patience unto love." Dora winds up the music-box, and lo, a spirit sits within, playing the beloved tune! She puts her hand within her husband's, and they look at each other with affectionate humility. But neither of them speak the resolution they form, while the voice of their early love falls on their ears, like the sounds of a fairy guitar.

Memory, thus aided, does teach patience unto love. No slackened string now sends discord through the domestic tune. Fioretta is passing into maidenhood, beautiful as an opening flower. She practises on the guitar, while the dear good father sits with his arm across her chair, singing from a manuscript tune of her own composing. In his eyes, this first effort of her genius cannot seem otherwise than beautiful. Ever and anon certain notes occur, and they look at each other and smile, and Dora smiles also. "Fioretta could not help bringing in *that* theme," she says, "for it was sung to her in her cradle." The father replies, "But the variations are extremely pretty and tasteful;" and a flush of delight goes over the expressive face of his child. The setting sun glances across the guitar, and just touches a rose in the maiden's bosom. The happy mother watches the dear group earnestly, and sketches rapidly on the paper before her. And now she, too, works privately in her own room, and has a secret to keep. On Fioretta's fifteenth birth-day, she sends by her hands, a covered present to the father. He opens it and finds a lovely picture of himself and daughter, the rose and the guitar. The sunlight glances across them in a bright shower of fine soft rays, and touches on the manuscript, as with a golden finger, the few beloved notes, which had made them smile. As the father shrined within his divine art the memory of their first hour of mutual love, so the mother has embalmed in *her* beautiful art the first musical echo from the heart of their child.

But now the tune of life passes into a sadder mode. Dora, pale and emaciated, lies propped up with pillows, her hand clasped within Fioretta's, her head resting on her husband's shoulder.

All is still—still. Their souls are kneeling reverently before the Angel of Death. Heavy sunset guns from a neighbouring fort, boom through the air. The vibrations shake the music-box, and it starts up like a spirit, and plays the cherished tune. Dora presses her daughter's hand, and she, with a faint smile, warbles the words they have so often sung. The dying one looks up to Alessandro, with a deep expression of unearthly tenderness. Gazing thus, with one long-drawn sigh, her affectionate soul floats away on the wings of that ethereal song. The memory that taught endurance unto love leaves a luminous expression, a farewell glory, on the lifeless countenance. Attendant angels smile, and their blessing falls on the mourners' hearts, like dew from heaven. Fioretta remains to the widowed one, the graceful blossom of his lonely life, the incarnation of his beloved tune.

ELIZABETH WILSON.

THE following story is founded upon facts which occurred during the latter part of the eighteenth century. The leading incidents are still in the memory of many of the inhabitants of Chester county, Pennsylvania.

ELIZABETH WILSON was of humble, though respectable parentage. From infancy she was remarked for beauty, and a delicate nervous organization. Her brother William, two years older, was likewise a handsome child, with a more sturdy and vigorous frame. He had a gentle, loving heart, which expended its affections most lavishly on his mother and little sister. In their early years, Lizzy was his constant shadow. If he went to the barn to hunt for eggs, the little one was sure to run prattling along with him, hand in hand. If he pelted walnuts from the tree, she was sure to be there with her little basket, to pick them up. They sat on the same blue bench to eat their bread and milk, and with the first jack-knife he ever owned, the affectionate boy carved on it the letters W. and E. for William and Elizabeth. The sister lavishly returned his love. If a pie was baked for her, she would never break it till Willie came to share; and she would never go to sleep unless her arms were about his neck.

Their mother, a woman of tender heart and yielding temper, took great delight in her handsome children. Often, when she went out to gather chips or brush, she stopped to look in upon them, as they sat on the blue bench, feeding each other from their little porringers of bread and milk. The cross-lights from side-window threw on them a reflection of the lilac ushes, so that they seemed seated in a flowering rove. It was the only picture the poor woman had; but none of the old masters could have equalled its beauty.

The earliest and strongest development of Lizzy's character was love. She was always caressing her kitten, or twining her arms about Willie's neck, or leaning on her mother's lap, begging for a kiss. A dozen times a day she would look earnestly into her mother's eyes, and inquire, most beseechingly, "*Does* you love your little Lizzy?" And if the fond answer did not come as promptly as usual, her beautiful eyes, always plaintive in their expression, would begin to swim with tears. This "strong necessity of loving," which so pervades the nature of woman, the fair child inherited from her gentle mother; and from her, too, inherited a deficiency of firmness, of which such natures have double need. To be every thing, and do every thing, for those she loved, was the paramount law of her existence.

Such a being was of course born for sorrow. Even in infancy, the discerning eye might already see its prophetic shadow resting on her expressive countenance. The first great affliction of her life was the death of her mother, when she was ten years old. Her delicate nerves were shattered by the blow, and were never after fully restored to health. The dead body of her beloved mother, with large coins on the eye-lids, was so awfully impressed on her imagination, that the image followed her everywhere, even into her dreams. As she slept, tears often dropped from her tremulous eye-lashes, and nightmare visions made her start and scream. There was no gentle voice near to soothe her perturbed spirit; none to throw an angel's shining robe over the hideous spectre, that lay so cold and stiff in the halls of memory. Her father fed and clothed his children, and caused them to be taught to read and write. It did not occur to him that anything more was included in parental duty. Of clothing for the mind, or food for the heart, he knew nothing; for his own had never been clothed and fed. He came home weary from daily toil, ate his supper, dozed in his chair awhile, and then sent the children to bed. A few times, after the death of his wife, he kissed his daughter; but she never ventured to look into *his* eyes, and ask, "*Does* you love your little Lizzy?" Willie was her only consolation; and all he could do was to weep passionately with her, at everything which reminded them of their mother.

Nature, as usual, reflected back the image of the soul that gazed upon her. To Lizzy's excited mind, everything appeared mysterious and awful, and all sounds seemed to wail and sigh. The rustling of the trees in the evening wind went through her, like the voice of a spirit; and when the nights were bright, she would hide her head in her brother's bosom, and whisper, "Willie, dear, I wish the moon would not keep looking at me. She seems to *say* something to me; and it makes me afraid."

All susceptible souls have felt thus; particularly when under the influence of grief.

> "The snow of deepest silence
>   O'er everything doth fall,
> So beautiful and quiet,
>   And yet so like a pall—
> As if all life were ended,
>   And rest were come to all."

Such a state of feeling, long indulged, could not be otherwise than injurious to a bodily frame originally delicate. The sensitive child soon became subject to fits, the severity of which at times threatencd her life. On coming out of these spasms, with piteous tones and bewildered looks, she would ask, "Where is my mother?"

At the end of a year, an important change came over the lonely household. A strong active step-mother was introduced. Her loud voice and energetic tread, so different from her own quiet and timid mother, frightened poor Lizzy. Her heart more than ever turned back upon itself, and listened to the echoes of its own yearnings. Willie, being old enough to work on the farm, was now absent most of the day; and the fair girl, so richly endowed by nature with all deep feelings and beautiful capacities, so lavish of her affections, so accustomed to free outpourings of love, became reserved, and apparently cold and stupid. When the step-mother gave birth to an infant, the fountain of feeling was again unsealed. It was her delight to watch the babe, and minister to its wants. But this development of the affections was likewise destined to be nipped in the bud. The step-mother, though by no means hard-hearted, was economical and worldly-wise. She deemed it most profitable to employ a healthy, stout niece of her own, somewhat older than Elizabeth, and to have her step-daughter bound out in some family where she could do light labour. It was also determined that William should go to service; and his place of destination was fifty miles from that of his sister.

The news of this arrangement was very bitter to the children. Both answered their father, very meekly, that they were willing to go; but their voices were deep, sad, and almost inaudible. Without saying another word, the boy put on his hat, and the girl her sun-bonnet, and taking each other by the hand, they went forth, and roamed silently to their mother's grave. There they stood for a long time, in silence, and their tears dropped fast on the green sod. At last, Elizabeth sobbed out, "Oh, if dear mother was alive, Willie, we should not have to go away from home." But Willie could only answer by a fresh outburst of grief. A little clump of wild flowers nodded over the edge of the mound. The affectionate boy cut two of them, and said, "Let us keep these, Lizzy, to remember mother by."

The flowers were carefully pressed between the leaves of Lizzy's Testament, and when the sorrowful day of parting came, one was nicely folded in a paper for Willie. "Now, dear sis, give me that nice little curl," said he, putting his finger on a soft, golden-brown ringlet, that nestled close to her ear, and lay caressingly on her downy cheek. She glanced in the fragment of a glass, which served them for a mirror, and with eyes brimful of tears she answered, "Oh, Willie, I cannot give you *that*. Don't you remember how dear mother used to wet my head all over with cold water, to make my hair curl? She used to laugh when I shook my head, and made the curls go all over my forehead; and she would kiss that little curl in particular. She said it was such a darling little curl." Thus childishly did the innocent ones speak together. The brother twisted the favorite curl round his finger, and kissed it, and a bright tear fell on it, and glittered in the sunshine.

William left home a few days earlier than his sister, and bitterly did the lonely one sob herself to sleep that night. She shuddered in the dark, and when the moon looked in at the window, its glance seemed more mournful than ever. The next morning, she fell from the breakfast table in a fit more severe than usual. But as she soon recovered, and as these spasms now occurred only at distant intervals, her step-mother thought she had better be in readiness to depart at the appointed time.

The wagon was brought to the door, and the father said to her, "Lizzy, put on your bonnet, and bring your bundle. It is time to go." Oh, how the poor child lingered in her little bed-room, where she and Willie slept in their infant days, and where the mother used to hear them say their prayers, and kiss them both, as they lay folded in each other's arms. To the strong step-mother she easily said good bye; but she paused long over the cradle of her baby-brother, and kissed each of his little fingers, and fondly turned a little wave of sunny hair on his pure white forehead.

Her heart swelled, and she had to swallow hard to keep down the sobs; for it was *her* cradle, and she was thinking how her mother used to sing her to sleep. Her father spoke to her in a tone of unusual tenderness, as if he too remembered her infancy, and the gentle one who used to rock her in that cradle. "Come, Lizzy," said he, "it is time to go. You shall come back and see the baby before long." With blinded eyes she stumbled into the wagon, and turned and looked back as long as she could see the old elm-tree by her bed-room window, where all the summers of her young life she had watched the swallows come and go.

It is a dreary fate for a loving and sensitive child to be bound out at service among strangers, even if they are kind-hearted. The good woman of the house received Lizzy in a very friendly manner, and told her to make herself at home. But the word only sent a mournful echo through her heart. For a few days, she went about in a state of abstraction, that seemed like absolute stupidity. Her step-mother had prepared them for this, by telling them there was something strange about Lizzy, and that many people thought her fits affected her mind. Being of coarser and stronger natures, they could none of them imagine that the slow stagnation of the heart might easily dim the light of intellect in a creature so keenly susceptible. But by degrees the duties required of her roused her faculties into greater activity; and when night came, she was fortunately too weary to lie awake and weep. Sometimes she dreamed of Willie, and her dreams of him were always bright and pleasant; but her mother sometimes fondled her with looks of love, and sometimes came as the pale cold spectre. Thus the months passed slowly away. Her father came to see her at distant intervals, and once in a great while, a letter came from Willie, in a large stiff hand. Unaccustomed to writing, he could not, through that medium, tell much that was passing in his heart. That he wanted badly to see his sister, and often kissed the flower they plucked from the dear mother's grave, was the substance of all his epistles.

In the mean time, Lizzy was passing into womanhood. Childhood and youth kissed each other, with new and glowing beauty. Her delicate cheeks mantled with a richer colour, and her deep blue eyes, shaded with long fringes of the darkest brown, looked out upon life with a more earnest and expressive longing. Plain and scanty garments could not conceal the graceful outline of her figure, and her motions were like a willow in the breeze. She was not aware of her uncommon loveliness, though she found it pleasant to look in the glass, and had sometimes heard strangers say to each other, "See that pretty girl!"

There were no young men in the immediate neighbourhood, and she had not been invited to any of the rustic dances or quilting frolics. One bashful lad in the vicinity always contrived to drive his cows past the house where she lived, and eagerly kept watch for a glimpse of her, as she went to the barn with her milking pails. But if she happened to pass near enough to nod and smile, his cheeks grew red, and his voice forsook him. She could not know, or guess, that he would lie awake long that night, and dream of her smile, and resolve that some time or other he would have courage to tell her how handsome she was, and how the sight of her made his heart throb. She did not yet know that she could love anybody better than she had loved Willie. She had seen her darling brother but twice, during their three years of separation; but his image was ever fresh and bright in memory. When he came to see her, she felt completely happy. While he gazed upon her with delighted eyes, her affectionate nature was satisfied with love: for it had not yet been revealed to her in the melting glance of passion. Yet the insidious power already began to foreshadow itself in vague restlessness and romantic musings. For she was at an age,

> "To feel a want, yet scarce know what it is;
> To seek one nature that is always new,
> Whose glance is warmer than another's kiss;
> Such longing instinct fills the mighty scope
> Of the young heart with one mysterious hope."

At last, an important event occurred in Lizzy's monotonous existence. A young girl in the village was to be married, and she was invited to the quilting party. It was the first invitation of the kind she had ever received, and of course it occupied her thoughts day and night. Could she have foreseen how this simple occurrence would affect her whole future destiny, she would have pondered over it still more deeply. The bridegroom brought a friend with him to the party, a handsome dark-eyed young man, clerk of a store in a neighbouring town. Aware of his personal attractions, he dressed himself with peculiar care. Elizabeth had never seen anything so elegant;

and the moment his eye glanced on her, he decided that he had never seen anything half so beautiful. He devoted himself to her in a manner sufficiently marked to excite envy; and some of the rich farmers' daughters made critical remarks about her dress, which they concluded was passably genteel, for a girl who lived out at service. However, Lizzy was queen of the evening, by virtue of nature's own impress of royalty. When the quilt was finished, romping games were introduced according to the fashion of the times; and the young men took care that the forfeits paid by the pretty girls should generally involve kissing some of their own number. Among the forfeits required of the dark-eyed stranger, he was ordered to beg on his knees for the identical little curl that Willie had asked of his sister. In the midst of her mirthfulness, this brought a shadow over her countenance, and she could not answer playfully. However, this emotion passed away with the moment, and she became the gayest of the gay. Never before had she been half so handsome, for never before had she been half so happy. The joyful consciousness of pleasing everybody, and the attractive young stranger in particular, made her eyes sparkle, and her whole countenance absolutely radiant with beauty. When the party were about to separate, the young man was very assiduous about placing her shawl, and begged permission to accompany her home. Little was said during this walk; yet enough to afford entrance into both hearts for that unquiet passion, which tangles the web of human life more than all the other sentiments and instincts of our mysterious being. At parting, he took her hand, to say good night. He continued to hold it, and leaning against the gate, they stood for a few moments, gazing at the clear, silvery orb of night. Ah, how different the moon seemed to Lizzy *now!* Earth's spectral robe had changed to a veil of glory. Her bonnet had fallen back, and the evening breeze played gently with her ringlets. In soft insinuating tones, the young man said, "Will you not give me that little curl I asked for?" She blushed deeply and answered, in her child-like way, "I cannot give you that, because my mother used to kiss it so often." "No wonder she kissed it," he replied; "it looks so roguish, lying there on your pretty cheek." And before she was aware of it, he had kissed it too. Trembling and confused, she turned to open the gate, but he held it fast, until she had promised that the next time he came she would give him one of her curls.

Poor Lizzy went to bed that night with an intoxicated heart. When she braided her hair at the glass, next morning, she smiled and blushed, as she twined the favourite ringlet more carefully than ever. She was so childishly happy with her pretty little curl! The next Sunday evening, as she sat at the window, she heard the sound of a flute. *He* had promised to bring his flute; and he had not forgotten her. She listened—it came nearer and nearer, through the wood. Her heart beat audibly, for it was indeed the handsome dark-eyed stranger.

All summer long, he came every Sunday afternoon; and with him came moonlight walks, and flute-warblings, and tender whisperings, and glances, such as steal away a woman's heart. This was the fairy-land of her young life. She had somebody now into whose eyes she could gaze, with all the deep tenderness of her soul, and ask, "*Do* you love your own Lizzy?"

The young man did love, but not as she loved him; for hers was a richer nature, and gave more than he could return. He accompanied her to her father's, and they were generally understood to be betrothed. He had not seen brother William, but he was told a thousand affectionate anecdotes of his kind good heart. When they returned from the visit to the homestead, they brought with them the little blue bench marked W. and E. Lizzy was proud of her genteel lover; and the only drop which it now seemed possible to add to her cup of happiness was to introduce him to William. But her brother was far off; and when the autumn came, her betrothed announced the necessity of going to a distant city, to establish himself in business. It was a bitter, bitter parting to both. The warmest letters were but a cold substitute for those happy hours of mutual confidence; and after awhile, his letters became more brief and cool. The fact was, the young man was too vain to feel deeply; and among his new acquaintance in the city was a young good-looking widow, with a small fortune, who early evinced a preference for him. To be obviously, and at the same time modestly preferred, by a woman of any agreeable qualities, is what few men, even of the strongest character, can withstand. It is the knowledge of this fact, and experience with regard to the most delicate and acceptable mode of expressing preference, which, as Samuel Weller declares, makes "a widow equal to twenty-five other women." Lizzy's lover was not a strong character, and he was vain and selfish. It is no wonder, therefore, that his letters to the pretty girl, who lived out at service, should become more cool and infrequent. She was very slow to believe it thus; and when, at last, news reached her that he was positively engaged to be married to another, she refused to listen to it. But he came not to vindicate himself, and he ceased to answer her letters. The poor deluded girl awoke to a full consciousness of her misery, and suffered such intensity of wretchedness as only keenly sensitive natures *can* suffer. William had promised to come and see her the latter part of the winter, and her heart had been filled with pleasant and triumphant anticipations of introducing to him her handsome lover. But now the pride of her heart was humbled, and its joy turned into mourning. She was cast off, forsaken; and, alas, that was not the worst. As she sobbed on the neck of her faithful brother, she felt, for the first time, that there was something she could not tell him. The keenest of her wretched feelings she dared not avow. He pitied and consoled her, as well as he could; but to her it seemed as if there was no consolation but in death. Most earnestly did he wish that he had a home to shelter her, where he could fold her round with the soft wings of brotherly love. But they were both poor, and poverty fetters the impulses of the heart. And so they must part again, he guessing but half of her great sorrow. If the farewell was sad to him, what must it have been to her, who now felt so utterly alone in the wide world? Her health sank under the conflict, and the fits returned upon her with increased violence. In her state of gloomy abstraction and indifference, she hardly noticed the significant glances and busy whispers of neighbours and acquaintance. With her, the agony of death was past. The world seemed too spectral for her to dread its censure. At last she gave birth to a dead infant, and for a long time her own life trembled in the balance. She recovered in a state of confirmed melancholy, and with visible indications of intellect, more impaired than ever.

> "A shadow seemed to rise
> From out her thoughts, and turned to dreariness
> All blissful hopes and sunny memories."

She was no longer invited to visit with the young people of the neighbourhood; and the envy excited by her uncommon beauty showed itself in triumph over her blighted reputation. Her father thought it a duty to reprove her for sin, and her step-mother said some cutting words about the disgrace her conduct had brought upon the family. But no kind Christian heart strengthened her with the assurance that one false step in life might be forgiven and retrieved. Thus was the lily broken in its budding beauty, and its delicate petals blighted by harsh winds.

Poor Lizzy felt this depressing atmosphere of neglect and scorn; but fortunately with less keenness than she would have done, before brain was stultified, and heart congealed by shame and sorrow. She no longer showed much feeling about anything, except the little blue bench marked W. and E. Every moment that she could steal from household labours, she would retire to her little room, and, seated on this bench, would read over William's letters, and those other letters, which had crushed her loving heart. She would not allow any person to remove the bench from her bedside, or to place a foot upon it. To such inanimate objects does the poor human heart cling in its desolation.

Years passed away monotonously with Elizabeth; years of loneliness and labour. Some young men, attracted by her beauty, and emboldened by a knowledge of her weakness, approached her with familiarity, which they intended for flattery. But their profligacy was too thinly disguised to be dangerous to a nature like hers. She turned coldly from them all, with feelings of disgust and weariness.

When she was about twenty-three years old, she went to Philadelphia to do household work for a family that wished to hire her. Important events followed this change, but a veil of obscurity rests over the causes that produced them. After some months residence in the city, her health failed more and more, and she returned to the country. She was still competent to discharge the lighter duties of household labour, but she seemed to perform them all mechanically, and with a dull stupor. After a time, it became obvious that she would again be a mother. When questioned, her answers were incoherent and contradictory. Some said she must be a very base low creature to commit this second fault; but more kindly natures said, "She was always soft-hearted and yielding, from childhood; and she is hardly a responsible being; for trouble and continual fits have made her almost an idiot." At last she gave birth to twins. She wept when she saw them; but they seemed to have no power to withdraw her mind from its disconsolate wanderings. When they were a few moths old, she expressed a wish to return to Philadelphia; and a lad, belonging to the family where she had remained during her illness, agreed to convey her part of the way in a wagon. When they came into the public road, she told him she could walk the rest of the way, and begged him to return. He left her seated on a rock, near a thick grove, nursing her babes. She was calm and gentle, but sad and abstracted as usual. That was in the morning. Where or how she spent the day was never known. Toward night she arrived in Philadelphia, at the house where she had formerly lived. She seemed very haggard and miserable; what few words she said were abrupt and unmeaning; and her attitudes and motions had the sluggish apathy of an insane person.

The next day, there was a rumour afloat that two strangled infants had been found in a grove on the road from Chester. Of course this circumstance soon became connected with her name. When she was arrested, she gave herself up with the same gloomy indifference that marked all her actions. She denied having committed the murder: but when asked who she supposed had done it, she sometimes shuddered and said nothing, sometimes said she did not know, and sometimes answered the children were still living. When conveyed to prison, she asked for pen and ink, and in a short letter, rudely penned, she begged William to come to her, and to bring from her bed-room the little blue bench they used to sit upon in the happy days of childhood. He came at once, and long did the affectionate couple stand locked in each other's arms, sobbing, and without the power to speak. It was not until the second interview, that her brother could summon courage to ask whether she really committed the crime of which she was accused.

"Oh no, William," she replied, "you could not suppose I did."

"You must indeed have been dreadfully changed, dear Lizzy," said he; "for you used to have a heart that could not hurt a kitten."

"I am dreadfully changed," she answered, "but I never wanted to harm anything."

He took her hand, played sadly with the emaciated fingers, and after a strong effort to control his emotions, he said, in a subdued voice, "Lizzy, dear, can you tell me who did do it?"

She stared at him with a wild intense gaze, that made him shudder. Then looking fearfully toward the door, she said, in a strange muffled whisper, "Did *what?*" Poor William bowed his head over the hand that he held in his own, and wept like a child.

During various successive interviews, he could obtain no satisfactory answer to the important question. Sometimes she merely gazed at him with a vacant inane expression; sometimes she faintly answered that she did not know; and sometimes she said she believed the babes were still alive. She gradually became more quiet and rational under her brother's soothing influence; and one day, when he had repeatedly assured her that she could safely trust her secrets to his faithful heart, she said with a suppressed whisper, as if she feared the sound of her own voice, "*He* did it."

"Who is he?" asked the brother, gently.

"The father," she replied.

"Did you know he meant to do it?"

"No. He told me he would meet me and give me some money. But when I asked him for something to support the children, he was angry, and choked them. I was frightened, and felt faint. I don't know what I did. I woke up and found myself on the ground alone, and the babies lying among the bushes."

"What is his name, and where does he live?" inquired the brother.

She gave him a wild look of distress, and said—"Oh, don't ask me. I ought not to have done so. I am a poor sinner—a poor sinner. But everybody deserted me; the world was very cold; I had nobody to love; and he was *very* kind to me."

"But tell me his name," urged the brother.

She burst into a strange mad laugh, picked nervously at the handkerchief she held in her hand, and repeated, idiotically, "Name? name? I guess the babies are alive now. I don't know—I don't know; but I guess they are."

To the lawyer she would say nothing, except to deny that she committed the murder. All their exertions could wring from her nothing more distinct than the story she had briefly told her brother. During her trial, the expression of her countenance was stupid and vacant. At times, she would drum on the railing before her, and stare round on the crowd with a bewildered look, as if unconscious where she was. The deranged state of her mind was strongty urged by her lawyer; but his opponent replied that all this might be assumed. To the story she had told in prison, it was answered that her not telling of the murder at the time made her an accomplice. After the usual display of legal ingenuity on both sides, the jury brought her in guilty of murder, and the poor forlorn demented creature was sentenced to be hung at Chester.

The wretched brother was so stunned by the blow, that at first he could not collect his thoughts. But it soon occurred to him that the terrible doom might still be arrested, if the case could be brought suitably before the governor. A petition was accordingly drawn up, setting forth the alienation of mind to which she had been subject, in consequence of fits, and the extreme doubtfulness whether she committed the murder. Her youth, her beauty, the severe sorrows of her life, and the obviously impaired state of her reason, touched many hearts, and the petition was rapidly signed. When William went to her cell to bid her adieu, he tried to cheer her with the hope of pardon. She listened with listless apathy. But when he pressed her hand, and with a mournful smile said, "Good-bye, dear Lizzy, I shall come back soon; and I hope with good news," she pointed tearfully to the little blue bench and said, "Let what will happen, Willie, take care of *that*, for my sake." He answered with a choked voice; and as he turned away, the tears flowed fast down his manly cheeks. She listened to the echoes of his steps, and when she could hear them no longer, she threw herself on the floor, laid her head down on the little blue bench, kissed the letters carved upon it, and sobbed as she had not sobbed since she was first deserted by her false lover. When the jailor went in to carry her supper, he found her asleep thus. Rich masses of her glossy brown hair fell over her pale, but still lovely face, on which rested a serene smile, as if she were happy in her dreams. He stood and gazed upon her, and his hard hand brushed away a tear. Some motion that he made disturbed her slumber. She opened her eyes, from which there beamed for a moment a rational and happy expression, as she said, "I was out in the woods, behind the house, holding my little apron to catch the nuts that Willie threw down. Mother smiled at me from a blue place between two clouds, and said, 'Come to me, my child.'"

The next day a clergyman came to see her. He spoke of the penalty for sin, and the duty of being resigned to the demands of justice. She heard his words, as a mother hears street sounds when she is watching a dying babe. They conveyed to her no import. When asked if she repented of her sins, she said she had been a weak erring creature, and she hoped that she was penitent; but that she never committed the murder.

"Are you resigned to die, if a pardon should not be obtained?" he asked.

"Oh yes," she replied, "I want to die."

He prayed with her in the spirit of real human love; and this soothed her heart. She spoke seldom, after her brother's departure; and often she did not appear to hear when she was spoken to. She sat on the little blue bench, gazing vacantly on the floor, like one already out of the body.

In those days, there was briefer interval between sentence and execution, than at present. The atal day and hour soon arrived, and still no tidings from the governor. Men came to lead her to the gallows. She seemed to understand what they said to her, and turned meekly to obey their orders. But she stopped suddenly, gazed on the little blue bench, and said in a gasping tone, "Has William come?" When they told her no, a shudder seemed to go over her, and her pale face became still paler. A bit of looking-glass hung on the wall in front of her; and as she raised her head, she saw the little curl, that had received her mother's caresses, and the first kiss of love. With a look of the most intense agony, she gave a loud groan, and burying her face in her hands, fell forward on the shoulder of the sheriff.

* * * * *

Poor William had worked with the desperate energy of despair, and the governor, after brief delay, granted a pardon. But in those days, the facilities for travelling were few; and it happened that the country was inundated with heavy rains, which everywhere impeded his progress. He stopped neither for food nor rest; but everywhere the floods and broken roads hindered him. When he came to Darby Creek, which was usually fordable, it was swollen too high to be crossed, and it was sometime before a boat could be obtained. In agony of mind he pressed onward, till his horse fell dead under him. Half frantic, he begged for another at any price, mounted, and rode furiously. From the top of a hill, he saw a crowd assembled round the place of execution. He waved his handkerchief, he shouted, he screamed. But in the excitement of the moment he was not heard or noticed. All eyes were fastened on the gallows; and soon the awful object came within his own vision. Father of mercies! There are a woman's garments floating in the air. There is a struggling, a quivering—and all is still.

With a shriek that pierced the ears of the multitude, the desperate rider plunged forward; his horse fell under him, and shouting, "A pardon! A pardon!" he rolled senseless on the ground. He came too late. The unhappy Elizabeth was dead. The poor young creature, guilty of too much heart, and too little brain to guide it, had been murdered by law, and men called it justice.

Pale as a ghost, with hair suddenly whitened by excess of anguish, the wretched brother bent over the corpse of that beautiful sister, whom he had loved so well. They spoke to him of resignation to God's will. He answered not; for it was not clear to him that the cruelty of man *is* the will of God. Reverently and tenderly, he cut from that fair brow the favourite little curl, twined about with so many sacred memories, and once a source of girlish innocent joy to the yearning heart, that slept so calmly now. He took the little bench from its cold corner in the prison, and gathering together his small personal property, he retired to a lonely cave in Dauphin county. He shunned all intercourse with his fellow men, and when spoken to, answered briefly and solemnly. There he died a few years ago, at an advanced age. He is well remembered in the region round about, as William the Hermit.

THE NEIGHBOUR-IN-LAW.

WHO blesses others in his daily deeds,
Will find the healing that his spirit needs;
For every flower in others' pathway strewn,
Confers its fragrant beauty on our own.

"So you are going to live in the same building with Hetty Turnpenny," said Mrs. Lane to Mrs. Fairweather, "You will find nobody to envy you. If her temper does not prove too much even for your good-nature, it will surprise all who know her. We lived there a year, and that is as long as anybody ever tried it."

"Poor Hetty!" replied Mrs. Fairweather, "She has had much to harden her. Her mother died too early for her to remember; her father was very severe with her, and the only lover she ever had, borrowed the savings of her years of toil, and spent them in dissipation. But Hetty, notwithstanding her sharp features, and sharper words, certainly has a kind heart. In the midst of her greatest poverty, many were the stockings she knit, and the warm waistcoats she made, for the poor drunken lover, whom she had too much good sense to marry. Then you know she feeds and clothes her brother's orphan child."

"If you call it feeding and clothing," replied Mrs. Lane. "The poor child looks cold, and pinched, and frightened all the time, as if she were chased by the East wind. I used to tell Miss Turnpenny she ought to be ashamed of herself, to keep the poor little thing at work all the time, without one minute to play. If she does but look at the cat, as it runs by the window, Aunt Hetty gives her a rap over the knuckles. I used to tell her she would make the girl just such another sour old crab as herself."

"That must have been very improving to her disposition," replied Mrs. Fairweather, with a good-humoured smile. "But in justice to poor Aunt Hetty, you ought to remember that she had just such a cheerless childhood herself. Flowers grow where there is sunshine."

"I know you think everybody ought to live in the sunshine," rejoined Mrs. Lane; "and it must be confessed that you carry it with you wherever you go. If Miss Turnpenny *has* a heart, I dare say you will find it out, though I never could, and I never heard of any one else that could. All the families within hearing of her tongue call her the neighbour-in-law."

Certainly the prospect was not very encouraging; for the house Mrs. Fairweather proposed to occupy, was not only under the same roof with Miss Turnpenny, but the buildings had one common yard in the rear, and one common space for a garden in front. The very first day she took possession of her new habitation, she called on the neighbour-in-law. Aunt Hetty had taken the precaution to extinguish the fire, lest the new neighbour should want hot water, before her own wood and coal arrived. Her first salutation was, "If you want any cold water, there's a pump across the street; I don't like to have my house slopped all over."

"I am glad you are so tidy, neighbour Turnpenny," replied Mrs. Fairweather; "It is extremely pleasant to have neat neighbours. I will try to keep everything as bright as a new five cent piece, for I see that will please you. I came in merely to say good morning, and to ask if you could spare little Peggy to run up and down stairs for me, while I am getting my furniture in order. I will pay her sixpence an hour."

Aunt Hetty had begun to purse up her mouth for a refusal; but the promise of sixpence an hour relaxed her features at once. Little Peggy sat knitting a stocking very diligently, with a rod lying on the table beside her. She looked up with timid wistfulness, as if the prospect of any change was like a release from prison. When she heard consent given, a bright colour flushed her cheeks. She was evidently of an impressible temperament, for good or evil. "Now mind and behave yourself," said Aunt Hetty; "and see that you keep at work the whole time. If I hear one word of complaint, you know what you'll get when you come home." The rose-colour subsided from Peggy's pale face, and she answered, "Yes, ma'am," very meekly.

In the neighbour's house all went quite otherwise. No switch lay on the table, and instead of, "mind how you do that. If you don't I'll punish you," she heard the gentle words, "There, dear, see how carefully you can carry that up stairs. Why, what a nice handy little girl you are!" Under this enlivening influence, Peggy worked like a bee, and soon began to hum much more agreeably than a bee. Aunt Hetty was always in the habit of saying, "Stop your noise, and mind your work." But the new friend patted her on the head, and said, "What a pleasant voice the little girl has. It is like the birds in the fields. By and by, you shall hear my music-box." This opened wide the windows of the poor little shut-up heart, so that the sunshine could stream in, and the birds fly in and out, carolling. The happy child tuned up like a lark, as she tripped lightly up and down stairs, on various household errands. But though she took heed to observe all the directions given her, her head was all the time filled with conjectures what sort of a thing a music-box might be. She was a little afraid the kind lady would forget to show it to her. She kept at work, however, and asked no questions; she only looked very curiously at everything that resembled a box. At last Mrs. Fairweather said, "I think your little feet must be tired, by this time. We will rest awhile, and eat some gingerbread." The child took the offered cake, with a humble little courtesy, and carefully held out her apron to prevent any crumbs from falling on the floor. But suddenly the apron dropped, and the crumbs were all strewn about. "Is that a little bird?" she exclaimed eagerly. "Where is he? Is he in this room?" The new friend smiled, and told her that was the music-box; and after awhile she opened it, and explained what made the sounds. Then she took out a pile of books from one of the baskets of goods, and told Peggy she might look at the pictures, till she called her. The little girl stepped forward eagerly to take them, and then drew back, as if afraid. "What is the matter?" asked Mrs. Fairweather; "I am very willing to trust you with the books. I keep them on purpose to amuse children." Peggy looked down with her finger on her lip, and answered in a constrained voice, "Aunt Turnpenny won't like it if I play." "Don't trouble yourself about that. I will make it all right with Aunt Hetty," replied the friendly one. Thus assured, she gave herself up to the full enjoyment of the picture books; and when she was summoned to her work, she obeyed with a cheerful alacrity that would have astonished her stern relative. When the labours of the day were concluded, Mrs. Fairweather accompanied her home, paid for all the hours she had been absent, and warmly praised her docility and diligence. "It is lucky for her that she behaved so well," replied Aunt Hetty; "if I had heard any complaint, I should have given her a whipping, and sent her to bed without her supper."

Poor little Peggy went to sleep that night with a lighter heart than she had ever felt, since she had been an orphan. Her first thought in the morning was whether the new neighbour would want her service again during the day. Her desire that it should be so, soon became obvious to Aunt Hetty, and excited an undefined jealousy and dislike of a person who so easily made herself beloved. Without exactly acknowledging to herself what were her own motives, she ordered Peggy to gather all the sweepings of the kitchen and court into a small pile, and leave it on the frontier line of her neighbour's premises. Peggy ventured to ask timidly whether the wind would not blow it about, and she received a box on the ear for her impertinence. It chanced that Mrs. Fairweather, quite unintentionally, heard the words and the blow. She gave Aunt Hetty's anger time enough to cool, then stepped out into the court, and after arranging divers little matters, she called aloud to her domestic, "Sally, how came you to leave this pile of dirt here? Didn't I tell you Miss Turnpenny was very neat? Pray make haste and sweep it up. I wouldn't have her see it on any account. I told her I would try to keep everything nice about the premises. She is so particular herself, and it is a comfort to have tidy neighbours." The girl, who had been previously instructed, smiled as she came out with brush and dust-pan, and swept quietly away the pile, that was intended as a declaration of border war.

But another source of annoyance presented itself, which could not so easily be disposed of. Aunt Hetty had a cat, a lean scraggy animal, that looked as if she were often kicked and seldom fed; and Mrs. Fairweather had a fat, frisky little dog, always ready for a caper. He took a distaste to poor poverty-stricken Tab, the first time he saw her; and no coaxing could induce him to alter his opinion. His name was Pink, but he was anything but a pink of behaviour in his neighbourly relations. Poor Tab could never set foot out of doors without being saluted with a growl, and a short sharp bark, that frightened her out of her senses, and made her run into the house, with her fur all on end. If she even ventured to doze a little on her own door step, the enemy was on the watch, and the moment her eyes closed, he would wake her with a bark and a box on the ear, and off he would run. Aunt Hetty vowed she would scald him. It was a burning shame, she said, for folks to keep dogs to worry their neighbours' cats. Mrs. Fairweather invited Tabby to dine, and made much of her, and patiently endeavoured to teach her dog to eat from the same plate. But Pink sturdily resolved he would be scalded first; that he would. He could not have been more obstinate in his opposition, if he and Tab had belonged to different sects in Christianity. While his mistress was patting Tab on the head, and reasoning the point with him, he would at times manifest a degree of indifference, amounting to toleration; but the moment he was left to his own free will, he would give the invited guest a hearty cuff with his paw, and send her home spitting like a small steam engine. Aunt Hetty considered it her own peculiar privilege to cuff the poor animal, and it was too much for her patience to see Pink undertake to assist in making Tab unhappy. On one of these occasions, she rushed into her neighbour's apartments, and faced Mrs. Fairweather, with one hand resting on her hip, and the forefinger of the other making very wrathful gesticulations. "I tell you what, madam, I wont put up with such treatment much longer," said she; "I'll poison that dog; see if I don't; and I shan't wait long, either, I can tell you. What you keep such an impudent little beast for, I don't know, without you do it on purpose to plague your neighbours."

"I am really sorry he behaves so," replied Mrs. Fairweather, mildly. "Poor Tab!"

"Poor Tab!" screamed Miss Turnpenny; "What do you mean by calling her poor? Do you mean to fling it up to me that my cat don't have enough to eat?"

"I didn't think of such a thing," replied Mrs. Fairweather. "I called her poor Tab, because Pink plagues her so, that she has no peace of her life. I agree with you, neighbour Turnpenny; it is *not* right to keep a dog that disturbs the neighbourhood. I am attached to poor little Pink, because he belongs to my son, who has gone to sea. I was in hopes he would soon leave off quarrelling with the cat; but if he won't be neighbourly, I will send him out in the country to board. Sally, will you bring me one of the pies we baked this morning? I should like to have Miss Turnpenny taste of them."

The crabbed neighbour was helped abundantly; and while she was eating the pie, the friendly matron edged in many a kind word concerning little Peggy, whom she praised as a remarkably capable, industrious child.

"I am glad you find her so," rejoined Aunt Hetty: "I should get precious little work out of her, if I didn't keep a switch in sight."

"I manage children pretty much as the man did the donkey," replied Mrs. Fairweather. "Not an inch would the poor beast stir, for all his master's beating and thumping. But a neighbour tied some fresh turnips to a stick, and fastened them so that they swung directly before the donkey's nose, and off he set on a brisk trot, in hopes of overtaking them."

Aunt Hetty, without observing how very closely the comparison applied to her own management of

Peggy, said, "That will do very well for folks that have plenty of turnips to spare."

"For the matter of that," answered Mrs. Fairweather, "whips cost something, as well as turnips; and since one makes the donkey stand still, and the other makes him trot, it is easy to decide which is the most economical. But, neighbour Turnpenny, since you like my pies so well, pray take one home with you. I am afraid they will mould before we can eat them up."

Aunt Hetty had come in for a quarrel, and she was astonished to find herself going out with a pie. "Well, Mrs. Fairweather," said she, "you *are* a neighbour. I thank you a thousand times." When she reached her own door, she hesitated for an instant, then turned back, pie in hand, to say, "Neighbour Fairweather, you needn't trouble yourself about sending Pink away. It's natural you should like the little creature, seeing he belongs to your son. I'll try to keep Tab in doors, and perhaps after awhile they will agree better."

"I hope they will," replied the friendly matron: "We will try them awhile longer, and if they persist in quarreling, I will send the dog into the country." Pink, who was sleeping in a chair, stretched himself and gaped. His kind mistress patted him on the head, "Ah, you foolish little beast," said she, "what's the use of plaguing poor Tab?"

"Well, I do say," observed Sally, smiling, "you are a master woman for stopping a quarrel."

"I learned a good lesson when I was a little girl," rejoined Mrs. Fairweather. "One frosty morning, I was looking out of the window into my father's barn-yard, where stood many cows, oxen, and horses, waiting to drink. It was one of those cold snapping mornings, when a slight thing irritates both man and beast. The cattle all stood very still and meek, till one of the cows attempted to turn round. In making the attempt, she happened to hit her next neighbour; whereupon the neighbour kicked and hit another. In five minutes, the whole herd were kicking and hooking each other, with all fury. Some lay sprawling on the ice, others were slipping about, with their hind heels reared in the air. My mother laughed, and said, 'See what comes of kicking when you're hit. Just so I've seen one cross word set a whole family by the ears, some frosty morning.' Afterward, if my brothers or myself were a little irritable, she would say, 'Take care, children. Remember how the fight in the barn-yard began. Never give a kick for a hit, and you will save yourself and others a deal of trouble.'"

That same afternoon, the sunshiny dame stepped into Aunt Hetty's rooms, where she found Peggy sewing, as usual, with the eternal switch on the table beside her. "I am obliged to go to Harlem, on business," said she: "I feel rather lonely without company, and I always like to have a child with me. If you will oblige me by letting Peggy go, I will pay her fare in the omnibus."

"She has her spelling lesson to get before night," replied Aunt Hetty. "I don't approve of young folks going a pleasuring, and neglecting their education."

"Neither do I," rejoined her neighbour; "but I

think there is a great deal of education that is not found in books. The fresh air will make Peggy grow stout and active. I prophesy that she will do great credit to your bringing up." The sugared words, and the remembrance of the sugared pie, touched the soft place in Miss Turnpenny's heart, and she told the astonished Peggy that she might go and put on her best gown and bonnet. The poor child began to think that this new neighbour was certainly one of the good fairies she read about in the picture books. The excursion was enjoyed as only a city child *can* enjoy the country. The world seems such a pleasant place, when the fetters are off, and Nature folds the young heart lovingly on her bosom! A flock of real birds and two living butterflies put the little orphan in a perfect ecstasy. She ran and skipped. One could see that she might be graceful, if she were only free. She pointed to the fields covered with dandelions, and said, "See how pretty! It looks as if the stars had come down to lie on the grass." Ah, our little stinted Peggy has poetry in her, though Aunt Hetty never found it out. Every human soul has the germ of some flowers within, and they would open, if they could only find sunshine and free air to expand in.

Mrs. Fairweather was a practical philosopher, in her own small way. She observed that Miss Turnpenny really liked a pleasant tune; and when Winter came, she tried to persuade her that singing would be excellent for Peggy's lungs, and perhaps keep her from going into a consumption.

"My nephew, James Fairweather, keeps a singing school," said she; "and he says he will teach her gratis. You need not feel under great obligation; for her voice will lead the whole school, and her ear is so quick, it will be no trouble at all to teach her. Perhaps you would go with us sometimes, neighbour Turnpenny? It is very pleasant to hear the children's voices."

The cordage of Aunt Hetty's mouth relaxed into a smile. She accepted the invitation, and was so much pleased, that she went every Sunday evening. The simple tunes, and the sweet young voices, fell like dew on her dried-up heart, and greatly aided the genial influence of her neighbour's example. The rod silently disappeared from the table. If Peggy was disposed to be idle, it was only necessary to say, "When you have finished your work, you may go and ask whether Mrs. Fairweather wants any errands done." Bless me, how the fingers flew! Aunt Hetty had learned to use turnips instead of the cudgel.

When Spring came, Mrs. Fairweather busied herself with planting roses and vines. Miss Turnpenny readily consented that Peggy should help her, and even refused to take any pay from such a good neighbour. But she maintained her own opinion that it was a mere waste of time to cultivate flowers. The cheerful philosopher never disputed the point; but she would sometimes say, "I have no room to plant this rose-bush. Neighbour Turnpenny, would you be willing to let me set it on your side of the yard? It will take very little room, and will need no care." At another time, she would say, "Well, really my ground is too full. Here is a root of Lady's-delight. How bright and pert it looks. It seems a pity to throw it away. If you are willing, I will let Peggy plant it in what she calls her garden. It will grow of itself, without any care, and scatter seeds, that will come up and blossom in all the chinks of the bricks. I love it. It is such a bright good-natured little thing." Thus by degrees, the crabbed maiden found herself surrounded by flowers; and she even declared, of her own accord, that they did look pretty.

One day, when Mrs. Lane called upon Mrs. Fairweather, she found the old weed-grown yard bright and blooming. Tab, quite fat and sleek, was asleep, in the sunshine, with her paw on Pink's neck, and little Peggy was singing at her work, as blithe as a bird.

"How cheerful you look here," said Mrs. Lane. "And so you have really taken the house for another year. Pray, how do you manage to get on with the neighbour-in-law?"

"I find her a very kind, obliging neighbour," replied Mrs. Fairweather.

"Well, this *is* a miracle!" exclaimed Mrs. Lane, "Nobody but you would have undertaken to thaw out Aunt Hetty's heart."

"That is probably the reason why it was never thawed," rejoined her friend. "I always told you, that not having enough of sunshine was what ailed the world. Make people happy, and there will not be half the quarrelling, or a tenth part of the wickedness, there is."

From this gospel of joy preached and practised, nobody derived so much benefit as little Peggy. Her nature, which was fast growing crooked and knotty, under the malign influence of constraint and fear, straightened up, budded and blossomed, in the genial atmosphere of cheerful kindness.

Her affections and faculties were kept in such pleasant exercise, that constant lightness of heart made her almost handsome. The young music-teacher thought her more than almost handsome; for her affectionate soul shone more beamingly on him than on others, and love makes all things beautiful.

When the orphan removed to her pleasant little cottage, on her wedding-day, she threw her arms round the blessed missionary of sunshine, and said, "Ah, thou dear good Aunt, it is thou who hast made my life Fairweather."

SHE WAITS IN THE SPIRIT LAND.

A Romance founded on an Indian Tradition.

A bard of many breathings
Is the wind in sylvan wreathings,
O'er mountain tops and through the woodland groves·
Now fifing and now drumming,
Now howling and now humming,
As it roves.

Though the wind a strange tone waketh
In every home it maketh,
And the maple tree responds not as the larch,
Yet harmony is playing
Round *all* the green arms swaying
Neath heaven's arch.

Oh, what can be the teaching
Of these forest voices preaching?
'Tis that a brother's creed, though not like mine,
May blend about God's altar,
And help to fill the psalter,
That's divine.

ELIZA COOK

PU-KEE-SHE-NO-QUA was famous among her tribe for her eloquent manner of relating stories. She treasured up all the old traditions, and though she repeated them truly, they came from her mouth in brighter pictures than from others, because she tipped all the edges with her own golden fancy. One might easily conjecture that there was poetry in the souls of her ancestry also; for they had given her a name which signifies, "I light from flying." At fourteen years old, she was shut up in a hut by herself, to fast and dream, according to the custom of the Indians. She dreamed that the Morning Star came down and nestled in her bosom, like a bird; therefore she chose it for the Manitou, or Protecting Spirit of her life, and named her first-born son Wah-bu-nung-o, an Indian word for the Morning Star. The boy was handsome, brave and gentle; and his childhood gave early indications that he inherited the spiritual and poetic tendencies of his mother. At the threshold of his young life, he too was set apart to fast and dream. He dreamed of a wild rose bush, in full bloom, and heard a voice saying, "She will wait for thee in the spirit-land. Do not forsake her." The Wild Rose was accordingly adopted as his Manitou.

In a neighbouring wigwam, was a girl named O-ge-bu-no-qua, which signifies the Wild Rose. When she, at twelve years old, was sent into retirement to fast and dream, she dreamed of a Star; but she could tell nothing about it, only that it was mild, and looked at her. She was a charming child, and grew into beautiful maidenhood. Her dark cheek looked like a rich brown autumn leaf, faintly tinged with crimson. Her large eyes, shaded with deep black fringe, had a shy and somewhat mournful tenderness of expression. Her voice seemed but the echo of her glance, it was so low and musical in tone, so plaintive in its cadences. Her well-rounded figure was pliant and graceful, and her motions were like those of some pretty, timid animal, that has always stepped to sylvan sounds.

The handsome boy was but two years older than the beautiful girl. In childhood, they swung together in the same boughs, hand in hand they clambered the rocks, and gathered the flowers and berries of the woods. Living in such playful familiarity with the deer and the birds, the young blood flowed fresh and strong, their forms were vigorous, and their motions flexile and free. The large dark eyes of Wah-bu-nung-o were tender and sad, and had a peculiarly deep, spiritual, inward-looking expression, as if he were the destined poet and prophet of his tribe. But the lofty carriage of his head, the Apollo curve of his parted lips, and his aquiline nose, with open well-defined nostrils, expressed the pride and daring of a hunter and a warrior.

It was very natural that the maiden should sometimes think it a beautiful coincidence that a Star was her guardian spirit, and this handsome friend of her childhood was named the Morning Star. And when he told her of the Wild Rose of his dream, had he not likewise some prophetic thoughts? Fortunately for the free and beautiful growth of their love, they lived out of the pale of civilization. There was no Mrs. Smith to remark how they looked at each other, and no Mrs. Brown to question the propriety of their rambles in the woods. The simple philosophy of the Indians had never taught that nature was a sin, and therefore nature was troubled with no sinful consciousness. When Wah-bu-nung-o hunted squirrels, O-ge-bu-no-qua thought it no harm to gather basket-stuff in the same woods. There was a lovely crescent-shaped island opposite the village, profusely covered with trees and vines, and carpeted with rich grasses and mosses, strewn with flowers. Clumps of young birches shone among the dark shrubbery, like slender columns of silver, and willows stooped so low to look in the mirror of the waters, that their graceful tresses touched the stream. Here, above all other places, did the maiden love to go to gather twigs for baskets, and the young man to select wood for his bows and arrows. Often, when day was declining, and the calm river reflected the Western sky, glowing with amber light, and fleckered with little fleecy rose-coloured clouds, his canoe might be seen gliding across the waters. Sometimes O-ge-bu-no-qua was waiting for him on the island, and sometimes he steered the boat for the grove of willows, while she urged it forward with the light swift stroke of her paddle.

Civilized man is little to be trusted under such circumstances; but nature, subjected to no false restraints, manifests her innate modesty, and even in her child-like abandonment to impulse, rebukes by her innocence the unclean self-consciousness of artificial society. With a quiet grave tenderness, the young Indian assisted his beautiful companion in her tasks, or spoke to her from time to time, as they met by brook or grove, in the pursuit of their different avocations. Her Manitou, the Morning Star of the sky, could not have been more truly her protecting spirit.

It was on her sixteenth birth day, that they, for the first time, lingered on the island after twilight. The Indians, with an untaught poetry of modesty, never talk of love under the bright staring gaze of day. Only amid the silent shadows do they yield to its gentle influence. O-ge-bu-no-qua was born with the roses; therefore this birth-night of their acknowledged love was in that beautiful month, named by the Indians "the Moon of Flowers." It was a lovely evening, and surpassingly fair was the scene around them. The picturesque little village of wigwams, on the other side of the river, gave a smiling answer to the sun's farewell. The abrupt heights beyond were robed in the richest foliage, through which the departing rays streamed like a golden shower. In the limitless forest, the tall trees were of noble proportions, because they had room enough to grow upward and outward, with a strong free grace. In the flowery glades of the islands, flocks of pigeons, and other smaller birds, cooed and chirped. Soon all subsided into moon-silence, and the elysian stillness was interrupted only by the faint ripple of the sparkling river, the lone cry of the whippowill, or the occasional plash of some restless bullfrog. The lovers sat side by side on a grassy knoll. An evening breeze gave them a gentle kiss as it passed, and brought them a love-token of fragrance from a rose-bush that grew at their feet. Wah-bu-nung-o gathered one of the blossoms, by the dim silvery light, and placing it in the hand of O-ge-bu-no-qua, he said, in a voice tender and bashful as a young girl's, "Thou knowest the Great Spirit has given me the wild rose for a Manitou. I have told thee my dream; but I have never told thee, thou sweet rose of my life, how sadly I interpret it."

She nestled closer in his bosom, and gazing earnestly on a bright star in the heavens, the Manitou of her own existence, she murmured almost inaudibly, "How *dost* thou?" His brave strong arm encircled her in a closer embrace, as he answered with gentle solemnity, "The Rose will go to the spirit-land, and leave her Star to mourn alone." The maiden's eyes filled with tears, as she replied, "But the Rose will wait for her Star. Thus said the voice of the dream."

They sat silently leaning on each other, till Wah-bu-nung-o took up the pipe, that lay beside him, and began to play. Birds sing only during their mating season; their twin-born love and music pass away together, with the roses; and the Indian plays on his pipe only while he is courting. It is a rude kind of flute, with two or three stops, and very limited variety of tone. The life of a savage would not be fitly expressed in rich harmonies; and life in any form never fashions to itself instruments beyond the wants of the soul. But the sounds of this pipe, with its perpetual return of sweet simple chords, and its wild flourishes, like the closing strain of a bob o' link, was in pleasing accord with the primeval beauty of the scene. When the pipe paused for awhile, O-ge-bu-no-qua warbled a wild plaintive little air, which her mother used to sing to her, when she swung from the boughs in her queer little birch-bark cradle. Indian music, like the voices of inanimate nature, the wind, the forest, and the sea, is almost invariably in the minor mode; and breathed as it now was to the silent moon, and with the shadow of the dream interpretation still resting on their souls, it was oppressive in its mournfulness. The song hushed; and O-ge-bu-no-qua, clinging closer to her lover's arm, whispered in tones of superstitious fear, "Does it not seem to you as if the Great Spirit was looking at us?" "Yes, and see how he smiles," replied Wah-bu-nung-o, in bolder and more cheerful accents, as he pointed to the sparkling waters: "The deer and the birds are not sad; let us be like them."

He spoke of love; of the new wigwam he would build for his bride, and the game he would bring down with his arrow. These home-pictures roused emotions too strong for words. Stolid and imperturbable as the Indian race seem in the presence of spectators, in these lonely hours with the beloved one, they too learn that love is the glowing wine, the exhilarating "fire-water" of the soul.

* * * * * * *

When they returned, no one questioned them. It was the most natural thing in the world that they should love each other; and natural politeness respected the freedom of their young hearts. No marriage settlements, no precautions of the law, were necessary. There was no person to object, whenever he chose to lead her into his wigwam, and by that simple circumstance she became his wife. The next day, as O-ge-bu-no-qua sat under the shadow of an elm, busily braiding mats, Wah-bu-nung-o passed by, carrying poles, which he had just cut in the woods. He stopped and spoke to her, and the glance of her wild melancholy eye met his with a beautiful expression of timid fondness. The next moment, she looked down and blushed very deeply. The poles were for the new wigwam, and so were the mats she was braiding; and she had promised her lover that as soon as the wigwam was finished, she would come and live with him. He conjectured her thoughts; but he did not smile, neither did he tell her that her blush was as beautiful as the brilliant flower of the Wickapee; but that bashful loving glance filled him with an inward warmth. Its beaming, yet half-veiled tenderness passed into his soul, and was never afterward forgotten.

That afternoon, all the young men of the tribe went a few miles up the river to fish. Sad tidings awaited their return. Ong-pa-tonga, the Big Elk, chief of a neighbouring tribe, in revenge for some trifling affront, had attacked the village in their absence, wounded some of the old warriors, and carried off several of the women and children. The blooming Wild Rose was among the captives. Wah-bu-nung-o was frantic with rage and despair. A demon seemed to have taken possession of his brave, but usually gentle soul. He spoke few words, but his eyes gleamed with a fierce unnatural fire. He painted himself with the colours of eternal enmity to the tribe of Big Elk, and secretly gloated over plans of vengeance. An opportunity soon offered to waylay the transgressors on their return from a hunting expedition. Several women accompanied the party, to carry their game and blankets. One of these, the wife of Big Elk, was killed by an arrow, and some of the men were wounded. This slight taste of vengeance made the flames of hatred burn more intensely. The image of his enemy expiring by slow tortures was the only thought that brought pleasure to the soul of Wah-bu-nung-o. Twice he had him nearly in his power, but was baffled by cunning. In one of the skirmishes between the contending tribes, he took captive a woman and her two children. Being questioned concerning the fate of O-ge-bu-no-qua, she said that Big Elk, in revenge for the loss of his wife, had killed her with his war club. For a moment, Wah-bu-nung-o stood as if suddenly changed to stone; then his Indian firmness forsook him, he tore his hair, and howled in frantic agony. But in the midst of this whirlwind of grief, the memory of his dream came like a still small voice, and whispered, "She waits for thee in the spirit land. Do not forsake her." The mad fire of his eye changed to the mildest and deepest melancholy. He promised the captive that she and her children should be treated kindly, and allowed to return to her tribe, if she would guide him to the maiden's grave.

Leaving her children in his own village, as a security against treachery, he followed her through the forest, till they came to a newly-made mound, with a few stones piled upon it. This she said was O-ge-bu-no-qua's grave. The young warrior gazed on it silently, with folded arms. No cry, or groan, escaped him; though in the depths of his soul was sorrow more bitter than death. Thus he remained for a long time. At last, he turned to take a careful inspection of the scene around him, and marked a tree with the point of his arrow. Then commanding the woman to walk before him, he strode homeward in perfect silence. A monotonous accompaniment of tree-whispering alone responded to the farewell dirge in his heart. As he looked on the boundless wilderness, and gazed into its dark mysterious depths, wild and solemn reveries came over him; vast shadowy visions of life and death; but through all the changes of his thought sounded the ever-recurring strain, "She waits for thee in the spirit-land." Then came the dread that Big Elk would go there before him, and would persecute his beloved, as he had done during her life in the body. An impatient shudder went over him, and he longed for death; but he had been taught to consider suicide a cowardly act, and he was awe-stricken before the great mystery of the soul. The dreadful conflict terminated in one calm fixed resolution. He determined to relinquish all his cherished plans of vengeance, and during the remainder of his life to watch over Big Elk, and guard him from danger, that he might not go to the spirit-land till he himself was there to protect his beloved.

The day after his return home, he told his mother that he must go away to fulfil a vow, and he knew not when he should return. He earnestly conjured his brothers to be kind and reverent to their mother; then bidding them a calm but solemn farewell, he stepped into his canoe, and rowed over to the Isle of Willows. Again he stood by the grassy knoll where the loved one had lain upon his breast. The rose-bush was there, tall and vigorous, though the human Rose had passed away, to return no more. He shed no tears, but reverently went through his forms of worship to the tutelary spirit of his life. With measured dance, and strange monotonous howls, he made a vow of utter renunciation of everything, even of his hopes of vengeance, if he might be permitted to protect his beloved in the spirit-land. He brought water from the brook in a gourd, from which they had often drunk together; he washed from his face the emblems of eternal enmity to Big Elk, and with solemn ceremonial poured it on the roots of the rose. Then he rowed far up the river, and landed near the grave, on which he kindled a fire, that the dear departed might be lighted to the spirit-land, according to the faith of his fathers. He buried the gourd in the mound, saying, "This I send to thee, my Rose, that thou mayest drink from it in the spirit-land." Three nights he tended the fire, and then returned for the rose-bush, which he planted at the head of the grave. He built a wigwam near by, and dwelt there alone. He feared neither wild beast nor enemies; for he had fulfilled his duties to the dead, and now his only wish was to go and meet her. Big Elk and his companions soon discovered him, and came upon him with their war-clubs. He stood unarmed, and quietly told them he had consecrated himself by a vow to the Great Spirit, and would fight no more. He gazed steadily in the face of his enemy, and said, if they wanted his life, they were welcome to take it. The deep, mournful, supernatural expression of his eyes inspired them with awe. They thought him insane; and all such are regarded by the Indians with superstitious fear and reverence. "He has seen the door of the spirit-land opened," they said; "the moon has spoken secrets to him; and the Great Spirit is angry when such are harmed." So they left him in peace. But he sighed as they turned away; for he had hoped to die by their hands. From that time he followed Big Elk like his shadow; but always to do him service. At first, his enemy was uneasy, and on his guard; but after awhile, he became accustomed to his presence, and even seemed to be attached to him. At one time, a fever brought the strong man to the verge of the grave. Wah-bu-nung-o watched over him with trembling anxiety, and through weary days and sleepless nights tended him as carefully as a mother tends her suffering babe. Another time, when Big Elk was wounded by an enemy, he drew out the arrow, sought medicinal herbs, and healed him. Once, when he was about to cross a wide deep ditch, bridged by a single tree, Wah-bu-nung-o perceived a rattle-snake on the bridge, and just as the venomous reptile was about to spring, his arrow nailed him to the tree.

Thus weary months passed away. The mourner, meek and silent, held communion with his Manitou, the rose-bush, to which he repeated often, "Bid her look to the Morning Star, and fear nothing. I will protect her. Tell her we shall meet again in the spirit-land, as we met in the Isle of Willows." Sadly but mildly his eye rested on the murderer of his beloved, and he tended upon him with patient gentleness, that seemed almost like affection. Very beautiful and holy was this triumph of love over hatred, seeking no reward but death. But the "twin-brother of sleep" came not where he was so much desired. Others who clung to life were taken, but the widowed heart could not find its rest. At last, the constant prayer of his faithful love was answered. By some accident, Big Elk became separated from his hunting companions, late in the afternoon of a winter's day. There came on a blinding storm of wind and snow and sleet. The deep drifts were almost impassable, and the keen air cut the lungs, like particles of sharpened steel. Night came down in robes of thick darkness. Nothing interrupted her solemn silence, but the crackling of ice from the trees, and the moaning and screaming of the winds. The very wolves hid themselves from the fury of the elements. While light enough remained to choose a shelter, the wanderers took refuge in a deep cleft screened by projecting rocks. The morning found them stiff and hungry, and almost buried in snow. With much difficulty they made their way out into the forest, completely bewildered, and guided only by the sun, which glimmered gloomily through the thick atmosphere. Two days they wandered without food. Toward night, Wah-bu-nung-o discovered horns projecting through the snow; and digging through the drift, he found a few moose bones, on which the wolves had left some particles of flesh. He resisted the cravings of hunger, and gave them all to his famishing enemy. As twilight closed, they took shelter in a large hollow tree, near which Wah-bu-nung-o, with the watchful eye of love and faith, observed a rose-bush, with a few crimson seed-vessels shining through the snow. He stripped some trees, and covered Ong-pa-tonga with the bark; then piling up snow before the entrance to the tree, to screen him from the cold, he bade him sleep, while he kept watch. Ong-pa-tonga asked to be awakened, that he might watch in his turn; but to this his anxious guardian returned no answer. The storm had passed away and left an atmosphere of intense cold. The stars glittered in the deep blue sky, like points of steel. Weary, faint, and starving, Wah-bu-nung-o walked slowly back and forth. When he felt an increasing numbness stealing over his limbs, a disconsolate smile gleamed on his countenance, and he offered thanks to the Manitou bush by his side. It was the first time he had smiled since his Wild Rose was taken from him. Presently, the howl of wolves was heard far off. He kept more carefully near the tree where his enemy slept, and listened to ascertain in what direction the ravenous beasts would come. "They shall eat me first, before they find their way to him," he said; "She would be so frightened to see his spirit, before mine came to protect her." But the dismal sounds died away in the distance, and were heard no more. Panting and staggering, the patient sufferer fell on the ground, at the foot of the rose-bush, and prayed imploringly, "Let not the wild beasts devour him, while I lie here insensible. Oh, send me to the spirit-land, that I may protect her!" He gasped for breath, and a film came over his eyes, so that he could no longer see the stars. How long he remained thus, no one ever knew.

Suddenly all was light around him. The rose-bush bloomed, and O-ge-bu-no-qua stood before him, with the same expression of bashful love he had last seen in her beautiful eyes. "I have been ever near thee," she said; "Hast thou not seen me?"

"Where am I, my beloved?" he exclaimed: "Are we in the Isle of Willows?"

"We are in the spirit-land," she answered: "Thy Rose has waited patiently for the coming of her Morning Star."

A POET'S DREAM OF THE SOUL.

For, as be all bards, he was born of beauty,
And with a natural fitness to draw down
All tones and shades of beauty to his soul,
Even as the rainbow-tinted shell, which lies
Miles deep at bottom of the sea, hath all
Colours of skies and flowers, and gems and plumes.—FESTUS.

Forms are like sea-shells on the shore; they show
Where the mind ends, and not how far it has been.—IBID.

HIDDEN among common stones, in a hill-side of Germany, an agate reposed in deep tranquillity. The roots of a violet twined about it, and as they embraced more and more closely, year by year, there grew up a silent friendship between the stone and the flower. In Spring, when the plant moved above the surface of the earth, it transmitted genial sun-warmth, and carried dim amethystine light into the dark home of the mineral. Lovingly it breathed forth the secrets of its life, but the agate could not understand its speech; for a lower form of existence has merely a vague feeling of the presence of the grade above it. But from circling degrees of vegetable life, spirally, through the violet, passed a subtle influence into the heart of the agate. It wanted to grow, to spread, to pass upward into the light. But the laws of its being girdled it round like a chain of iron.

A shepherd came and stretched himself fondly by

the side of the violet, and piped sweet pastoral music, thinking the while of the fragrant breath and deep blue eyes of her he loved. The flower recognised the tones as a portion of its own soul, and breathed forth perfumes in harmony. Her deeply moved inward joy was felt by the mineral, and kindled enthusiastic longing. Under the glow which renders all forms fluid, the chain of necessity relaxed, and the agate expressed its aspiration for vegetable life, in the form of mosses, roots, and leaves. But soon it touched the wall of limitation; upward it could not grow.

A compounder of medicines and amulets came digging for roots and minerals. He pounded the moss-agate to dust, and boiled it with the violet. The souls passed away from the destroyed forms, to enter again at some perfect union of Thought and Affection, a marriage between some of the infinitely various manifestations of this central duality of the universe. The spirit of the agate floated far, and was finally attracted toward a broad inland lake in the wilds of unknown America. The water-lilies were making love, and it passed into the seed to which their union gave birth. In the deep tranquillity of the forest, it lived a snowy lily with a golden heart, gently swayed on the waters, to the sound of rippling murmurs. Brightly solemn was the moon-stillness there. It agitated the breast of the lily; for the mild planet shed dewy tears on his brow, as he lay sleeping, and seemed to say mournfully, "I too am of thy kindred, yet thou dost not know me."

Soon came the happy days when the lily wooed his bride. Gracefully she bowed toward him, and a delicious languor melted his whole being, as he fondly veiled her in a golden shower of aroma. Its spiritual essence pervaded the atmosphere. The birds felt its influence, though they knew not whence it was. The wood-pigeons began to coo, and the mocking-bird poured forth all the loves of the forest. The flowers thrilled responsive to their extremest roots, and all the little blossoms wanted to kiss each other.

The remembrance of mineral existence had passed away from the lily; but with these sounds came vague reminiscences of kindred vibrations, that wrote the aspiration of the agate in mossy hieroglyphics on its bosom. Among the tall trees, a vine was dancing and laughing in the face of the sun. "It must be a pleasant life to swing so blithely high up in the air," thought the lily: "O, what would I give to be so much nearer to the stars!" He reared his head, and tried to imitate the vine; but the waters gently swayed him backward, and he fell asleep on the bosom of the lake. A troop of buffaloes came to drink, and in wild sport they pulled up the lilies, and tossed them on their horns.

The soul, going forth to enter a new body, arrived on the southern shores of the Rhone, at the courting time of blossoms, and became a winged seed, from which a vine leaped forth. Joyous was its life in that sunny clime of grapes and olives. Beautiful rainbow-tinted fairies hovered about it in swarms. They waltzed on the leaves, and swung from the tendrils, playing all manner of merry tricks. If a drowsy one fell asleep in the flower-bells, they tormented him without mercy, tickling his nose with a butterfly's feather, or piping through straws in his ear. Not a word of love could the vine-blossoms breathe to each other, but the mischievous fairies were listening; and with a zephyry laugh of silvery sweetness, they would sing, "Aha, we hear you!" Then the blossoms would throw perfumes at them, and they would dance away, springing from leaf to leaf, still shouting, "Aha, we heard you!" The next minute, the whole troop would be back again, making ugly faces from a knot-hole in the tree, pelting the blossoms with dew-drops, or disturbing their quiet loves with a serenade of musquito trumpets, and a grotesque accompaniment of cricket-rasping. But the blossoms delighted in the frolicksome little imps; for their capers were very amusing, and at heart they were real friends to love, and always ready to carry perfumes, or presents of golden flower-dust, from one to another, on their tiny wands. They could not reveal secrets, if they would; because the flowers and the fairies have no secrets; but many a graceful song they sang of Moth-feather kissed by Fly-wing, as she lay pretending to be asleep in a Fox-glove; or how Star-twinkle serenaded Dew-drop in the bosom of a Rose.

It was a pleasant life the vine led among the butterflies and fairies; but the stars seemed just as far off as when he was a lily; and when he saw the great trees spread their branches high above him, he wished that he could grow strong, brave, and self-sustaining, like them. While such wishes were in his heart, a traveller passed that way, singing light carols as he went. With careless gayety he switched the vine, the stem broke, and it hung fainting from the branches.

The fairies mourned over the drooping blossoms, and sang sweet requiems as its spirit passed away.

On the heights of Mount Helicon, oak-blossoms were tremulous with love when the vine-spirit floated over them. He entered into an acorn, and became an oak. Serenely noble was his life, in a grove consecrated to the Muses. With calm happiness he gazed upon the silent stars, or watched his own majestic shadow dancing on the verdant turf, enamelled with flowers, which filled the whole air with fragrance. The olive trees, the walnuts, and the almonds, whispered to him all the stories of their loves; and the zephyrs, as they flew by, lingered among his branches, to tell marvellous stories of the winds they had kissed in foreign climes. The Dryads, as they leaned against him, and lovingly twined each other with vernal crowns from his glossy leaves, talked of primal spirits, veiled in never-ending varieties of form, gliding in harmonies through the universe. The murmur of bees, the music of pastoral flutes, and the silvery flow of little waterfalls, mingled ever with the melodious chime of these divine voices. Sometimes, long processions of beautiful youths, crowned with garlands, and bearing branches of laurel, passed slowly by, singing choral hymns in worship of the Muses. The guardian Nymphs of fountains up among the hills leaned forward on their flowing urns, listening to the tuneful sounds; and often the flash of Apollo's harp might be seen among the trees, lightening the forest with a golden fire.

Amid this quiet grandeur, the oak forgot the prettiness of his life with the nimble fairies. But when he looked down on little streams fringed with oleander and myrtle, or saw bright-winged butterflies and radiant little birds sporting in vine-festoons, he felt a sympathy with the vines and the blossoms, as if they were somehow allied to his own being. The motion of the busy little animals excited a vague restlessness; and when he saw goats skip from rock to rock, or sheep following the flute of the shepherd far over the plain, the sap moved more briskly in his veins, and he began to ask, "How is it beyond those purple hills? Do trees and Dryads live there? And these moving things, are their loves more lively and perfect than ours? Why cannot I also follow that music? Why must I stand still, and wait for all things to come to me?" Even the brilliant lizard, when he crawled over his bark, or twined about his stems, roused within him a faint desire for motion. And when the winds and the trees whispered to him their pastoral romances, he wondered whether the pines, the hazels, and the zephyrs, there beyond, could tell the story of love between the moon and the hills, that met so near them, to bid each other farewell with such a lingering kiss. There came no answer to these queries; but the marble statue of Euterpe, in the grove below, smiled significantly upon him, and the bright warblings of a flute were heard, which sounded like the utterance of her smile. A Dryad, crowned with laurel, and bearing a branch of laurel in her hands, was inspired by the Muse, and spake prophetically: "That was the divine voice of Euterpe," she says; "be patient, and I will reveal all things."

Long stood the oak among those Grecian hills.

The whisperings of the forest became like the voices of familiar friends. But those grand choral hymns, accompanied by warblings of Euterpe's flute, with harmonic vibrations from Erato's silver lyre, and Apollo's golden harp, remained mysteries profound as the stars. Yet all his fibres unconsciously moved in harmony, the unintelligible sounds passed into his inmost being, and modified his outward growth. In process of time, a woodcutter felled the magnificent tree, for pillars to an altar of Jove; and weeping Dryads threw mosses and green garlands over the decaying roots.

A beautiful lizard, with bright metallic hues, glided about on the trees and temples of Herculaneum. He forgot that he had ever been an oak, nor did he know that he carried on his back the colours of the faëry songs he had heard as a vine. He led a pleasant life under the shadow of the leaves, but when Autumn was far advanced, he found a hole in the ground, under one of the pillars of the theatre, and crept into the crevice of a stone to sleep. A torpor came over him, at first occasionally startled by the sharp clash of cymbals, or the deep sonorous voice of trombones, from within the building. But the wind blew sand into the crevice, the earth covered him, and the unconscious lizard was entombed alive. Processions of drunken Bacchantes, with all their furious uproar, did not rouse him from his lethargy. Vesuvius roared, as it poured out rivers of fire, but he heard it not. Through the lapse of silent centuries, he lay there within a buried city, in a sepulchre of lava. But not even that long, long sleep, without a dream, could efface the impressions of his past existences. At last, some workmen, digging for a well; struck upon a statue, and the lost city was discovered. Breaking away the lava with pickaxes and hammers, they dashed in pieces the stone into which the lizard had crept. He gasped when the fresh air came upon him, and died instantly. His lizard-life had passed without aspiration, and long imprisonment had made him averse to light. He slipped under ground, and became a mole, blind as when he was an agate. He could not see the beauty of the flowers, or the glory of the stars. But music, the universal soul of all things, came to him also. A lark built her nest on the ground near by; and when she returned to her little ones, the joyful trill of her gushing tones was so full of sunlight, that it warmed the heart of the poor little mole. He could not see where the lark went, when he heard her clear notes ascending far into the sky; but he felt the expression of a life more free and bright than his own, and he grew weary of darkness and silence. As he came out oftener to feel the sunshine, his rich brown glossy fur attracted the attention of a boy, who caught him in a trap.

The emancipated spirit passed where birds were mating on the sea shore, and became a halcyon. He wooed a lady-bird, and she was enamoured of his beauty, though neither of them knew that the lark's song was painted in rainbow-tints upon his plumage. Their favourite resort was a cave in the Isle of Staffa. Season after season, he and his successive lady-loves went there to rear their young, in a deep hole of the rock, where the tide, as it ebbs and flows, makes strange wild melody. As the mother brooded over her nest, he sat patiently by her side, listening to the measured rhythm of the sea, and the wild crescendo of the winds. When storms subsided, and rainbows spanned the rocky island, sirens and mermaids came riding on the billows, with pearls in their hair, singing of submarine gardens, where groves of fan-coral bend like flexile willows, and yellow and crimson seaweeds float in their fluid element, as gracefully as banners on the wind. The halcyons, as they glided above the white wave-wreaths, or sat on the rocks watching for food, often saw these fantastic creatures swimming about, merrily pelting each other with pebbles and shells; and their liquid laughter, mingled with snatches of song, might be heard afar, as they went deep down to their grottoes in the sea.

When Winter approached, the happy birds flew to more Southern climes. During these inland visits, the halcyon again heard the song of the lark. It moved him strangely, and he tried to imitate it; but the sounds came from his throat in harsh twirls, and refused to echo his tuneful wishes. One day, as the beautiful bird sat perched on a twig, gazing intently into the stream, and listening to woodland warbles, a sportsman pointed his gun at him, and killed him instantly.

The spirit, hovering over Italian shores, went into the egg of a nightingale, and came forth into an earthly paradise of soft sunny valleys, and vine-clad hills, with urns and statues gleaming amid dark groves of cypress and cedar. When the moon rose above the hills, with her little one, the evening star, by her side, and twilight threw over the lovely landscape a veil of rose-coloured mist, the bird felt the pervading presence of the beautiful, and poured forth his soul in songs of exquisite tenderness. Plaintive were the tones; for the moon spoke into his heart far more sadly than when he was a water-lily, and with her solemn voice was mingled the chime of vesper bells across the water, the melancholy cry of gondoliers, and the measured plash of their oars. When the sun came up in golden splendour, flooding hill and dale with brilliant light, the nightingale nestled with his lady-love in cool sequestered groves of cypress and ilex, and listened in dreamy revery to the trickling of many fountains. Fairies came there and danced in graceful undulations, to music of liquid sweetness. In their wildest mirth, they were not so giddy-paced as the pretty caperers of the Rhone, and more deeply passionate were the love-stories they confided to the sympathizing nightingale. When the solemn swell of the church organ rose on the breeze, the fairies hid away timidly under leaves, while human voices chanted their hymns of praise. The nightingale, too, listened with awe; the majestic sounds disturbed him, like echoes of thunder among the hills. His mate had built her nest in low bushes, on the shore of a broad lagune, and there he was wont to sing to her at eventide. The gondolas, as they glided by, with lights glancing on the water, passed his home more slowly, that passengers might listen to the flowing song. One night, a violinist in the gondola responded to his lay. The nightingale answered with an eager gush. Again the violin replied, more at length. Sadly, and with a lingering sweetness, the nightingale resumed; but suddenly broke off, and went silent. The musician stept on shore, and played a long time under the shadow of the groves, to the ears of his lady-love, who leaned from her balcony to listen. Wildly throbbed the pulses of the nightingale. What was this enchanting voice? It repeated the sky-tone of the lark, the drowsy contemplations of the water-lily communing with the moon, the trills of fairies frisking among the vine-blossoms, the whispers of winds, and trees, and streams, the siren's song, and the mermaid's laugh. With all these he had unconsciously acquired sympathy, in the progress of his being; but mingled with them was a mysterious utterance of something deeper and more expansive, that thrilled his little bosom with an agony of aspiration. When the violin was itself a portion of trees, the music of winds, and leaves, and streams, and little birds, had passed into its heart. The poet's soul likewise listens passively to the voices of nature, and receives them quietly, as a divine influx. The violin knew by the poet's manner of questioning, that he could understand her, and she told him all the things she had ever heard. But by reason of this divine harmony between them, his human soul breathed through her, and made her the messenger of joys and sorrows far deeper than her own. This it was that troubled the breast of the nightingale. The next evening he flooded the whole valley with a rich tide of song. Men said, "Did ever bird sing so divinely?" But he felt how far inferior it was to those heavenly tones, which repeated all the things he had ever heard, and oppressed him with a prophecy of things unknown. Evening by evening, his song grew more sad in its farewell sweetness, and at last was heard no more. He had pined away and died, longing for the voice of the violin.

In a happy German home, a young wife leaned lovingly on the bosom of her chosen mate. They were not aware that the spirit of a nightingale was circling round them and would pass into the soul of their infant son, whom they named Felix Mendelssohn. The poet-musician, as he grew to manhood, lost all recollection of his own transmigrations. But often when his human eyes gazed on lovely scenes for the first time, Nature looked at him so kindly, and all her voices spoke so familiarly, that it seemed as if his soul must have been there before him. The moon claimed kindred with him, and lulled him into dreamy revery, as she had done when the undulating waters cradeled him as a lily. In music, he asked the fair planet concerning all this, and why she and the earth always looked into each other's eyes with such saddened love. Poets, listening to the Concerto,* heard in it the utterance of their souls also; and they will give it again in painting, sculpture, and verse. Thus are all forms intertwined by the pervading spirit which flows through them.

The sleeping flowers wakened vague reminiscences of tiny radiant forms. Mendelssohn called to them in music, and the whole faëry troop came dancing on moon-beams into his "Midsummer Night's Dream."

* Concerto for the piano, in G Minor.

The sight of temples and statues brought shadowy dreams of Druids, and consecrated groves, of choral hymns, and the rich vibrations of Apollo's harp. Serene in classic beauty, these visions float through the music of "Antigone."

The booming of waves, and the screaming of gulls, stirred halcyon recollections. He asked in music whence they came, and Euterpe answered in the picturesque sea-wildness of his "Fingal's Cave."

The song of the nightingale brought dim memories of a pure brilliant atmosphere, of landscapes tinted with prismatic splendour, of deep blue lakes dimpled with sun-flecks; and gracefully glides the gondola, under the glowing sky of Italy, through the flowing melody of his "Songs without Words."

But music is to him as the violin was to the nightingale. It repeats, with puzzling vagueness, all he has ever known, and troubles his spirit with prophecies of the infinite unknown. Imploringly he asks Euterpe to keep her promise, and reveal to him all the secrets of the universe. Graciously and confidingly she answers. But as it was with the nightingale, so is it with him; the utterance belongs to powers above the circle of his being, and he cannot comprehend it now. Through the gate which men call Death, he will pass into more perfect life, where speech and tone dwell together forever in a golden marriage.

THE BLACK SAXONS.

Tyrants are but the spawn of ignorance,
Begotten by the slaves they trample on;
Who, could they win a glimmer of the light,
And see that tyranny is *always* weakness,
Or fear with its own bosom ill at ease,
Would laugh away in scorn the sand-wove chain,
Which their own blindness feigned for adamant.
Wrong ever builds on quicksands; but the Right
To the firm centre lays its moveless base.—J. R. LOWELL.

MR. DUNCAN was sitting alone in his elegantly furnished parlour, in the vicinity of Charleston, South Carolina. Before him lay an open volume, Thierry's History of the Norman Conquest. From the natural kindliness of his character, and democratic theories deeply imbibed in childhood, his thoughts dwelt more with a nation prostrated and kept in base subjection by the strong arm of violence, than with the renowned robbers, who seized their rich possesions, and haughtily trampled on their dearest rights.

"And so that bold and beautiful race became slaves!" thought he. "The brave and free-souled Harolds, strong of heart and strong of arm; the fair-haired Ediths, in their queenly beauty, noble in soul as well as ancestry; these all sank to the condition of slaves. They tamely submitted to their lot, till their free, bright beauty passed under the heavy cloud of animal dullness, and the contemptuous Norman epithet of 'base Saxon churls' was but too significantly true. Yet not without efforts did they thus sink. How often renewed, or how bravely sustained, we know not; for Troubadours rarely sing of the defeated, and conquerors write their own History. That they did not relinquish freedom without a struggle, is proved by Robin Hood and his bold followers, floating in dim and shadowy glory on the outskirts of history; brave outlaws of the free forest, and the wild mountain-passes, taking back, in the very teeth of danger, a precarious subsistence from the rich possessions that were once their own; and therefore styled thieves and traitors by the robbers who had beggared them. Doubtless they had minstrels of their own; unknown in princely halls, untrumpeted by fame, yet singing of their exploits in spirit-stirring tones, to hearts burning with a sense of wrong. Troubled must be the sleep of those who rule a conquered nation!"

These thoughts were passing through his mind, when a dark mulatto opened the door, and making a servile reverence, said, in wheedling tones, "Would massa be so good as gib a pass to go to Methodist meeting?"

Mr. Duncan was a proverbially indulgent master; and he at once replied, "Yes, Jack, you may have a pass; but you must mind and not stay out all night."

"Oh, no, massa. Tom neber preach more than two hours."

Scarcely was the pass written, before another servant appeared with a similar request; and presently another; and yet another. When these interruptions ceased, Mr. Duncan resumed his book, and quietly read of the oppressed Saxons, until the wish for a glass of water induced him to ring the bell. No servant obeyed the summons. With an impatient jerk of the rope, he rang a second time, muttering to himself, "What a curse it is to be waited upon by slaves! If I were dying, the lazy loons would take their own time, and come dragging their heavy heels along, an hour after I was in the world of spirits. My neighbours tell me it is because I never flog them. I believe they are in the right. It is a hard case, too, to force a man to be a tyrant, whether he will or no."

A third time he rang the bell more loudly; but waited in vain for the sound of coming footsteps. Then it occurred to him that he had given every one of his slaves a pass to go to the Methodist meeting. This was instantly followed by the remembrance, that the same thing had happened a few days before.

We were then at war with Great Britain; and though Mr. Duncan often boasted the attachment of his slaves, and declared them to be the most contented and happy labourers in the world, who would not take their freedom if they could, yet, by some coincidence of thought, the frequency of Methodist meetings immediately suggested the common report that British troops were near the coast, and about to land in Charleston. Simultaneously came the remembrance of Big-boned Dick, who many months before had absconded from a neighbouring planter, and was suspected of holding a rendezvous for runaways, in the swampy depths of some dark forest. The existence of such a gang was indicated by the rapid disappearance of young corn, sweet potatoes, fat hogs, &c., from the plantations for many miles round.

"The black rascal!" exclaimed he: "If my boys *are* in league with him"—

The coming threat was arrested by a voice within, which, like a chorus from some invisible choir, all at once struck up the lively ballad of Robin Hood; and thus brought Big-boned Dick, like Banquo's Ghost, unbidden and unwelcome, into incongruous association with his spontaneous sympathy for Saxon serfs, his contempt of "base Saxon churls," who tamely submitted to their fate, and his admiration of the bold outlaws, who lived by plunder in the wild freedom of Saxon forests.

His republican sympathies, and the "system entailed upon him by his ancestors," were obviously out of joint with each other; and the skilfullest soldering of casuistry could by no means make them adhere together. Clear as the tones of a cathedral bell above the hacks and drays of a city, the voice of Reason rose above all the pretexts of selfishness, and the apologies of sophistry, and loudly proclaimed that his sympathies were right, and his practice wrong. Had there been at his elbow some honest John Woolman, or fearless Elias Hicks, that hour might perhaps have seen *him* a freeman, in giving freedom to his serfs. But he was alone; and the prejudices of education, and the habits of his whole life, conjured up a fearful array of lions in his path; and he wist not that they were phantoms. The admonitions of awakened conscience gradually gave place to considerations of personal safety, and plans for ascertaining the real extent of his danger.

The next morning he asked his slaves, with assumed nonchalance, whether they had a good meeting.

"Oh, yes, massa; bery good meeting."

"Where did you meet?"

"In the woods behind Birch Grove, massa."

The newspaper was brought, and found to contain a renewal of the report that British troops were prowling about the coast. Mr. Duncan slowly paced the room for some time, apparently studying the figures of the carpet, yet utterly unconscious whether he trod on canvass or the greensward. At length, he ordered his horse and drove to the next plantation. Seeing a gang at work in the fields, he stopped; and after some questions concerning the crop, he said to one of the most intelligent, "So you had a fine meeting last night?"

"Oh, yes, massa, bery nice meeting."

"Where was it?

The slave pointed far *east* of Birch Grove. The white man's eye followed the direction of the bondman's finger, and a deeper cloud gathered on his brow. Without comment he rode on in another direction, and with apparent indifference made similar inquiries of another gang of labourers. They pointed *north* of Birch Grove, and replied, "In the Hugonot woods, massa."

With increasing disquietude, he slowly turned his horse toward the city. He endeavoured to conceal anxiety under a cheerful brow; for he was afraid to ask counsel, even of his most familiar friends, in a community so prone to be blinded by insane fury under the excitement of such suspicions. Having purchased a complete suit of negro clothes, and a black mask well fitted to his face, he returned home, and awaited the next request for passes to a Methodist meeting.

In a few days, the sable faces again appeared before him, one after another, asking permission to hear Tom preach. The passes were promptly given, accompanied by the cool observation, "It seems to me, boys, that you are all growing wonderfully religious of late."

To which they eagerly replied, "Ah, if massa could hear Tom preach, it make his hair stand up. Tom make ebery body tink weder he hab a soul."

When the last one had departed, the master hastily assumed his disguise, and hurried after them. Keeping them within sight, he followed over field and meadow, through woods and swamps. As he went on, the number of dark figures, all tending toward the same point, continually increased. Now and then, some one spoke to him; but he answered briefly, and with an effort to disguise his voice. At last, they arrived at one of those swamp islands, so common at the South, insulated by a broad, deep belt of water, and effectually screened from the main-land by a luxuriant growth of forest trees, matted together by a rich entanglement of vines and underwood. A large tree had been felled for a bridge; and over this dusky forms were swarming, like ants into their new-made nest.

Mr. Duncan had a large share of that animal instinct called physical courage; but his heart throbbed almost audibly, as he followed that dark multitude.

At the end of a rough and intricate passage, there opened before him a scene of picturesque and imposing grandeur. A level space, like a vast saloon, was enclosed by majestic trees, uniting their boughs over it, in fantastic resemblance to some Gothic cathedral. Spanish moss formed a thick matted roof, and floated in funereal streamers. From the points of arches hung wild vines in luxuriant profusion, some in heavy festoons, others lightly and gracefully leaping upward. The blaze of pine torches threw some into bold relief, and cast others into a shadowy background. And here, in this lone sanctuary of Nature, were assembled many hundreds of swart figures, some seated in thoughtful attitudes, others scattered in moving groups, eagerly talking together. As they glanced about, now sinking into dense shadow, and now emerging into lurid light, they seemed to the slaveholder's excited imagination like demons from the pit, come to claim guilty souls. He had, however, sufficient presence of mind to observe that each one, as he entered, prostrated himself, till his forehead touched the ground, and rising, placed his finger on his mouth. Imitating this signal, he passed in with the throng, and seated himself behind the glare of the torches. For some time, he could make out no connected meaning amid the confused buzz of voices, and half-suppressed snatches of songs. But, at last, a tall man mounted the stump of a decayed tree, nearly in the centre of the area, and requested silence.

"When we had our last meeting," said he, "I suppose most all of you know, that we all concluded it was best for to join the British, if so be we could get a good chance. But we didn't all agree about our masters. Some thought we should never be able to keep our freedom, without we killed our masters, in the first place; others didn't like the thoughts of that; so we agreed to have another meeting to talk about it. And now, boys, if the British land here in Caroliny, what shall we do with our masters?"

He sat down, and a tall, sinewy mulatto stepped into his place, exclaiming, with fierce gestures, "Ravish wives and daughters before their eyes, as they have done to *us!* Hunt them with hounds, as they have hunted *us!* Shoot them down with rifles, as they have shot *us!* Throw their carcasses to the crows, they have fattened on *our* bones; and then let the Devil take them where they never rake up fire o' nights. Who talks of *mercy* to our masters?"

"I do," said an aged black man, who rose up before the fiery youth, tottering as he leaned both hands on an oaken staff. "I do;—because the blessed Jesus always talked of mercy. I know we have been fed like hogs, and shot at like wild beasts. Myself found the body of my likeliest boy under the tree where buckra* rifles reached him. But thanks to the blessed Jesus, I feel it in my poor old heart to forgive them. I have been member of a Methodist church these thirty years; and I've heard many preachers, white and black; and they all tell me Jesus said, Do good to them that do evil to you, and pray for them that spite you. Now I say, let us love our enemies;

* Buckra is the negro term for white man.

let us pray for them ; and when our masters flog us, and sell our piccaninnies, let us break out singing :

"You may beat upon my body,
But you cannot harm my soul;
I shall join the forty thousand by and by.

"You may sell my children to Georgy,
But you cannot harm their soul;
They will join the forty thousand by and bye.

"Come, slave-trader, come in too;
The Lord 's got a pardon here for you;
You shall join the forty thousand by and bye.

"Come, poor nigger, come in too;
The Lord 's got a pardon here for you;
You shall join the forty thousand by and bye.

"My skin is black, but my soul is white;
And when we get to Heaven we 'll all be alike;
We shall join the forty thousand by and bye.

That's the way to glorify the Lord."

Scarcely had the cracked voice ceased the tremulous chant in which these words were uttered, when a loud altercation commenced ; some crying out vehemently for the blood of the white men, others maintaining that the old man's doctrine was right. The aged black remained leaning on his staff, and mildly replied to every outburst of fury, "But Jesus said, do good for evil." Loud rose the din of excited voices ; and the disguised slaveholder shrank deeper into the shadow.

In the midst of the confusion, an athletic, gracefully-proportioned young man sprang upon the stump, and throwing off his coarse cotton garments, slowly turned round and round, before the assembled multitude.

Immediately all was hushed; for the light of a dozen torches, eagerly held up by fierce revengeful comrades, showed his back and shoulders deeply gashed by the whip, and still oozing with blood. In the midst of that deep silence, he stopped abruptly, and with stern brevity exclaimed, "Boys! *shall* we not murder our masters?"

"Would you murder *all?*" inquired a timid voice at his right hand. "They don't all cruellize their slaves."

"There's Mr. Campbell," pleaded another; "he never had one of his boys flogged in his life. You wouldn't murder *him*, would you?"

"Oh, no, no, no," shouted many voices; "we wouldn't murder Mr. Campbell. He's always good to coloured folks."

"And I wouldn't murder *my* master," said one of Mr. Duncan's slaves; "and I'd fight anybody that set out to murder him. I an't a going to work for him for nothing any longer, if I can help it; but he shan't be murdered; for he's a good master."

"Call him a good master, if ye like!" said the bleeding youth, with a bitter sneer in his look and tone. "I curse the word. The white men tell us God made them our masters; I say it was the Devil. When they don't cut up the backs that bear their burdens; when they throw us enough of the grain we have raised, to keep us strong for another harvest; when they forbear to shoot the limbs, that toil to make *them* rich; there *are* fools who call them good masters. Why should *they* sleep on soft beds, under silken curtains, while *we*, whose labour bought it all, lie on the floor at the threshold, or miserably coiled up in the dirt of our own cabins? Why should I clothe my master in broadcloth and fine linen, when he knows, and I know, that he is my own brother? and I, meanwhile, have only this coarse rag to cover my aching shoulders?" He kicked the garment scornfully, and added, "Down on your knees, if ye like, and thank them that ye are not flogged and shot. Of *me* they'll learn another lesson!"

Mr. Duncan recognised in the speaker, the reputed son of one of his friends, lately deceased; one of that numerous class, which southern vice is thoughtlessly raising up, to be its future scourge and terror.

The high, bold forehead, and flashing eye, indicated an intellect too active and daring for servitude; while his fluent speech and appropriate language betrayed the fact that his highly educated parent, from some remains of instinctive feeling, had kept him near his own person, during his lifetime, and thus formed his conversation on another model than the rude jargon of slaves.

His poor, ignorant listeners stood spell-bound by the magic of superior mind; and at first it seemed as if he might carry the whole meeting in favour of his views. But the aged man, leaning on his oaken staff, still mildly spoke of the meek and blessed Jesus; and the docility of African temperament responded to his gentle words.

Then rose a man of middle age, short of stature, with a quick roguish eye, and a spirit of knowing drollery lurking about his mouth. Rubbing his head in uncouth fashion, he began: "I don't know how to speak like Bob; for I never had no chance. He says the Devil made white men our masters. Now dat's a ting I've thought on a heap. Many a time I've axed myself how pon arth it was, that jist as sure as white man and black man come togeder, de white man sure to git he foot on de black man. Sometimes I tink one ting, den I tink anoder ting; and dey all be jumbled up in my head, jest like seed in de cotton, afore he put in de gin. At last, I find it all out. White man *always* git he foot on de black man; no mistake in *dat*. But how he do it? I'll show you how!"

Thrusting his hand into his pocket, he took out a crumpled piece of printed paper, and smoothing it carefully on the palm of his hand, he struck it significantly with his finger, and exclaimed triumphantly, "Dat's de way dey do it! Dey got de *knowledge!* Now, it'll do no more good to rise agin our masters, dan put de head in de fire and pull him out agin; and may be you can't pull him out agin. When I was a boy, I hear an old conjuring woman say she could conjure de Divil out of anybody. I ask her why she don't conjure her massa, den; and she tell me, 'Oh, nigger neber conjure buckra—can't do't.' But I say nigger *can* conjure buckra. How he do it? Get de knowledge! Dat de way. We make de sleeve wide, and fill full of de tea and de sugar, ebery time we get in missis' closet. If we take half so much pains to get de knowledge, de white man take he foot off de black man. Maybe de British land, and maybe de British no land; but tell you sons to marry de free woman, dat know how to read and write; and tell you gals to marry de free man, dat know how to read and write; and den, by'm bye, you be de British *yourselves!* You want to know how I manage to get de knowledge? I tell you. I want right bad to larn to read. My old boss is the most begrudgfullest massa, and I know he won't let me larn. So, when I see leetle massa wid he book, (he about six year old,) I say to him, What you call dat? He tell me dat is A. Oh, dat is A! So I take old newspaper, and I ax missis, may I hab dis to rub my brasses? She say yes. I put it in my pocket, and by'm by, I look to see I find A; and I look at him till I know him bery well. Den I ask my young massa, What you call dat? He say, dat is B. So I find him on my paper, and look at him, till I know him bery well. Den I ask my young massa what C A T spell? He tell me cat. Den, after great long time, I can read de newspaper. And what you tink I *find* dere? I read British going to land! Den I tell all de boys British going to land; and I say what you *do*, s'pose British land? When I stand behind massa's chair, I hear him talk, and I tell all de boys what he say. Den Bob say must hab Methodist meeting, and tell massa, Tom going to preach in de woods. But what you tink I did toder day? You know Jim, massa Gubernor's boy? Well, I want mighty bad to let Jim know British going to land. But he lib ten mile off, and old boss no let me go. Well, massa Gubernor he come dine my massa's house; and I bring he horse to de gate; and I make my bow, and say, massa Gubernor, how Jim do? He tell me Jim bery well. Den I ax him, be Jim good boy? He say yes. Den I tell him Jim and I leetle boy togeder; and I want mighty bad send Jim someting. He tell me Jim hab enough of ebery ting. Oh, yes, massa Gubernor, I know you bery good massa, and Jim hab ebery ting he want; but when leetle boy togeder, dere is always someting *here* (laying his hand on his heart). I want to send a leetle backy to Jim. I know he hab much backy he want; but Jim and I leetle boy togeder, and I want to send Jim someting. Massa Gubernor say, bery well, Jack. So I gib him de backy, done up in de bery bit o' newspaper dat tell British going to land! And massa Gubernor *himself* carry it! And massa Gubernor *himself* carry it!!"

He clapped his hands, kicked up his heels, and turned somersets like a harlequin. These demonstrations were received with loud shouts of merriment; and it was sometime before sufficient order was restored to proceed with the question under discussion.

After various scenes of fiery indignation, gentle expostulation, and boisterous mirth, it was finally decided, by a considerable majority, that in case the British landed, they would take their freedom *without* murdering their masters; not a few, however, went away in wrathful mood, muttering curses deep.

With thankfulness to Heaven, Mr. Duncan again found himself in the open field, alone with the stars. Their glorious beauty seemed to him, that night, clothed in new and awful power. Groups of shrubbery took to themselves startling forms; and the sound of the wind among the trees was like the unsheathing of swords. Again he recurred to Saxon history, and remembered how he had thought that troubled must be the sleep of those who rule a conquered people. A new significance seemed given to Wat Tyler's address to the insurgent labourers of *his* day; an emphatic, and most unwelcome application of *his* indignant question why serfs should toil unpaid, in wind and sun, that lords might sleep on down, and embroider their garments with pearl.

"And these Robin Hoods, and Wat Tylers, were my Saxon ancestors," thought he. "Who shall so balance effects and causes, as to decide what portion of my present freedom sprung from their seemingly defeated efforts? Was the place I saw to-night, in such wild and fearful beauty, like the haunts of the *Saxon* Robin Hoods? Was not the spirit that gleamed forth as brave as *theirs*? And who shall calculate what even such hopeless endeavours may do for the future freedom of this down-trodden race?"

These cogitations did not, so far as I ever heard, lead to the emancipation of his bondmen; but they did prevent his revealing a secret, which would have brought hundreds to an immediate and violent death. After a painful conflict between contending feelings and duties, he contented himself with advising the magistrates to forbid all meetings whatsoever among the coloured people until the war was ended.

He visited Boston several years after, and told the story to a gentleman, who often repeated it in the circle of his friends. In brief outline it reached my ears. I have told it truly, with some filling up by imagination, some additional garniture of language, and the adoption of fictitious names, because I have forgotten the real ones.

HILDA SILFVERLING.

A Fantasy.

> "Thou hast nor youth nor age;
> But, as it were, an after dinner's sleep,
> Dreaming on both."—MEASURE FOR MEASURE.

HILDA GYLLENLOF was the daughter of a poor Swedish clergyman. Her mother died before she had counted five summers. The good father did his best to supply the loss of maternal tenderness; nor were kind neighbors wanting, with friendly words, and many a small gift for the pretty little one. But at the age of thirteen, Hilda lost her father also, just as she was receiving rapidly from his affectionate teachings as much culture as his own education and means afforded. The unfortunate girl had no other resource than to go to distant relatives, who were poor, and could not well conceal that the destitute orphan was a burden. At the end of a year, Hilda, in sadness and weariness of spirit, went to Stockholm, to avail herself of an opportunity to earn her living by her needle, and some light services about the house.

She was then in the first blush of maidenhood, with a clear innocent look, and exceedingly fair complexion. Her beauty soon attracted the attention of Magnus Andersen, mate of a Danish vessel then lying at the wharves of Stockholm. He could not be otherwise than fascinated with her budding loveliness ; and alone as she was in the world, she was naturally prone to listen to the first words of warm affection she had heard since her father's death. What followed is the old story, which will continue to be told as long as there are human passions and human laws. To do the young man justice, though selfish, he was not deliberately unkind ; for he did not mean to be treacherous to the friendless young creature who trusted him. He sailed from Sweden with the honest intention to return and make her his wife ; but he was lost in a storm at sea, and the earth saw him no more.

Hilda never heard the sad tidings ; but, for another cause, her heart was soon oppressed with shame and sorrow. If she had had a mother's bosom on which to lean her aching head, and confess all her faults and all her grief, much misery might have been saved. But there was none to whom she dared to speak of her anxiety and shame. Her extreme melancholy attracted the attention of a poor old woman, to whom she sometimes carried clothes for washing. The good Virika, after manifesting her sympathy in various ways, at last ventured to ask outright why one so young was so very sad. The poor child threw herself on the friendly bosom, and confessed all her wretchedness. After that, they had frequent confidential conversations ; and the kind-hearted peasant did her utmost to console and cheer the desolate orphan. She said she must soon return to her native village in the Norwegian valley of Westfjordalen ; and as she was alone in the world, and wanted something to love, she would gladly take the babe, and adopt it for her own.

Poor Hilda, thankful for any chance to keep her disgrace a secret, gratefully accepted the offer. When the babe was ten days old, she allowed the good Virika to carry it away; though not without bitter tears, and the oft-repeated promise that her little one might be reclaimed, whenever Magnus returned and fulfilled his promise of marriage.

But though these arrangements were managed with great caution, the young mother did not escape suspicion. It chanced, very unfortunately, that soon after Virika's departure, an infant was found in the water, strangled with a sash very like one Hilda had been accustomed to wear. A train of circumstantial evidence seemed to connect the child with her, and she was arrested. For some time, she contented herself with assertions of innocence, and obstinately refused to tell anything more. But at last, having the fear of death before her eyes, she acknowledged that she had given birth to a daughter, which had been carried away by Virika Gjetter, to her native place, in the parish of Tind, in the Valley of Westfjordalen. Inquiries were accordingly made in Norway, but the answer obtained was that Virika had not been heard of in her native valley, for many years. Through weary months, Hilda lingered in prison, waiting in vain for favourable testimony; and at last, on strong circumstantial evidence, she was condemned to die.

It chanced there was at that time a very learned chemist in Stockholm; a man whose thoughts were all gas, and his hours marked only by combinations and explosions. He had discovered a process of artificial cold, by which he could suspend animation in living creatures, and restore it at any prescribed time. He had in one apartment of his laboratory a bear that had been in a torpid state five years, a wolf two years, and so on. This of course excited a good deal of attention in the scientific world. A metaphysician suggested how extremely interesting it would be to put a human being asleep thus, and watch the reunion of soul and body, after the lapse of a hundred years. The chemist was half wild with the magnificence of this idea; and he forthwith petitioned that Hilda, instead of being beheaded, might be delivered to him, to be frozen for a century. He urged that her extreme youth demanded pity; that his mode of execution would be a very gentle one, and, being so strictly private, would be far less painful to the poor young creature than exposure to the public gaze.

His request, being seconded by several men of science, was granted by the government; for no one suggested a doubt of its divine right to freeze human hearts, instead of chopping off human heads, or choking human lungs. This change in the mode of death was much lauded as an act of clemency, and poor Hilda tried to be as grateful as she was told she ought to be.

On the day of execution, the chaplain came to pray with her, but found himself rather embarrassed in using the customary form. He could not well allude to her going in a few hours to meet her final judge; for the chemist said she would come back in a hundred years, and where her soul would be meantime was more than theology could teach. Under these novel circumstances, the old nursery prayer seemed to be the only appropriate one for her to repeat:

"Now I lay me down to sleep,
I pray the Lord my soul to keep:
If I should die before I wake,
I pray the Lord my soul to take."

The subject of this curious experiment was conveyed in a close carriage from the prison to the laboratory. A shudder ran through soul and body, as she entered the apartment assigned her. It was built entirely of stone, and rendered intensely cold by an artificial process. The light was dim and spectral, being admitted from above through a small circle of blue glass. Around the sides of the room, were tiers of massive stone shelves, on which reposed various objects in a torpid state. A huge bear lay on his back, with paws crossed on his breast, as devoutly as some pious knight of the fourteenth century. There was in fact no inconsiderable resemblance in the proceedings by which both these characters gained their worldly possessions; they were equally based on the maxim that "might makes right." It is true, the Christian obtained a better name, inasmuch as he paid a tithe of his gettings to the holy church, which the bear never had the grace to do. But then it must be remembered that the bear had no soul to save, and the Christian knight would have been very unlikely to pay fees to the ferryman, if he likewise had had nothing to send over.

The two public functionaries, who had attended the prisoner, to make sure that justice was not defrauded of its due, soon begged leave to retire, complaining of the unearthly cold. The pale face of the maiden became still paler, as she saw them depart. She seized the arm of the old chemist, and said, imploringly, "You will not go away, too, and leave me with these dreadful creatures?"

He replied, not without some touch of compassion in his tones, "You will be sound asleep, my dear, and will not know whether I am here or not. Drink this; it will soon make you drowsy."

"But what if that great bear should wake up?" asked she, trembling.

"Never fear. He cannot wake up," was the brief reply.

"And what if I should wake up, all alone here?"

"Don't disturb yourself," said he, "I tell you that you will not wake up. Come, my dear, drink quick; for I am getting chilly myself."

The poor girl cast another despairing glance round the tomb-like apartment, and did as she was requested. "And now," said the chemist, "let us shake hands, and say farewell; for you will never see me again."

"Why, wont you come to wake me up?" inquired the prisoner; not reflecting on all the peculiar circumstances of her condition.

"My great-grandson may," replied he, with a smile. "Adieu, my dear. It is a great deal pleasanter than being beheaded. You will fall asleep as easily as a babe in his cradle."

She gazed in his face, with a bewildered drowsy look, and big tears rolled down her cheeks. "Just step up here, my poor child," said he; and he offered her his hand.

"Oh, don't lay me so near the crocodile!" she exclaimed. "If he *should* wake up!"

"You wouldn't know it, if he did," rejoined the patient chemist; "but never mind. Step up to this other shelf, if you like it better."

He handed her up very politely, gathered her garments about her feet, crossed her arms below her breast, and told her to be perfectly still. He then covered his face with a mask, let some gasses escape from an apparatus in the centre of the room, and immediately went out, locking the door after him.

The next day, the public functionaries looked in, and expressed themselves well satisfied to find the maiden lying as rigid and motionless as the bear, the wolf, and the snake. On the edge of the shelf where she lay was pasted an inscription: "Put to sleep for infanticide, Feb. 10, 1740, by order of the king. To be wakened Feb. 10, 1840."

The earth whirled round on its axis, carrying with it the Alps and the Andes, the bear, the crocodile, and the maiden. Summer and winter came and went; America took place among the nations; Bonaparte played out his great game, with kingdoms for pawns; and still the Swedish damsel slept on her stone shelf with the bear and the crocodile.

When ninety-five years had passed, the bear, having fulfilled his prescribed century, was waked according to agreement. The curious flocked round him, to see him eat, and hear whether he could growl as well as other bears. Not liking such close observation, he broke his chain one night, and made off for the hills. How he seemed to his comrades, and what mistakes he made in his recollections, there were never any means of ascertaining. But bears, being more strictly conservative than men, happily escape the influence of French revolutions, German philosophy, Fourier theories, and reforms of all sorts; therefore Bruin doubtless found less change in *his* fellow citizens, than an old knight or viking might have done, had he chanced to sleep so long.

At last, came the maiden's turn to be resuscitated. The populace had forgotten her and her story long ago; but a select scientific few were present at the ceremony, by special invitation. The old chemist and his children all "slept the sleep that knows no waking." But carefully written orders had been transmitted from generation to generation; and the duty finally devolved on a great grandson, himself a chemist of no mean reputation.

Life returned very slowly; at first by almost imperceptible degrees, then by a visible shivering through the nerves. When the eyes opened, it was as if by the movement of pulleys, and there was something painfully strange in their marble gaze. But the lamp within the inner shrine lighted up, and gradually shone through them, giving assurance of the presence of a soul. As consciousness returned, she looked in the faces round her, as if seeking for some one; for her first dim recollection was of the old chemist. For several days, there was a general sluggishness of soul and body; an overpowering inertia, which made all exertion difficult, and prevented memory from rushing back in too tumultuous a tide.

For some time, she was very quiet and patient; but the numbers who came to look at her, their perpetual questions how things seemed to her, what was the state of her appetite and her memory, made her restless and irritable. Still worse was it when she went into the street. Her numerous visitors pointed her out to others, who ran to doors and windows to stare at her, and this soon attracted the attention of boys and lads. To escape such annoyances, she one day walked into a little shop, bearing the name of a woman she had formerly known. It was now kept by ner grand-daughter, an aged woman, who was evidently as afraid of Hilda, as if she had been a witch or a ghost.

This state of things became perfectly unendurable. After a few weeks, the forlorn being made her escape from the city, at dawn of day, and with money which had been given her by charitable people, she obtained a passage to her native village, under the new name of Hilda Silfverling. But to stand, in the bloom of sixteen, among well-remembered hills and streams, and not recognise a single human face, or know a single human voice, this was the most mournful of all; far worse than loneliness in a foreign land; sadder than sunshine on a ruined city. And all these suffocating emotions must be crowded back on her own heart; for if she revealed them to any one, she would assuredly be considered insane or bewitched.

As the thought became familiar to her that even the

little children she had known were all dead long ago, her eyes assumed an indescribably perplexed and mournful expression, which gave them an appearance of supernatural depth. She was seized with an inexpressible longing to go where no one had ever heard of her, and among scenes she had never looked upon. Her thoughts often reverted fondly to old Virika Gjetter, and the babe for whose sake she had suffered so much; and her heart yearned for Norway. But then she was chilled by the remembrance that even if her child had lived to the usual age of mortals, she must have been long since dead; and if she had left descendants, what would they know of *her?* Overwhelmed by the complete desolation of her lot on earth, she wept bitterly. But she was never utterly hopeless; for in the midst of her anguish, something prophetic seemed to beckon through the clouds, and call her into Norway.

In Stockholm, there was a white-haired old clergyman, who had been peculiarly kind, when he came to see her, after her centennial slumber. She resolved to go to him, to tell him how oppressively dreary was her restored existence, and how earnestly she desired to go, under a new name, to some secluded village in Norway, where none would be likely to learn her history, and where there would be nothing to remind her of the gloomy past. The good old man entered at once into her feelings, and approved her plan. He had been in that country himself, and had staid a few days at the house of a kind old man, named Eystein Hansen. He furnished Hilda with means for the journey, and gave her an affectionate letter of introduction, in which he described her as a Swedish orphan, who had suffered much, and would be glad to earn her living in any honest way that could be pointed out to her.

It was the middle of June when Hilda arrived at the house of Eystein Hanson. He was a stout, clumsy, red-visaged old man, with wide mouth, and big nose, hooked like an eagle's beak; but there was a right friendly expression in his large eyes, and when he had read the letter, he greeted the young stranger with such cordiality, she felt at once that she had found a father. She must come in his boat, he said, and he would take her at once to his island-home, where his good woman would give her a hearty welcome. She always loved the friendless; and especially would she love the Swedish orphan, because her last and youngest daughter had died the year before. On his way to the boat, the worthy man introduced her to several people, and when he told her story, old men and young maidens took her by the hand, and spoke as if they thought Heaven had sent them a daughter and a sister. The good Brenda received her with open arms, as her husband had said she would. She was an old weather-beaten woman, but there was a whole heart full of sunshine in her honest eyes.

And this new home looked so pleasant under the light of the summer sky! The house was embowered in the shrubbery of a small island, in the midst of a fiord, the steep shores of which were thickly covered with pine, fir, and juniper, down to the water's edge.

The fiord went twisting and turning about, from promontory to promontory, as if the Nereides, dancing up from the sea, had sportively chased each other into nooks and corners, now hiding away behind some bold projection of rock, and now peeping out suddenly, with a broad sunny smile. Directly in front of the island, the fiord expanded into a broad bay, on the shores of which was a little primitive romantic-looking village. Here and there a sloop was at anchor, and picturesque little boats tacked off and on from cape to cape, their white sails glancing in the sun. A range of lofty blue mountains closed in the distance. One giant, higher than all the rest, went up perpendicularly into the clouds, wearing a perpetual crown of glittering snow. As the maiden gazed on this sublime and beautiful scenery, a new and warmer tide seemed to flow through her stagnant heart. Ah, how happy might life be here among these mountain homes, with a people of such patriarchal simplicity, so brave and free, so hospitable, frank and hearty!

The house of Eystein Hansen was built of pine logs, neatly white-washed. The roof was covered with grass, and bore a crop of large bushes. A vine, tangled among these, fell in heavy festoons that waved at every touch of the wind. The door was painted with flowers in gay colours, and surmounted with fantastic carving. The interior of the dwelling was ornamented with many little grotesque images, boxes, bowls, ladles, &c., curiously carved in the close-grained and beautifully white wood of the Norwegian fir. This was a common amusement with the peasantry, and Eystein being a great favourite among them, received many such presents during his frequent visits in the surrounding parishes.

But nothing so much attracted Hilda's attention as a kind of long trumpet, made of two hollow half cylinders of wood, bound tightly together with birch bark. The only instrument of the kind she had ever seen was in the possession of Virika Gjetter, who called it a *luhr*, and said it was used to call the cows home in her native village, in Upper Tellemarken. She showed how it was used, and Hilda, having a quick ear, soon learned to play upon it with considerable facility.

And here in her new home, this rude instrument reappeared; forming the only visible link between her present life and that dreamy past! With strange feelings, she took up the pipe, and began to play one of the old tunes. At first, the tones flitted like phantoms in and out of her brain; but at last, they all came back, and took their places rank and file. Old Brenda said it was a pleasant tune, and asked her to play it again; but to Hilda it seemed awfully solemn, like a voice warbling from the grave. She would learn other tunes to please the good mother, she said; but this she would play no more; it made her too sad, for she had heard it in her youth.

"Thy youth!" said Brenda, smiling." One sees well that must have been a long time ago. To hear thee talk, one might suppose thou wert an old autumn leaf, just ready to drop from the bough, like myself."

Hilda blushed, and said she felt old, because she had had much trouble.

"Poor child," responded the good Brenda: "I hope thou hast had thy share."

"I feel as if nothing could trouble me here," replied Hilda, with a grateful smile; "all seems so kind and peaceful." She breathed a few notes through the *luhr*, as she laid it away on the shelf where she had found it. "But, my good mother," said she, "how clear and soft are these tones! The pipe I used to hear was far more harsh."

"The wood is very old," rejoined Brenda: "They say it is more than a hundred years. Alerik Thorild gave it to me, to call my good man when he is out in the boat. Ah, he was such a Berserker* of a boy! and in truth he was not much more sober when he was here three years ago. But no matter what he did; one could never help loving him."

"And who is Alerik?" asked the maiden.

Brenda pointed to an old house, seen in the distance, on the declivity of one of the opposite hills. It overlooked the broad bright bay, with its picturesque little islands, and was sheltered in the rear by a noble pine forest. A water-fall came down from the hill-side, glancing in and out among the trees; and when the sun kissed it as he went away, it lighted up with a smile of rainbows.

"That house," said Brenda, "was built by Alerik's grandfather. He was the richest man in the village. But his only son was away among the wars for a long time, and the old place has been going to decay. But they say Alerik is coming back to live among us; and

* A warrior famous in the Northern Sagas for his stormy and untamable character.

he will soon give it a different look. He has been away to Germany and Paris, and other outlandish parts, for a long time. Ah! the rogue! there was no mischief he didn't think of. He was always tying cats together under the windows, and barking in the middle of the night, till he set all the dogs in the neighbourhood a howling. But as long as it was Alerik that did it, it was all well enough: for everybody loved him, and he always made one believe just what he liked. If he wanted to make thee think thy hair was as black as Noeck's* mane, he *would* make thee think so."

Hilda smiled as she glanced at her flaxen hair, with here and there a gleam of paly gold, where the sun touched it. "I think it would be hard to prove *this* was black," said she.

"Nevertheless," rejoined Brenda, "if Alerik undertook it, he would do it. He always has his say, and does what he will. One may as well give in to him first as last."

This account of the unknown youth carried with it that species of fascination, which the idea of uncommon power always has over the human heart. The secluded maiden seldom touched the *luhr* without thinking of the giver; and not unfrequently she found herself conjecturing when this wonderful Alerik would come home.

Meanwhile, constant but not excessive labour, the mountain air, the quiet life, and the kindly hearts around her, restored to Hilda more than her original

* An elfish spirit, which, according to popular tradition in Norway, appears in the form of a coal black horse.

loveliness. In her large blue eyes, the inward-looking sadness of experience now mingled in strange beauty with the out-looking clearness of youth. Her fair complexion was tinged with the glow of health, and her motions had the airy buoyancy of the mountain breeze. When she went to the mainland, to attend church, or rustic festival, the hearts of young and old greeted her like a May blossom. Thus with calm cheerfulness her hours went by, making no noise in their flight, and leaving no impress. But here was an unsatisfied want! She sighed for hours that did leave a mark behind them. She thought of the Danish youth, who had first spoken to her of love; and plaintively came the tones from her *luhr*, as she gazed on the opposite hills, and wondered whether the Alerik they talked of so much, was indeed so very superior to other young men.

Father Hansen often came home at twilight with a boat full of juniper boughs, to be strewed over the floors, that they might diffuse a balmy odour, inviting to sleep. One evening, when Hilda saw him coming with his verdant load, she hastened down to the water's edge to take an armful of the fragrant boughs. She had scarcely appeared in sight, before he called out, "I do believe Alerik has come! I heard the organ up in the old house. Somebody was playing on it like a Northeast storm; and surely, said I, that must be Alerik."

"Is there an organ there?" asked the damsel, in surprise.

"Yes. He built it himself, when he was here three years ago. He can make anything he chooses.

An organ, or a basket cut from a cherry stone, is all one to him.

When Hilda returned to the cottage, she of course repeated the news to Brenda, who exclaimed joyfully, "Ah, then we shall see him soon! If he does not come before, we shall certainly see him at the weddings in the church to-morrow.

"And plenty of tricks we shall have now," said Father Hansen, shaking his head with a good-natured smile. "There will be no telling which end of the world is uppermost, while he is here."

"Oh yes, there will, my friend," answered Brenda, laughing; "for it will certainly be whichever end Alerik stands on. The handsome little Berserker! How I should like to see him!"

The next day there was a sound of lively music on the waters; for two young couples from neighbouring islands were coming up the fiord, to be married at the church in the opposite village. Their boats were ornamented with gay little banners, friends and neighbours accompanied them, playing on musical instruments, and the rowers had their hats decorated with garlands. As the rustic band floated thus gayly over the bright waters, they were joined by Father Hansen, with Brenda and Hilda in his boat.

Friendly villagers had already decked the simple little church with ever-greens and flowers, in honour of the bridal train. As they entered, Father Hansen observed that two young men stood at the door with clarinets in their hands. But he thought no more of it, till, according to immemorial custom, he, as clergy man's assistant, began to sing the first lines of the hymn that was given out. The very first note he sounded, up struck the clarinets at the door. The louder they played, the louder the old man bawled; but the instruments gained the victory. When he essayed to give out the lines of the next verse, the merciless clarinets brayed louder than before. His stentorian voice had become vociferous and rough, from thirty years of halloing across the water, and singing of psalms in four village churches. He exerted it to the utmost, till the perspiration poured down his rubicund visage; but it was of no use. His rivals had strong lungs, and they played on clarinets in F. If the whole village had screamed fire, to the shrill accompaniment of rail-road whistles, they would have over-topped them all.

Father Hansen was vexed at heart, and it was plain enough that he was so. The congregation held down their heads with suppressed laughter; all except one tall vigorous young man, who sat up very serious and dignified, as if he were reverently listening to some new manifestation of musical genius. When the people left church, Hilda saw this young stranger approaching toward them, as fast as numerous hand-shakings by the way would permit. She had time to observe him closely. His noble figure, his vigorous agile motions, his expressive countenance, hazel eyes with strongly marked brows, and abundant brown hair, tossed aside with a careless grace, left no doubt in her mind that this was the famous Alerik Thorild; but what made her heart beat more wildly was his strong resemblance to Magnus the Dane. He went up to Brenda and kissed her, and threw his arms about

Father Hansen's neck, with expressions of joyful recognition. The kind old man, vexed as he was, received these affectionate demonstrations with great friendliness. "Ah, Alerik," said he, after the first salutations were over, "that was not kind of thee."

"Me! What!" exclaimed the young man, with well-feigned astonishment.

"To put up those confounded clarinets to drown my voice," rejoined he bluntly. "When a man has led the singing thirty years in four parishes, I can assure thee it is not a pleasant joke to be treated in that style. I know the young men are tired of my voice, and think they could do things in better fashion, as young fools always do; but I may thank thee for putting it into their heads to bring those cursed clarinets."

"Oh, dear Father Hansen," replied the young man, in the most coaxing tones, and with the most caressing manner, "you *couldn't* think I would do such a thing!"

"On the contrary, it is just the thing I think thou couldst do," answered the old man: "Thou need not think to cheat me out of my eye-teeth, this time. Thou hast often enough made me believe the moon was made of green cheese. But I know thy tricks. I shall be on my guard now; and mind thee, I am not going to be bamboozled by thee again."

Alerik smiled mischievously; for he, in common with all the villagers, knew it was the easiest thing in the world to gull the simple-hearted old man. "Well, come, Father Hansen," said he, "shake hands and be friends. When you come over to the village, to-morrow, we will drink a mug of ale together, at the Wolf's Head."

"Oh yes, and be played some trick for his pains," said Brenda.

"No, no," answered Alerik, with great gravity; "he is on his guard now, and I cannot bamboozle him again." With a friendly nod and smile, he bounded off, to greet some one whom he recognised. Hilda had stepped back to hide herself from observation. She was a little afraid of the handsome Berserker; and his resemblance to the Magnus of her youthful recollections made her sad.

The next afternoon, Alerik met his old friend, and reminded him of the agreement to drink ale at the Wolf's head. On the way, he invited several young companions. The ale was excellent, and Alerik told stories and sang songs, which filled the little tavern with roars of laughter. In one of the intervals of merriment, he turned suddenly to the honest old man, and said, "Father Hansen, among the many things I have learned and done in foreign countries, did I ever tell you I had made a league with the devil, and am shot-proof?"

"One might easily believe thou hadst made a league with the devil, before thou wert born," replied Eystein, with a grin at his own wit; "but as for being shot-proof, that is another affair."

"Try and see," rejoined Alerik. "These friends are winesses that I tell you it is perfectly safe to try. Come, I will stand here; fire your pistol, and you will soon see that the Evil One will keep the bargain he made with me."

"Be done with thy nonsense, Alerik," rejoined his old friend.

"Ah, I see how it is," replied Alerik, turning towards the young men. "Father Hansen used to be a famous shot. Nobody was more expert in the bear or the wolf-hunt than he; but old eyes grow dim, and old hands will tremble. No wonder he does not like to have us see how much he fails."

This was attacking honest Eystein Hansen on his weak side. He was proud of his strength and skill in shooting, and he did not like to admit that he was growing old. "I not hit a mark!" exclaimed he, with indignation: "When did I ever miss a thing I aimed at?"

"Never, when you were young," answered one of the company; "but it is no wonder you are afraid to try now."

"Afraid!" exclaimed the old hunter, impatiently. "Who the devil said I was afraid?"

Alerik shrugged his shoulders, and replied carelessly, "It is natural enough that these young men should think so, when they see you refuse to aim at me, though I assure you that I am shot proof, and that I will stand perfectly still."

"But art thou really shot-proof?" inquired the guileless old man. "The devil has helped thee to do so many strange things, that one never knows what he will help thee to do next."

"Really, Father Hansen, I speak in earnest. Take up your pistol and try, and you will soon see with your own eyes that I am shot-proof."

Eystein looked round upon the company like one

perplexed. His wits, never very bright, were somewhat muddled by the ale. "What shall I do with this wild fellow?" inquired he. "You see he *will* be shot."

"Try him, try him," was the general response. "He has assured you he is shot-proof; what more do you need?"

The old man hesitated awhile, but after some further parley, took up his pistol and examined it. "Before we proceed to business," said Alerik, "let me tell you that if you do *not* shoot me, you shall have a gallon of the best ale you ever drank in your life. Come and taste it, Father Hansen, and satisfy yourself that it is good."

While they were discussing the merits of the ale, one of the young men took the ball from the pistol. "I am ready now," said Alerik: "Here I stand. Now don't lose your name for a good marksman."

The old man fired, and Alerik fell back with a deadly groan. Poor Eystein stood like a stone image of terror. His arms adhered rigidly to his sides, his jaw dropped, and his great eyes seemed starting from their sockets. "Oh, Father Hansen, how *could* you do it!" exclaimed the young men.

The poor horrified dupe stared at them wildly, and gasping and stammering replied, "Why he said he was shot-proof; and you all told me to do it."

"Oh yes," said they; "but we supposed you would have sense enough to know it was all in fun. But don't take it too much to heart. You will probably forfeit your life; for the government will of course consider it a poor excuse, when you tell them that you fired at a man merely to oblige him, and because he said he was shot-proof. But don't be too much cast down, Father Hansen. We must all meet death in some way; and if worst comes to worst, it will be a great comfort to you and your good Brenda that you did not intend to commit murder."

The poor old man gazed at them with an expression of such extreme suffering, that they became alarmed, and said, "Cheer up, cheer up. Come, you must drink something to make you feel better." They took him by the shoulders, but as they led him out, he continued to look back wistfully on the body.

The instant he left the apartment, Alerik sprang up and darted out of the opposite door; and when Father Hansen entered the other room, there he sat, as composedly as possible, reading a paper, and smoking his pipe.

"There he is!" shrieked the old man, turning paler than ever.

"Who is there?" inquired the young men.

"Don't you see Alerik Thorild?" exclaimed he, pointing, with an expression of intense horror.

They turned to the landlord, and remarked, in a compassionate tone, "Poor Father Hansen has shot Alerik Thorild, whom he loved so well; and the dreadful accident has so affected his brain, that he imagines he sees him."

The old man pressed his broad hand hard against his forehead, and again groaned out, "Oh, don't you see him?"

The tones indicated such agony, that Alerik had

not the heart to prolong the scene. He sprang on his feet, and exclaimed, "Now for your gallon of ale, Father Hansen! You see the devil did keep his bargain with me."

"And *are* you alive?" shouted the old man.

The mischievous fellow soon convinced him of that, by a slap on the shoulder, that made his bones ache.

Eystein Hansen capered like a dancing bear. He hugged Alerik, and jumped about, and clapped his hands, and was altogether beside himself. He drank unknown quantities of ale, and this time sang loud enough to drown a brace of clarinets in F.

The night was far advanced when he went on board his boat to return to his island home. He pulled the oars vigorously, and the boat shot swiftly across the moon-lighted waters. But on arriving at the customary landing, he could discover no vestige of his white-washed cottage. Not knowing that Alerik, in the full tide of his mischief, had sent men to paint the house with a dark brown wash, he thought he must have made a mistake in the landing; so he rowed round to the other side of the island, but with no better success. Ashamed to return to the mainland, to inquire for a house that had absconded, and a little suspicious that the ale had hung some cobwebs in his brain, he continued to row hither and thither, till his strong muscular arms fairly ached with exertion. But the moon was going down, and all the landscape settling into darkness; and he at last reluctantly concluded that it was best to go back to the village inn.

Alerik, who had expected this result much sooner,

had waited there to receive him. When he had kept him knocking a sufficient time, he put his head out of the window, and inquired who was there.

"Eystein Hansen," was the disconsolate reply. "For the love of mercy let me come in and get a few minutes sleep, before morning. I have been rowing about the bay these four hours, and I can't find my house any where."

"This is a very bad sign," replied Alerik, solemnly. "Houses don't run away, except from drunken men. Ah, Father Hansen! Father Hansen! what *will* the minister say?"

He did not have a chance to persecute the weary old man much longer; for scarcely had he come under the shelter of the house, before he was snoring in a profound sleep.

Early the next day, Alerik sought his old friends in their brown-washed cottage. He found it not so easy to conciliate them as usual. They were really grieved; and Brenda even said she believed he wanted to be the death of her old man. But he had brought them presents, which he knew they would like particularly well; and he kissed their hands, and talked over his boyish days, till at last he made them laugh. "Ah now," said he, "you have forgiven me, my dear old friends. And you see, father, it was all your own fault. You put the mischief into me, by boasting before all those young men that I could never bamboozle you again."

"Ah thou incorrigible rogue!" answered the old man. "I believe thou hast indeed made a league with the devil; and he gives thee the power to make every body love thee, do what thou wilt."

Alerik's smile seemed to express that he always had a pleasant consciousness of such power. The *luhr* lay on the table beside him, and as he took it up, he asked, "Who plays on this? Yesterday, when I was out in my boat, I heard very wild pretty little variations on some of my old favourite airs."

Brenda, instead of answering, called, "Hilda! Hilda!" and the young girl came from the next room, blushing as she entered. Alerik looked at her with evident surprise. "Surely, this is not your Gunilda?" said he.

"No," replied Brenda, "She is a Swedish orphan, whom the all-kind Father sent to take the place of our Gunilda, when she was called hence."

After some words of friendly greeting, the visitor asked Hilda if it was she who played so sweetly on the *luhr*. She answered timidly, without looking up. Her heart was throbbing; for the tones of his voice were like Magnus the Dane.

The acquaintance thus begun, was not likely to languish on the part of such an admirer of beauty as was Alerik Thorild. The more he saw of Hilda, during the long evenings of the following winter, the more he was charmed with her natural refinement of look, voice, and manner. There was, as we have said, a peculiarity in her beauty, which gave it a higher character than mere rustic loveliness. A deep, mystic, plaintive expression in her eyes; a sort of graceful bewilderment in her countenance, and at times in the carriage of her head, and the motions of her body; as if her spirit had lost its way, and was listening intently. It was not strange that he was charmed by her spiritual beauty, her simple untutored modesty. No wonder she was delighted with his frank strong exterior, his cordial caressing manner, his expressive eyes, now tender and earnest, and now sparkling with merriment, and his "smile most musical," because always so in harmony with the inward feeling, whether of sadness, fun, or tenderness. Then his moods were so bewitchingly various. Now powerful as the organ, now bright as the flute, now *naive* as the oboe. Brenda said every thing he did seemed to be alive. He carved a wolf's head on her old man's cane, and she was always afraid it would bite her.

Brenda, in her simplicity, perhaps gave as good a description of genius as *could* be given, when she said everything it did seemed to be alive. Hilda thought it certainly was so with Alerik's music. Sometimes all went madly with it, as if fairies danced on the grass, and ugly gnomes came and made faces at them, and shricked, and clutched at their garments; the fairies pelted them off with flowers, and then all died away to sleep in the moonlight. Sometimes, when he played on flute, or violin, the sounds came mournfully as the midnight wind through ruined towers; and they stirred up such sorrowful memories of the past, that Hilda pressed her hand upon her swelling heart, and said, "Oh, not such strains as that, dear Alerik." But when his soul overflowed with love and happiness, oh, then how the music gushed and nestled!

"The lark could scarce get out his notes for joy,
But shook his song together, as he neared
His happy home, the ground."

The old *luhr* was a great favourite with Alerik; not for its musical capabilities, but because it was entwined with the earliest recollections of his childhood. "Until I heard thee play upon it," said he, "I half repented having given it to the good Brenda. It has been in our family for several generations, and my nurse used to play upon it when I was in my cradle. They tell me my grandmother was a foundling. She was brought to my great-grandfather's house by an old peasant woman, on her way to the valley of Westfjordalen. She died there, leaving the babe and the *luhr* in my great-grandmother's keeping. They could never find out to whom the babe belonged; but she grew up very beautiful, and my grandfather married her."

"What was the old woman's name?" asked Hilda; and her voice was so deep and suppressed, that it it made Alerik start.

"Virika Gjetter, they have always told me," he replied. "But my dearest one, what *is* the matter?"

Hilda, pale and fainting, made no answer. But when he placed her head upon his bosom, and kissed her forehead, and spoke soothingly, her glazed eyes softened, and she burst into tears. All his entreaties, however, could obtain no information at that time. "Go home now," she said, in tones of deep despondency. "To-morrow I will tell thee all. I have had many unhappy hours; for I have long felt that I ought to tell thee all my past history; but I was afraid to do it, for I thought thou wouldst not love me any more; and that would be worse than death. But come to-morrow, and I will tell thee all."

"Well, dearest Hilda, I will wait," replied Alerik; "but what my grandmother, who died long before I was born, can have to do with my love for thee, is more than I can imagine."

The next day, when Hilda saw Alerik coming to claim the fulfilment of her promise, it seemed almost like her death-warrant. "He will not love me any more," thought she, "he will never again look at me so tenderly; and then what can I do, but die?"

With much embarrassment, and many delays, she at last began her strange story. He listened to the first part very attentively, and with a gathering frown; but as she went on, the muscles of his face relaxed into a smile; and when she ended by saying, with the most melancholy seriousness, "So thou seest, dear Alerik, we cannot be married; because it is very likely that I am thy great-grandmother"—he burst into immoderate peals of laughter.

When his mirth had somewhat subsided, he replied, "Likely as not thou art my great-grandmother, dear Hilda; and just as likely I was thy grandfather, in the first place. A great German scholar* teaches that our souls keep coming back again and again into new bodies. An old Greek philosopher is said to have come back for the fourth time, under the name of Pythagoras. If these things are so, how the deuce is a man ever to tell whether he marries his grandmother or not?"

* Lessing.

"But, dearest Alerik, I am not jesting," rejoined she. "What I have told thee is really true. They did put me to sleep for a hundred years."

"Oh, yes," answered he, laughing, "I remember reading about it in the Swedish papers; and I thought it a capital joke. I will tell thee how it is with thee, my precious one. The elves sometimes seize people, to carry them down into their subterranean caves; but if the mortals run away from them, they, out of spite, forever after fill their heads with gloomy insane notions. A man in Drontheim ran away from them, and they made him believe he was an earthen coffee-pot. He sat curled up in a corner all the time, for fear somebody would break his nose off."

"Nay, now thou art joking, Alerik; but really"—

"No, I tell thee, as thou hast told me, it was no joke at all," he replied. "The man himself told me he was a coffee-pot."

"But be serious, Alerik," said she, "and tell me, dost thou not believe that some learned men can put people to sleep for a hundred years?"

"I don't doubt some of my college professors could," rejoined he; "provided their tongues could hold out so long."

"But, Alerik, dost thou not think it possible that people may be alive, and yet not alive?"

"Of course I do," he replied; "the greater part of the world are in that condition."

"Oh, Alerik, what a tease thou art! I mean, is it not possible that there are people now living, or staying somewhere, who were moving about on this earth ages ago?"

"Nothing more likely," answered he; "for instance, who knows what people there may be under the ice-sea of Folgefond? They say the cocks are heard crowing down there, to this day. How a fowl of any feather got there is a curious question; and what kind of atmosphere he has to crow in, is another puzzle. Perhaps they are poor ghosts, without sense of shame, crowing over the recollections of sins committed in the human body. The ancient Egyptians thought the soul was obliged to live three thousand years, in a succession of different animals, before it could attain to the regions of the blest. I am pretty sure I have already been a lion and a nightingale. What I shall be next, the Egyptians know as well as I do. One of their sculptors made a stone image, half woman and half lioness. Doubtless his mother had been a lioness, and had transmitted to him some dim recollection of it. But I am glad, dearest, they sent thee back in the form of a lovely maiden; for if thou hadst come as a wolf, I might have shot thee; and I shouldn't like to shoot my—great-grandmother. Or if thou hadst come as a red herring, Father Hansen might have eaten thee in his soup; and then I should have had no Hilda Silfverling."

Hilda smiled, as she said, half reproachfully, "I see well that thou dost not believe one word I say."

"Oh yes, I do, dearest," rejoined he, very seriously. "I have no doubt the fairies carried thee off some summer's night and made thee verily believe thou hadst slept for a hundred years. They do the strangest things. Sometimes they change babies in the cradle; leave an imp, and carry off the human to the metal mines, where he hears only clink! clink! Then the fairies bring him back, and put him in some other cradle. When he grows up, how he does hurry skurry after the silver! He is obliged to work all his life, as if the devil drove him. The poor miser never knows what is the matter with him; but it is all because the gnomes brought him up in the mines, and he could never get the clink out of his head. A more poetic kind of fairies sometimes carry a babe to Æolian caves, full of wild dreamy sounds; and when he is brought back to upper earth, ghosts of sweet echoes keep beating time in some corner of his brain, to something which *they* hear, but which nobody else is the wiser for. I know that is true; for I was brought up in those caves myself."

Hilda remained silent for a few minutes, as he sat looking in her face with comic gravity. "Thou wilt do nothing but make fun of me," at last she said. "I do wish I could persuade thee to be serious. What I told thee was no fairy story. It really happened. I remember it as distinctly as I do our sail round the islands yesterday. I seem to see that great bear now, with his paws folded up, on the shelf opposite to me."

"He must have been a great bear to have staid there," replied Alerik, with eyes full of roguery. "If I had been in his skin, may I be shot if all the drugs and gasses in the world would have kept *me* there, with my paws folded on my breast."

Seeing a slight blush pass over her cheek, he added, more seriously, "After all, I ought to thank that wicked elf, whoever he was, for turning thee into a stone image; for otherwise thou wouldst have been in the world a hundred years too soon for me, and so I should have missed my life's best blossom."

Feeling her tears on his hand, he again started off into a vein of merriment. "Thy case was not so very peculiar," said he. "There was a Greek lady, named Niobe, who was changed to stone. The Greek gods changed women into trees, and fountains, and all manner of things. A man couldn't chop a walking-stick in those days, without danger of cutting off some lady's finger. The tree might be—his great-grandmother; and she of course would take it very unkindly of him."

"All these things are like the stories about Odin and Frigga," rejoined Hilda. "They are not true, like the Christian religion. When I tell thee a true story, why dost thou always meet me with fairies and fictions?"

"But tell me, best Hilda," said he, "what the Christian religion has to do with penning up young maidens with bears and crocodiles? In its marriage ceremonies, I grant that it sometimes does things not very unlike that, only omitting the important part of freezing the maiden's heart. But since thou hast mentioned the Christian religion, I may as well give thee a bit of consolation from that quarter. I have read in my mother's big Bible, that a man must not marry his grandmother; but I do not remember that it said a single word against his marrying his *great*-grandmother."

Hilda laughed, in spite of herself. But after a pause, she looked at him earnestly, and said, "Dost thou indeed think there would be no harm in marrying, under these circumstances, if I were really thy great-grandmother? Is it thy earnest? Do be serious for once, dear Alerik!"

"Certainly there would be no harm," answered he. "Physicians have agreed that the body changes entirely once in seven years. That must be because the soul outgrows its clothes; which proves that the soul changes every seven years, also. Therefore, in the course of one hundred years, thou must have had fourteen complete changes of soul and body. It is therefore as plain as daylight, that if thou wert my great-grandmother when thou fell asleep, thou couldst not have been my great-grandmother when they waked thee up."

"Ah, Alerik," she replied, "it is as the good Brenda says, there is no use in talking with thee. One might as well try to twist a string that is not fastened at either end."

He looked up merrily in her face. The wind was playing with her ringlets, and freshened the colour on her cheeks. "I only wish I had a mirror to hold before thee," said he; "that thou couldst see how very like thou art to a—great grandmother."

"Laugh at me as thou wilt," answered she; "but I assure thee I have strange thoughts about myself sometimes. Dost thou know," added she, almost in a whisper, "I am not always quite certain that I have not died, and am now in heaven?"

A ringing shout of laughter burst from the light-hearted lover. "Oh, I like that! I like that!" exclaimed he. "That is good! That a Swede coming to Norway does not know certainly whether she is in heaven or not."

"Do be serious, Alerik," said she imploringly. "Don't carry thy jests too far."

"Serious? I am serious. If Norway is not heaven, one sees plainly enough that it must have been the scaling place, where the old giants got up to heaven; for they have left their ladders standing. Where else wilt thou find clusters of mountains running up perpendicularly thousands of feet right into the sky? If thou wast to see some of them, thou couldst tell whether Norway is a good climbing place into heaven."

"Ah, dearest Alerik, thou hast taught me that already," she replied, with a glance full of affection; "so a truce with thy joking. Truly one never knows how to take thee. Thy talk sets everything *in* the world, and *above* it, and *below* it, dancing together in the strangest fashion."

"Because they all do dance together," rejoined the perverse man.

"Oh, be done! be done, Alerik!" she said, putting her hand playfully over his mouth. "Thou wilt tie my poor brain all up into knots."

He seized her hand and kissed it, then busied himself with braiding the wild spring flowers into a garland for her fair hair. As she gazed on him earnestly, her eyes beaming with love and happiness, he drew her to his breast, and exclaimed fervently, "Oh, thou art beautiful as an angel; and here or elsewhere, with thee by my side, it seemeth heaven."

They spoke no more for a long time. The birds

now and then serenaded the silent lovers with little twittering gushes of song. The setting sun, as he went away over the hills, threw diamonds on the bay, and a rainbow ribbon across the distant waterfall. Their hearts were in harmony with the peaceful beauty of Nature. As he kissed her drowsy eyes, she murmured, "Oh, it was well worth a hundred years with bears and crocodiles, to fall asleep thus on thy heart."

* * * * *

The next autumn, a year and a half after Hilda's arrival in Norway, there was another procession of boats, with banners, music and garlands. The little church was again decorated with evergreens; but no clarinet players stood at the door to annoy good Father Hansen. The worthy man had in fact taken the hint, though somewhat reluctantly, and had good-naturedly ceased to disturb modern ears with his clamorous vociferation of the hymns. He and his kind-hearted Brenda were happy beyond measure at Hilda's good fortune. But when she told her husband anything he did not choose to believe, they could never rightly make out what he meant by looking at her so slily, and saying, "Pooh! Pooh! tell that to my——great-grandmother."

ROSENGLORY.

A stranger among strange faces, she drinketh the wormwood of dependence;
She is marked as a child of want; and the world hateth poverty.
She is cared for by none upon earth, and her God seemeth to forsake her.
Then cometh, in fair show, the promise and the feint of affection;
And her heart, long unused to kindness, remembereth her brother, and loveth;
And the traitor hath wronged her trust, and mocked and flung her from him;
And men point at her and laugh, and women hate her as an outcast;
But elsewhere, far other judgment may seat her among the martyrs.

Proverbial Philosophy.

Oh, moralists, who treat of happiness and self-respect in every sphere of life, go into the squalid depths of deepest ignorance, the uttermost abyss of man's neglect, and say can any hopeful plant spring up in air so foul that it extinguishes the soul's bright torch as soon as it is kindled? Oh, ye Pharisees of the nineteen hundredth year of Christian knowledge, who soundingly appeal to human nature, see that it *be* human first. Take heed that during your slumber, and the sleep of generations, it has not been transformed into the nature of the beasts.—*Dickens.*

Jerry Gray and his sister Susan were the children of a drunken father, and of a poor woman, who saved them from starvation by picking up rags in the street, and washing them for the paper-makers. In youth, she had been a rustic belle, observable for her neat and tasteful attire. But she was a weak, yielding character; and sickness, poverty, and toil, gradually broke down the little energy with which nature had endowed her. "What's the use of patching up my old rags?" she used to say to herself; "there's nobody now to mind how I look." But she had a kind, affectionate heart; and love for her children preserved her from intemperance, and sustained her in toiling for their daily bread.

The delight she took in curling her little daughter's glossy brown ringlets was the only remaining indication of early coquetish taste. Though often dirty and ragged herself, Susan was always clean and tidy. She was, in fact, an extremely lovely child; and as she toddled through the streets, holding by her mother's skirts, Napoleon himself could not have been more proud of popular homage to his little King of Rome, than was the poor rag-woman of the smiles and kisses bestowed on her pretty one. Her large chestnut-coloured eyes had been saddened in their expression by the sorrows and privations of her mother, when the same life-blood sustained them both; but they were very beautiful; and their long dark fringes rested on cheeks as richly coloured as a peach fully ripened in the sunshine. Like her mother, she had a very moderate share of intellect, and an extreme love of pretty things. It was a gleam in their souls of that intense love of the beautiful, which makes poets and artists of higher natures, under more favourable circumstances.

A washerwoman, who lived in the next room, planted a Morning-Glory seed in a broken tea-pot; and it bore its first blossom the day Susan was three years old. The sight of it filled her with passionate joy. She danced, and clapped her hands; she returned to it again and again, and remained a long time stooping down, and looking into the very heart of the flower. When it closed, she called out, impatiently, "Wake up! wake up, pretty posy!" When it shrivelled more and more, she cried aloud, and refused to be comforted. As successive blossoms opened day by day, her friendship for the vine increased, and the conversations she held with it were sometimes quite poetic, in her small way.

One day, when her mother was hooking up rags from the dirty gutters of the street, with the little ones trudging behind her, a gentleman passed with a large bouquet in his hand. Susan's eyes brightened, as she exclaimed, "Oh, mammy, look at the pretty posies!"

The gentleman smiled upon her and said, "Would you like one, my little girl?"

She eagerly held out her hand, and he gave her a flower, saying, "There's a rose for you."

"Thank the good gentleman," said her mother. But she was too much occupied to attend to politeness. Her head was full of her pet Morning-Glory, the first blossom she had ever looked upon; and she ran to her brother shouting joyfully, "See my Rosenglory!"

The gentleman laughed, patted her silky curls, and said, "You are a little Rosenglory yourself; and I wish you were mine."

Jerry, who was older by two years, was quite charmed with the word. "Rosenglory," repeated he; "what a funny name! Mammy, the gentleman called our Susy a Rosenglory."

From that day, it became a favourite word in the wretched little household. It sounded there with mournful beauty, like the few golden rays which at sunset fell aslant the dingy walls and the broken crockery. When the weary mother had washed her basket of rags, she would bring water for Susan's hands, and a wooden comb to smooth her hair, and gazing fondly in that infant face, her only vision of beauty in a life otherwise all dark and dreary, she would say, " Now kiss your poor mammy, my little Rosenglory." Even the miserable father, when his senses were not stupified with drink, would take the pretty little one on his knee, twine her shining ringlets round his coarse fingers, and sigh deeply as he said, " Ah, how many a rich man would be proud to have my little Rosenglory for his own!"

But it was brother Jerry who idolized her most of all. He could not go to bed on his little bunch of straw, unless her curly head was nestled on his bosom. They trudged the streets together, hand in hand, and if charity offered them an apple or a slice of bread, the best half was always reserved for her. A proud boy was he when he received an old tatterdemalion rocking-horse from the son of a gentleman, for whom his father was sawing wood. " Now Rosenglory shall ride," said he; and when he placed her on the horse, and watched her swinging back and forth, his merry shouts of laughter indicated infinite satisfaction. But these pleasant scenes occurred but seldom. More frequently, they came home late and tired, every body was hungry and cross, and they were glad to steal away in silence to their little bed. When the father was noisy in his intoxication, the poor boy guarded his darling with the thoughtfulness of maturer years. He patiently warded off the random blows, or received them himself; and if harm accidentally came to her, it was affecting to see his tearful eyes, and hear his grieved whisper, "Mammy! he struck Rosenglory!"

Poor child! her young life was opening in dark and narrow places; though, like the vine in the broken tea-pot, she caught now and then a transient gleam of sunshine. It would be well if men could spare time from the din of theological dispute, and the drowsiness of devotional routine, to reflect whether such ought to be the portion of any of God's little ones, in this broad and beautiful earth, which He created for the good of all.

Many a hungry day, and many a night of pinching cold, this brother and sister went struggling through their blighted youth, till the younger was eight years old. At that period, the father died of delirium tremens, and the mother fell into a consumption, brought on by constant hardship and unvarying gloom. The family were removed to the almshouse, and found it an improvement in their condition. The coarse food was as good as that to which they had been accustomed, there was more air and a wider scope for the eye to range in. Blessed with youthful impressibility to the bright and joyous, Jerry and Susan took more notice of the clear silvery moon and the host of bright stars, than they did of the deformity, paleness, and sad looks around them. The angels watch over childhood, and keep it from understanding the evil that surrounds it, or retaining the gloom which is its shadow.

The poor weak mother was daily wasting away, but they only felt that her tones were more tender, her endearments more fond. One night, when they were going to bed, she held them by the hand longer than usual. The rough hireling nurse felt the eloquence of her sad countenance, and had not the heart to hurry them away. No one knew what deep thought, what agony of anxious love, was in the soul of the dying one; but she gazed earnestly and tearfully into their clear young eyes, and said, with a troubled voice, "My children, *try* to be good." She kissed them fervently, and spoke no more. The next day, the nurse told them their mother was dead. They saw her body laid in a white pine coffin, and carried away in a cart to the burying ground of the poor. It was piled upon a hundred other nameless coffins, in a big hole dug in the sandy hill side. She was not missed from the jostling crowd; but the orphans wept bitterly, for she was all the world to them.

In a few days, strangers came to examine them, with a view to take them into service. Jerry was bound to a sea-captain, and Susan to a grocer's wife, who wanted her to wait upon the children. She was, indeed, bound; for Mrs. Andrews was entirely forgetful that anything like freedom or enjoyment might be necessary or useful to servants. All day long she lugged the heavy baby, and often sat up late at night, to pacify its fretfulness as she best could, while her master and mistress were at balls, or the Bowery. While the babe was sleeping, she was required to scour knives, or scrub the pavement. No one talked to her, except to say, "Susy do this;" or "Susy, why didn't you do as I bade you?"

Now and then she had a visit from Jerry, when his

master was in port. He was always very affectionate, and longed for the time when he should be a man, and able to have his sister live with him. But after a few years, he came no more ; and as neither of them could write, they had no means of communication.

When Susan grew older, and there were no more babes to tend, she was mostly confined to the cellar kitchen, from which she looked out upon stone steps and a brick wall. Her mistress had decided objections to her forming acquaintances in the neighbourhood, and for several years the young girl scarcely held communion with any human being, except the old cook. Even her beauty made her less a favourite ; for when company came in, it was by no means agreeable to Mrs. Andrews to observe that the servant attracted more attention than her own daughter. Her husband spent very little of his time at home, and when there, was usually asleep. But one member of the family was soon conscious of a growing interest in the orphan. Master Robert, a year older than herself, had been a petulant, over-indulged boy, and was now a selfish, pleasure-seeking lad. In juvenile days, he had been in the habit of ordering the little servant to wash his dog, and of scolding at her, if she did not black his shoes to his liking. But as human nature developed within him, his manners toward her gradually softened ; for he began to notice that she was a very handsome girl.

Having obtained from his sister a promise not to reveal that he had said anything, he represented that Susy ought to have better clothes, and be allowed to go to meeting sometimes. He said he was sure the neighbours thought she was very meanly clad, and he had heard that their servants made remarks about it. He was not mistaken in supposing that his mother would be influenced by such arguments. She had never thought of the alms-house child in any other light than as a machine for her convenience; but if the neighbours talked about her meanness, it was certainly necessary to enlarge Susy's privileges. In answer to her curious inquiries, her daughter repeated that Mrs. Jones's girl had said so and so, and that Mrs. Smith, at the next door, had made a similar remark to Mrs. Dickson. Whether this gossip was, or was not, invented by Robert, it had the effect he desired.

Susan, now nearly sixteen years of age, obtained a better dress than she had ever before possessed, and was occasionally allowed to go to meeting on Sunday afternoon. As Mrs. Andrews belonged to a very genteel church, she could not, of course, take a servant girl with her. But the cook went to a Methodist meeting, where "the *poor* had the gospel preached to them," and there a seat was hired for Susan also. Master Robert suddenly became devotional, and was often seen at the same meeting. He had no deliberately bad intentions; but he was thoughtless by nature, and selfish by education. He found pleasant excitement in watching his increasing power over the young girl's feelings; and sometimes, when he queried within himself whether he was doing right to gain her affections, and what would come of it all, he had floating visions that he might possibly educate Susan, and make her his wife. These very vague ideas he impressed so definitely on the mind of the old cook, aided by occasional presents, that she promised to tell no tales. Week after week, the lovers sat together in the same pew, and sang from the same hymn-book. Then came meetings after the family had retired to rest, to which secresy gave an additional charm. The concealment was the only thing that troubled Susan with a consciousness of wrong; and he easily persuaded her that this was a duty, in order to screen him from blame. "Was it his fault that he loved her?" he asked; "he was sure he could not help it."

She, on her part, could not help loving *him* deeply and fervently. He was very handsome, and she delighted in his beauty, as naturally as she had done in the flower, when her heart leaped up and called it a Rosenglory. Since her brother went away, there was no other human bosom on which she could rest her weary head; no other lips spoke lovingly to her, no other eye-beams sent warmth into her soul. If the gay, the prosperous, and the flattered find it pleasant to be loved, how much more so must it be to one whose life from infancy had been so darkened? Society reflects its own pollution on feelings which nature made beautiful, and does cruel injustice to youthful hearts by the grossness of its interpretations. Thus it fared with poor Susan. Late one summer's night, she and Robert were sitting by the open window of the breakfast-room. All was still in the streets; the light of the moon shone mildly on them, and hushed their souls into quiet happiness. The thoughtless head of sixteen rested on the impressible heart of seventeen, and thus they fell asleep.

Mrs. Andrews had occasion for some camphor, in the course of the night, and it chanced to be in the closet of that room. When she entered in search of it, she started back, as if she had heard the report of a pistol. No suspicion of the existing state of things had ever crossed her mind; and now that she discovered it, it never occurred to her that she herself was much to blame. Her own example, and incidental remarks not intended as education, but which in fact were so, had taught her son that the world was made for him to get as much pleasure in as possible, without reference to the good of others. She had cautioned him against the liability of being cheated in money matters, and had instructed him how to make the cheapest bargains, in the purchase of clothing or amusement; but against the most inevitable and most insidious temptations of his life, he had received no warning. The sermons he heard were about publicans and pharisees, who lived eighteen hundred years ago; none of them met the wants of his own life, none of them interpreted the secrets of his own heart, or revealed the rational laws of the senses.

As for Susan, the little fish, floated along by the tide, were not more ignorant of hydrostatics, than she was of the hidden dangers and social regulations, in the midst of which she lived. Robert's love had bloomed in her dreary monotonous life, like the Morning-Glory in the dark dismal court; and she welcomed it, and gazed into it, and rejoiced in it, much after the same fashion.

All these thoughts were, however, foreign to the mind of Mrs. Andrews. She judged the young couple as if they had her experience of forty years, and were encased in her own hard crust of worldly wisdom. The dilemma would have been a trying one, even for a sensible and judicious mother; and the management of it required candour and delicacy altogether beyond her shallow understanding and artificial views. She wakened them from their dream with a storm of indignation. Her exaggerated statements were in no degree adapted to the real measure of wrong doing, and therefore, instead of producing humility and sorrow, they roused resentment against what was felt to be unjust accusation. The poor heedless neglected child of poverty was treated as if she were already hardened in depravity. No names were too base to be bestowed upon her. As the angry mistress drove her to her garret, the concluding words were, "You ungrateful, good-for-nothing hussy, that I took out of the alms-house from charity! You vile creature, you, thus to reward all my kindness by trying to ruin and seduce my only son!"

This was reversing matters strangely. Susan was sorely tempted to ask for what kindness she was expected to be grateful; but she did not. She was ashamed of having practised concealment, as every generous nature is; but this feeling of self-reproach was overpowered by a consciousness that she did not deserve the epithets bestowed upon her, and she timidly said so. "Hold your tongue," replied Mrs. Andrews. "Leave my house to-morrow morning, and never let me see you again. I always expected you'd come to some bad end, since that fool of a painter came here and asked to take your likeness, sweeping the side-walk. This comes of setting people up above their condition."

After talking the matter over with her husband, Mrs. Andrews concluded to remain silent about Robert's adventure, to send him forthwith into the country, to his uncle the minister, and recommend Susan to one of her friends, who needed a servant, and had no sons to be endangered. At parting, she said, "I shall take away the cloak I gave you last winter. The time for which you were bound to me isn't up by two years; and the allowance Mr. Jenkins makes to me isn't enough to pay for my disappointment in losing your services just when you are beginning to be useful, after all the trouble and expense I have had with you. He has agreed to pay you every month, enough to get decent clothing; and that's more than you deserve. You ought to be thankful to me for all the care I have taken of you, and for concealing your bad character; but I've done expecting any such thing as gratitude in this world." The poor girl wept, but she said nothing. She did not know what to say.

No fault was found with the orphan in the family of Mr. Jenkins, the alderman. His wife said she was capable and industrious; and he himself took a decided fancy to her. He praised her cooking, he praised the neatness with which she arranged the table, and after a few days, he began to praise her glossy hair and glowing cheeks. All this was very pleasant to the human nature of the young girl. She thought it was very kind and fatherly, and took it all in good part. She made her best courtesy wnen he presented her with a handsome calico gown; and she began to think she had fallen into the hands of real friends. But when he chucked her under the chin, and said such a pretty girl ought to dress well, she blushed and was confused by the expression of his countenance, though she was too ignorant of the world to understand his meaning. But his demonstrations soon became too open to admit of mistake, and ended with offers of money. She heard him with surprise and distress. To sell herself without her affections, had never been suggested to her by nature, and as yet she was too little acquainted with the refinements of high civilization, to acquire familiarity with such an idea.

Deeming it best to fly from persecutions which she could not avoid, she told Mrs. Jenkins that she found the work very hard, and would like to go to another place as soon as possible. "If you go before your month is up I shall pay you no wages," replied the lady; "but you may go if you choose." In vain the poor girl represented her extreme need of a pair of shoes. The lady was vexed at heart, for she secretly suspected the cause of her departure; and though she could not in justice blame the girl, and was willing enough that she should go, she had a mind to punish her. But when Susan, to defend herself, hinted that she had good reasons for wishing to leave, she brought a storm on her head, at once. "You vain, impertinent creature!" exclaimed Mrs. Jenkins, "because my husband gave you a new gown, for shame of the old duds you brought from Mrs. Andrews, do you presume to insinuate that his motives were not honourable? And he a gentleman of high respectability, an alderman of the city! Leave my house; the sooner the better; but don't expect a cent of wages."

Unfortunately, a purse lay on the work table, near which Susan was standing. She had no idea of stealing; but she thought to herself, "Surely I have a right to a pair of shoes for my three weeks of hard labour." She carried off the purse, and went into the service of a neighbour, who had expressed a wish to hire. That very evening she was arrested, and was soon after tried and sentenced to Blackwell's Island. A very bold and bad woman was sentenced at the same time, and they went in company. From her polluting conversation and manners, poor Susan received a new series of lessons in that strange course of education, which a Christian community had from the beginning bestowed upon her. Her residence on the Island rapidly increased her stock of evil knowledge. But she had no natural tendencies to vice; and though her ideas of right and wrong were inevitably confused by the social whirlpool into which she was born, she still wished to lead a decent and industrious life. When released from confinement, she tried to procure a situation at service; but she had no references to give, except Mrs. Andrews and Mrs. Jenkins. When she called a second time, she uniformly met the cold reply, "I hear you have been on Blackwell's Island. I never employ people who have lost their character."

From the last of these attempts, she was walking away hungry and disconsolate, doubtful where to obtain shelter for the night, when she met the magistrate, who had sentenced her and the other woman. He spoke to her kindly, gave her a quarter of a dollar, and asked her to call upon him that evening. At parting, he promised to be a friend to her, if she behaved herself, and then murmured something in a lower tone of voice. What were his ideas of behaving herself were doubtless implied by the whisper; for the girl listened with such a smile as was never seen on her innocent face, before he sent her to improve her education on the Island. It is true she knew very little, and thought still less, about the machinery of laws, and regulations for social protection; but it puzzled her poor head, as it does many a wiser one, why men should be magistrates, when they practise the same things for which they send women to Blackwell's Island. She had never read or heard anything about "Woman's Rights;" otherwise it might have occurred to her that it was because men made all the laws, and elected all the magistrates.

The possible effect of magisterial advice and protection is unknown; for she did not accept the invitation to call that evening. As she walked away from the tempter, thinking sadly of Robert Andrews, and her dear brother Jerry, she happened to meet the young man who had gained her first youthful love, unmixed with thoughts of evil. With many tears, she told him her adventures since they parted. The account kindled his indignation and excited his sympathy to a painful degree. Had he lived in a true and rational state of society, the impulse then given to his better feelings might have eventually raised his nature to noble unselfishness and manly frankness. But as it was, he fell back upon deception and false pride. He hired apartments for Susan, and, by some pretence, wheedled his mother out of the means of paying for them. Those who deem the poor girl unpardonable for consenting to this arrangement, would learn mercy if they were placed under similar circumstances of poverty, scorn, and utter loneliness.

* * * * *

Ten years passed since Jerry last parted with his blooming sister, then fourteen years old. He had been shipwrecked twice, and returned from sea in total blindness, caused by mismanagement of the small pox. He gained a few coppers by playing a clarinet in the street, led by a little ragged boy. Everywhere he inquired for his sister, but no one could give him any tidings of her. One day, two women stopped to listen, and one of them put a shilling into the boy's hand. "Why, Susy, what possesses you to give so much to hear that old cracked pipe?" said one.

"He looks a little like somebody I knew when I was a child," replied the other; and they passed on.

The voices were without inflexions, rough and animal in tone, indicating that the speakers led a merely sensual existence. The piper did not recognise either of them; but the name of Susy went through his heart, like a sunbeam through November clouds. Then she said he looked like somebody she had known! He inquired of the boy whether the woman called Susy was handsome.

He replied, "No. She is lean and pale; her cheek-bones stand out, and her great staring dark eyes look crazy."

The blind man hesitated a moment, and then said, "Let us walk quick and follow them." They did go, but lost sight of the women at the turning of a dirty alley. For six weeks, the blind piper kept watch in the neighbourhood, obviously a very bad one. In many houses he inquired if any one knew a woman by the name of Susan Gray; but he always received an answer in the negative. At last an old woman said that a girl named Susan Andrews boarded with her for a while; that she was very feeble, and lived in a street near by. He followed the directions she gave, and stopped before the house to play. People came to the door and windows, and in a few minutes the boy pressed his hand and said, "There is the woman you want to find."

He stopped abruptly, and exclaimed, "Susy!" There was an anxious tenderness in his tones, which the bystanders heard with loud laughter. They shouted, "Susy, you are called for! Here's a beau for you!" and many a ribald jest went round.

But she, in a sadder voice than usual, said, "My poor fellow, what do you want of me?"

"Did you give me a shilling a few weeks ago?" he asked.

"Yes, I did; but surely that was no great thing."

"Had you ever a brother named Jerry?" he inquired.

"Oh, Heavens! tell me if you know any thing of *him!*" she exclaimed.

He fell into her arms, sobbing, "My sister! My poor sister!"

The laughter hushed instantly, and many eyes were filled with tears. There were human hearts there also; and they felt at once the poor piper was Susy's long-lost brother, and that he had come home to her blind.

For an instant, she clasped him convulsively to her heart. Then thrusting him away with a sudden movement, she said, "Don't touch me, Jerry! Don't touch me!"

"Why not? dear sister," he asked. But she only replied, in a deep, hollow tone of self-loathing, "Don't touch me!"

Not one of the vicious idlers smiled. Some went away weeping; others, with affectionate solicitude, offered refreshments to the poor blind wanderer. Alas, he would almost have *wished* for blindness, could he have seen the haggard spectre that stood before him, and faintly recognised, in her wild melancholy eyes, his own beloved Rosenglory.

From that hour, he devoted himself to her with the most assiduous attention. He felt that her steps trembled when she leaned on his arm, he observed that her breath came with difficulty, and he knew that she spoke truly when she said she had not long to live. A woman, who visited the house, told him of a charitable institution in Tenth Avenue, called the Home, where women who have been prisoners, and sincerely wish to reform, can find shelter and employment. He went and besought that his sister might be allowed to come there and die.

There, in a well ventilated room, on a clean and comfortable bed, the weary pilgrim at last reposed in the midst of true friends. "Oh, if I had only met with such when my poor mother first died, how different it might all have been," she was wont to say. The blind brother kissed her forehead, and said, "Don't grieve for that now, dear. It was not your fault that you had no friends."

One day, a kind sympathizing lady gave him a bunch of flowers for his sister. Hitherto an undefined feeling of delicacy had restrained him, when he thought of using the pet word of their childhood. But thinking it might perhaps please her, he stepped into the room, and said, cheerfully, "Here, Rosenglory! See what I have brought you!" It was too much for the poor nervous sufferer. "Oh, don't call me *that!*" she said; and she threw herself on his neck, sobbing violently.

He tried to soothe her; and after awhile, she said in a subdued voice, "I am bewildered when I think about myself. They tell me that I am a great sinner: and so I am. But I never injured any human being; I never hated any one. Only once, when Robert married that rich woman, and told me to keep out of his way, and get my living as others in my situation did—then for a little while, I hated him; but it was not long. Dear Jerry, I did not mean to be wicked; I never wanted to be wicked. But there seemed to be no place in the world for me. They all wronged me; and my heart dried up. I was like a withered leaf, and the winds blew me about just as it happened."

He pressed her hand to his lips, and hot tears fell

upon it. "Oh, bless you, for your love!" she said. "Poor outcast as I am, *you* do not think I have sinned beyond forgiveness. Do you?"

Fervently he embraced her, and answered, "I too have sinned; but God only knows the secret history of our neglected youth, our wrongs, sufferings, and temptations; and say what they will, I am sure He will not judge u so harshly as men have done."

He knelt down by the bed-side in silent prayer, and with her hand clasped in his, they both fell asleep. He dreamed that angels stood by the pillow and smiled with sad pitying love on the dying one. It was the last night he watched with her. The next day, her weary spirit passed away from this world of sin and suffering. The blind piper was all alone.

As he sat holding her emaciated hand, longing once more to see that dear face, before the earth covered it forever, a visitor came in to look at the corpse. She meant to be kind and sympathizing; but she did not understand the workings of the human heart. To the wounded spirit of the mourner, she seemed to speak with too much condescension of the *possibility* of forgiveness *even* to so great a sinner. He rose to leave the room, and answered meekly, "She was a good child. But the paths of her life were dark and tangled, and she lost her way."

A LEGEND

OF THE FALLS OF ST. ANTHONY.

Founded on Indian Tradition.

From all its kind
  This wasted heart,
This moody mind
  Now drifts apart;
It longs to find
  The tideless shore,
Where rests the wreck
  Of Heretofore—
The great heart-break
  Of loves no more.

I drift alone,
For all are gone,
Dearest to me;
And hail the wave
That to the grave
  On hurrieth me:
Welcome, thrice welcome, then,
  Thy wave, Eternity.

MOTHERWELL.

WEE-CHUSH-TA-DOO-TA was a powerful Sioux chief. He numbered many distinguished warriors among his ancestors, and was as proud of his descent as was ever feudal noble. His name simply signified The Red Man; but he was "a great brave," and the poet of his tribe, whose war-songs were sung on all great occasions. In one of the numerous battles of the

Sioux with their enemies the Chippewas, he took prisoner a very handsome little girl. A widowed woman begged to adopt her, to supply the place of a daughter, who had gone to the spirit-land; and thus the pretty young creature was saved from the general massacre of prisoners. As she approached womanhood, the heart of the poet-chieftain inclined towards her, and he made her his wife.

Their first-born was a daughter. When she was two years old, the mother, struck by a peculiarity in the expression of her eyes, named her Zah-gah-see-ga-quay, which, in her own language, signified Sun-beams breaking through a Cloud. As she grew older, this poetic name became more and more appropriate; for when she raised her large deeply-shaded eyes, their bright lucid expression was still more obviously veiled with timidity and sadness. Her voice, as usual with young Indian women, was low and musical, and her laugh was gentle and childlike.

There was a mixed expression in her character, as in her eyes. She was active, buoyant, and energetic, in her avocations and amusements; yet from childhood she was prone to serious moods, and loved to be alone in sequestered places, watching the golden gleam of sunset on the green velvet of the hills, till it passed away, and threw their long twilight-shadows across the solitude of the prairies.

Her father, proud of her uncommon intelligence and beauty, resolved to mate her with the most renowned of warriors, and the most expert of hunters. In the spring of 1765, when she had just passed her fourteenth birth-day, she attracted the attention of one worthy to claim the prize. Nee-hee-o-ee-woo, The Wolf of the Hill, was a noble-looking young chief, belonging to the neighbouring tribe of Shiennes. He was noted for bold exploits, superb horsemanship, and the richness of his savage attire. The first time he saw the beautiful Sioux, he looked at her with earnest eyes; and he soon after returned, bringing Wee-chush-ta-doo-ta a valuable present of furs. The maiden understood very well why his courting-flute was heard about the wigwam till late into the night, but the sounds excited no lively emotions in her heart. The dashing young warrior came too late. The week previous, a Frenchman, drawn thither by thirst for new adventures, had arrived with a company of fur traders from Quebec. He was a handsome man; but Zah-gah-see-ga-quay was less attracted by his expressive face and symmetrical figure, than by his graceful gallantry toward women, to which she had been hitherto unaccustomed. His power of fascinating was increased by the marked preference bestowed upon herself. She received his attentions with childish delight and pretty bashfulness, like a coy little bird. The lustrous black hair, which he praised, was braided more neatly than ever; her dress of soft beaver-skins was more coquetishly garnished with porcupine quill-work, and her moccasons were embroidered in gayer patterns.

The beauty of this forest nymph pleased the Frenchman's fancy, and his vanity was flattered by the obvious impression he had made on her youthful imagination. He was incapable of love. A volatile temperament, and early dissipation, had taken from him that best happiness of human life. But Indian lands were becoming more and more desirable to his ambitious nation, and Wee-chush-ta-doo-ta had the disposal of broad and valuable tracts. He had an aversion to marriage; but this he knew would be but the shadow of a fetter; for he could dissolve the bond at any moment, with as little loss of reputation as if it were a *liaison* in Paris. Thus reasoned civilized man, while the innocent child of the woods was as unconscious of the possibility of such selfish calculations, as is a robin in the mating season.

Her father had encountered white men, and was consequently more on his guard. When Jerome de Rancé offered rich presents, and asked his daughter in marriage, he replied, "Zah-gah-see-ga-quay must mate with a chieftain of her own people. If a pale-face marries an Indian woman, he calls her his wife while he likes to look upon her, but when he desires another, he walks away and says she is not his wife. Such are not the customs of the red men."

Though Jerome de Rancé had secretly rejoiced over the illegality of an Indian marriage, being highly civilized, he of course made the most solemn protestations of undying love and everlasting good faith. But the proud chieftain had set his heart upon an alliance with the magnificent Wolf of the Hill, and he listened coldly. Obstacles increased the value of the prize, and the adventurous Frenchman was determined to win his savage bride at any price. With the facility of his pliant nation, he accommodated himself to all the customs of the tribe; he swore to adopt all their friendships and all their enmities;

he exercised himself in all performances requiring strength and skill, and on all possible occasions he exhibited the most reckless courage. These things made him very popular, and gained the admiration of the chief more than was shown by his grave countenance and indifferent manner. Still he could not easily overcome a reluctance to mix his proud race with foreign blood.

De Rancé, considering himself the one who stooped in the proposed alliance, was piqued by what seemed to him a ridiculous assumption of superiority. Had it not been for the tempting Indian lands, of which he hoped to come in possession, he would have gained the loving maiden on his own terms, and left her when he chose, without seeking to conciliate her father. But the fulfilment of his ambitious schemes required a longer probation. With affected indifference, he made arrangements for departure. He intended to re-appear among them suddenly, in a few weeks, to test his power over the Clouded Sunbeam; but he said he was going to traffic with a neighbouring tribe, and it was doubtful whether he should see them again, or return to Canada by a different route. That she would pine for him, he had no doubt; and he had observed that Wee-chush-ta-doo-ta, though bitter and implacable to his enemies, was tenderhearted as a child toward his own family.

He was not mistaken in his calculations. Zah-gah-see-ga-quay did not venture to dispute the will of her father; but her sweet voice was no more heard in songs; the sunbeam in her eyes went more and more behind the cloud, and the bright healthy colour of her cheek grew pale. Her listless movements and languid glance pained her mother's heart, and the stern father could not endure the mournfulness of their beseeching looks. He spoke no words, but called together a few of his companions, and went forth apparently to hunt in the forest. Before the moon had traversed half her monthly orbit, he and Jerome entered the wigwam together. Zah-gar-see-ga-quay was seated in a dark corner. Her head leaned despondingly on her hand, and her basket-work lay tangled beside her. As she looked up, a quick blush mantled her face, and her eyes shone like stars. Wee-chush-ta-doo-ta noticed the sudden change, and, in tones of deep tenderness, said, "My child, go to the wigwam of the stranger; that your father may again see you love to look on the rising sun and the opening flowers." There was mingled joy and modesty in the upward glance of The Clouded Sunbeam, and when she turned away bashfully from his triumphant gaze, the Frenchman smiled with a consciousness of unlimited power over her simple heart.

That evening, they rambled alone, under the friendly light of the moon. When they returned, a portion of the scarlet paint from her brown cheek was transferred to the face of her lover. Among his Parisian acquaintance, this would have given rise to many a witty jest; but the Indians, with more natural politeness, observed it silently. A few days after, the gentle daughter of the Sioux passed into the tent of the stranger, and became his wife.

Years passed on, and she remained the same devoted, submissive friend. In all domestic avocations of the Indians, she was most skilful. No one made more beautiful matting, or wove into it such pretty patterns. The beaver skins she dressed were as soft and pliable as leather could be. She rowed her canoe with light and vigorous stroke, and the flight of her arrow was unerring. Her husband loved her as well as was possible for one of his butterfly temperament and selfish disposition; but the deferential courtesy of the European lover gradually subsided into something like the lordly indifference of the men around him. He was never harsh; but his affectionate bride felt the change in his manner, and sometimes wept in secret. When she nestled at his feet, and gazed into his countenance with her peculiarly pleading plaintive look, she sometimes obtained a glance such as he had given her in former days. Then her heart would leap like a frolicsome lamb, and she would live cheerfully on the remembrance of that smile through wearisome days of silence and neglect. Her love amounted to passionate idolatry. If he wished to cross the river, she would ply the oar, lest he should suffer fatigue. She carried his quiver and his gun through the forest, and when they returned at twilight, he lounged indolently on the bottom of the boat, while she dipped her oars in unison with her low sweet voice, soothing him with some simple song, where the same plaintive tones perpetually came, and went away in lullaby-cadence.

To please him, she named her son and daughter Felicie and Florimond, in memory of his favourite brother and sister. On these little ones, she could lavish her abundant love without disappointment or fear. The children inherited their parents' beauty; but Felicie, the eldest, was endowed with a double portion. She had her mother's large lucid eye, less deeply shaded with the saddening cloud; but her other features resembled her handsome father. Her oval cheeks had just enough of the Indian tint to give them a rich warm colouring. At thirteen years old, her tall figure combined the graceful elasticity of youth, with the rounded fulness of womanhood. She inherited her father's volatile temperament, and was always full of fun and frolic. As a huntress, she was the surest eye, and the fleetest foot; and her pretty canoe skimmed the waters like a stormy petrel. It was charming to see this young creature, so full of life, winding about among the eddies of the river, or darting forward, her long black hair streaming on the wind, and her rich red lips parted with eagerness. She sported with her light canoe, and made it play all manner of gambols in the water. It dashed and splashed, and whirled round in pirouettes, like an opera-dancer; then, in the midst of swift circles, she would stop at once, and laugh, as she gracefully shook back the hair from her glowing face. Jerome de Rancé had never loved anything, as he did this beautiful child. But something of anxiety and sadness, mingled with his pride, when he saw her caracoling on her swift little white horse of the prairies, or leaping into the chase, or making her canoe caper like a thing alive. Buoyant and free was her Indian childhood; but she was approaching the period, when she would be claimed as a wife; and he could not endure the thought, that the toilsome life of a squaw, would be the portion of his beautiful daughter. He taught her to dance to his flute, and hired an old Catholic priest to instruct her in reading and writing. But these lessons were irksome to the Indian girl, and she was perpetually eluding her father's vigilance, to hunt squirrels in the woods, or sport her canoe among the eddies. He revolved many plans for her future advancement in life; and sometimes, when he turned his restless gaze from daughter to mother, the wife felt troubled, by an expression she did not understand. In order to advance his ambitious views, it was necessary to wean Felicie from her woodland home; and he felt that his Clouded-Sunbeam, though still beautiful, would be hopelessly out of place in Parisian saloons. Wee-chush-ta-doo-ta and his wife were dead, and their relatives were too much occupied with war and hunting, to take particular notice of the white man's movements. The acres of forest and prairie, which he had received, on most advantageous terms, from his Indian father-in-law, were sold, tract after tract, and the money deposited in Quebec. Thither, he intended to convey first his daughter,.and then his son, on pretence of a visit, for the purposes of education, but in reality, with the intention of deserting his wife, to return no more.

According to Indian custom, the mother's right to her offspring amounts to unquestioned law. If her husband chooses to leave the tribe, the children must remain with her. It was therefore necessary to proceed artfully. De Rancé became more than usually affectionate; and Zah-gah-see-ga-quay, grateful for such gleams of his old tenderness, granted his earnest prayer, that Felicie might go to Quebec, for a few moons only. The Canadian fur-traders made their annual visit at this juncture, and he resolved to accept their escort for himself and daughter. His wife begged hard to accompany them; humbly promising, that she would not intrude among his white friends, but would remain with a few of her tribe, hidden in neighbouring woods, where she could now and then get a glimpse of their beloved faces. Such an arrangement, was by no means pleasing to the selfish European. The second time she ventured to suggest it, he answered briefly and sternly, and the beautiful shaded eyes filled with unnoticed tears. Felicie was the darling of her heart; she so much resembled the handsome Frenchman, as she had first known him. When the parting hour came, she clung to her daughter with a passionate embrace, and then starting up with convulsive energy, like some gentle animal when her young is in danger, she exclaimed, "Felicie is *my* child, and I will not let her go." De Rancé looked at her, as he had never looked before, and raised his arm to push her away. Frightened at the angry expression of his eye, she thought he intended to strike her; and with a deep groan she fell on the earth, and hid her face in the long grass.

Felicie sobbed, and stretched out her arms imploringly towards her mother; but quick as a flash, her father lifted her on the horse, swung himself lightly into the same saddle, and went off at a swift gallop. When the poor distracted mother rose from the ground, they were already far off, a mere speck on the wide prairie. This rude parting would perhaps have killed her heart, had it not been for her handsome boy of seven summers. With a sad countenance, he gravely seated himself by her side. She spoke no word to him, but the tears rolled slowly down, as she gazed at him, and tried to trace a resemblance to his unkind father.

The promised period of return arrived; but moon after moon passed away, and nothing was heard from the absent ones. A feeling that she had been intentionally deceived gradually grew strong within the heart of the Indian mother; and the question often arose, "Will he seek to take my boy away also?" As time passed on, and suspicion changed into certainty, she became stern and bitter. She loved young Florimond intensely; but even this love was tinged with fierceness, hitherto foreign to her nature. She scornfully abjured his French name, and called him Mah-to-chee-ga, The Little Bear. Her strongest wish seemed to be to make him as hard and proud as his grandfather had been, and to instil into his bosom the deadliest hatred of white men. The boy learned her lessons well. He was the most inveterate little savage that ever let fly an arrow. Already, he carried at his belt the scalp of a boy older and bigger than himself, the son of a chief, with whom his tribe were at war. The Sioux were proud of his vigour and his boldness, and considered his reckless courage almost a sufficient balance to the disadvantage of mixed blood.

Such was the state of things, when Jerome de Rancé returned to the shores of the Mississippi, after an absence of three years. He was mainly induced to make this visit by a wish to retain some hold upon his Indian boy, and preserve a good understanding with the tribe, as an advantage in future speculations. He had some dread of meeting the Clouded Sunbeam, and was not without fear that she might have exasperated her people against him. But he trusted much to her tenderness for him, and still more to his own adroitness. He was, however, surprised at the cold indifference with which she met him. He had expected deep resentment, but he was not prepared for such perfect apathy. He told a mournful and highly-wrought story of Felicie's sudden death, by being thrown from her horse, in their passage through the forest; and sought to excuse his long absence, by talking of his overwhelming grief, and his reluctance to bring sad tidings. The bereaved mother listened without emotion; for she did not believe him. She thought, and thought truly, that Felicie was in her father's native land, across the wide ocean. All his kind glances and endearing epithets were received with the same stolid indifference. Only when he talked with her Little Bear, did she rouse from this apparent lethargy. She watched over him like a she-wolf, when her young are in danger. She hoped that the hatred of white men, so carefully instilled, would prove a sufficient shield against all attempts to seduce him from her. But in the course of a few weeks, she saw plainly enough that the fascinating and insidious Frenchman was gaining complete power over the boy, as he had over her own youthful spirit. She was maddened with jealousy at her own diminished influence; and when Mah-to-chee-ga at last expressed a wish to go to Canada with his father, the blow was too severe for her deeply lacerated soul. The one thought that he would be enticed away from her took complete possession of her mind, and night and day she brooded over plans of vengeance. More than once, she nearly nerved her hand to murder the father of her son. But his features recalled the image of the handsome young Frenchman, who had carried her arrows through the woods, and kissed the moccason he stooped to tie; and she could not kill him.

As the time approached for de Rancé to return to Canada with the traders, her intense anxiety increased almost to frenzy. One day, when he had gone to a neighbouring tribe to traffic for furs, she invited Mah-to-chee-ga to go up the river with her, to fish. She decked herself in her most richly embroidered skins, and selected the gaudiest wampum-belt for her Little Bear. When the boy asked why they were dressed so carefully, she replied, "Because we are going to meet your grandfather, who was a great brave, and a mighty hunter." He was puzzled by the answer, but when he questioned of her meaning, she remained silent. When they came to the waterside, she paused and looked back on the forest, where she had spent her happy childhood, and enjoyed her brief dream of love. The beautiful past, followed by a long train of dark shadows, rushed through memory, and there seemed no relief for her but death.

She entered the boat with a calm countenance, and began to chant one of those oppressively mournful songs, which must have been suggested to her people by the monotonous minor cadences of the rustling forest. As they approached the Falls of St. Anthony, and heard more and more plainly the rush of waters, she gazed on her child with such a wild expression of vehement love, that the boy was frightened. But his eye was spell-bound to hers, and he could not escape its concentrated magnetic power. At length, his attention was roused by the violent motions of the boat; and he screamed, "Mother! mother! the canoe is going over the rapids!"

"We go to the spirit-land together," she replied: "he cannot come there to separate us."

With whirl and splash, the boat plunged down the cataract. The white foam leaped over it, and it was seen no more.

The sky soon after darkened, and the big rain fell in torrents.

The Indians believe that the spirits of the drowned ones, veiled in a winding-sheet of mist, still hover over the fatal spot. When they see the vapour rising, they say, "Let us not hunt to-day; a storm will certainly come; for Zah-gah-see-ga-quay and her son are going over the Falls of St. Anthony."

Felicie was informed of the death of her mother and brother, and wept for them bitterly, though she never knew the painful circumstances of their exit. She married a wealthy Frenchman, and was long pointed out in society as "*La Belle Indienne.*"

THE BROTHERS.

Three pure heavens opened, beaming in three pure hearts, and nothing was in them but God, love, and joy, and the little tear-drop of earth which hangs upon all our flowers.—*Richter.*

Few know how to estimate the precious gem of friendship at its real worth; few guard it with the tender care which its rarity and excellence deserves. Love, like the beautiful opal, is a clouded gem, which carries a spark of fire in its bosom; but true friendship, like a diamond, radiates steadily from its transparent heart.

This sentiment was never experienced in greater depth and purity than by David and Jonathan Trueman, brothers, of nearly the same age. Their friendship was not indeed of that exciting and refreshing character, which is the result of a perfect accord of very different endowments. It was unison, not harmony. In person, habits, and manners, they were as much alike as two leaves of the same tree. They were both hereditary members of the Society of Friends, and remained so from choice. They were acquainted in the same circle, and engaged in similar pursuits. "Their souls wore exactly the same frock-coat and morning-dress of life; I mean two bodies with the same cuffs and collars, of the same colour, button-holes, trimmings and cut."

Jonathan was a little less sedate than his older brother; he indulged a little more in the quiet, elderly sort of humour of the "Cheeryble Brothers." But it was merely the difference between the same lake perfectly calm, or faintly rippled by the slightest breeze. They were so constantly seen together, that they were called the Siamese Twins. Unfortunately, this similarity extended to a sentiment which does not admit of partnership. They both loved the same maiden.

Deborah Winslow was the only daughter of one of those substantial Quakers, whom a discriminating observer would know, at first sight, was "well to do in the world;" for the fine broadcloth coat and glossy hat spoke that fact with even less certainty than the perfectly comfortable expression of countenance. His petted child was like a blossom planted in sunny places, and shielded from every rude wind. All her little lady-like whims were indulged. If the drab-coloured silk was not exactly the right shade, or the Braithwaite muslin was not sufficiently fine and transparent, orders must be sent to London, that her daintiness might be satisfied. Her countenance was a true index of life passed without strong emotions. The mouth was like a babe's, the blue eyes were mild and innocent, and the oval face was unvarying in the delicate tint of the Sweet Pea blossom. Her hair never straggled into ringlets, or played with the breeze; its silky bands were always like molasses-candy, moulded to yellowish whiteness, and laid in glossy braids.

There is much to be said in favour of this unvarying

serenity; for it saves a vast amount of suffering. But all natures cannot thus glide through an unruffled existence. Deborah's quiet temperament made no resistance to its uniform environment; but had I been trained in her exact sect, I should inevitably have boiled over and melted the moulds.

She had always been acquainted with the Trueman brothers. They all attended the same school, and they sat in sight of each other at the same meeting; though Quaker custom, ever careful to dam up human nature within safe limits, ordained that they should be seated on different sides of the house, and pass out by different doors. They visited the same neighbours, and walked home in company. She probably never knew, with positive certainty, which of the brothers she preferred; she had always been in the habit of loving them both; but Jonathan happened to ask first, whether she loved him.

It was during an evening walk, that he first mentioned the subject to David; and he could not see how his limbs trembled, and his face flushed. The emotion, though strong and painful, was soon suppressed; and in a voice but slightly constrained, he inquired, "Does Deborah love thee, brother?"

The young man replied that he thought so, and he intended to ask her, as soon as the way opened.

David likewise thought, that Deborah was attached to him; and he had invited her to ride the next day, for the express purpose of ascertaining the point. Never had his peaceful soul been in such a tumult. Sometimes he thought it would be right and honourable, to tell Deborah that they both loved her, and ask her to name her choice. "But then if she should prefer *me*," he said to himself," it will make dear Jonathan very unhappy; and if she should choose *him*, it will be a damper on their happiness, to known that I am disappointed. If she accepts him, I will keep my secret to myself. It is a heavy cross to take up; but William Penn says, 'no cross, no crown.' In this case, I would be willing to give up the crown, if I could get rid of the cross. But then if I lay it down, poor Jonathan must bear it. I have always found that it brought great peace of mind to conquer selfishness, and I will strive to do so now. As my brother's wife, she will still be a near and dear friend; and their children will seem almost like my own."

A current of counter thoughts rushed through his mind. He rose quickly and walked the room, with a feverish agitation he had never before experienced. But through all the conflict, the idea of saving his brother from suffering remained paramount to his own pain.

The promised ride could not be avoided, but it proved a temptation almost too strong for the good unselfish man. Deborah's sweet face looked so pretty under the shadow of her plain bonnet; her soft hand remained in his so confidingly, when she was about to enter the chaise, and turned to speak to her mother; she smiled on him so affectionately, and called him Friend David, in such winning tones, that it required all his strength to avoid uttering the question, which for ever trembled on his lips: "Dost thou love me, Deborah?" But always there rose between them the image of that dear brother, who slept in his arms in childhood, and shared the same apartment now. "Let him have the first chance," he said to himself. If he is accepted, I will be resigned, and will be to them both a true friend through life. A very slight pressure of the hand alone betrayed his agitation, when he opened the door of her house, and said, "Farewell, Deborah."

In a few days, Jonathan informed him that he was betrothed; and the magnanimous brother wished him joy with a sincere heart, concealing that it was a sad one. His first impulse was to go away, that he might not be daily reminded of what he had lost; but the fear of marring their happiness enabled him to choose the wiser part of making at once the effort that must be made. No one suspected the sacrifice he laid on the altar of friendship. When the young couple were married, he taxed his ingenuity to furnish whatever he thought would please the bride, by its peculiar neatness and elegance. At first, he found it very hard to leave them by their cozy pleasant fireside, and go to his own solitary apartment, where he never before had dwelt alone; and when the bride and bridegroom looked at each other tenderly, the glance went through his heart like an arrow of fire. But when Deborah, with gentle playfulness, apologized for having taken his brother away from him, he replied, with a quiet smile, "Nay, my friend, I have not lost a brother, I have only gained a sister." His self-denial seemed so easy, that the worldly might have thought it cost him little effort, and deserved no praise; but the angels loved him for it.

By degrees he resumed his wonted serenity, and became the almost constant inmate of their house. A stranger might almost have doubted which was the husband; so completely were the three united in all their affections, habits, and pursuits. A little son and daughter came to strengthen the bond; and the affectionate uncle found his heart almost as much cheered by them, as if they had been his own. Many an agreeable young Friend would have willingly superintended a household for David; but there was a natural refinement in his character, which rendered it impossible to make a marriage of convenience. He felt, more deeply than was apparent, that there was something wanting in his earthly lot; but he could not marry, unless he found a woman whom he loved as dearly as he had loved Deborah; and such a one never again came to him.

Their years flowed on with quiet regularity, disturbed with few of the ills humanity is heir to. In all the small daily affairs of life, each preferred the other's good, and thus secured the happiness of the whole. Abroad, their benevolence fell with the noiseless liberality of dew. The brothers both prospered in business, and Jonathan inherited a large portion of his father-in-law's handsome property. Never were a family so pillowed and cushioned on the carriage-road to heaven. But they were so simply and naturally virtuous, that the smooth path was less dangerous to them than to others.

Reverses came at last in Jonathan's affairs. The failure of others, less careful than himself, involved him in their disasters. But David was rich, and the idea of a separate purse was unknown between them; therefore the gentle Deborah knew no change in her household comforts and elegancies, and felt no necessity of diminishing their large liberality to the poor.

At sixty-three years old, the younger brother departed this life, in the arms of his constant friend. The widow, who had herself counted sixty winters, had been for some time gradually declining in health. When the estate was settled, the property was found insufficient to pay debts. But the kind friend, with the same delicate disinterestedness which had always characterized him, carefully concealed this fact. He settled a handsome fortune upon the widow, which she always supposed to be a portion of her husband's estate. Being executor, he managed affairs as he liked. He borrowed his own capital; and every quarter, he gravely paid her interest on his own money. In the refinement of his generosity, he was not satisfied to support her in the abundance to which she had been accustomed; he wished to have her totally unconscious of obligation, and perfectly free to dispose of the funds as she pleased.

His goodness was not limited to his own household. If a poor seamstress was declining in health, for want of exercise and variety of scene, David Trueman was sure to invite her to Niagara, or the Springs, as a particular favour to him, because he needed company. If there was a lone widow, peculiarly friendless, his carriage was always at her service. If there was a maiden lady uncommonly homely, his arm was always ready as an escort to public places. Without talking at all upon the subject, he practically devoted himself to the mission of attending upon the poor, the unattractive, and the neglected.

Thus the good old bachelor prevents his sympathies from congealing, and his heart from rusting out. The sunlight was taken away from his landscape of life; but little birds sleep in their nests, and sweet flowers breathe their fragrance lovingly through the bright moonlight of his tranquil existence.

FINIS.

CPSIA information can be obtained at www.ICGtesting.com
Printed in the USA
BVOW01s1810110315

391292BV00010B/85/P